There Is Another Way!

Also Available from ASQ Quality Press:

Charting Your Course: Lessons Learned During the Journey Toward Performance Excellence
John G. Conyers and Robert Ewy

Quality Across the Curriculum: Integrating Quality Tools and PDSA with Standards
Jay Marino and Ann Haggerty Raines

Permission to Forget: And Nine Other Root Causes of America's Frustration with Education
Lee Jenkins

Improving Student Learning: Applying Deming's Quality Principles in the Classroom, 2nd Edition
Lee Jenkins

Successful Applications of Quality Systems in K–12 Schools
The ASQ Quality Education Division

Futuring Tools for Strategic Quality Planning in Education
William F. Alexander and Richard W. Serfass

Insights to Performance Excellence 2005: An Inside Look at the 2005 Baldrige Award Criteria
Mark L. Blazey

Thinking Tools for Kids: An Activity Book for Classroom Learning
Barbara A. Cleary and Sally J. Duncan

From Baldrige to the Bottom Line: A Road Map for Organizational Change and Improvement
David W. Hutton

There Is Another Way!

Launch a Baldrige-Based Quality Classroom

Margaret A. Byrnes
with
Jeanne C. Baxter

ASQ Quality Press
Milwaukee, Wisconsin

American Society for Quality, Quality Press, Milwaukee 53203

Printed in the United States of America
12 11 10 5

Library of Congress Cataloging-in-Publication Data

Byrnes, Margaret A.
There is another way! : launch a Baldrige-based quality classroom / Margaret A. Byrnes with Jeanne C. Baxter.
p. cm.
Includes bibliographical references and index.
ISBN 0-87389-653-X (hardback : alk. paper)
1. Educational leadership—United States. 2. School management and organization—United States. 3. Total quality management—United States. 4. Education—Aims and objectives—United States. I. Baxter, Jeanne, 1934– II. Title.
LB2805.B97 2005
371.2—dc22 2005003588

Publisher: William A. Tony
Acquisitions Editor: Annemieke Hytinen
Project Editor: Paul O'Mara
Production Administrator: Randall Benson

ASQ Mission: The American Society for Quality advances individual, organizational, and community excellence worldwide through learning, quality improvement, and knowledge exchange.

Attention Bookstores, Wholesalers, Schools, and Corporations: ASQ Quality Press books, videotapes, audiotapes, and software are available at quantity discounts with bulk purchases for business, educational, or instructional use. For information, please contact ASQ Quality Press at 800-248-1946, or write to ASQ Quality Press, P.O. Box 3005, Milwaukee, WI 53201-3005.

To place orders or to request a free copy of the ASQ Quality Press Publications Catalog, including ASQ membership information, call 800-248-1946. Visit our Web site at www.asq.org or http://qualitypress.asq.org.

♾ Printed on acid-free paper

Quality Press
600 N. Plankinton Avenue
Milwaukee, Wisconsin 53203
Call toll free 800-248-1946
Fax 414-272-1734
www.asq.org
http://qualitypress.asq.org
http://standardsgroup.asq.org
E-mail: authors@asq.org

To Larry and Dick

You have shown us the way to excellence by your unselfish love, unfailing support, and eternal patience. You inspire us to make a difference through example.

"Here is Edward Bear, coming downstairs now, bump, bump, bump, on the back of his head, behind Christopher Robin. It is, as far as he knows, the only way of coming downstairs, but sometimes, he feels that there really is another way . . . if only he could stop bumping for a moment and think of it."

Winnie-the-Pooh
A.A. Milne

Contents

CD-ROM Contents

Figures and Tables

Figures

Tables

Foreword

Since the Malcolm Baldrige Award was established in 1987 and the quality movement began taking hold in the 1990s, more business, healthcare, and education organizations have learned the value of systems thinking. Learning organizations, of course, have no finish line when it comes to accomplishing the aim of the system. Continuous improvement is a life-long journey, and those who embark will come to realize that hard work and effort must be sustained over time. The Baldrige Criteria provide a framework for systems that includes leadership and strategic planning among the seven criteria. But leadership, as important as it is, cannot do it alone. As evidenced by corporations and other types of organizations engaged in a systems approach, excellent results will not occur until the "study and practice" permeates the organization.

There Is Another Way! Launch a Baldrige-Based Quality Classroom is among the first, if not the first book, to combine the Baldrige framework and quality issues where they count, inside the classroom. The teacher and the students represent the true culture of the school system and how it operates. Here is a practical guide that teams of teachers, the teacher with his or her students, the school, or the district can use in their quality journey. In embracing this book, those who use it must recognize that this is not a program that has a start and a finish. It is not a fad that will come and go, as the media and other cultural factors might suggest. Entailed is a major cultural shift for teachers and students. It will take knowledge gained from studying this book, courage, and perseverance to ensure success, but it is not overstating the critical need when one observes our current educational system and the students who are not making it in schools across this nation.This is a book for classroom teachers and their students of all ages. It should be used by teacher leaders who yearn for a way to learn how to change the classroom system so that all students achieve success. If you are among those teachers who choose it as your mentor and guide, I wish you every success. This book would have been an outstanding resource for our teachers had it been available when we started our continuous improvement journey. Incorporating the principles and processes in this book will result in having empowered self-directed students who learn more and exhibit higher levels of satisfaction and enthusiasm for their learning.

Robert A. McKanna, Ed.D., CQIA
Superintendent of Schools
Community Consolidated School District 15
Palatine, Illinois
2003 Malcolm Baldrige Award-Winning District

Preface

We are all shaped by our life's experiences, and I am no exception. When I began my teaching career in physical education years ago, the principal way I was evaluated was (1) how many girls dressed for gym class, and (2) of those, how many took showers. Teaching in a high school with 5000 students in suburban Chicago, with a teaching load of seven 45-minute classes each day and 90 students per class, I asked myself, "Is this my purpose?" That question began my quality journey long before it was introduced in education.

The questions continued as I moved from that school district to another in Michigan, where the curricula had not changed in 30 years (the same number of years the department chair had been in the district). Students were disinterested and bored, and frankly so was I. I asked myself, "Why aren't the students interested in learning this stuff?" I wrote a training manual for the students, explaining body types and specific exercises to address problem areas. Next I changed the way we started class to make students responsible for setting personal physical goals. It helped, but wasn't a cure.

When my husband went back to graduate school, I changed districts again and after a year became the department chair. Faced with a change in state legislation (P.E., as a requirement for graduation, was cut from four years to one), a building project that took away all physical education facilities except one gym and the pool, and the real possibility that the district would dismiss at least half of all physical education teachers, I knew we had to take dramatic action.

First, this was a wake-up call because although I was the department chair I was also the most recently hired, which according to our bargaining agreement meant that I would be the first to go. Second, I realized that *students were our customers* and unless we met their needs, few would sign up for physical education as an elective. Third, I realized that the traditional approach to physical education with a heavy emphasis on team sports simply wasn't meeting the needs of many girls. Fourth, while I felt swimming was an important life survival skill, many girls stayed out of the pool more days than they were in. They simply didn't want to get their hair wet. Finally, I had the opportunity to make changes that theretofore were not possible. It was the urgency of the moment that led to the changes we were able to implement and thus not only "save the day" and save everyone's jobs, but also change the future of physical education programs around the country. We had the first coed physical education program in the state and possibly in the nation.

The first step was to define my purpose—to help all students learn the mind/body connections and gain skills that would serve them over a lifetime to remain healthy adults. This led to a scrutiny of the curriculum and a decision about the most important things girls and young women needed to learn. This meant changing the ninth-grade curriculum to something we called "All About You" and requiring the girls to set individual weight and fitness goals, keep track of personal wellness data, and create their own exercise program and work it. We required everyone to take swimming, creative dance movement that included balancing activities, and self-defense.

We spent a lot of time asking the girls what they wanted to learn about their bodies and found as many experts (hair stylists, make-up, clothing) as we could to give demonstrations and offer common-sense advice. (Yes, we screened these folks and were careful about the message they brought to our students.) Other than that, we set a curriculum with one team and one individual sport choice each three weeks. Those who preferred team sports could make that choice. Students were not tracked and had the freedom to choose three times each semester. Sophomore girls were able to make similar choices. We also eliminated grading on the athletic model of winners and losers and began grading on individual achievement against personally set goals. This helped immensely as the overweight girls and students who were not athletically inclined had hope that they could succeed.

During that school year, we would have to share one gym, a pool, a wrestling closet, the cafeteria, and hallways around the gym area. This provided us with leverage to convince the male physical education teachers to institute a co-ed class for junior/senior students that would be based entirely on lifelong activities. We were able to teach golf, bowling, skiing, bridge, fly casting, and tennis. We instituted a policy of "appropriate clothes for physical activity" and defined that for the kids, but we didn't require any specific clothing. Fortunately, we were able to use community facilities and actually taught golf at a local course; it was the same with bowling and skiing. We team-taught all these classes. While the men still offered football, baseball, and basketball to junior and senior guys, we no longer offered any other option. As it turned out, nearly every student in the school signed up for physical education, they learned important skills, and they had fun.

It was the most amazing experience of my teaching career because it taught me a lot about purpose, the need to identify the customer and plan for success, students' need for freedom and choice, and the importance of setting goals and collecting data. I also learned how to engage students in making improvements and how much fun it is when everyone works together to achieve a common purpose. Perhaps most amazing of all was the change in the attitudes of our students. No longer was it a hassle to get the girls to class on time or to have everyone in the pool nearly every day. I witnessed how rewarding it is for students who act as facilitators of learning as well as those who are the recipients of their work. It was amazing! It was the start of my quality journey.

I have learned that it's all about leadership and not at all about "boss management" or coercion. It is psychology; it is a different way of looking at the world—the glass is half full, not half empty. It is about optimism and hope and making decisions to improve based on the data, not on intuition, as I did in the beginning. In those early days I was going on gut instinct based on thoughtful reflection, but nonetheless, there were no training manuals or guides available to me. Dr. Deming? Who ever heard of him? There was no Malcolm Baldrige National Quality Award Program—or criteria for performance excellence. After the Michigan experience, however, my purpose has never wavered.

Through the years it became important to learn as much as possible to help more people be successful. I went back to school for advanced degrees in educational psychology with an emphasis on learning theory, early childhood learning, and guidance and counseling. After that, as my work experiences changed, I founded a vocational school for disadvantaged adults. I began to learn from Drs. Deming, Juran, and the other Quality gurus and became a Stephen Covey *(Seven Habits of Highly Effective People)* trainer. I was appointed to the Board of Examiners for the Baldrige Program, becoming a senior examiner in

2001. Every one of these experiences gave me a perspective that I have honed from providing training to thousands of teachers and administrators around the nation.

—Margaret A. Byrnes

How to Use This Book

This training guide represents one way to look at the Baldrige Criteria and use it to improve classroom systems. It is designed for classroom teachers at all levels as well as teachers in training. The approach described here has proven helpful to teachers all across the nation.

We are aware that in a perfect world, a school district will embrace the Baldrige framework and align and integrate all systems and processes to create districtwide systemic change and improvement. In this somewhat less than perfect world, a school administrator may see the value of the Baldrige approach even if the district has not seen fit to do so. In such a situation, the changes made will affect everyone in this particular school. If neither the school district nor your administrator has knowledge of Baldrige or the desire to embrace this performance excellence model, you have the ability to move forward to help your students make the improvements needed for their success. We urge you not to use a lack of administrative support as a reason for not creating a Baldrige-based quality (BBQ) classroom. When teachers understand the Baldrige framework and how it applies to their work and when systemic changes are made based on the criteria, everyone wins. We encourage administrators and other school leaders to use this training guide to learn about BBQ classrooms, that they may lead and support teachers in their efforts to change.

We have organized this training guide with an introduction to quality theory and the Baldrige framework in the belief that this knowledge will help you better understand what we think is a logical approach to a complex subject, system re-creation. At times we were challenged because a Baldrige-based approach is not linear; it is one where all processes are aligned and integrated. *One problem in classroom systems is that many teachers are linear thinkers; linear thinking often fails to embrace integration of processes.* So, if that is your normal cognitive approach, you may have to reread and make adjustments. Included are examples from different regions of the country, different educational levels, and a variety of classes with the hope that you will be able to relate your own situation to the one we have described.

We have included the tools and embedded them just-in-time for the appropriate activity, and have included a Tools Selection Chart in Chapter 1. This placement is to help you refer immediately to the tools instructions for each activity, but with the Tools Selection Chart you can easily find instructions for each tool when applying them to your own journey.

Our approach is practical; the many activities have been tested and improved in our training sessions with real teachers. We urge you to make this training guide your resource while you become an active learner. *It is not a book that you should read and put on a shelf; it is a book intended for "doers." Depending on your learning style, however, you may need a "first read-through" to give you an overview before you begin.* Practice the activities, the approaches, the Plan-Do-Study-Act, and the tools until you feel comfortable enough to go before a class of students. That is the best way to learn.

Imagine we are sitting together while you read this training guide. Each chapter begins with a personal conversation. These conversations are similar to how we would be conversing if you were right beside us, and it is our hope that they stimulate your thinking as well as set the stage for learning. It will help if you have the opportunity to learn with peers or colleagues in your school or district. If, however, a partner is not available, don't let that keep you from launching the approach.

Is a BBQ classroom for you? You need only ask the following questions to decide whether the use of the Baldrige framework and quality improvement approach would help: Are you satisfied with the student learning results? Are you convinced that *all* students are learning to their maximum potential? How do you know? Is the atmosphere in the classroom one of enthusiasm for learning and excitement that arises from learning new, more difficult skills and knowing how to apply these new skills and knowledge? Are the students challenged appropriately? Are students treating one another with care and respect? Are there fewer interruptions caused by undisciplined students? Are you, the students' leader, enjoying the process of guiding them to greater learning? Are parents satisfied that their children are safe and engaged and learning what they need to learn? Is the next-teacher-in-line satisfied that the students have gained the skills needed on which to build future success?

If your answer to any of these questions is "No" or "I'm not sure," then *There Is Another Way! Launch a Baldrige-Based Quality Classroom* is meant for you!

Acknowledgments

There are many people to thank who have helped make this training guide a reality. We are deeply indebted to Hubert Minn, Candace (Allen) Smith, Valerie Stowell-Hart, and Bette Wilson, who are exceptional educators and continuously inspire us and with whom we originally developed many of the activities contained in this guide. Dr. Charles Holmes from Savannah, Georgia, Joe Washington from the Chicago Public Schools, the wonderful people at the Hawaii Quality Network, and the entire staff at Voyager Charter School in Honolulu have, by example, thoughtful discussion, and persistence, helped shape our overall philosophy and improve our approach. Bob Ewy and Carol Ann Rush from CCSD15, Palatine, Illinois, pushed our thinking beyond good to great. Their insights, questions, and support have been invaluable. Sherry Bright, an exceptional fellow senior Baldrige examiner, gave us a professional critique that immensely improved the final product. We also want to thank Paul O'Mara, our editor, for his expertise, insights, ideas, and patience, and Amanda Hosey at Thistle Hill Publishing Services for her attention to every detail and her confidence that we could "get it right." To those school districts, teachers, and administrators who have given us permission to share their work and ideas, we are appreciative and believe this has improved our ability to make some key points. Last, there are thousands of teachers and administrators who have touched our lives over the years, pushing us to analyze and practice what we preach—continuous improvement. This book is the result of all those efforts. Thanks to you all.

—Margaret A. Byrnes
—Jeanne C. Baxter

1

QUALITY AND THE BALDRIGE FRAMEWORK

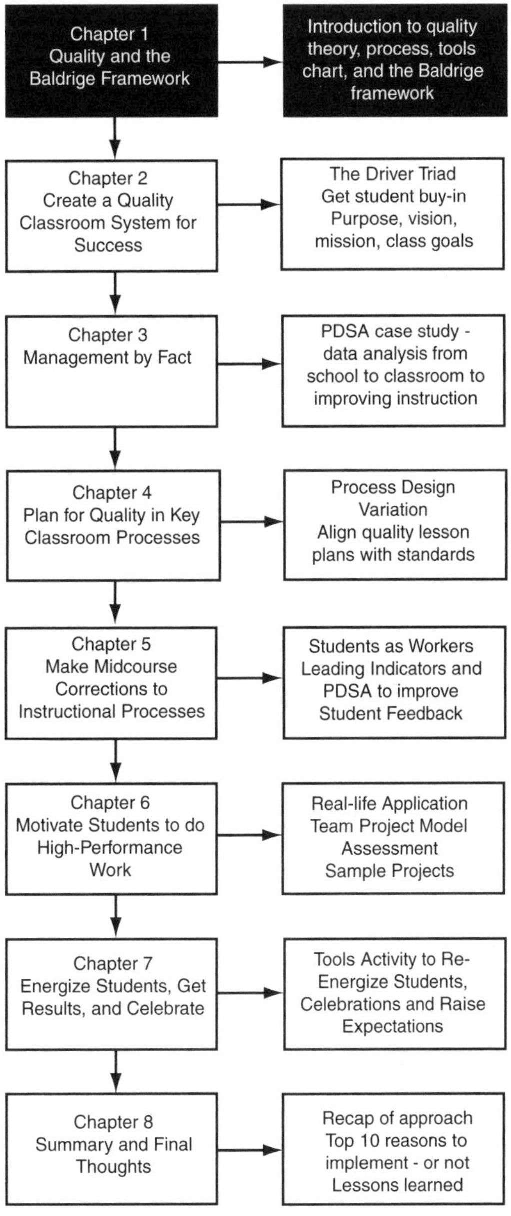

Chapter 1
Quality and the Baldrige Framework
Introduction to quality theory, process, tools chart, and the Baldrige framework
Chapter 2
Create a Quality Classroom System for Success
The Driver Triad
Get student buy-in
Purpose, vision, mission, class goals
Chapter 3
Management by Fact
PDSA case study - data analysis from school to classroom to improving instruction
Chapter 4
Plan for Quality in Key Classroom Processes
Process Design
Variation
Align quality lesson plans with standards
Chapter 5
Make Midcourse Corrections to Instructional Processes
Students as Workers
Leading Indicators and PDSA to improve Student Feedback
Chapter 6
Motivate Students to do High-Performance Work
Real-life Application
Team Project Model
Assessment
Sample Projects
Chapter 7
Energize Students, Get Results, and Celebrate
Tools Activity to Re-Energize Students, Celebrations and Raise Expectations
Chapter 8
Summary and Final Thoughts
Recap of approach
Top 10 reasons to implement - or not
Lessons learned

Conversation with the Teacher

Why do some students learn faster than others? And why do some never quite "get it"? How concerned are you about your students achieving the annual yearly progress required by the No Child Left Behind Act? Adding new programs (textbooks, software, kits, and so on) may provide some improvement, but unless you understand your classroom system and the root causes of why some students don't learn, you can never be certain that you have optimized learning and the educational experience for all students. Have you ever experienced a situation where you feel compelled to add more rules, becoming more structured in response to a problem, only to discover that after a short while the problem returns and sometimes is even worse than before? Help is on the way, as you will learn a better way to address classroom issues.

Teachers who have created Baldrige-based quality classrooms routinely have students who learn more and enjoy learning. Teachers who have created Baldrige-based quality classrooms report they are less stressed, have more fun watching students get excited about learning, and have a greater sense of efficacy. While we don't purport to have the answer to every problem, and we realize learning the approach might at times be overwhelming and may cause cognitive dissonance for a time, the end result will prove worthwhile. You don't have to take our word for this; just join the thousands of your peers we've trained, have faith, and enjoy the journey. You'll be amazed at how students blossom in an environment where the teachers trust them and engage them as true partners in changing the classroom system.

In this chapter you will learn about:

- The theory of Total Quality Education
- Classroom Systems
- The Plan-Do-Study-Act Improvement Cycle and an overview of the quality tools
- The Baldrige Framework for Performance Excellence

What Quality Is and What It Isn't

Total Quality Education (TQE) is a planned approach to systemic improvement. It requires (1) visionary leaders (2) to maintain a customer focus and have the humility to realize that (3) workers are in the best position to analyze and help seek solutions to system and process problems. (Students are both customers and workers in the classroom, and therefore they play an important role in problem solving.) Leaders/teachers must practice excellent communication skills and willingly empower and support others in risk taking, the use of a systematic approach to problem solving, and commitment to learning and acting based on data. True leaders must stay the course, encouraging those within the organization and enlightening external customers while remaining passionate about the need for improvement leading to excellence. TQE requires persistence and patience, and improves quality by removing the root causes of problems in the system. *This inevitably leads to improved student learning!*

The goal is to improve effectiveness and efficiency throughout the system. This can be applied at any aspect of a school district, individual schools, or classrooms, but this training guide will focus on the classroom. We'll begin by looking at the three key aspects mentioned earlier and explore the relationships between them, finally learning how it all fits together to achieve Quality.

Figure 1.1 shows the relationship between leadership and customer focus. Teachers are leaders in the classroom. It is important to know who your customers are and what they need and expect. When teachers understand this and are able to create a system that focuses on customer needs and expectations, the result is high satisfaction. Naturally, leaders must also have methods to build and sustain relationships with their primary customers. These are the four most important customers of any classroom, in priority order:

1. Students
2. Next-teacher-in-line
3. Parents
4. Building administration

Figure 1.1 Leadership and customer focus.

Is it important that students and other stakeholders are satisfied? Consider the consequences of dissatisfied students and discuss this with a partner.

Directions: Fill in the chart below by identifying some behaviors you might expect from satisfied or dissatisfied students. How might these behaviors impact learning?

	Satisfied Students	Dissatisfied Students
Likely Behavior		

Figure 1.2 gives insight into the relationship between customer focus and continuous process improvement. This shows that the way to continuously improve is to stay focused on satisfying customer needs/expectations, knowing that the *most important things* a teacher can change are the key classroom processes. Unless data are collected and analyzed, any changes will be based on intuition, which may or may not be accurate and may or may not address the root cause of any problems. Therefore, it is imperative

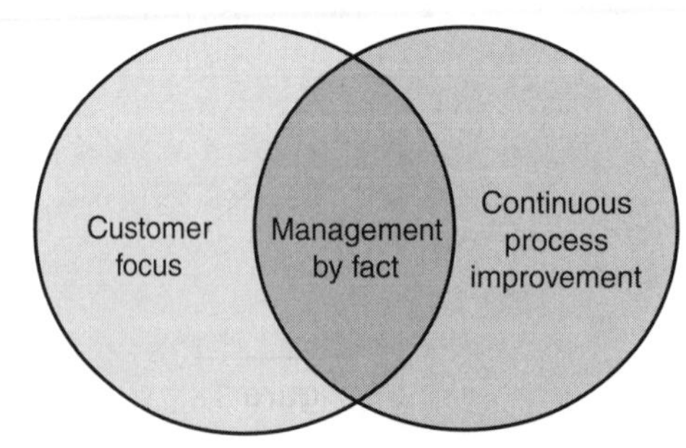

Figure 1.2 Customer focus and continuous process improvement.

that teachers understand that management by fact *is* the approach to use to achieve process improvement, which will turn into greater customer satisfaction.

Teachers pride themselves on being problem solvers. It might be a natural reaction to give more math homework if quiz results show students have not mastered the math operations. However, this may not necessarily resolve the problem. Recall a time when you may have forgotten the importance of maintaining a customer focus and decided to change a process based on intuition or in reaction to a perceived problem. What was the immediate result? What was the long-term result? Figure 1.2 shows that management by fact is the most effective approach to eliminating problems if long-term solutions are the desired result.

A look at the relationship between continuous process improvement and visionary leaders in Figure 1.3 demonstrates that leaders must be involved in improving the system and held accountable for the results. It is wise for us to recall the admonition by the Father of Modern Quality, Dr. W. Edwards Deming, that your system yields exactly the results it was designed to get. If leaders (teachers) are not able or willing to continuously improve every key classroom process, it will be impossible to predict increased learning results and joy of learning or decreased behavior problems and absenteeism. The continuous process improvement model for any Quality organization is called Plan-Do-Study-Act, or PDSA. PDSA is a systematic, structured, scientific approach to eliminating problems and increasing effectiveness and efficiency of any process. You will have the opportunity to practice several PDSA approaches when reading this guide.

While each circle in Figures 1.1–1.3 and its intersections is important, it is not until these are integrated into a whole (Figure 1.4) that leaders have a holistic picture of a highly effective and efficient system, which we call Total Quality Education.

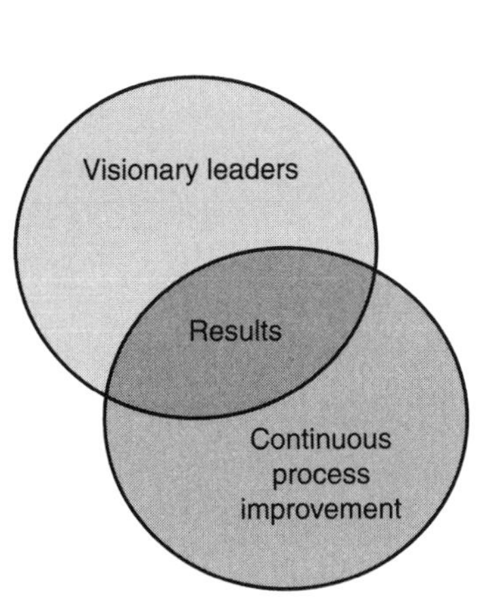

Figure 1.3 Visionary leaders and continuous process improvement.

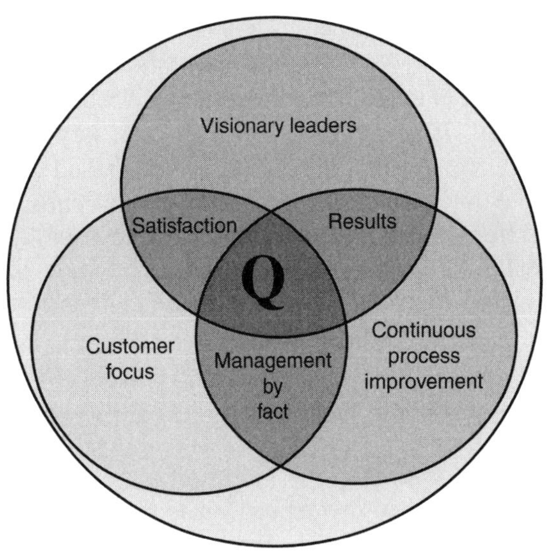

Figure 1.4 A quality system.

The Baldrige criteria that will be discussed later in this chapter are the framework, building blocks, and glue that lead to organizational performance excellence.

> *Deciding to enter into a quality process in education is* not *because good things are not happening but because of a desire to have good things happen regularly, consistently, and predictably at every level of the school system.*
>
> *Random acts of excellence have little effect on the desired strategic results.*

Quality is not a quick fix or a silver bullet. It is not a race. It has no finish line because the world and customer expectations are constantly in a state of flux, so the requirements for success continue to increase. Therefore, there is a need to stay ahead of the curve through researching the latest and most innovative approaches to learning, understanding and using new knowledge in your content area, and adapting your instructional activities so your students are prepared to meet any challenge that lies ahead of them. Be aware that these strategies alone, without system change, won't optimize your results.

Dr. Deming emphasizes that leaders must drive out fear! Teachers and administrators seldom realize how fear influences learning on a daily basis, but the brain-research experts confirm how devastating fear is to anyone attempting to learn. What are the causes of fear in school today? One major cause is the high-stakes testing approach to accountability. Teachers are fearful of the pressures caused by the No Child Left Behind Act and the Annual Yearly Progress requirements. (Students are afraid too because of the enormous pressure put on them by the school, teachers, and frequently parents.) It has not been our experience that teachers reject standards, but many are confused about how to do their job to predict success and achieve the desired results. Many districts have adopted new texts or software in an attempt to reach the state requirements, only to find that progress continues to be sporadic and unpredictable. This leads many educators to blame students or parents, or even the previous teacher, for the failure of some students to meet grade level requirements.

Another aspect of this fear comes from the challenges teachers must meet today. High among these is the fear of violence such as happened at Columbine or at the school in Beslan, Russia. Other challenges include the increase in numbers of students who lack English-speaking skills, who lack civility, who are undisciplined or disrespectful, who cannot read, and whose parents don't seem to care and the barrage of edicts coming from central administration and the state and federal governments. Add to this the perception of not enough time in the school day/year to accomplish the daunting task of getting everyone to do well on the state standards test and you have teachers who are tense at the start of the year and who become more anxious as the testing date draws closer. Who could think of creating a system focused on learning when they feel the pressure to "cover the curriculum" and ensure high test scores? How can teachers get students with major deficiencies to master subjects or meet grade level expectations when they work in a system that encourages short-term memorization, as described in *Permission to Forget,* a thoughtful book by Lee Jenkins?

On the other hand, students face many fears in the classroom too. Among these are bullying and intimidation by both students and teachers; too many and too strict rules—or no rules; too much or not enough structure; no freedom to make decisions; not enough or too much attention from the teacher; expectations from parents or the school/district that seem too high; and the threat of being held back a grade because of low test scores. If a student with limited English skills is required by his or her family to speak their native language at home, this can result in feelings of isolation, intimidation, and ridicule from their classmates. A student who "looks different" from the others often experiences similar treatment from classmates.

Those who cannot read, however, experience the worst fear. The fact that these students even come to school is quite amazing, because the fear of being discovered brings about the greatest shame. This fear is compounded each year. Is it any wonder that nonreaders are more likely to act out or drop out? If there are students in your classes who fall into this category—overage and unable to read—you know what we're talking about. This raises many questions for teachers as they seek ways to bring these nonreaders up to grade level. Throughout this guide you'll learn strategies for creating a system that will increase the chances for every student to be successful.

A Systems View

Dr. Deming says, "A system is a network of interdependent components that work together to try to accomplish the aim of the system. . . . Without an aim, there is no system. . . . An aim . . . must always relate to a better life for everyone" (*The New Economics,* 2nd edition, pages 50 and 52). In a school district, the system (district) has three levels. Levels one and two, as shown in Figure 1.5, provide an example. Note that at each of these levels, there are many subsystems. The third level, which is the system level this manual focuses on, is the classroom. Figure 1.6 on page 8 provides an overview of the complexity and elements of a classroom system.

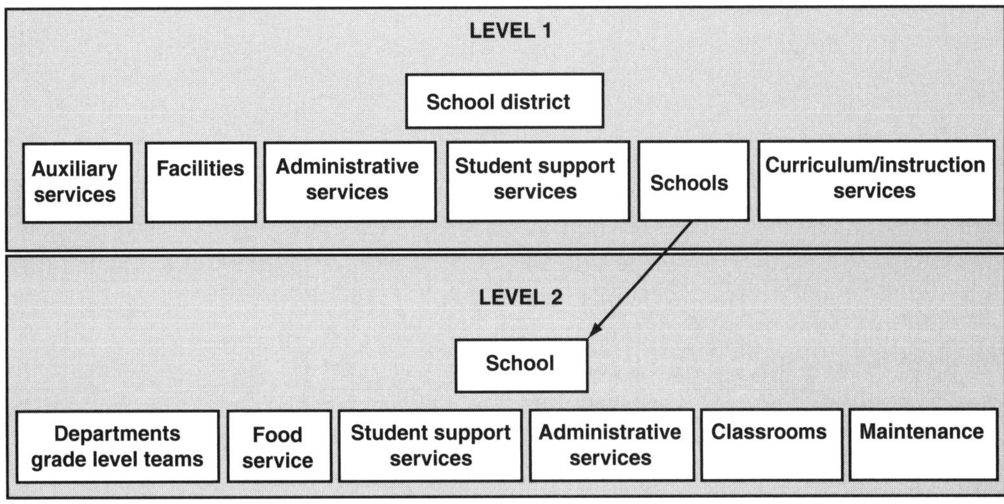

Figure 1.5 High altitude look—levels of district subsystems.

A former superintendent from New York, Dr. Al Mammary, once shared this message with his teachers: "Never, ever lower your standards for students who 'won't,' and, only after trying every approach, would you negotiate standards for students who 'can't.'" Dr. Mammary's message was that most often teachers quickly lower standards and expectations for students, thinking that they "can't," when really it is because the students *don't want to learn in the ways the teacher wants to teach.* This is an important message for anyone working with students regardless of mental capacity. It has been my experience that many more students fall into the "won't" category than into the "can't."

The aim or purpose of every classroom ought to be to facilitate learning and a love of learning among all students. This requires teachers to take a different view of their own purpose. If you have the view that your purpose is to teach, and once taught it is no longer your problem if students don't learn, you will create a classroom system based on the athletic model of winners and losers. On the other hand, teachers who view themselves as *facilitators of learning* realize their success is measured by how many students gain the skills, knowledge, and abilities required within the semester or school year. These teachers will leave no stone uncovered in their quest for all students to achieve success, and they will not lower their standards.

Let's take a closer look at Figure 1.6 and some of the key terms. *Inputs* into the system are things (people, policies, materials, mandates, curriculum, and attitudes) that influence the system. Note the second input from Figure 1.6 is *teacher's personal biases, attitudes, knowledge, skills, and feelings of efficacy.* While we often insist that students leave their personal "baggage" outside the classroom, teachers frequently bring their own baggage in, and it *does* matter because it influences the relationship between teacher and student and often impedes learning. More on this later when we get into classroom strategic planning.

When problems arise within the system, or if the results are not as desired, look to the *key processes* (see Figure 1.6 for examples) for answers. A process is a series of steps taken to achieve a task. The way to improve is to use the Plan-Do-Study-Act (PDSA) improvement cycle, which will be described in more detail throughout this training guide. The way to manage key processes is through systematic collection and analysis of in-process data,

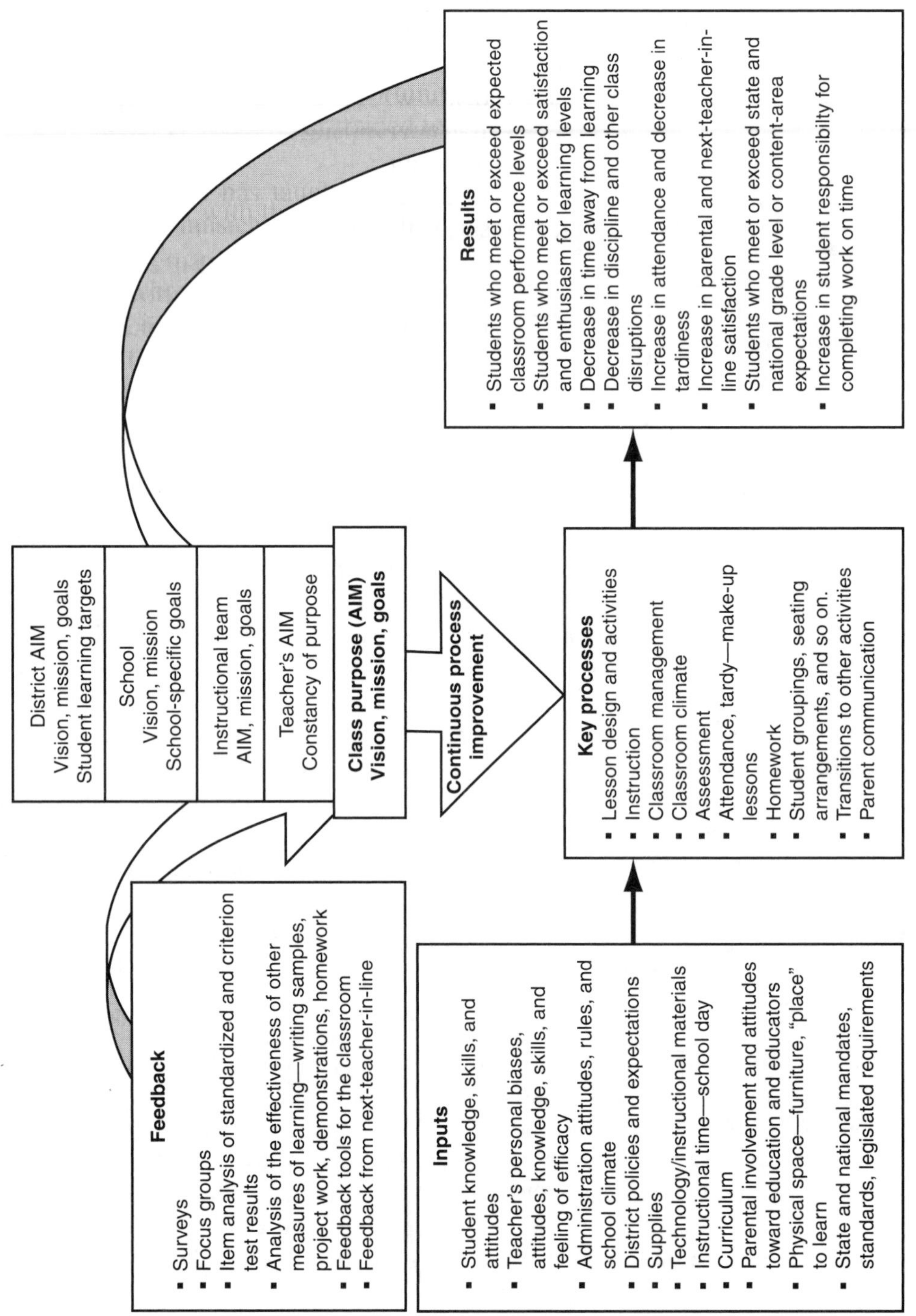

Figure 1.6 Classroom system diagram.

and using the information it yields to make midcourse corrections in order to predict that good things will happen regularly and consistently.

Results are the product of your system. These include student learning results, student and stakeholder satisfaction, student enthusiasm for learning, behavioral results, attendance/tardy results. These data are used to prepare for the next strategic planning cycle and to inform leadership and stakeholders how effective and efficient the system was. They are not useful for ensuring or for predicting success in that cycle. By the time results are collected, it is too late to build in quality. Students will be gone, and opportunities for improvement will be lost with that group. The traditional bell curve (see Glossary), shown in Figure 1.7, means an abundance of rework is required of the next-teacher-in-line. The bandwidth of variation represents the spread of all data points for any process, and the greater the bandwidth of variation (see Glossary), the more rework required, and ultimately the loss of time. We all agree that instructional time is scarce, and each year the numbers of students who don't meet the standards exponentially grows, taking additional time away from learning the skills at that grade or course level.

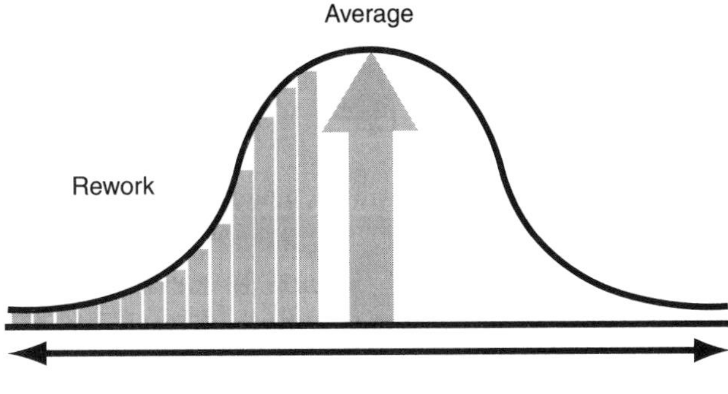

Figure 1.7 Bell curve—traditional systems.

This is why it is essential to collect in-process data and apply the PDSA cycle of improvement to all key processes *during the school year, on a regular and systematic basis.* Figure 1.8 shows what happens in Baldrige-based classrooms. Note how the average is raised and the bandwidth of variation is decreased. The amount of rework dramatically decreases as many more students meet the requirements.

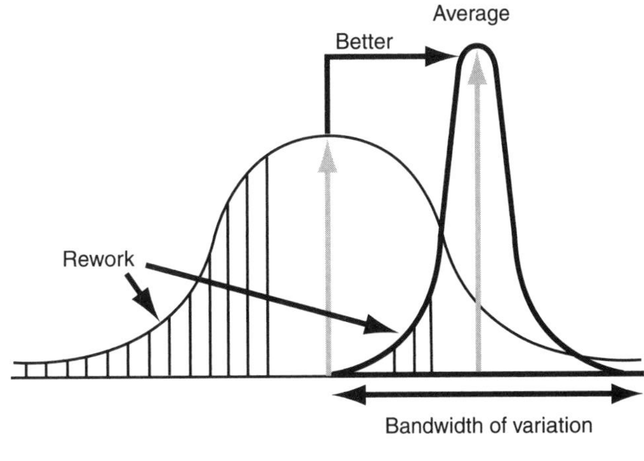

Figure 1.8 Improved learning results in a BBQ system.

How does this happen? Your system is informed through various *feedback* mechanisms. The more frequent and systematically feedback is sought from students as workers and as customers as well as from the next-teacher-in-line and other stakeholders, the better your chances of improving the system to remove barriers to student success. Feedback is *not useful if it is not used to improve.*

> *If you don't want to know what students and stakeholders think, don't ask. If you ask, don't take the answers personally; take them as "gifts" to help you improve the system by removing the barriers identified through the feedback mechanisms. In other words, become a leader, not a boss-manager. The worst thing any teacher can do is become defensive and react negatively.*

Equally important in a Baldrige-based quality classroom is the elimination of things that detract from the purpose and reduce instructional time, such as discipline issues, transitional time, and tardiness. In this case, the goal of an effective and efficient system is to lower the average number of negative incidents until all are extinguished. Figure 1.9 shows what this might look like. Lost instructional time and students' learning opportunities are the most significant resources wasted.

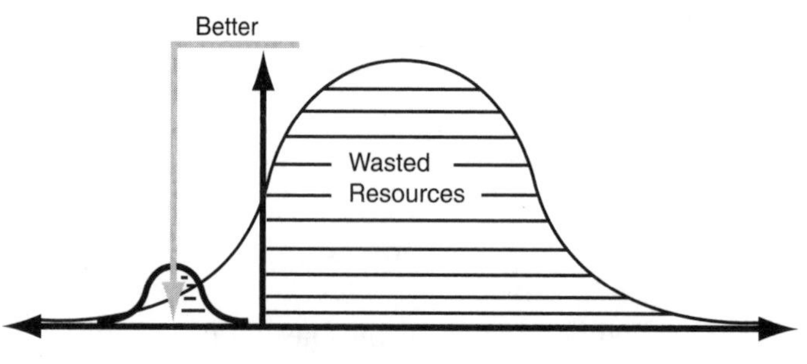

Figure 1.9 Improve effectiveness and efficiency of processes and reduce negative behavior or results.

It behooves you to ask, "Am I satisfied with the current results?" Remember, *management creates the system into which the workers must "fit."* Students are workers in the classroom system created by the teacher. If some of the students are not successful in the system you've created, *it is your responsibility to find out what barriers exist,* change the system to drive out fear, and empower workers to solve problems. *Nothing will give you sustained improved results unless the system is changed.*

System improvement begins with trust. Students must be able to trust their teacher and the other adults in the classroom. Teachers set the tone and expectations of civility and respect, and they must become comfortable knowing a dynamic system allows for continual improvement and retains the hope and expectation that everyone can succeed. The number one issue of at-risk children is "no hope for the future." Teachers have an obligation to instill hope by changing the classroom system.

The students are incapable of "fixing" the classroom system on their own. They do not have the authority unless teachers give it to them. Teachers in Quality classrooms quickly realize they have nothing to fear from seeking help from students to eliminate system problems. Asking students for help requires *teachers to listen nonjudgmentally and accept their suggestions* or explain why it is not possible to do so. When teachers become upset and insist on the "my way or the highway" approach, trust is lost and other problems will surface that may never be able to be resolved. *Therefore, the decision to enter into the Baldrige-based quality approach should not be taken lightly. Once you've made the decision, you cannot go back to traditional, boss-management approaches even when feeling overwhelmed.*

Remember, the aim of education is to facilitate learning and a love of learning. If students are happy in your classroom but not learning or meeting expectations, there are barriers keeping them from success. It is essential that students leave your classroom with the skills, knowledge, and abilities required to meet future challenges. Foremost among these are the fundamental skills of literacy and math. However, it is also important for students to expand their cognitive and problem-solving abilities; to develop emotional intelligence, self-discipline, and civility; and to develop the ability to work with a team of diverse students, to accept personal responsibility for one's own actions, to accomplish tasks within a given amount of time, and to access information and analyze data. It requires a balance between working independently and with others to accomplish difficult tasks. Anything short of this would not be considered success, as these are the requirements for good citizenship and productive citizens.

As you begin to think about the classroom system you've created, it's a good idea to begin to identify the barriers that might be keeping some students from being successful.

Directions: Keep in mind, your system is yielding exactly the results it was designed to get. Reflect on how many students are successful in your system, as defined previously, and visualize the faces of those who struggle in your class. Write about what barriers you think exist in your classroom. Barriers to success might include, but are not limited to, the following: classroom organization, student involvement in decision-making, structure, time to accomplish tasks, instructional methods or instructional materials.

The Quality Improvement Process: Remove Barriers to Success

The Plan-Do-Study-Act Cycle

The process requires four sequential steps, as shown in Figure 1.10. Note that *Plan* takes half the total time and *Study* consumes about 50 percent of the remaining time. Many teachers and administrators complain that they don't have enough time to give to this sort of thing, that they have a curriculum to cover, and that this demonstrates how impractical the Quality theory is in education. In fact, taking a systems view, people realize this is what has caused so many recurring failures in education today.

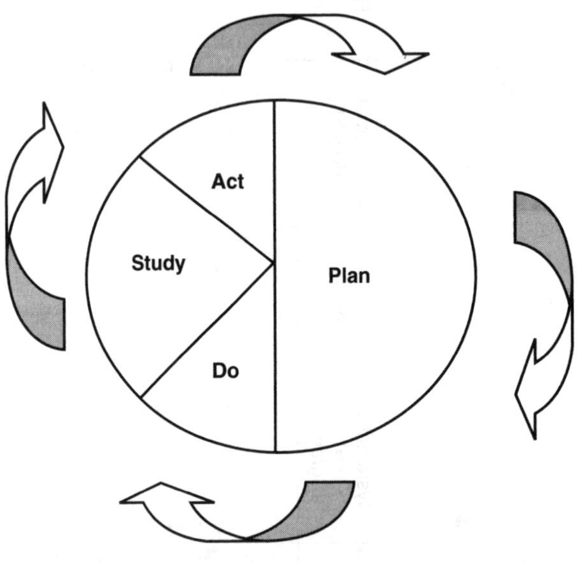

Figure 1.10 Plan-Do-Study-Act cycle.

Instead, teachers and administrators pride themselves on *Action* and seldom take time to understand the root cause of any problem before arriving at a "sure-fire solution." These solutions are based more on intuition or on copycatting other school districts or classrooms without realizing that each situation and culture is somewhat different and the root cause of problems is not always the same. These "solutions" seldom eliminate the original situation and sometimes make it worse. Most frequently, problems recur and take more time away from the purpose, which is to facilitate learning and create a joy of learning.

The structured problem-solving process (PDSA) uses graphical techniques to produce better solutions faster than an unstructured process. It recognizes that those involved in the work are in the best position to help resolve any issues because they know the job best. In the classroom, this means students will be involved in problem solving; throughout this book, you'll discover how this can happen efficiently.

The following table shows the variety of quality tools that can be used during the PDSA cycle and highlights the purpose of each tool. You will learn how to use some of these tools by following instructions in this book. Detailed instructions are provided for "just-in-time" tools training in each chapter. Careful selection of the tools saves a great deal of time when understanding root causes and problem solving. Even young students can learn and use the tools, including Pareto charts and scatter diagrams, which are the most difficult of them all.

Tool selection chart

If you want to:	Gather ideas	Group ideas	Analyze	Sequence steps	Draw a picture of the data	Collect or track data over time	Prioritize get group consensus	Show relationships
	Affinity diagram Page 127	Affinity diagram Page 127	Cause/effect diagram Page 90	Flow chart Page 107	Histogram Page 68	Check sheet Page 96	Multivoting Page 41	Radar chart Page 45
	Satellite diagram Page 182	Satellite diagram Page 182	Force field analysis Page 124	Gantt chart Page 184	Pareto chart Page 86	Run chart Page 66	*Nominal group technique	Relations digraph Page 128
	Brainstorm	Lotus diagram Page 175	Relations digraph Page 128	*Systematic (tree) diagram	Run chart Page 66	Line graph Page 81	Relations digraph Page 128	Scatter diagram Page 83
Use This Tool	Lotus diagram Page 175	Force field analysis Page 124	Pareto chart Page 86		Scatter diagram Page 83	Pareto chart Page 86		Enthusiasm and learning chart Page 157
	Force field analysis Page 124		Fast feedback Page 156		Radar chart Page 45	*Control chart		
			Plus/delta chart Page 194		Line graph Page 81			
			How helpful... Page 125		*Control chart			

*Tools not included in this book, but widely available through a number of resources. See recommended reading for details.
This chart is modified from *Charting Your Course* by John G. Conyers and Robert Ewy, ASQ Quality Press, 2004.

Tools of Quality

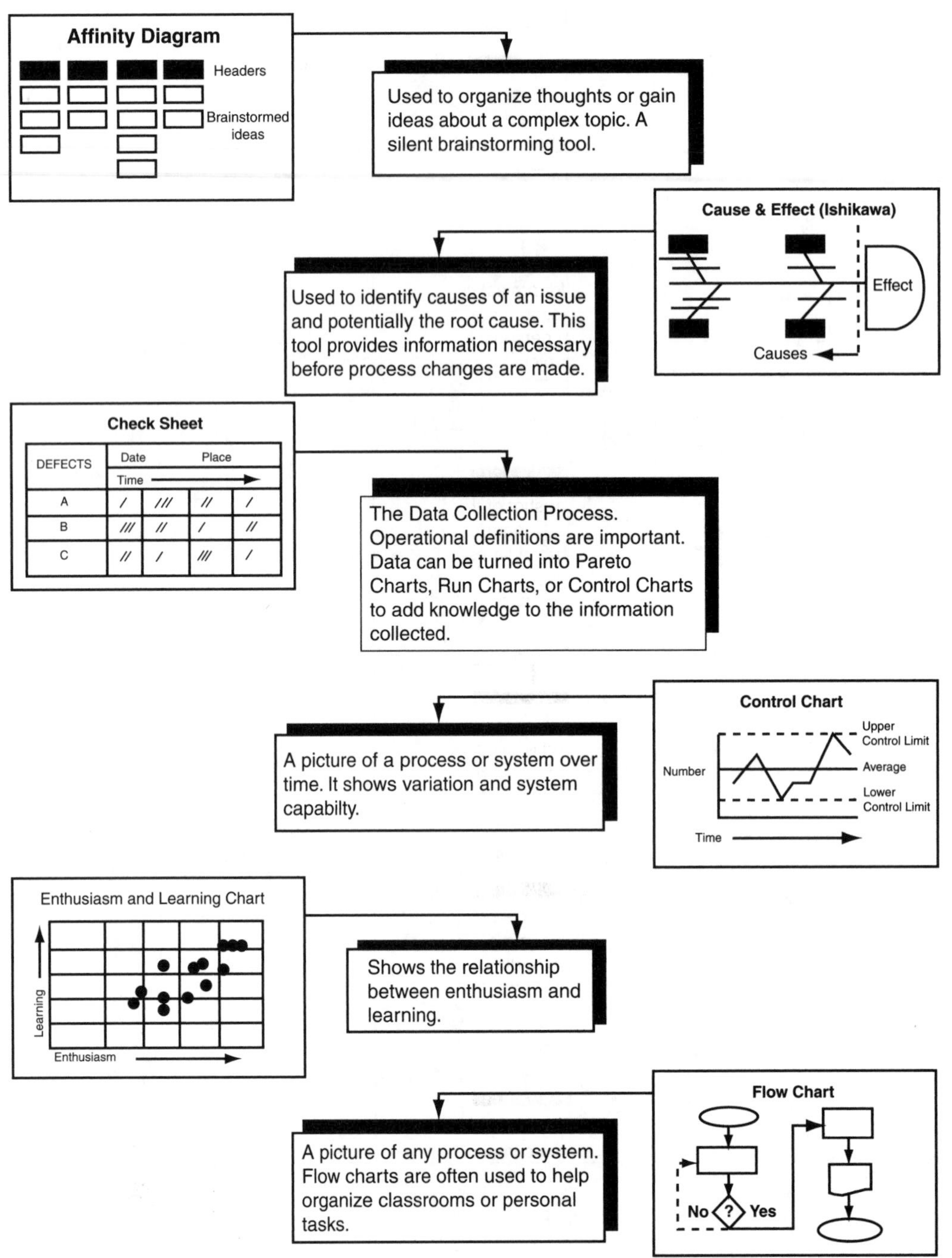
Affinity Diagram
Headers
Brainstormed ideas
Used to organize thoughts or gain ideas about a complex topic. A silent brainstorming tool.
Cause & Effect (Ishikawa)
Effect
Causes
Used to identify causes of an issue and potentially the root cause. This tool provides information necessary before process changes are made.
Check Sheet
DEFECTS
Date
Place
Time
A
B
C
The Data Collection Process. Operational definitions are important. Data can be turned into Pareto Charts, Run Charts, or Control Charts to add knowledge to the information collected.
Control Chart
Upper Control Limit
Average
Lower Control Limit
Number
Time
A picture of a process or system over time. It shows variation and system capabilty.
Enthusiasm and Learning Chart
Learning
Enthusiasm
Shows the relationship between enthusiasm and learning.
Flow Chart
No
?
Yes
A picture of any process or system. Flow charts are often used to help organize classrooms or personal tasks.

Tools of Quality

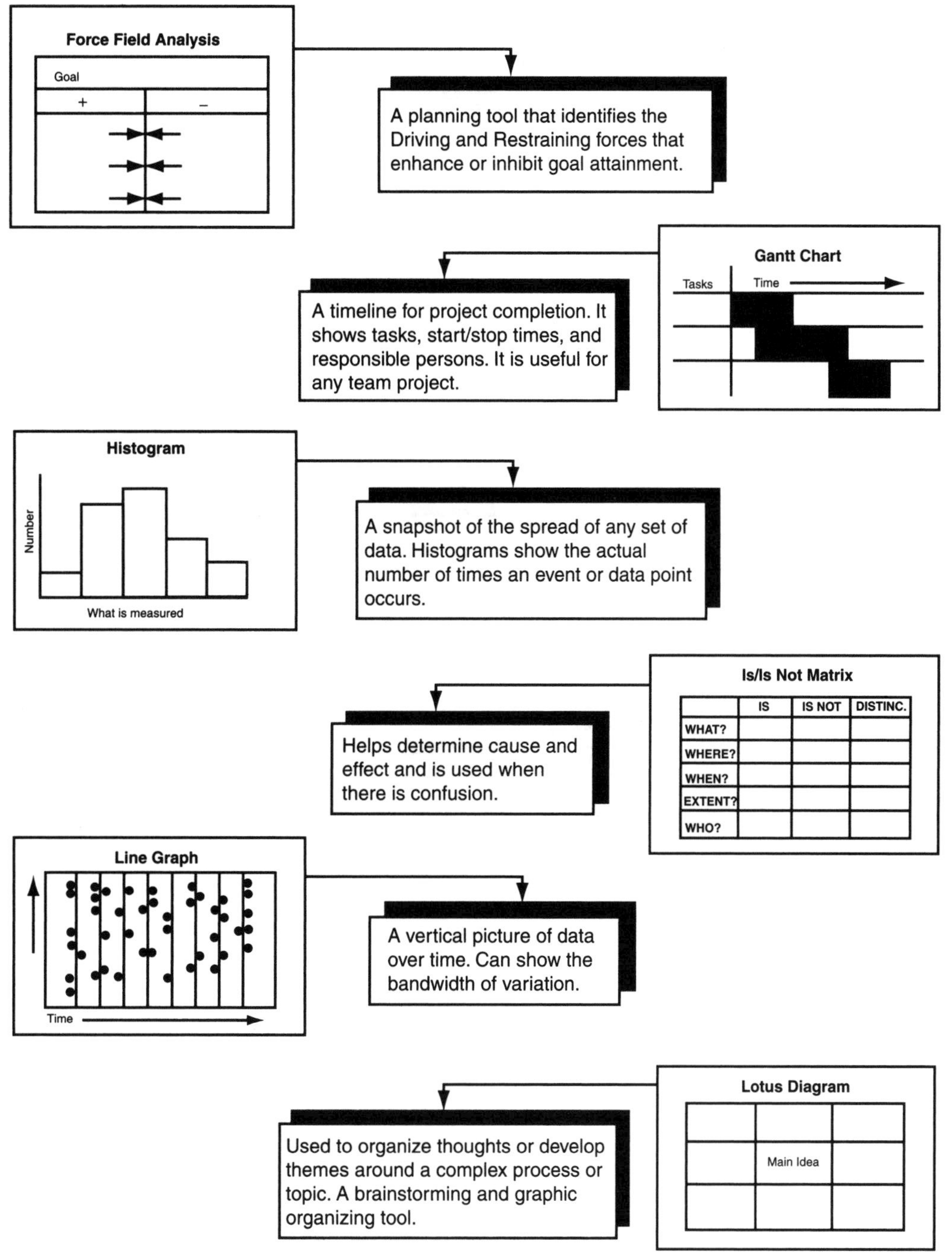

Tools of Quality

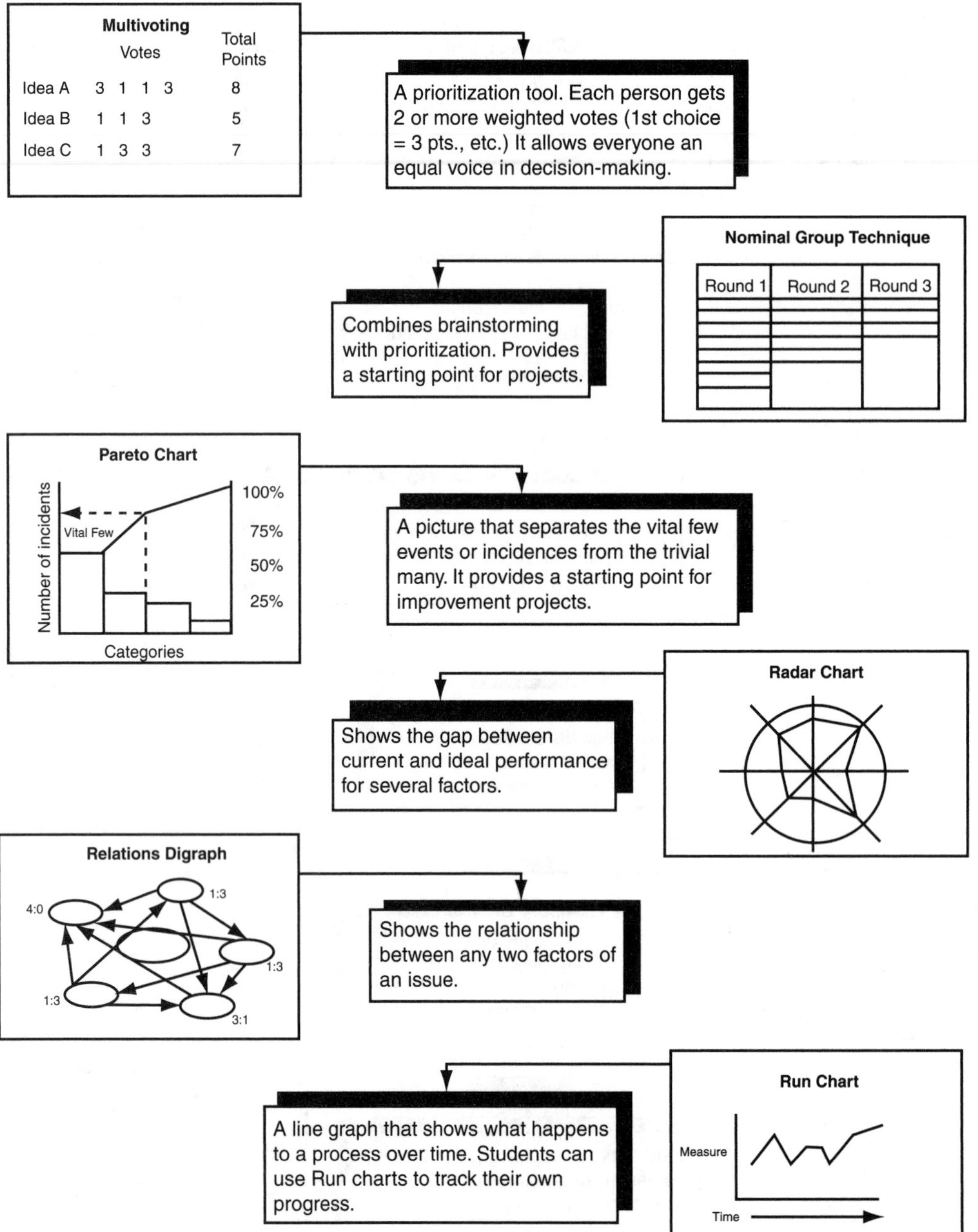

Multivoting
Votes
Total Points
Idea A 3 1 1 3 8
Idea B 1 1 3 5
Idea C 1 3 3 7
A prioritization tool. Each person gets 2 or more weighted votes (1st choice = 3 pts., etc.) It allows everyone an equal voice in decision-making.
Nominal Group Technique
Round 1
Round 2
Round 3
Combines brainstorming with prioritization. Provides a starting point for projects.
Pareto Chart
Number of incidents
Vital Few
100%
75%
50%
25%
Categories
A picture that separates the vital few events or incidences from the trivial many. It provides a starting point for improvement projects.
Radar Chart
Shows the gap between current and ideal performance for several factors.
Relations Digraph
4:0
1:3
1:3
1:3
3:1
Shows the relationship between any two factors of an issue.
Run Chart
Measure
Time
A line graph that shows what happens to a process over time. Students can use Run charts to track their own progress.

Tools of Quality

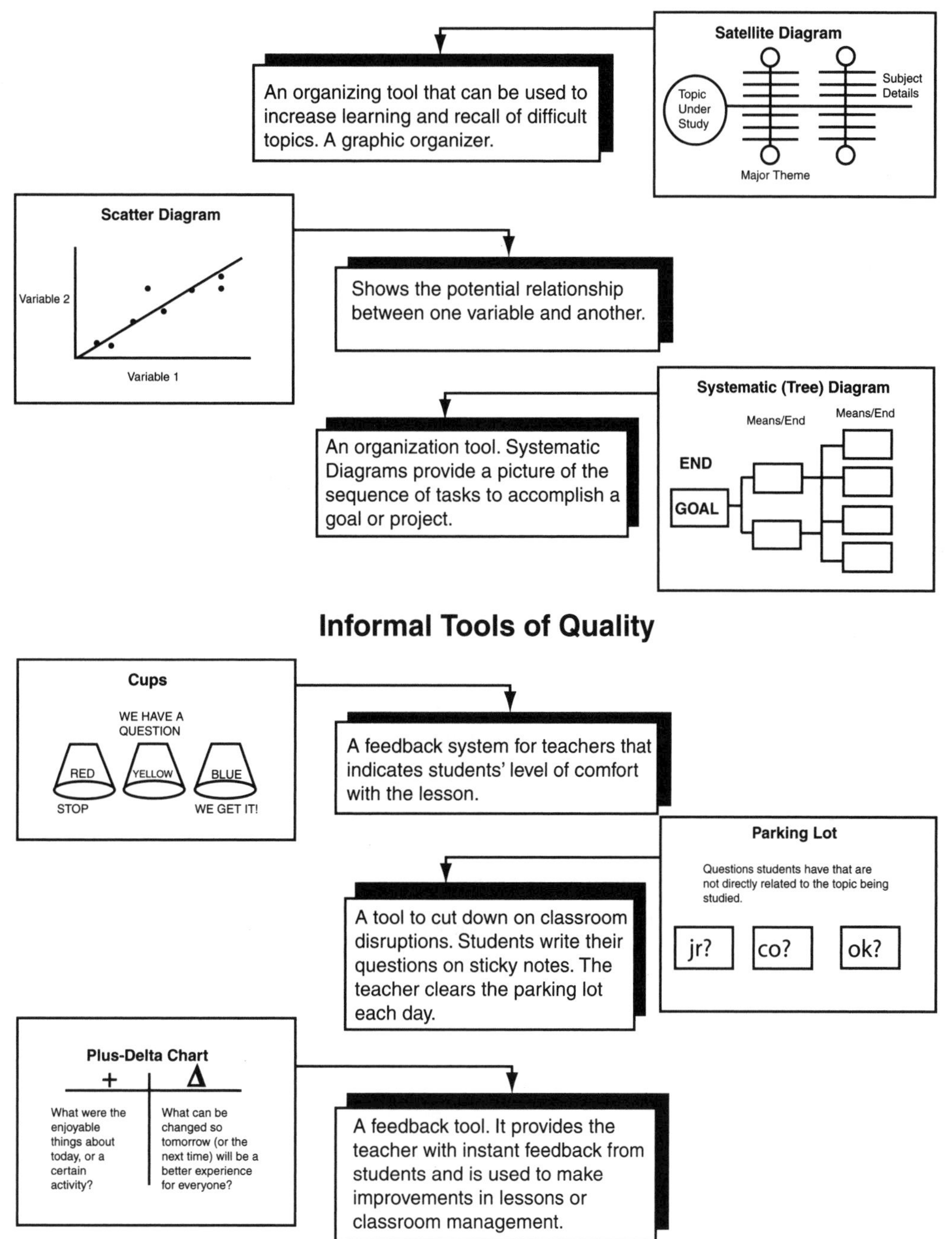

Baldrige: The Framework for Excellence

The Malcolm Baldrige National Quality Award Program was signed into law by President Reagan in August 1987 as a public/private partnership to recognize performance excellence in business. Named after former Secretary of Commerce Malcolm Baldrige, the award process now includes education, health care, and nonprofits. More than 40 states and many countries have programs modeled after the Baldrige Award. The criteria and framework are widely recognized as the most effective approach to organizational performance excellence. Since the inception of the Baldrige Award, three K-12 school districts have been awarded this high honor. They are Pearl River School District, Pearl River, NY; Chugach Schools, Anchorage, AK; and Community Consolidated School District 15, Palatine, IL. For contact information, check out their websites, which are listed on page 286.

The underpinnings of the Baldrige framework are the core values of:

- Visionary leadership
- Agility
- Management by fact
- Social responsibility
- Customer-driven excellence
- Focus on the future
- Managing for innovation
- Systems perspective
- Organization and personal learning
- Valuing employees and partners
- Focus on results and creating value

You'll discover these core values woven throughout this training guide.

The Baldrige Education Criteria for Performance Excellence (see the Glossary and website information) is a systemic framework that, if followed, *will* lead to improved student learning results and diminished behavior-related issues. Although the Baldrige categories, shown in Figure 1.11, are typically used by school districts or individual schools, the framework can also be applied to individual classrooms. This is possible because classrooms are subsystems of a school, which are subsystems of a school district.

Mark Blazey, in the book *Insights to Performance Excellence in Education 2003: An Inside Look at the 2003 Baldrige Award Criteria for Education,* deemed that the categories of (1) Leadership, (2) Strategic Planning, and (3) Student, Stakeholder, and Market Focus comprise the Driver Triad. This describes the way leaders set the tone and use feedback from students and stakeholders to understand their needs and expectations, and then turn these into a viable and motivating strategic plan that informs employees about how to reach the goals. Blazey describes (4) Measurement, Analysis, and Knowledge Management as the Brain Center. Category 4, as shown on the chart, informs every aspect of the system. This means that the collection and analysis of in-process (formative) data is

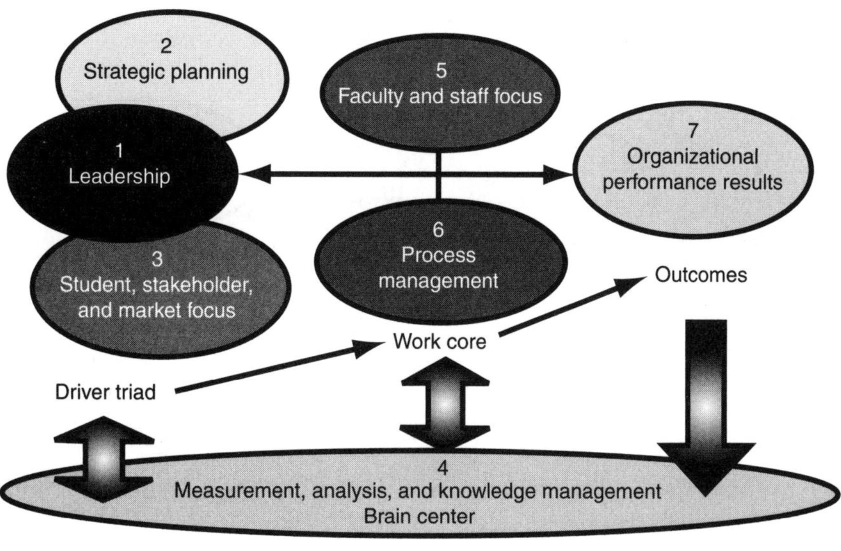

Figure 1.11 Malcolm Baldrige National Quality Award education framework.

a vital part of continuous process improvement and making midcourse corrections. Everyone must also be informed of (summative) results, which are used for annual strategic planning purposes. Categories 5 (Faculty and Staff Focus) and 6 (Process Management) represent the Work Core, because this is how and where the fundamental work of the organization takes place. Results (7) are the direct result of system and process alignment and integration, and organizational learning. The degree to which a teacher employs fact-based, systematic evaluation and improvement of key processes is the degree to which performance results will improve.

While it is crucial for teachers to align their classroom systems with other grade-level classrooms, and/or courses along a continuum, each must also align with the school's vision, mission, and goals. Likewise, each school must align itself with the district's vision, mission, and goals. It is because the classroom is where the "rubber meets the road" in education that there is a dramatic need for system overhaul at this level in addition to the district or building levels.

The processes used by teachers for instruction and to achieve various classroom tasks, and the approach used to tie all the processes together are what lead to improved student learning and fewer behavioral issues. The criteria emphasize the importance of alignment and integration of all aspects of the system. When accomplished, the results demonstrate effective and efficient processes where students learn more; students, parents and the next-teacher-in-line are more satisfied; and joy in learning is restored.

Figure 1.12 on the next page shows how the Baldrige framework fits a classroom. Note that the title of Category 5, "Student as Worker Focus," replaces "Staff and Faculty Focus." This is the only category whose title is altered.

What this diagram tells us is that all aspects of the system are linked together. The data are used to understand the current situation and inform the leader (teacher) about

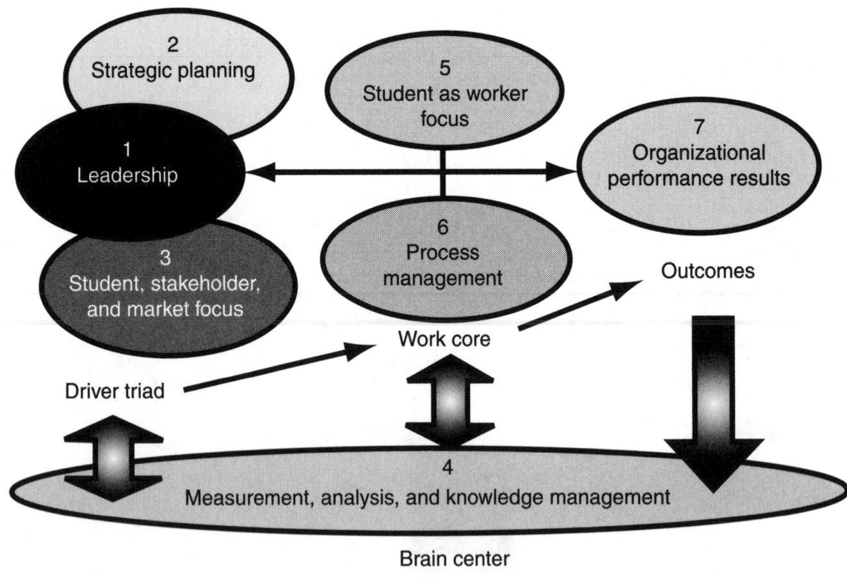

Figure 1.12 The Baldrige framework adapted for a quality classroom system.

what students and stakeholders need and want and how these can be ensured by careful strategic planning. In this model, the longer-term planning horizon would be the entire school year, while the shorter-term planning horizons would likely be marking periods (six weeks) or the semester.

Teachers are leaders in the classroom, and as such are responsible for relationship management among students, parents, stakeholders, and the next-teacher-in-line. A major part of this role is to seek information about the customers' needs and expectations, and that means identifying the customers and learning how to build positive relationships with each.

Take a closer look at the Driver Triad (Figure 1.13). You, the teacher, are the Leader (Baldrige Category 1) in the classroom. It is up to you to drive performance excellence,

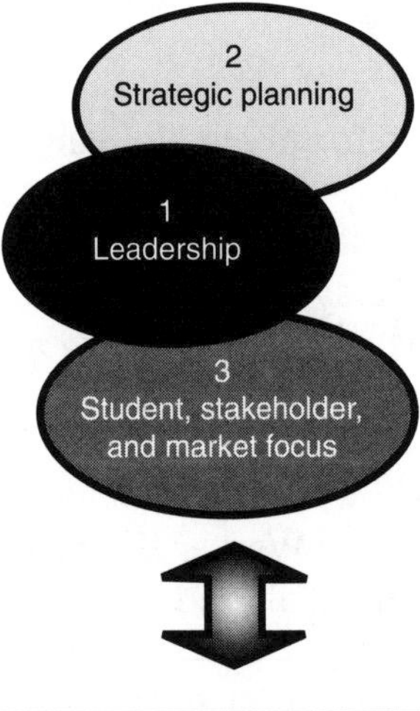

Figure 1.13 Driver Triad.

but you must do this by (Category 3) understanding student and stakeholder needs and expectations. This category recognizes the need to build and maintain relationships, providing pathways for individuals and groups to express satisfaction or dissatisfaction and make complaints. The way to determine what customers need and expect is to engage in two-way communication often through surveys, focus groups, face-to-face communication, and the use of feedback tools that you will practice later during this training. The way to manage these relationships is to make improvements based on the feedback students and stakeholders provide. First, however, it is important to know who your customers, partners, and stakeholders are.

ACTIVITY: *Identify the Relationship*

Directions: Place the following groups into the slots that best describe their relationship to your grade level class, course, or services. Several may appear more than once, but be clear about how you describe and justify the relationship. Depending on your position, the relationship may differ somewhat.

Instructional aides	Parents/guardians	Students	Community
Next-teacher-in-line	Student support services	Administration	State
World of work	Previous teacher	Previous school	District
Pre-K programs			

Internal customers Those inside the system who receive services or products of the system	**Partner** Individual or group not paid by the system, but who render services or support	**Stakeholder** Groups affected by an organization's actions and success	**Supplier** Groups or individuals who provide materials or students	**Worker** Individuals engaged in processes that affect the finished product

Teacher/leaders are responsible for leading the classroom strategic planning process (CSPP, or Category 2), taking into account an analysis of results and information gleaned from customers and stakeholders. It is during the CSPP that a success-for-all climate begins to take shape by having students assist in setting purpose, vision, mission, and class goals and establishing the expectation that they will help improve key processes to meet the class goals and expectations.

Next, let's look more closely at the Work Core, Categories 5 and 6, shown in Figure 1.14. Action plans leading from class strategic plans give students the roadmap for how work will get done. The way students work in the classroom constitute its "work system," and the assessment or evaluation approaches are the performance management system for the workers (students). The education and training portions of Category 5 are the opportunities teachers give students to learn how to improve their skills and how to improve the system. How teachers look after their students' well-being by creating a climate for success, by encouraging students to help each other, and by refusing to allow bullying, teasing, or other destructive behaviors creates the final element of Category 5.

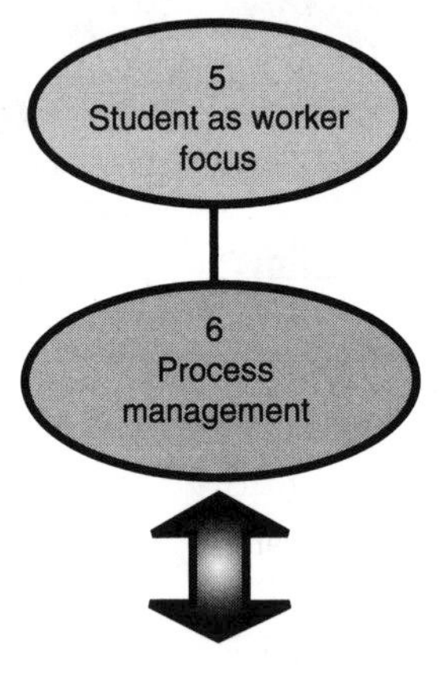

Figure 1.14 The Work Core.

Category 6, Process Management, reflects the instructional process and classroom support processes that allow students to learn to their optimal ability. A crucial part of Category 6 is the process used to improve instruction and engage students by using the Plan-Do-Study-Act cycle for continuous process improvement.

Notice that Category 4, Measurement, Analysis, and Knowledge Management, is the Brain Center. As you can see from Figure 1.15, the use of data is key to all aspects of the framework. Results (Category 7) inform Leadership and become the basis for changes in strategic goals and action plans, which is particularly important for planning for the following year or semester. Further, in-process measures (note the two-way arrow going from the Brain Center to the Driver Triad and Work Core) inform students and the teacher about the need to make midcourse corrections whenever it becomes clear that a key process is not effective or efficient. The ability and commitment to make changes in-process, based on data and a root cause analysis, allows more students to be successful.

Each classroom is unique, with different students and therefore different challenges. Complete the profile on the next several pages to set the stage for understanding your system. It will give you insight into your current situation and what it will take to create and implement a Baldrige-based classroom.

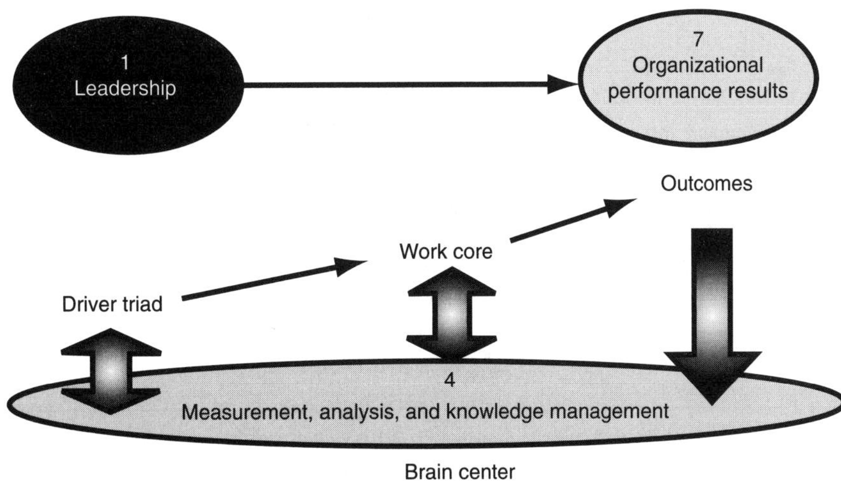

Figure 1.15 Leadership and the Brain Center are tied to results.

Type of school and grades (e.g., public, K–6, etc.)	
Assignment (e.g., 3rd grade; Honors Calculus, etc.)	
Size of school and your class size (e.g., school 800; class 29)	
Student demographics (ethnicity, gender, f/r lunch, SPED, ages)	
School day–instructional minutes per class (e.g., 50 min./5 × week)	
How do you set the tone for the class (mission, rules, expectations)?	
What communication methods do you use with parents, administration, and others about student progress?	
How do you assure a safe classroom and foster responsible, honest, respectful student behavior?	
How do you measure student performance and what is regularly measured?	
On a daily basis how do you know how students are doing relative to class learning and behavior goals?	
How do you determine opportunities for innovation? Are these based on student performance measures?	
How are you evaluated?	
What materials and/or technology are used to teach these students?	
Budget for which you have control (amount and how allocated)	
Instructional approaches used and frequency (e.g., hands-on activities once a day; lecture 3×/week, computer lab 2 × 20 min. /week, etc.)	
How do your students perform relative to those in similar classes and with similar demographics in the rest of your district, region, state, and nationally?	
What are the most significant challenges you currently face?	
What are the key measures you have for meeting or surpassing district, state, or national requirements?	
How do you anticipate and proactively prepare for concerns with your services and operations?	
Who are the key groups you work with? How do you support and strengthen these groups, thereby contributing to their improvement?	

Figure 1.16 My class profile: establish the context.

Performance Review System: Teachers

Are You . . .	Yes	No
Receiving higher quality work from your students?		
Involving students in planning and decision making?		
Seeking feedback from the next-teacher-in-line about skills students need to succeed?		
Providing learning experiences dealing with real-life application and using a variety of teaching strategies that address multiple intelligences, incorporate the latest brain research, and use differentiated instruction?		
Setting personal goals and measuring progress toward them? A role model for continuous improvement?		
Using quality tools to enhance your effectiveness as a teacher?		
Becoming a Quality learning risk taker?		
Sharing your "lessons learned" with colleagues?		
Becoming more a facilitator of learning and less a boss-manager?		
Able to analyze data to know what to change? Becoming a better problem solver?		
Seeking feedback from students regularly to eliminate barriers to their success?		

Organizational Review System: Classroom

Does your classroom have . . .	Yes	No
A collaboratively established vision and mission? Is it signed by all and posted in the classroom?		
A climate that demonstrates the two principles of "I am responsible for my own learning" and "I am response-able to the success of the group"?		
Measurable class learning goals? Are they posted prominently in the classroom? Are there charts on the walls showing progress toward the learning goals?		
Charts and graphs posted that show evidence of improvement of key classroom processes?		
Well-defined procedures that are reviewed for best practice and improved as needed?		
Students who are enthusiastic about learning; few discipline problems; high attendance rates; and low tardy rates?		
Community members and parents involved?		

Performance Review System: Teacher-Students

Are your students . . .	Yes	No
Involved in planning learning activities?		
Setting personal goals? Are they measuring progress toward their goals?		
Working cooperatively in teams on projects?		
Improving the quality of their work?		
Becoming better listeners?		
Becoming learning risk takers?		
Making suggestions to improve classroom procedures?		
Using the PDSA process to improve?		
Familiar with quality tools and using them to improve learning?		
Becoming better problem solvers and making better choices?		

Summary

You have now learned a little about the theory underpinning this approach. Use this book as your guide for the BBQ (Baldrige-based quality) journey ahead. We urge you to have the courage to *take the first steps* in changing your classroom system. Next, we encourage you to learn from your mistakes, relax a bit, and have fun learning with your students. Above all, *keep going!* Remember, it's all about continuous improvement!

Reflections

2

CREATE A QUALITY CLASSROOM SYSTEM FOR SUCCESS

The Foundation for Increased Student Enthusiasm and Improved Learning Results

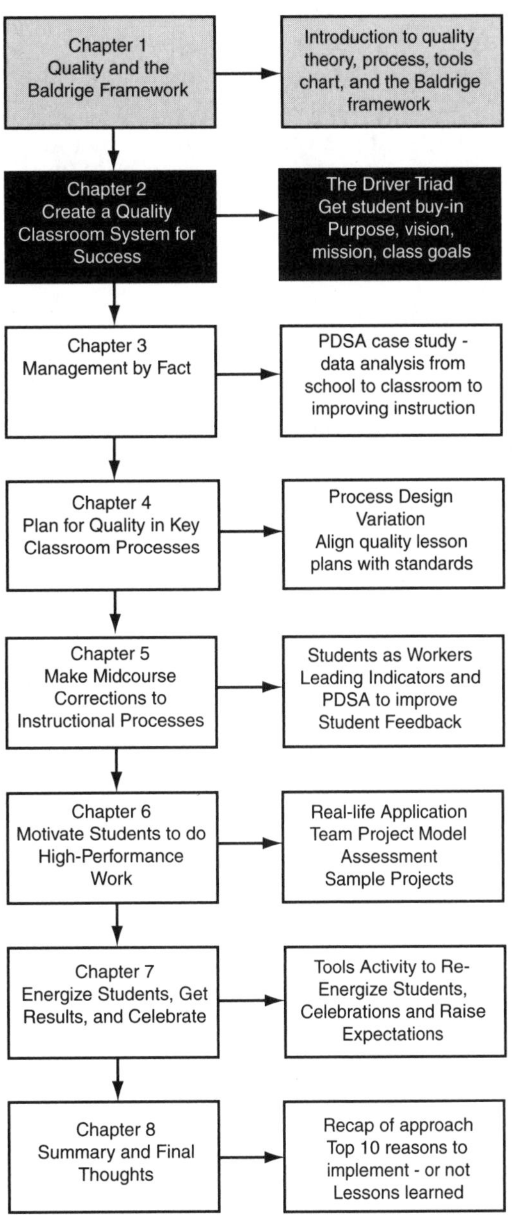

Conversation with the Teacher

Does it sometimes seem that the expectations of national, state, or local policymakers are unrealistic, given the students with whom you work? Perhaps it is the emphasis on accountability and the use of high-stakes testing results that causes you concern. It has been our observation that most teachers are doing the best job they can with their current knowledge, skills, and abilities. The difficulty is that traditional approaches work for some students, but not for all. In fact, this has always been the case, but now that educators are being held accountable for the results of all students, the issues have become more prominent.

The lessons learned for education are the same as those for manufacturing, business, and healthcare. Business has learned to focus on its core business; to align its mission, goals, and action plans; and to plan for the future to ensure success. Healthcare system problems lead to higher costs for malpractice insurance and to higher costs of doing business because of errors and inefficiencies. Education's challenges have caused districts to add more complexity to the system in response to governmental or school board mandates. A good example is the addition of character education curricula to address issues related to student cheating, lack of civility, and respect. This takes time and the focus away from the core work of the organization. We believe in the words "No Child Left Behind," and we believe firmly that it begins with teachers and students working together to create a climate for success.

In this chapter you will learn:

- The importance of a holistic approach to establish a Baldrige-based classroom climate for success for all students
- A systematic approach and detailed instructions for how to move through the steps to create the culture of a Baldrige-based quality classroom
- One way to measure mission specificity

Introduction to the Baldrige Framework and Classroom Application

Soccer Analogy

You are passionate about soccer and were delighted when the government enacted a law stating that every child from age 5 to 16 had to play soccer. You are convinced that this is the way to improve the health of the nation's youth and therefore decrease healthcare costs. The only hitch is that the government has assigned you (the coach) a group of 15 individuals who will form your team. The government has defined the goal, and it's your job to turn these children into an *effective team with a winning record.* You've called a team meeting and only five show up. You observe three to be eager to please and have some skills and two who have very good skills but don't listen very well. Of the 10 who didn't come,

you have been told that six are not interested in soccer, four have tried but have no skills and therefore don't want to play, and two have more important things to do. The government, however, insists that you work with all 15, and officials will be monitoring your progress as a coach. Since you cannot change the government's ruling, nor can you directly influence the team selection process, you must focus on ways to get the job done and achieve the goals.

ACTIVITY: ***Build on Your Knowledge***

Directions: Answer the following questions using what you've already learned about a Baldrige-based classroom and its criteria categories. You might want to refresh your memory by returning to Chapter 1, which introduces the Baldrige framework.

What are the first things you need to address? How might you go about changing things?

Once you get all the children to the field, how might you get them motivated to work as a team and continue coming to practice and games?

Once you have the group motivated, what steps will you take to achieve the goal? Remember, the goal is to have an *effective team with a winning record.*

Task	Approach	How will you know the approach worked?

Think: *How do the issues of a teacher or school leader relate to the soccer analogy?*

The Criteria Categories

To launch your Baldrige-based quality classroom, you're going to need to develop into a high-performing team with your students. Figure 2.1 shows you the whole framework, and to get good results you'll need to understand the following:

- *Leadership* sets the tone and vision, brings passion and care/concern for all stakeholders, is a key participant in classroom strategic planning, sets targets, and makes certain that action plans are aligned with the strategic plan. Leadership also makes sure resources are available to those who must carry out the action plans, and then carefully and consistently monitors progress and makes midcourse corrections. A primary function is to seek information about barriers to success and remove them.

- *Strategic Planning* must be aligned with the vision and mission of the organization. Focus on three or four primary goals that are key drivers of success. Create action plans specific to each goal. Establish targets and a measurement system (how, when, and what will be measured) aligned with the action plans and strategic goals.

- *Student, Stakeholder, and Market Focus* requires one to perform a needs assessment. What do the students need and expect? What do the stakeholders need and expect? The results of this are an essential part of the strategic plan. This focus refers to both needs/expectations and relationship management and satisfaction.

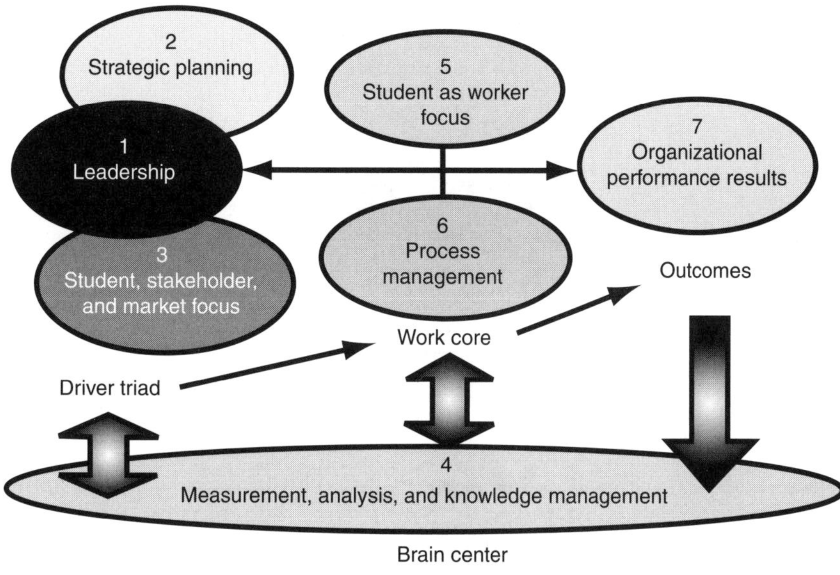

Figure 2.1 Baldrige framework adapted for a classroom system.

- *Measurement, Analysis, and Knowledge Management* relate to what is measured and analyzed and how the organization (school department, grade level, or classroom) *knows* how well individuals and groups are progressing toward the goals. Who has the information and how the information is used are key factors in success.
- *Student as Worker Focus* has to do with how work gets done, how work is evaluated, and how the work system is improved. Also of concern is how students are motivated and participate in their own education and development. Last, the question of how leadership takes care of students as workers and understands the key drivers of satisfaction/dissatisfaction is addressed.
- *Process Management* addresses both the learning-centered and support processes. How do these key processes flow and how are they improved? These must be aligned with the strategic goals and action plans.
- *Organizational Performance Results* reveal the results of the system. Results always tell the story of the effectiveness and efficiency of key processes. They also provide information about the effectiveness of action plans developed to address strategic goals. Results should inform the leadership about gaps in any of the previous sections.

The Driver Triad

Leadership

Leadership drives the system, as shown in Figure 2.2. Good leaders immediately begin to turn the class into a united whole and to transform the motivation from external to internal by creating a climate for success for all. Systematically set the tone and expectation that this class will be different from a traditional classroom. It is up to the teacher/leader to

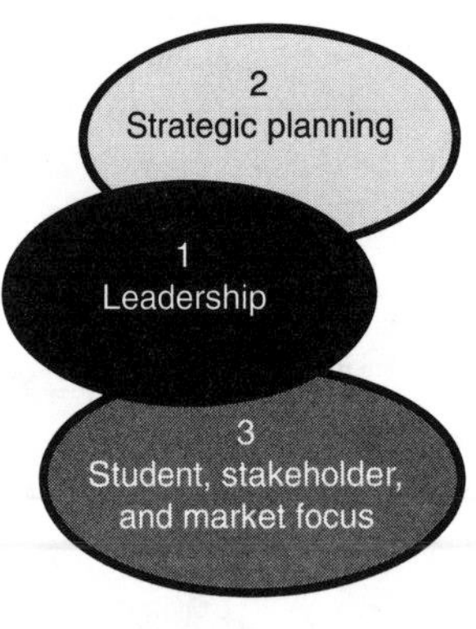

Figure 2.2 Driver Triad.

develop a personal constancy of purpose. Think first—develop a personal constancy of purpose. *Ask yourself if you are getting paid to teach or to facilitate learning.* If you think you are getting paid to teach, then you'll create a classroom with a teaching focus. In these classrooms, the mentality is, "I've taught it. It isn't my fault they didn't learn. Send me the 'right' students and they will learn and we'll all be successful." Or, "These students have so many different needs there is no way I can teach them all." Of course, we know that parents are not holding back the "right" children. Faulty thinking like this reflects a deeper problem for education, as it is fraught with hopelessness.

Turn your thinking around and refer to yourself as a *facilitator of learning.* We guarantee that this one thought alone will make a huge difference in the way you approach your work. Facilitators of learning know that they must create a learner-centered, learning-focused classroom. They also realize that their job is not finished until all students have mastered the skills, knowledge, and abilities required for future success. It *does* matter, and we will show you how to make this transformation in a systematic way. If you follow these steps it will change the way students act and react, and you'll be pleasantly surprised at the difference in learning and behavioral results.

> *A word of caution: These steps cannot be skipped and must be done in the order in which they are discussed in this chapter. Imagine yourself as a creator and you are beginning with a blank slate.*

Student and Stakeholder Focus

One key opportunity for building a system designed for success is this: *Learn as much as possible about the students.* Find out about their interests, learning styles, learning fears, past successes, and problem areas. (You can find survey examples in Appendix A.) It is also necessary to learn "how" your students like to learn. This information is used for classroom management, for managing learning activities, and for creating a system that addresses students' learning needs. In a BBQ classroom, there are often many activities going on simultaneously, with some students doing independent work (not busy work or "rework") while others work with buddies or in small groups. Figure 2.3 provides an example of a survey that can be used or

About me	
Circle the response that best fits you.	
I learn best	alone with a buddy in a small group as part of a large group
I learn best when I	watch others read about things move objects around listen talk through what I'm learning use the computer
When I am learning I need	someone to work with me quiet music or noise to move around
When I need help	I feel okay about asking the teacher to help me. I feel okay about asking a friend to help me. I don't like to ask for help. I am afraid others will laugh if I ask for help.
Things that get in the way of my learning are	music movement around me noise too complicated directions bright light too little light

Figure 2.3 Learn about your students.

modified to suit any level (elementary, middle, or high school) at the beginning of the school year or semester.

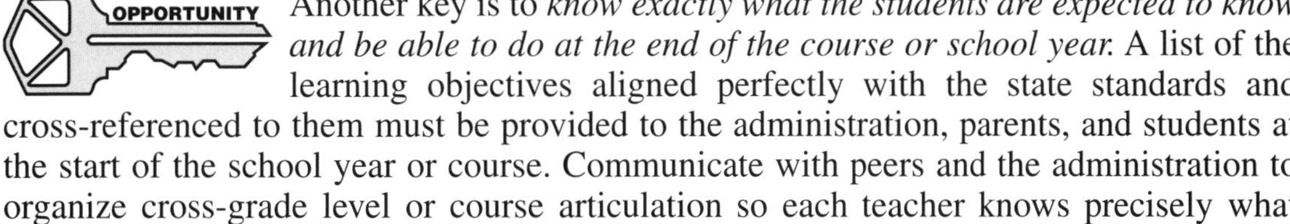

Another key is to *know exactly what the students are expected to know and be able to do at the end of the course or school year.* A list of the learning objectives aligned perfectly with the state standards and cross-referenced to them must be provided to the administration, parents, and students at the start of the school year or course. Communicate with peers and the administration to organize cross-grade level or course articulation so each teacher knows precisely what skills students must have to be successful in the next grade or class, postsecondary institutions, or the world of work.

Here is a partial example of reading and language arts skills that must be mastered by fourth grade students in Las Cruces Public Schools in New Mexico:

- Visualizes and recalls details, characterization, and sequence.
- Analyzes characters, events, and plots from different texts with supportive evidence.

- Reads common abbreviations.
- Reads over 200 English and 80 Spanish words automatically.
- Uses simple and compound sentences in speaking and writing.
- Combines short, related sentences using appositives, participial phrases, adjectives, adverbs, and prepositional phrases.
- Spells correctly roots, inflections, affixes, and common syllables.

An example of the minimum math mastery expectations of Community Consolidated School District 15 (D15) in Palatine, Illinois, by grade level are shown in the following list. Mastery is defined as rapid recall. Minimal expectations should be reached by the completion of the school year at each grade level.

Grade Level	Minimum Mastery Expectations
K	Number recognition, recognition and understanding of addition and subtraction
1	Understanding of addition and subtraction facts 1–20
2	Memorization of addition and subtraction facts 1–20
3	Review addition and subtraction facts. Memorize multiplication facts 0–10. Begin memorization of division facts of multipliers 0–10.
4	Review addition and subtraction facts. Memorize multiplication and division facts of multipliers 0–10.
5	Review addition, subtraction, multiplication, and division facts
6	Memorize multiplication and division facts of multipliers 0–12.

Examples from Aldine Independent School District in Texas and Minuteman Science and Technology High School in Lexington, Massachusetts, are found in Appendix B.

The final key opportunity is to seek feedback from parents or guardians about their expectations. Some teachers have discovered that parents or guardians often have conflicting expectations, and in some cases this has led to problems that could have been eliminated easily if teachers had spent the time during back-to-school night or in the fall surveying parents. So long as they feel listened to and respected, parents are more likely to want to help. Candace (Allen) Smith, formerly a social studies teacher at Centennial High School in Pueblo, Colorado, and an award-winning teacher for the use of Quality processes in her class, invited parents to a meeting each fall. During that time, she reviewed the curriculum and asked parents for feedback. Not only did she ask them to rank order their expectations, but she also asked in what ways they'd be willing to help. In this way, she made them partners. Many parents expressed these sentiments on their surveys, "No teacher has ever asked me what I expected before. It is a nice surprise and pleasure." Once again, we caution you. If you don't want to know, don't ask. Candace also followed up with surveys to parents at each marking period and then reported the results back to parents. Building relationships with parents and guardians is an important part of Category 3 (Student and Stakeholder Focus). On the occasion that she had to call parents to report issues with their child, she found the parents most willing to listen and help. Figure 2.4 is the survey Candace gave parents. Other examples are

Parent/Guardian Expectations Survey – Secondary
Your student is enrolled in a World Geography class for one semester. He/she has indicated his/her expectations and hoped-for outcomes for the class. Because you are most likely concerned about what is taught in the class, this survey is intended to explore those interests. Please answer the following questions. Thanks for your assistance. I will send a report informing you of how other parents/guardians have responded.
1. If you were the teacher of a world geography class, what would you think is most important to teach?
2. Other than content, is there anything else you hope your student will learn? (skills, attitudes, etc.)
3. Is there any way in which you might be able to assist in the teaching of the class; that is, do you have expertise that might add value to this particular class? Would you be willing or able to help in any particular way?
4. How could I be of assistance in helping to facilitate learning for your student?
5. Other comments, suggestions, expectations, etc.?
Please sign here if you're able to assist with this class. ______________________

Figure 2.4 Social studies survey example.

included in Appendix A. Naturally she charted the results and provided them to parents; then made certain her learning activities addressed their expectations.

When you've gathered feedback from all sources, it is time to set the stage and create a Baldrige-based quality (BBQ) classroom climate.

Classroom Strategic Planning: Set the Stage

Two principles comprise the foundation of a Baldrige-based quality classroom. Everything else is predicated on *everyone* holding these beliefs and demonstrating them each and every day. This includes the teacher, aides, volunteers, and of course, students.

> *I am responsible for my own learning.*
>
> *I am response-able to the success of the class.*

We recommend teachers make large banners with each principle and hang them in the classroom as a constant reminder.

Here's our recommended process for introducing the two principles to students. Use a whole-group approach if you teach young children, but with students from grades five up, it works equally well to divide the class into small groups for initial discussion of each principle and then have the groups report back to the class.

Ask, "How would I know you were being responsible for your own learning? What behaviors would I see?"

Potential answers might include: come on time, be prepared with materials, do homework, or ask questions.

Ask, "How would I know you were being response-able to the success of the class? What behaviors would I see that would show me you were able to respond to your classmates and therefore to the success of the class?"

Potential answers might include: help others by answering their questions if I know the information, work cooperatively with others, help the group stay focused on the tasks, and don't engage in disruptive behavior.

The "response-able" principle usually requires some role-playing and examples as students attempt to define what it means. *Being "response-able" means being able to respond to others* so the group can succeed. Do not confuse this with holding students and others accountable for the learning success of the class.

You might demonstrate a student disrupting class by coming in tardy or shoving another student's books aside. In each instance ask students whether this would lend itself to being "response-able" to the success of the group. Other ideas to explore include doing one's homework or participating in class discussions. Each time, ask the students whether such behavior lends itself to being "response-able" and if so, how. Follow this by a conversation about whether helping classmates who are having difficulty or those who don't understand the teachers' instructions would demonstrate being "response-able."

We cannot overstate the importance of the two principles and how they define student and teacher behavior. They must become manifest and permeate the classroom.

ACTIVITY: *Apply the principles to yourself.*

Directions: You are the leader and a significant partner in the classroom.

What does the principle "I am response-able to the success of the class" mean? What behaviors would the teacher use to demonstrate a commitment to this principle?

What does the principle "I am responsible for my own learning" mean? What are you (the teacher) responsible for learning about? How does this relate to the "response-able" principle?

"I am response-able to the success of the class" implies that teachers understand and act on Category 3 (Student and Stakeholder Focus) activities to discover needs and expectations of students, parents, the next-teacher-in-line and key stakeholders such as the district, state and national requirements. For teachers working with middle and secondary students, the community world of work and post-secondary expectations become more significant and must be considered part of the teacher's learning responsibilities prior to planning instructional activities and classroom projects and organization. It is also important to realize you are responsible for learning about yourself. Dig deep inside to discover your biases because these impact your relationships with students and parents and are at the core of your classroom system.

Helpful Tips

- Create large banners with the two principles and post on opposite walls of the classroom.
- Refer to the principles often, especially at the beginning of any new learning activity.

We realize classroom strategic planning, as it relates to creation of the purpose, vision, mission, and setting class goals, may seem overwhelming and consume too much instructional time. We suggest chunking the planning process along these lines: Day 1, purpose and vision; Day 2, mission; Day 3, Quality factors for students; Day 4, class goals. Teachers who use this approach *uniformly* tell us that the time spent on this process is regained as "found" instructional time each subsequent day.

Establish a Purpose

If students don't know why they are at school or in a particular class, they have no reason to become active, eager learners. Further, if *you* don't know what *your* own purpose is, *you will be unable* to stay focused, and a great deal of instructional time may be wasted. See Figure 2.5.

Purpose is the ray of light projecting pulsating energy from and beyond the vision to encompass everyone involved. It is the aim *of the classroom—the reason it exists.*

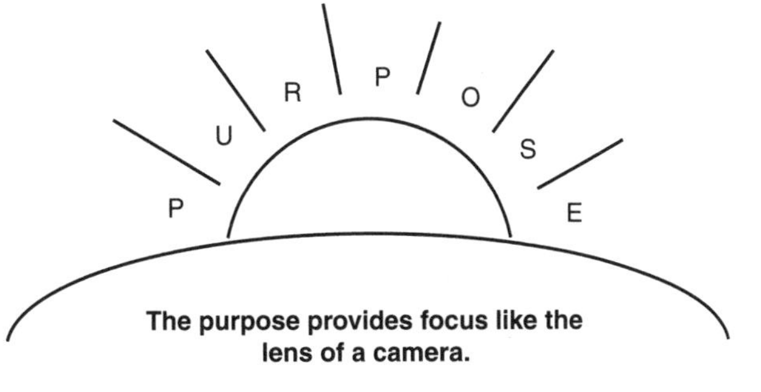
P
U
R
P
O
S
E
The purpose provides focus like the lens of a camera.

Figure 2.5 Purpose.

ACTIVITY: *Practice the Five Whys.*

Directions: Clarify your purpose and write down your response to each question and then use that answer as the basis for the next "why." Once you've gotten to the fifth "why," your true purpose will be revealed. Is it a noble purpose?
Ask yourself: **Why am I a teacher?** Response:
Why (use the answer from above):
Response:
Why:
Response:
Why:
Response:
Why:
Response:

My purpose is: ____

A *purpose is a short, succinct statement that describes the core reason for what you do.* Keep your purpose statement close so you can be reminded of it regularly. Frequently, the winds of life distract people from their purpose. Similarly, you can engage students in this exercise. We highly recommend that middle and high school students create their own purpose statements. It is the beginning of creating a successful future for them.

Your class purpose can be arrived at in a similar fashion. For elementary students, this is probably best done as a whole group, but with older students you might be able to have them work in small groups and then get the whole class together to agree on the best purpose statement. Actually, when the word *learning* is mentioned, you have the central purpose of the class.

Use the Five Whys instead of simply a broad discussion with the students. Be careful, however, not to go down a path that is a dead end. Responses as in the following example (see page 39) can lead to a problem. To avoid this problem, rephrase the "why" questions. For example, the second why question could be rephrased as: Why do parents think it is important for students to come to school? To avoid some of these pitfalls, you might want to practice with a friend or colleague before attempting to use the Five Whys with your class. Ask your training partner to respond as she or he thinks the students might respond.

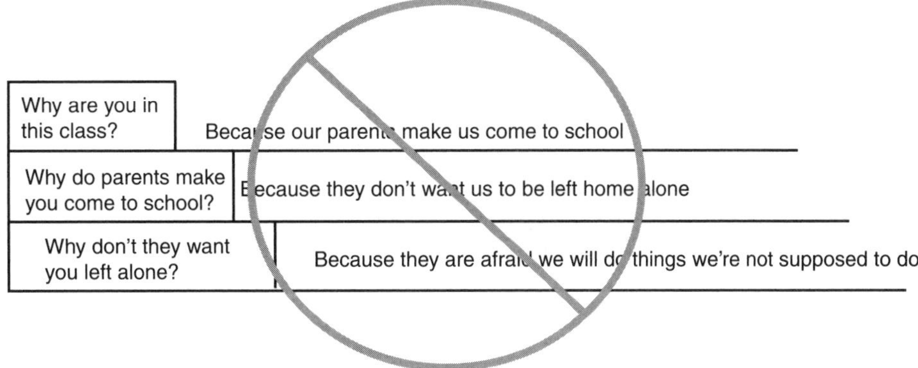

Why are you in this class?	Because it is required for graduation
Why is it required for graduation?	Because it is required to get into college
Why would a college want you to have this class for admission?	Because we need to have these skills to succeed in college
Why would these skills help you be successful in college?	Because we need a strong foundation to build on with the new concepts and skills to graduate and get a good job
Why do you want to graduate and get a good job?	Because we want to earn money to afford a nice lifestyle and enjoy the work we do

Our class purpose is: *To learn the skills taught in this class to improve our chances to be successful in the college and career of our choice so we can become employed and afford a nice lifestyle, while enjoying our chosen work.*

Once the purpose has been decided, be certain the students copy it in their class folders or organizers. This should also be posted prominently in the classroom. Include the class purpose on any communication pieces sent to parents. In this way, the focus of the class becomes indelibly forged on everyone's mind.

Helpful Tips

If the class purpose contains the word *learn,* a clear sense of the seriousness of learning will permeate the time students spend in class, completing homework, and doing other assignments.

Create a Class Vision

A vision is a brief statement or cluster of sentences that answer the "what" question. Vision is the long-term future. It must be inspirational and lead students to become internally motivated to "live" the two Quality principles, stay focused on their purpose, and learn as much as possible. Teachers, as leaders, provide the passion and inspiration for students to write the vision through their excitement, tonal quality, and passion for answering the "what" question. See Figure 2.6 on the next page.

Keep in mind that *you know* the district grade or course-level requirements and curriculum for your assignment (Category 3, Student and Stakeholder Focus). This gives you the opportunity to prompt the students with your passion for the subject matter immediately.

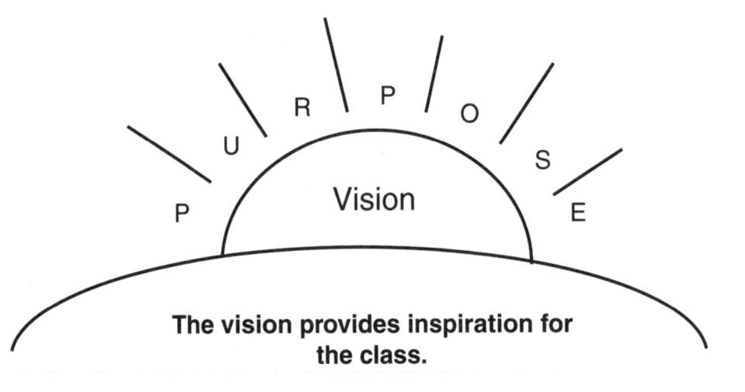

Figure 2.6 Vision.

So much of the visioning process rests on the teacher's ability to express his/her passion for the subject. Your body language, voice, and enthusiasm all are important during this exercise. You know the content of the subject. You know the requirements. You are the one who can bring it to life. For example, instead of simply accepting the idea that "we will learn things," you might add adjectives or more descriptive nouns to the thoughts students had, such as: We are scholars, Einsteins, or brilliant mathematicians. These words will lend much more enthusiasm to the class. Of course, you cannot use these words unless students concur. It is amazing how much a little passion and teacher enthusiasm lends to capturing students' attention and desire to learn.

Begin by asking the students, "What do we want to achieve in the time we'll be together? What will distinguish our class from all the others? What will we be noted for by ourselves, parents, and others?" Continue along these lines: "What will we want to be able do as a result of being in this class; at the end of our time together, what will we have accomplished?" "What would make us proud and others say, 'Wow, what a great class that was!'" By getting students involved in this activity, you actually are capturing some ideas about students' expectations (Category 3, Student and Stakeholder Focus). Even if an individual student's ideas are not prioritized into the final vision statement, you have heard what he or she has said and can use that information later when preparing learning activities.

You are asking students to brainstorm ideas. If your students have not experienced this activity before, you may need to "prime the pump" by making one or two suggestions. Resist the urge to give your suggestions before allowing at least 30 seconds for students to give theirs. Once they begin providing ideas, stop adding yours and continue again only if they seem to get stuck. Write all ideas on the board. Review each idea and, if there are any questions, ask the student who made the suggestion to clarify the idea. If there are like ideas or similar ones, ask for permission to combine them.

Have the students prioritize the remaining ideas to create the vision statement by using a multivoting technique. Explain the significance of the voting procedure, to ensure each student's voice is heard and considered. Multivoting is a *silent* activity. This ensures that each student makes up his or her mind without being influenced by the others. Give students a minute to make up their minds at their desks before anyone starts voting. Then they place their priority votes by going one by one to place dots next to the corresponding idea(s). Ask several students to total the scores for each idea. Eliminate ideas without any votes or those with just a few. The remaining ideas will be reworked into the vision by asking students to help compose sentences. If the ideas are already stated in sentence form, they may be adopted as written.

Develop the vision with elementary students or with special education classes as a whole class activity. Once the students have prioritized the lists, you might divide middle or high school age students into smaller groups. Each group can take the words and put them into sentences to create a vision. Each group reports out to the class, which can then select the one they like best or even edit several ideas to create a better vision statement.

Once the vision statement is written, ask for consensus from students, and when it is adopted, ask everyone in the class to sign it. (Remember, teachers and aides sign too.) Post the signed vision statement in a prominent place. Ask the students to write the class vision in their notebooks. Share it with parents, other classes, and the administration.

It is important that the vision come from the students and be written in their words, not yours. This begins to make the students feel empowered and take ownership of this class. Consequently, motivation for learning begins to flip from external to internal. By asking students to engage in defining the class vision, you are asking them to:

Imagine the result of their efforts—beyond the usual "pass this class" mentality.

Think about "excellence" and state it in writing.

Get involved in shaping the desired result of time spent together.

Multivoting

What

Multivoting is a prioritization tool. It helps the group reach consensus. This tool allows everyone to have a voice in the decision-making process.

How

1. Explain the tool and the benefits of it to the group.
2. Items to be multivoted on may come from a Brainstorming and Affinity Process, the items listed on a cause/effect diagram, or a simple list.
3. Ask the group to study the list carefully before voting.
4. Divide the total number of items by three or five. This will determine how many votes each person receives.
5. Determine the method of voting (for example, colored markers; colored dots; dimes, nickels, and pennies).
6. Assign a value to the method of voting. For example, a red dot = 3 points, yellow dot = 2 points, blue dot = 1 point.
7. Explain the voting procedure. Members may distribute their votes any way they choose. All the votes can go to one item if a person feels it is overwhelmingly the most important. Votes may also be split up among several items.
8. *Members silently vote* one at a time, placing the appropriate symbols next to their prioritized choices.
9. Add the point value of all votes for each item and determine the rank value of items on the list.
10. Record the results and discuss.

When

- Consensus is the desired outcome of any decision.
- Some students are shy and would be overpowered by more vocal, assertive students.
- It is necessary to determine from the group's perspective the most significant cause of something.
- There is a desire to have students learn prioritization skills.

Examples

The first example that follows comes from the results of a cause/effect diagram on "why homework is not turned in." The teacher decided to chunk the Assignments subcause responses and ask students to multivote only on this group.

Continued

Continued

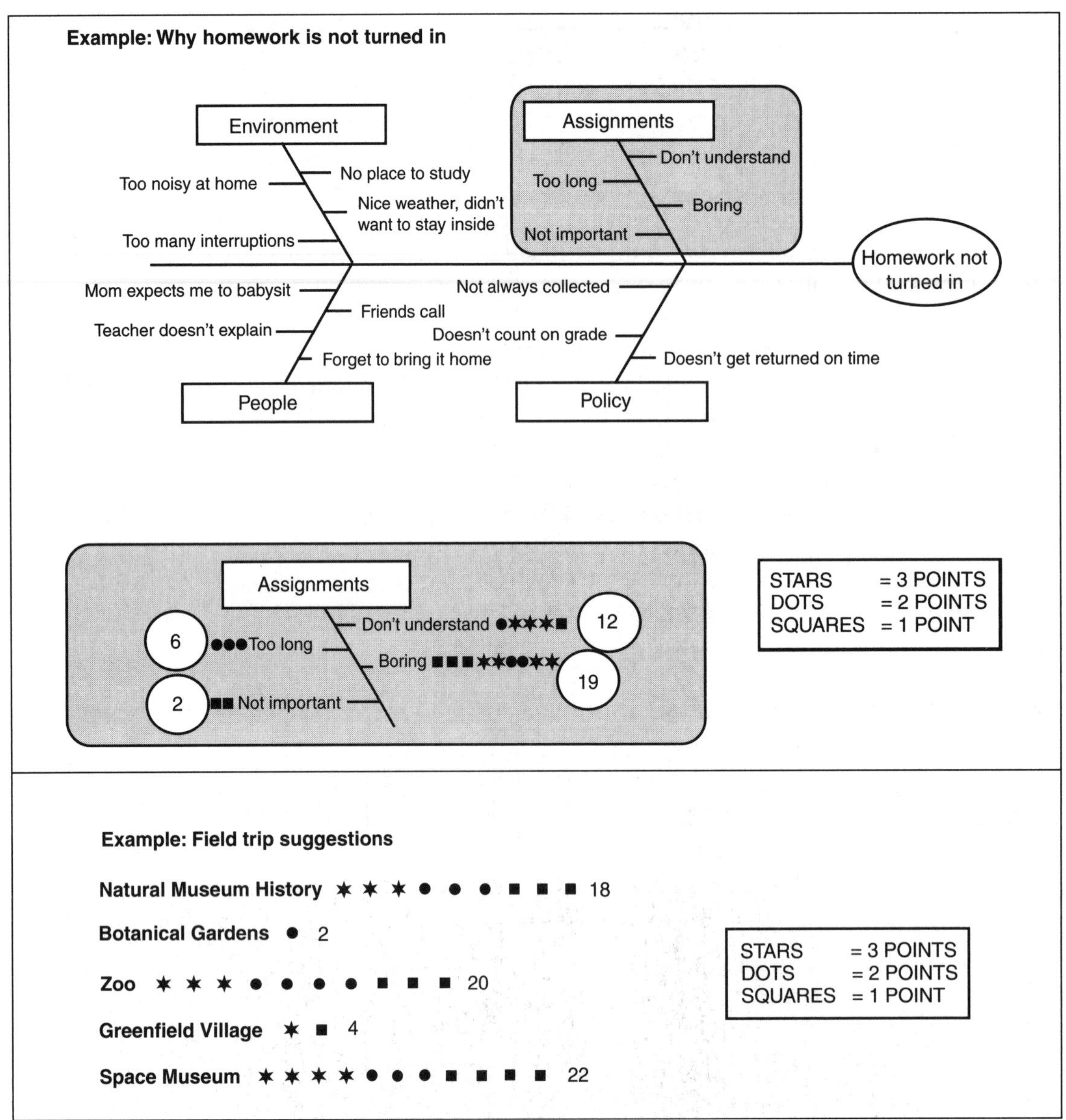

Helpful Tips

- Assign a leadership team of two or three students in advance to orient new students into the class.
- Change the team once a month. These students are responsible for orienting new students to the class purpose, two Quality principles, the vision, and the mission (coming next).
- As soon as possible, have new students sign the purpose and vision.
- Middle or high school teachers who teach more than one section of the same course might think about having each class (this does not work for different

courses) brainstorm the words and then having groups of students in each class put the words into a vision statement. Each class can vote on the statement they like best, or combine the elements of more than one to reach agreement on the final version of the vision.

Write a Class Mission

A mission is a cluster of sentences that answer the "how" question. It provides the behavioral pathway for the class to achieve the vision and embodies the two Quality principles. The mission keeps the focal point on the agreed-upon aim, or purpose of the class. See Figure 2.7.

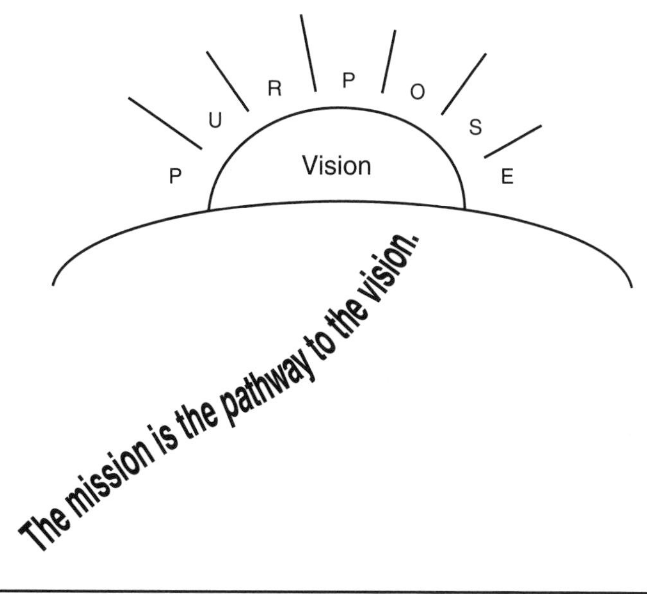

Figure 2.7 Mission.

Teachers begin by drawing a path leading toward the vision. Ask the question, "How will we have to work together during this year (semester) to achieve our vision? What are some behaviors that will help ensure that our vision is accomplished?"

Students follow the same brainstorming and multivoting approach as they used in creating the vision, although now students will be brainstorming *action words.* Once again you may need to prime the pump by making one or two suggestions. Resist the urge to give your suggestions first, as the important thing is that students are empowered to create "their" classroom and not just re-create "your" classroom. Here are some suggestions: cooperate, participate, be kind, have a sense of humor, respect, trust, and listen.

Throughout this process, you are gaining more and more information from your students (Category 3: Student and Stakeholder Focus) about what they need to be successful. It is important to make mental notes of the students with specific requests to guide you in your approach to these students, even if their suggestions are not included in the final version of the mission statement. Prior to multivoting, remind students their decisions need to be based on the words they believe are *the most important for everyone to remember* in order *to achieve the vision.* Have one or more students total the points and circle the top five words or more if there is a natural break in point value.

Ask students to provide sentences that incorporate all the agreed-upon words to make a mission statement for the class. Once consensus is reached, rewrite the class mission and have everyone sign it before posting in the classroom. Ask the students to copy the mission, put it in a prominent place in their folder or notebook, and take copies home.

Helpful Tips

- When the mission is written, ask the students whether they believe it is going to help them achieve the vision. If not, find out why and rewrite it.
- A mission statement developed by and for each class is important. It is not possible to write a global mission statement for all classes (for example, if you teach algebra I, geometry, and basic math classes).

Measure Mission Specificity

To stay focused on the transformation and help students understand that this approach is aimed at student ownership and accountability, it is necessary to measure progress. Mission statements are behaviors, and some might say it is impossible to measure progress; however, here is one approach that works. You can use a radar chart for measuring class or individual progress. Students can keep an individual radar chart with up to four weeks (one month) of data. This can be shared with parents along with report cards and/or during parent conferences. Class radar charts can be posted, with the entire class getting involved in suggestions for improving the results. If you intend to use the radar chart as a class assessment tool, depending on the age of the students, you might want to use it daily or weekly. Individual radar charts in the early grades could be done daily, especially for K-2 students. After that, weekly charting works well.

Remember, you want students to self-assess and be honest. If they feel they will be punished for honesty, they will resist or will give themselves an inflated score. Neither of these is desirable. When there is a conflict between your perception and that of a student, use your charm and gently remind him or her of an instance where you have a difference of opinion. These exercises should never be graded, but instead used as self-assessment and as an aid to accountability and taking responsibility for one's own actions. See instructions for the radar chart on page 45.

Class Goals

The next step is to establish class goals. Without a way to measure progress toward the vision, it will remain a series of words without importance (see Figure 2.8 on page 46). With the class, review the vision. Consider this first-grade example: *We are super learners and fantastic readers!*

The teacher asked, "How will we know when we are super learners?" From a brainstormed list, the class agreed on the following:

- When we all turn in our homework for 10 days in a row.
- When we can all add single digit numbers without mistakes.

Radar Chart

What

A chart that shows the gaps between current performance and ideal performance using a number of previously agreed upon key criteria (from the multi-voting technique).

How

1. Select and operationally define the characteristics to be rated. The chart can handle up to 10 characteristics, but six is optimal.
2. Construct the chart. Draw a large wheel with as many spokes as there are characteristics. Around the outside of the wheel, label each spoke (characteristic).
3. Scale the chart. If you would like to increase the behavior or results, write "0%" at the center of the wheel and "100%" at the outside end of each spoke. If the desire is to decrease the behavior or results, write "100%" at the center of the wheel and "0%" at the outside end of each spoke. For all charts, along each spoke, put hash marks indicating percentages moving toward the desired outcome, either 100% or 0%. (An alternative way to scale the chart is from 0 to 10.)
4. Put the data on the chart. Put a dot along each spoke corresponding to the numerical value of the data. When data are on the chart, connect the dots in a circular fashion.
5. Interpret the chart. The radar chart shows the gap between the goal and the current reality. Each radar chart can handle up to four sets of weekly or monthly data for the same characteristics. It is suggested that a different color marker be used each time data are put on the chart. The value of this is to show improvement or growing gaps that must be addressed.
6. Act to improve. Look at the gaps between the optimal rating and actual rating for each characteristic being measured. Engage students in a brief brainstorming activity to address the lowest area of performance. Ask for clarification regarding student suggestions and determine what will be done differently the following week. If there is little or no improvement in the way the radar chart looks, engage students in a cause/effect diagram to discover what is keeping the results stagnant.

When

- There is a desire to look at more than one characteristic at a time.
- You want the class or individuals to see the gap between current and desired results.
- You have a desire to have the group become more aware of where they need to improve.

Classroom Example-Social skills by class

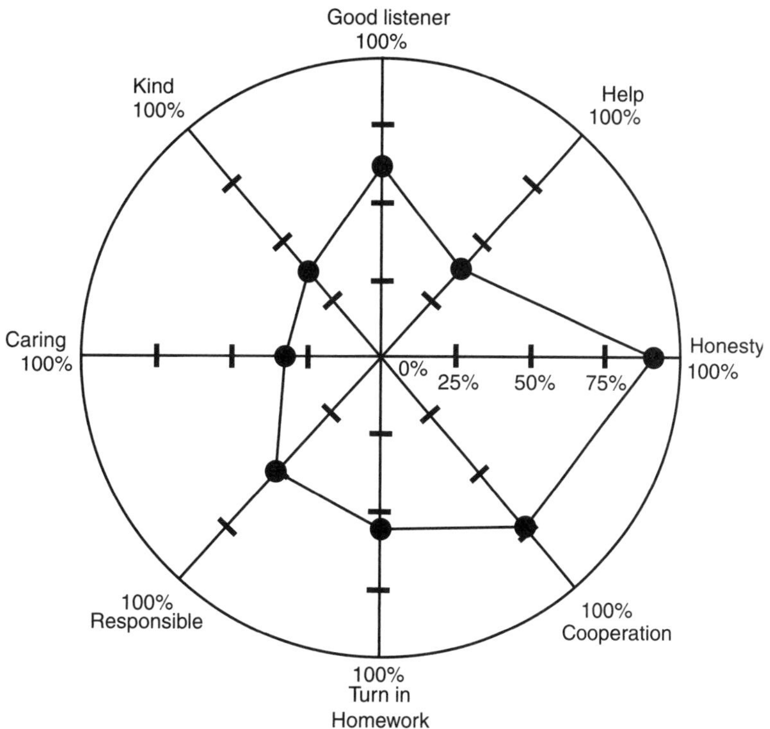

Continued

Continued

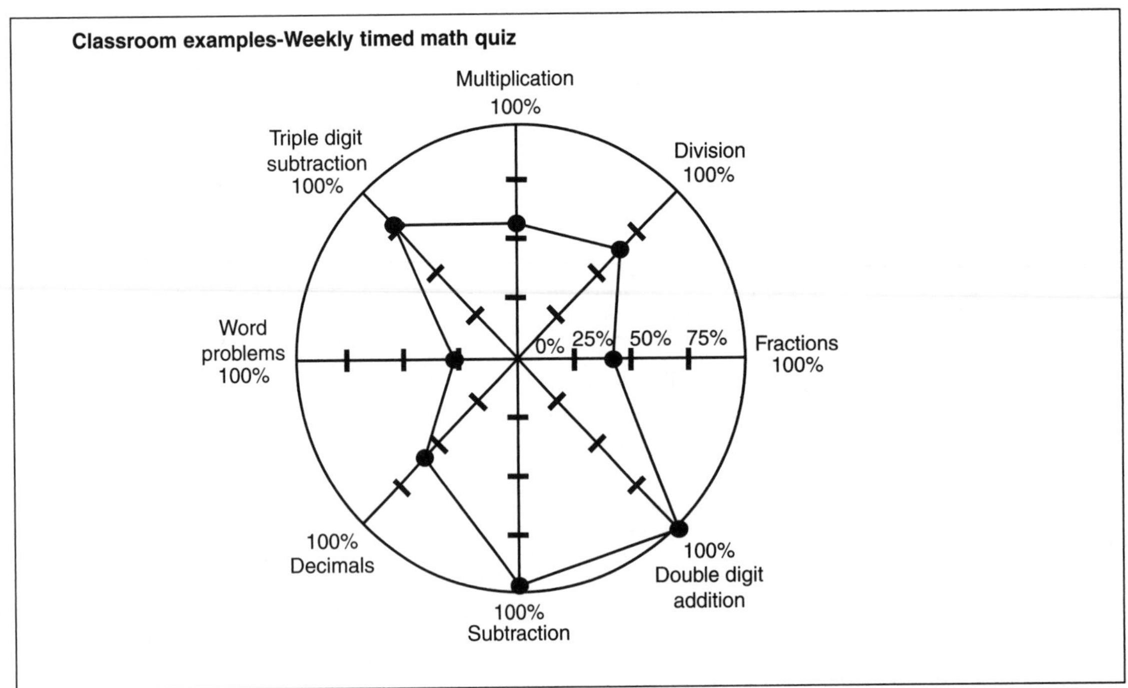

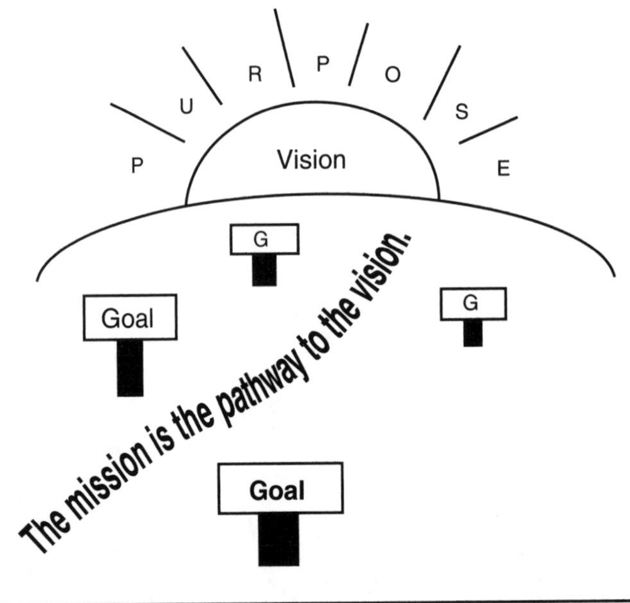

Figure 2.8 Class goals.

Next, "How will we know when we are fantastic readers?"

- When we all know all our [sight] words.
- When we read two books a week at home every week for four consecutive weeks.

Naturally, young students will require more prompting and information to state goals than older students will. It is important to have the class write the goals, then sign and post them as a constant reminder for the class.

Helpful Tips

- Keep the goals simple and measurable, focused on the vision and purpose.
- Measure progress toward the goals regularly and display the results.
- When each goal is met, celebrate, and then increase expectations!

Establish Quality Factors for Students

Quality Factors (QFs) are essential characteristics all students must exhibit to help achieve the class vision. Here are several approaches you can use to accomplish this task.

Elementary

- Draw an outline of a body on a large piece of butcher paper and give each student a blank sheet of 8½ by 11 paper. See Figure 2.9.
- Label the butcher paper: *Quality Student.*
- Ask students what they need to remember to be excellent students and help the class achieve the vision.
- Write the brainstormed characteristics down on the outlined body in the appropriate places. (Example: for "listen," draw a large ear and write "listen" in a bright color.) Continue until all the ideas are represented on the large outlined body.

Figure 2.9 Example: student quality factors.

- If the word "learn" has not been mentioned, you will need to remind the students of their purpose and ask whether their ideas will help them become better learners.
- Post this in a prominent place.
- Ask each student to draw a picture of himself or herself, label it "Quality Student-(Name)," and copy all the ideas from the butcher paper outline.

Middle or High School

Find an inspiring poster (example: someone climbing a mountain) and put a Post-it note flag at the top marked: Vision accomplished.

- Ask the students to jot down their ideas on Post-it notes or use index cards to identify characteristics that ensure that the class achieves its vision.
- On the poster, with the most frequently suggested ideas on the bottom (to form the foundation), work your way up to the apex of the mountain by listing the students' ideas.
- Label it "Quality Student" and post it in a prominent place.

For All Grade Levels

Go back through the list and write operational definitions for each of the Quality Factors. Operational definitions are concise and explain precisely what the Quality Factor means. For example, if the QF is be a good listener, the operational definition might be: *Look directly at the person speaking with your mouth closed; nod or respond in a meaningful manner to the person's comment.*

Helpful Tips

- Use these as a quick check-up at the end of the day. Ask, "How did we (as a class) do today on the QFs?" Ask the students to rate the class from 1 to 5. If there is a score less than 4, ask for details about where they failed to meet expectations and seek ideas for improvement for the next day.
- Be certain not to use this as a shame-and-blame exercise. The purpose is to bring to everyone's attention to the Quality Factors they defined.
- Keep in mind that students are workers as well as customers in the classroom, and therefore they receive services from the teacher.

Define a Quality Teacher

You can follow the activity of defining a Quality Student with defining a Quality Teacher. When doing so, it is important to make mental notes of what each student says. Some teachers have used butcher paper and drawn their silhouette on it and then had the class go through a similar exercise as they did to define a Quality Student. How you explain this to the students makes a large difference in the outcome as most young children generally like to please their teacher, so most of their ideas will revolve around concepts like "be nice to us" or "love us." While these are important traits, they are not sufficient.

Explain your purpose to the students (to *facilitate their learning* and to help make sure the class reaches its vision). If your students don't identify the behaviors they need from you, it is your obligation to point this out and even make a suggestion. Once you make a suggestion, give the students time to come up with their own ideas.

It is possible the class will come up with 20 or more things they want from you. These will be difficult for you to constantly remember. Therefore, once all the ideas are given ask the students to prioritize the five to seven *most important things you must remember every day* so that you can help them learn. Copy the prioritized list, and ask students to assess you weekly on each trait. "How did I do this week?"

You can use a radar chart to record their perceptions and then ask students for suggestions to help you improve the trait that scored the lowest. At the same time, it is important for you to weigh student learning results compared to the Quality Factors your students have identified for you.

> *If students rate you very highly on the Quality Factors for teacher but are not learning, there is a gap that needs analysis. It does no good for students to have you love them if they are not learning. Likewise, it does no good for students to love the teacher if they are not learning.*

Rules versus Procedures

If you have completed the preceding steps you will have created a climate conducive to everyone's success. Rules may be unnecessary (except for those mandated by the school or district) so long as the entire class has agreed, reached consensus, and signed onto the purpose, vision, mission, and Quality Factors for students described earlier in this chapter.

What may be missing, however, are procedures. *Procedures* is another name for processes. They are the steps taken to achieve a task. Examples of procedures include turning in homework, coming in late, using the bathroom, or transitioning from one activity to another. See Chapter 4 for more information on this topic.

Create a Measurement System for Strategic Goals

To date everything you've done is going to help, but one question remains: "How will you measure class performance, both at the end of the year (or semester) and during the school year?" These are significant and important decisions. If you collect data only at the end of the unit, course, or school year—lagging indicators—it is too late to improve the instructional process for that group of students. Therefore you can see the significance of creating a systematic formal measurement system that includes in-process-leading indicators. As you can see from Figure 2.10 on the next page, the Brain Center informs the leader not only about results, but also about process. When the organization learns

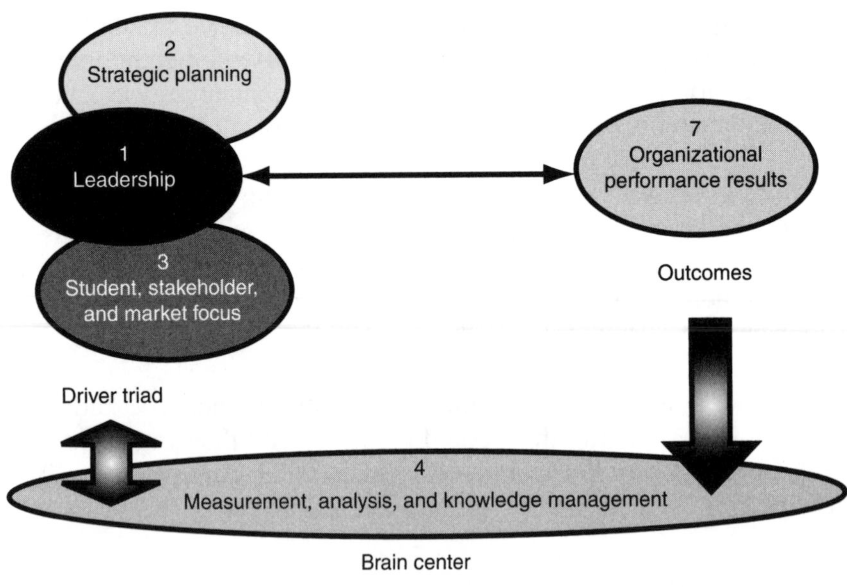

Figure 2.10 Driver Triad—Brain Center: Results.

from the data and makes informed decisions about what midcourse corrections must be made, there is a greater chance for all students to succeed.

A measurement system is developed by the leadership during strategic planning before the school year begins. (In this training guide, we focus on the classroom measurement system.) Leading indicators or in-process measures are key predictors of success. You need to determine what these would be for your class and each content area. For example, key indicators of reading success include comprehension, vocabulary, fluency, phonemic awareness, and phonemes. Examples of key indicators of math success include computing fluency, problem solving, logical reasoning, math operations, and math vocabulary.

To get started, first determine what data to collect, how often you will collect it, and how the data will be analyzed and used to monitor daily operations. You'll also need to set some targets and dates for meeting the class goals. The measurement system known as the Brain Center (Category 4) of the Baldrige framework is central to informing the leadership about the efficiency and effectiveness of the system. Without a measurement system, neither educators nor students will understand what needs to improve.

ACTIVITY: ***Identify the key predictors of success for your grade or subject.***

Content Taught	Key Predicators (Leading Indicators)

Set Targets for Goal Completion to Reach the Vision

You have just walked through the creation of a classroom culture built on the concept of success for all. Now we want to explore the concept of measurable targets. Category 2 of the Baldrige framework asks, "What are your performance projections for short- and longer-term planning time horizons?" Performance projections are used to track progress toward goal accomplishment and therefore the class vision. Without targeted projections and consistent ways to measure, it is easy to lose focus on the goal. Over the course of our lives, we probably can all cite at least one time when we lost focus, which resulted in not achieving a personal goal. This is a natural consequence of not having measurable targets along the way. What follows are examples at all three levels of the K–12 spectrum.

Here's an example from a high school Japanese I class.

Purpose: To learn Japanese so we can work for U.S. companies doing business in Japan.

Vision: *We are Japanese scholars who appreciate and can communicate the culture, history, music, and traditions of Japanese families. We act as goodwill bridges to U.S. companies desiring to market their products in Japan.*

Mission: *We will participate every day and help one another learn while having fun, asking questions, and using technology to communicate and create communication products. We will respect one another, cooperate, and do our homework.*

GOALS ▼ TARGETS ►	October	December	February	April
We will all learn 100% of our vocabulary words. (Percentage of students who know all words.)	40%	60%	80%	100%
We will write and send e-mail letters each week in Japanese to our pen pal families.	70%	100%	100%	100%
We will carry on a 10-minute conversation in Japanese with a native speaker.	0	10%	50%	100%
We will prepare marketing materials in Japanese for products of U.S. companies. (Percentage of projects started/completed.)	0	10/0	40/0	100/100

Here's an example from a middle school science class.

Purpose: To learn about science to solve difficult scientific problems and get important jobs as engineers, in medicine, or astronauts.

Vision: *We are the "Einsteins" of this school who discover and uncover things! We are prolific problem solvers and astound the adults with our inquisitive minds!*

Mission: *We will come to school every day, eagerly ask questions, help one another, work together, and keep our "job" promises to our classmates. We will use technology, have fun, and stay optimistic.*

GOALS ▼ TARGETS ►	October	December	February	May
We will all learn 100% of our science vocabulary words. (Percentage of students who know all words.)	40%	65%	100%	100%
We will write problems for the class to solve based on what we read, see, or hear. (Weekly starting in October.)	100%	100%	100%	100%
We will work in teams to solve at least one science-related community problem each semester and present our findings to community officials.	0	100%	0%	100%
We will all enter individual projects in the district science fair. (Percentage of projects started/ completed.)	5/0	20/0	100/100	

Here's an example from a first-grade class.

Purpose: To learn to read, write, and solve simple math problems.

Vision: *We are super, fantastic readers! We are geniuses who love learning!*

Mission: *We listen, ask questions, and are helpers for one another. We come to school every day, are kind to everyone, have fun, and work hard.*

GOALS ▼ TARGETS ►	October	December	February	May
We will all know and be able to write 100% of our words. (Percentage of students who know all words.)	40%	65%	80%	100%
We will write stories with sentences. (Percentage of students who demonstrate the skill.)	10%	30%	70%	100%
We will take out and read two library books at home each week.	100%	100%	100%	100%
We will all learn our math addition and subtraction facts to 10. (Percentage of students who demonstrate the skill.)	60%	90%	100%	100%

You see, the importance of having measurable goals and targets is that students have something concrete to work toward. If the vision is filled with passion and the mission statement outlines the behaviors necessary to reach the vision, and all students and adults in the classroom have signed off on each, there is every reason to believe that the students will reach the goals. Note the target for the last first grade goal is at 100% by February. As soon as students reach the target, continue to monitor, and select a new goal.

This gets to the issue that we brought up in Chapter 1 about teachers lowering standards and expectations for students who "won't," believing they "can't." In any BBQ classroom, it is vital to understand the significance of developing a culture for success. There is no reason to expect different results until you understand systems thinking and engage students in the process of creating the classroom system. This classroom system will reflect their needs/expectations/desires and, yes, interest in having fun learning.

In Chapter 5 you will learn how to make data available so students can monitor their own progress and help improve instruction. Appendix C provides information and templates for Student Data and Goal Setting books. When teachers have the expectation and teach students to track their progress, analyze results, and set goals and action plans, the principle "I am responsible for my own learning" becomes real.

It has been said that educators are data rich and information poor. This means, we collect data on everything, but we mostly *don't use it to inform the system* and therefore lose opportunities to drive midcourse corrections that lead to improved results.

A complete classroom measurement system (Figure 2.11) would include measures from Category 3 (Student, Stakeholder Focus), including student satisfaction with class culture or climate and next-teacher-in-line and parent satisfaction; Category 5 (Student as Worker Focus), student feedback on materials used and pacing; and Category 6 (Process Management), in-process (formative) learning measures and other measures of effectiveness and efficiency such as cycle time.

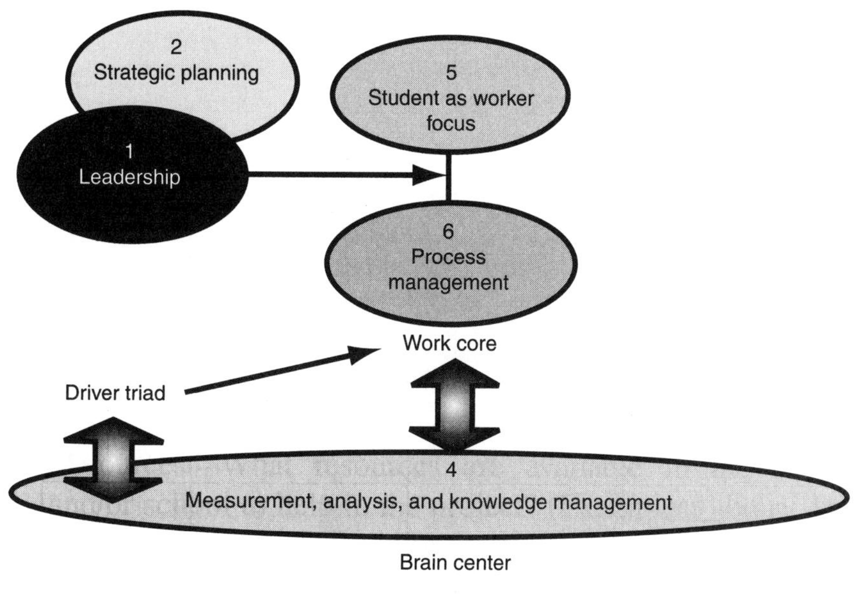

Figure 2.11 Measurement system ties the Driver Triad and Work Core.

You want to include hard data (things you can count, measure, time) as well as soft data (perception) in your measurement system. See Tables 2.1, 2.2, and 2.3 for examples of leading/lagging indicators of hard and soft data. The charts also give you suggestions for the frequency and best tool to use to understand the different types of data.

Here is a suggestion for how you might want to organize your measurement system.

What will be collected	How often	How will it be collected?	Who will collect the data?	How will it be used?
Example: Tardy	Daily Studied monthly for trends	Students not ready to learn 10 seconds after bell	Teacher or designated student	Relationship between tardy and learning Root cause analysis If school-based problem, information presented to faculty

Table 2.1 Examples of hard data in-process measures (leading indicators).

Type	What will be studied?	Measure	Tool used	Frequency	Tool used	Frequency
Hard data	Absenteeism	Number in class	Run chart	Daily	Bar graph	Daily
	Tardy	Number late	Run chart	Daily		
	Learning gains	Regular quizzes on in-process measures (e.g., vocabulary)	Class—line graph	Weekly	Student run chart	Weekly
		Portfolio rubrics	Histogram	Monthly		
		Pre-Unit test	Histogram	As appropriate		
		Writing rubrics	Histogram	Monthly	Run chart	Monthly
	Homework	Number turned in on time and accurate	Run chart	Daily or weekly	Bar graph	Daily/weekly
	Relationship between homework and learning	Completed homework and weekly quiz grades	Scatter	Weekly or monthly		
		Completed homework and unit test grades	Scatter	As appropriate		
	Relationship between attendance and learning gains	Attendance data and pre-post learning gains	Scatter	As appropriate		
	Reading fluency	Number of words right on timed reading	Run chart	Bi-monthly		
	Efficiency of learning	On time completion of assignments	Line graph	As appropriate		
	Discipline issues	Type/frequency	Check sheet to collect Run chart to graph	Daily (specified period of time)	Pareto to analyze	As appropriate
	Failure	Number who fail a quiz or unit test	Run chart	As appropriate		

Table 2.2 Examples of soft data in-process measures (leading indicators).

Type	What will be studied?	Measure	Tool used	Frequency	Tool used	Frequency
Soft Data	Student satisfaction	Learning climate and rapport	Satisfaction surveys	Weekly		
	Student satisfaction	Effectiveness of resources	How effective were these resources?	As appropriate	Pareto chart of analysis	
	Student satisfaction	Learning activities	Plus/delta chart	Daily or weekly		
	Student satisfaction	Effectiveness of instruction	Fast feedback	Daily	Histogram of analysis	
	Student satisfaction	Effectiveness of teacher	Radar chart of QFs for teacher	Weekly		
	Parent satisfaction	Teacher effectiveness	Prioritization survey	October		
	Next-teacher-in-line satisfaction	Students arrive with necessary skills	Satisfaction survey	Early fall		
	Learning environment	Faculty and staff trust and respect for students	Student satisfaction survey	At report card time	Histogram	To follow up on survey
	Enthusiasm for learning	Student active engagement in learning	Enthusiasm/learning chart	Daily or weekly End of units		

Table 2.3 Examples of hard and soft data results measures (lagging indicators).

Type	What will be studied?	Measure	Tool used	Frequency	Tool used	Frequency
Soft data	Student satisfaction	Learning climate and rapport	Satisfaction surveys	Semester or year-end		
	Parent satisfaction	Learning climate and rapport	Satisfaction surveys	Semester or year-end		
Hard data	Learning gains	Normed test results	Control charts	Yearly		
		Local exams	Run chart	Semester/yearly	Pareto (errors)	
		Portfolios	Histogram	Semester/yearly		
	Discipline issues	Referrals to office	Run chart	Semester/yearly		
	Failure	Rate of failure	Run chart	Semester/yearly		
	Retention	Students retained	Histogram	Year-end	Run chart	Year-end
	Parent involvement and student achievement	Volunteer hours and learning result	Scatter diagram	Year-end		

Leaders Determine the Action Plans

Keep in mind that this is a learner-centered system. The focus is on the leader as a facilitator of learning, so the job is not finished until everyone is successful. Action plans ought to include the approaches you believe will (1) engage students and (2) help them learn to achieve the goal.

Example:

Strategic goal (from the vision): 100% mastery of single-digit addition				
Action plan	**Current**	**Target: Sept. 1**	**Target: Jan. 31**	**Target: April 30**
3-D math addition problems to be solved with partners	0	1/week	2/week	3/week
Students silently write math stories from prompts to share with class	0	1/week	2/week	2/week
2-minute timed tests of numeric problems	1/week	2/week	3/week	1/week
2-minute timed tests of word addition problems	0	1/week	2/week	4/week

ACTIVITY: ***Practice creating action plans***

Strategic goal				
Action plan	**Current**	**Target:**	**Target:**	**Target:**

The Importance of Systems Thinking on Results

Many classroom management approaches fail to provide teachers with an understanding of systems. With the exception of having students collaborate on mission statements and perhaps helping write class rules, seldom are students empowered to create a classroom climate for success. The wise teacher will recognize that adding more rules or giving more homework, or teaching to a test will *not yield sustained, improved results over time.* Improved results come if the teacher aligns and integrates all aspects of the system, empowers students as workers, and is committed to personal and organizational improvement as shown in Figure 2.12 on the next page. If teachers don't accept that 90% or more of all system problems are due to faulty processes, they will forever blame students, parents, or the previous teacher.

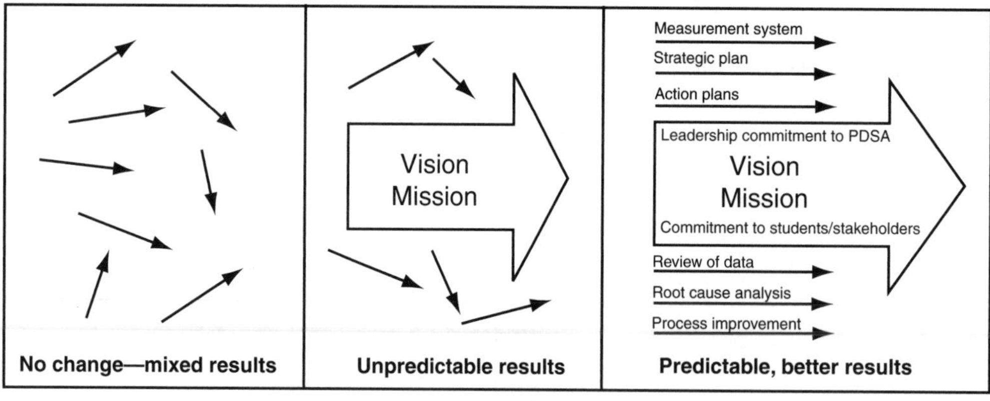

Figure 2.12 How systems thinking leads to improved results.

Summary

You have set the stage for your classroom system, one that conveys the expectation that all of your students can and will meet the learning standards. Further, you have created a system that empowers students to help create a class vision, mission, and goals based on the culture of internal motivation, responsibility for one's own learning, and the citizenship of becoming response-able to the success of the group. From this new culture, all activities flow and students feel safe knowing that everyone has agreed to help. Civility and character are built into this system. There is no need to directly teach "character education," because the behavior is modeled, expected, and practiced every day by everyone.

You may be feeling as though you have turned all your established routines upside down! You may even wonder if all the time spent on vision, mission, and class goals and the involvement of "student as worker" is worth it. Teachers who engage in this process, and who follow up with teaching students how to use PDSA and related tools, are able to "buy back" significant instructional time. If you have gone through this process as outlined, it will be a rare occurrence if you have to drag some students along. While creating this new climate for success is necessary, it is not sufficient for predicting improved student learning results. You must stay the course and continue learning how the rest of the Baldrige framework aligns work systems and processes to keep motivation high and students focused on doing high-performance work.

Reflections

3

MANAGEMENT BY FACT

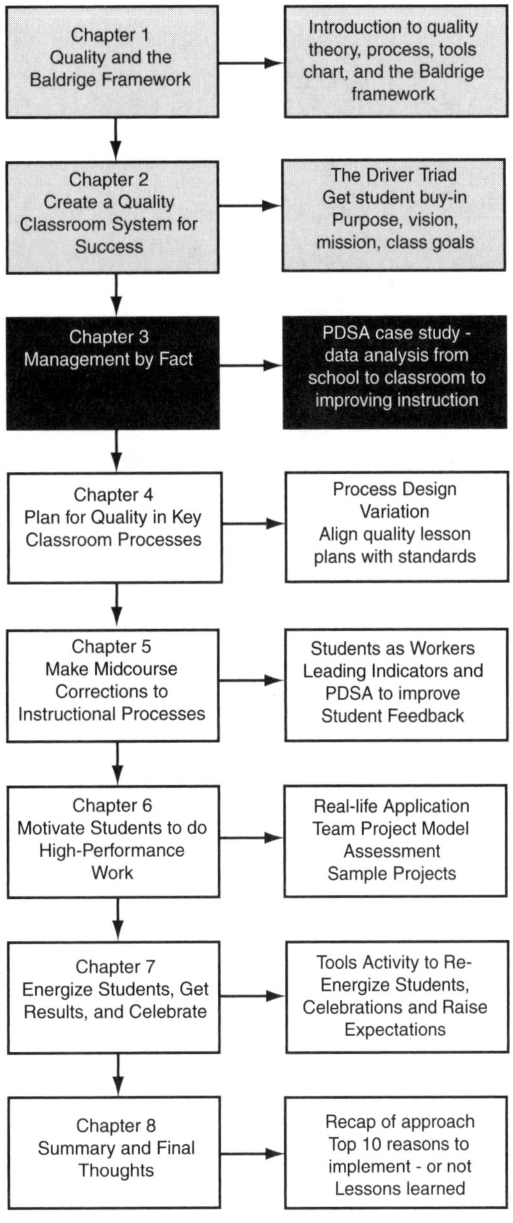

Conversation with the Teacher

There is some irony in the fact that data have been used to denigrate public school teachers and the work they do, causing frustration, fear, and some of the best to give up and quit the profession. Yet, without data there is no way to understand what is really happening, or how to analyze the root cause of problems. It is not easy to let down your guard and become comfortable with the notion that you need to rely less on intuition and canned curricula and much more on data analysis to make decisions about instructional approaches and activities, but it must be done.

Do you ever think about the consequences of moving ahead while leaving some students behind? If you are a first-grade teacher and at the end of the year pass along five students who do not know their sight words or how to read simple sentences, this leaves the second-grade teacher with 25% or more rework from the first day. If the second-grade teacher does not get all the students up to grade level in math or reading or writing, the third-grade teacher has that much more rework to do. As this pattern continues through the grades, each successive teacher inherits exponentially that much more rework, until finally the learning gaps are so large that it is nearly impossible to close them.

We know (because it has been proven) that application of the Plan-Do-Study-Act cycle of improvement to key classroom processes does yield system change and, therefore, leads to improved student learning results. This is, in many ways, a leap of faith because until you have learned the PDSA process and practiced it, you may say, "I can't do this. It takes too much time. I have to cover the curriculum." Acting under this assumption, think about how many students are left behind because you are covering the curriculum.

Remember your purpose and that you are a facilitator of learning. Remember the two principles of a Baldrige-based quality classroom (I am responsible and I am response-able), and let these guide your conscience and your dedication to learning how to use the Plan-Do-Study-Act Cycle. Use the PDSA to improve every key classroom process, as nearly all of them directly influence learning.

In this chapter you will learn:

- The basics of the Plan-Do-Study-Act cycle improvement process
- Some appropriate tools to use at specific steps of the PDSA process
- The importance of data analysis and of looking at data from more than one perspective
- The difference between in-process measures and outcomes measures and the use each has for planning purposes

Data-Driven Decision Making

As a routine part of planning before a new school year, we would hope that your school administration provides you with the results data from any state or national standardized test, including an item analysis of the error types your students made the previous year. If, however, that information is not provided, at a minimum you will want to request the results of your class and grade level. We are talking about the Brain Center, the Measurement,

It is not about shame or blame.

It is not about students or parents.

It is about your desire to become a true facilitator of learning and to realize that 90% or more of any problems with the results are because of faulty processes or systems.

Who creates the system? Leadership.

You are Leadership in the classroom. Therefore, you are the one who must step up to the data and learn how to analyze it from more than one point of view until you have a good idea of what it really says.

Analysis, and Knowledge Management (Category 4) of the Baldrige framework. From Figure 3.1 you can see how important this is for leadership, as it forms the beginning of knowledge that is fed into any strategic planning process. Make no mistake about it. Unless you are brave enough to look, analyze, and *own* your students' results, you will never be able to make informed decisions about how to improve instruction so future students can be more successful.

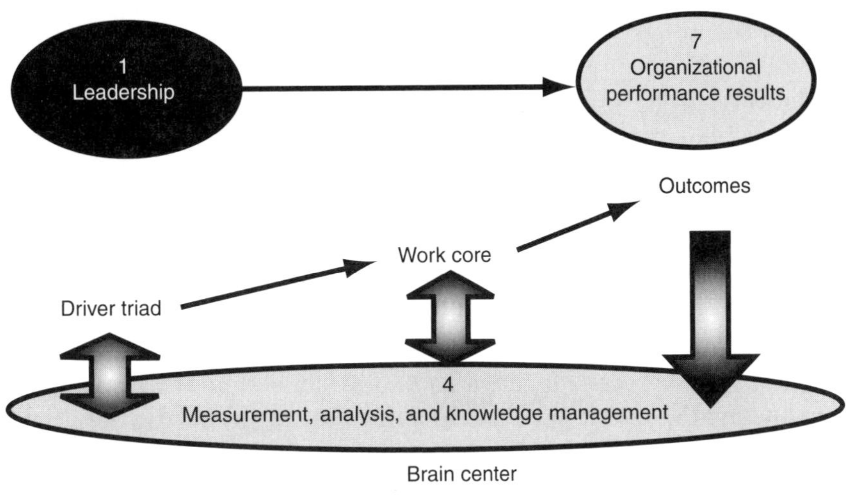

Figure 3.1 The line from leadership to results.

Plan-Do-Study-Act: The Quality Improvement Process

In Chapter 1 you were briefly introduced to the Plan-Do-Study-Act improvement cycle. Before we get into practice, it's a good idea to take a closer look at the specific steps in the process (see Figure 3.2 on the next page). Data are collected during steps 2 and 5 and

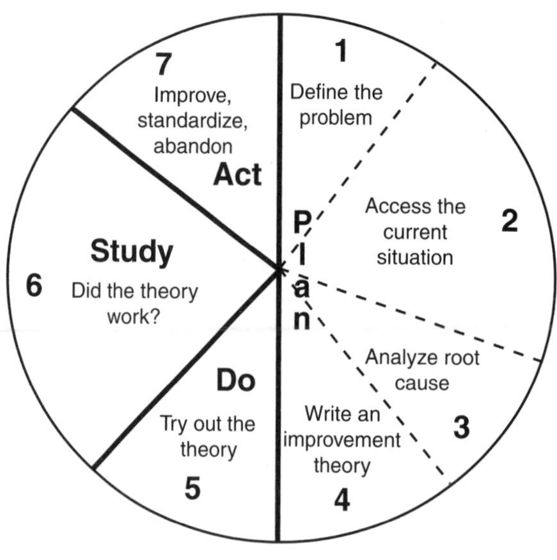

Figure 3.2 Steps of the PDSA process.

analyzed in steps 3 and 6. Decisions about what to change are not made until after a root cause analysis is completed. Change for the sake of change is risky business. It may yield better results, but it may also make matters worse. Often, when decisions are made on intuition, problems thought to be solved recur. This is a huge problem in education and one that ought to frustrate every teacher because it wastes tremendous amounts of time. Isn't it better to use a fact-based process, to learn from the data, and then to make decisions that lead to elimination of problems? Here are some true, albeit outrageous examples of the high cost of making decisions based on faulty or incomplete examination of the data and poor planning:

- District level—purchasing an additional set of texts for students to use at home to reduce back injuries from heavy book sacks
- School level—locking all the bathroom doors except one between classes to keep students from smoking
- Classroom—assigning additional pages of homework because many students don't "get" the concepts being taught

All three of these instances demonstrate a lack of systems thinking as changes were made without understanding the true root cause. Imagine the cost to the district to purchase additional textbooks without piloting other approaches first. These are lessons we all need to learn. The PDSA process is designed to continuously improve effectiveness and efficiency, thus saving resources and still attaining the desired goal.

There are tools to use at each step of the process. Refer to the Tool Selection Chart on page 13 for help in selecting the most appropriate tool to use. This will save you a lot of time and help you avoid mistakes. We believe that the best way to learn the PDSA process and the tools associated with it is through a case study. By following the case study directions you will experience "just-in-time" learning of most of the tools. We have chosen to imbed the tools throughout this training guide to help you avoid the annoyance of having to flip pages back and forth. Just remember, when you're working on your own PDSA process improvements, turn to the Tool Selection Chart and you'll find the page number for instructions for each tool.

The actual data you see is fictional, but it is formatted to resemble state and school district No Child Left Behind Annual Yearly Progress reports. Although we refer to Hawaii and its schools as examples, you should not infer that this is actual data or that good things are not happening there. They are, just as they are in every state in the union. But, we must face reality that the road to true improvement and meeting state and federal expectations requires dramatic system change and the use of PDSA to improve. Adding programs or more technology without changing the system may be necessary but is certainly not sufficient to meet the challenges of the 21st century.

The instructions for practicing the tools and charting the data are given in black boxes. Key notes to the teacher are given in a white box alongside or near the data. Once you go through this PDSA process and practice using the tools, use your own data to analyze the results of your students.

PDSA for Annual Planning Prior to Each New School Year

PLAN Step 1: Define the problem (background information)

Your school is facing some difficult issues with poor student learning results: levels that do not meet state guidelines. On the basis of the most recent state standards test, 44% of all students were below the "cut" score for reading and writing. The Hawaiian–Part-Hawaiian students have the highest failure rate. Attendance is below the expected levels, which may account for some of the low achievement scores, but we cannot be certain of this. All we can surmise is that when students are not in school, they miss the benefit of instruction. *What we don't know is whether or not the instruction is effective.*

The results indicate a gap between action plans, instructional strategies, staff development, and student services. Your school recognizes the problems and is determined to close the achievement gap among subgroups and increase the rates of learning to meet the Hawaii Standards, General Learner Outcomes, and Annual Yearly Progress (AYP) rates for the No Child Left Behind requirements.

The Project Statement—Raise student achievement by improving instruction.

PLAN Step 2: Assess the current situation

Begin by analyzing results (outcomes) data. These data come directly from the school system. They inform teachers, administrators, school boards, and the community about the effectiveness and efficiency of the system. Newspapers, however, most frequently report these results to compare districts and/or to compare schools within a district. Since newspaper publishers are in the business of selling papers and not necessarily committed to telling the whole story, they generally only print one year's worth of results. This type of reporting does not adequately inform the public about the effects of any improvement in student learning that only trend data reveals. We cannot change the media's ways (although we hope the school board takes up this cause), but we can control how we analyze results and use the information to improve instruction. Teachers cannot do their job without this information. It is at the heart of learning to improve so more students can master the skills required.

Figure 3.3 shows the percentage of third-, fifth-, and eighth-grade students who *met or exceeded the grade level requirements* on the state math test for the previous four years.

Test	School	**State math scores**			
Grade 3	**Ambacom**	2001	2002	2003	2004
	Hawaiian/part Hawaiian	5%	15%	6%	8%
	Asian-Pacific Islanders	10%	19%	11%	25%
	Caucasian	43%	50%	53%	52%
	Hispanic	40%	39%	31%	35%
	Black	40%	51%	52%	53%
	Free/reduced lunch	5%	3%	6%	8%
	Pay lunch	41%	39%	40%	40%

Test	School	**State math scores**			
Grade 5	**Ambacom**	2001	2002	2003	2004
	Hawaiian/part Hawaiian	15%	20%	18%	12%
	Asian-Pacific Islanders	33%	35%	26%	25%
	Caucasian	58%	65%	66%	55%
	Hispanic	30%	29%	29%	45%
	Black	35%	38%	39%	42%
	Free/reduced lunch	23%	20%	18%	8%
	Pay lunch	52%	50%	53%	50%

These data are useful for understanding gaps in results. *These results are best used for planning for the next school year. It is too late to build in quality for this group of students.*

The questions to ask are:

- What were the results for students in my classes over the same period of time?
- Have the ethnic groups in my classes performed at about the same level as all students in that grade?
- Do you know the preferred learning styles of these student groups?

Test	School	**State math scores**			
Grade 8	**Lielehai**	2001	2002	2003	2004
	Hawaiian/part Hawaiian	10%	18%	15%	12%
	Asian-Pacific Islanders	39%	40%	41%	45%
	Caucasian	50%	52%	49%	57%
	Hispanic	38%	39%	36%	40%
	Black	35%	49%	52%	43%
	Free/reduced lunch	25%	33%	26%	25%
	Pay lunch	48%	49%	55%	60%

Figure 3.3 State math proficiency results by subgroup.

ACTIVITY: ***Practice using a run chart.*** **See the following run chart instructions.**

Directions: Use a run chart for these data. Use a different color of marker for each subgroup with a legend at the side. Place all the data for each year on a separate chart. Scale the chart as shown to the right. Each set of data will have four points. Connect the dots for each subgroup.

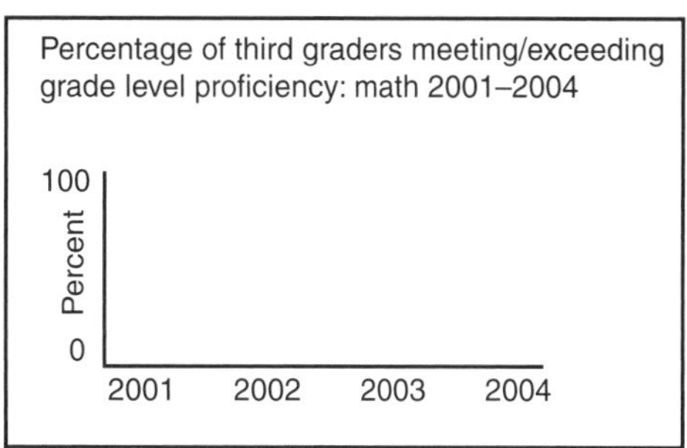

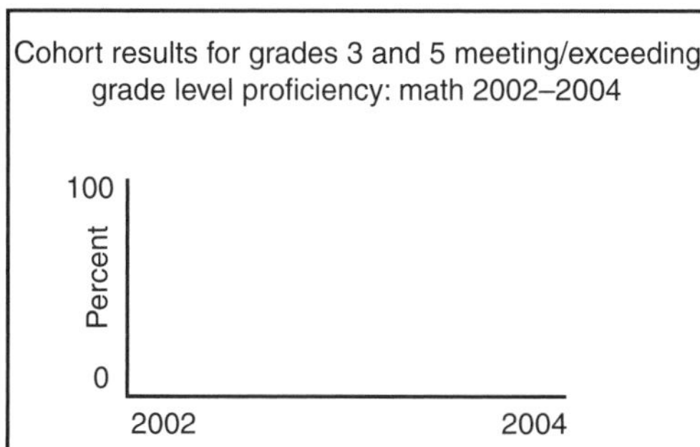

Directions: Chart the cohort data by using a run chart. These cohorts consist of grades 3 and 5 (2002, 2004) or grades 5 (2001) and 8 (2004). (See the glossary for a detailed definition of "cohort.") Use a different color of marker for each subgroup with a legend at the side. Scale the chart as shown to the left. Each run chart will have two data points. Connect the dots.

Look at the charts side by side. What do you see that is important and of concern? What do you see from looking at the cohort data that gives you a different perspective? These are schoolwide data, important because of success levels of ethnic groups and the free/reduced and pay lunch subgroups. It's important for you to examine the similar data from your classes over the past three to five years.

Further your familiarity with assessing the current situation and imagine you are Ms. Jane Smith, grade 8 math teacher. You've been at the same school for four years. The percentage breakdown of students representing each No Child Left Behind subgroup in your class is as follows: Hawaiian–Part Hawaiian, 40%; Asian–Pacific Islander, 30%; Caucasian, 13%; Hispanic, 2%; and Black, 15%. Seventy percent of your students are on free/reduced lunch. Go to Figure 3.4 on page 67 to find the results for Jane Smith's classes and follow the directions to look at how each subgroup has performed over the past four years.

We recommend you compare the results of your students with those of the school as a whole. You can probably obtain these data from the district assessment office. What does this information tell you?

Run Chart

What

A run chart is a picture of a process over time. It is a simple tool to use and young children from grades 1 on up can learn to plot and read run charts. A run chart is one form of a line graph.

How

1. Draw the horizontal axis (X) and vertical axis (Y).
2. Label the horizontal axis "Time" (dates, days of the week, months, and so on).
3. Label the vertical axis "What is being measured" (number right on test, number of students, number of sit-ups, and so on).
4. Plot the data by putting a dot at the intersection of the X axis (date) and the Y axis (measurement).
5. Plot all the data. When finished, connect the dots.

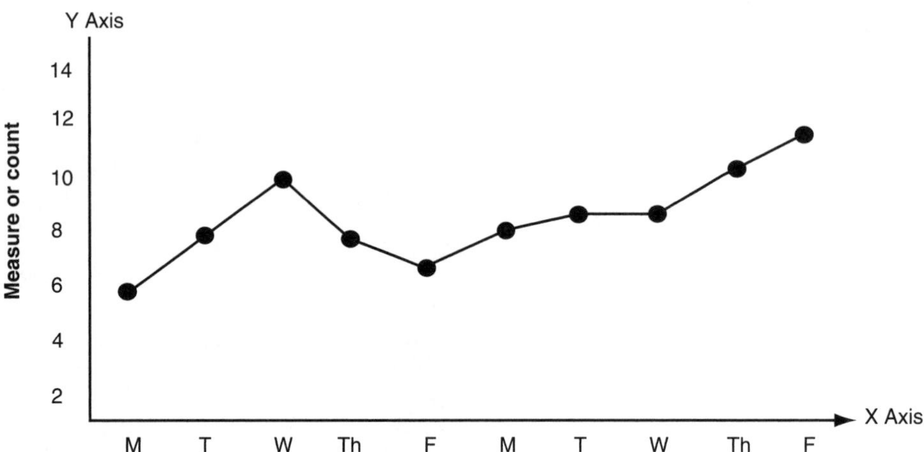

When

- You want to see the trend over a certain period of time.
- You need to know what the current situation is.
- It is important to know whether the average is changing.
- To have students track their own progress.

Classroom Examples

J. Smith's physical fitness record

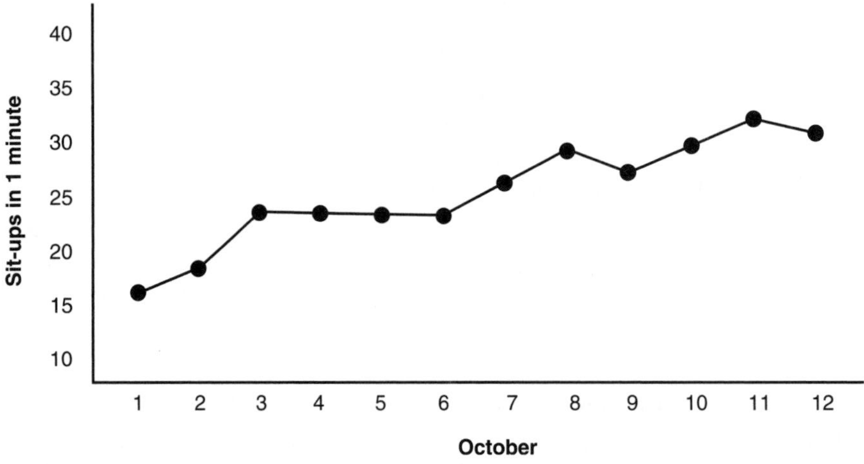

Continued

Continued

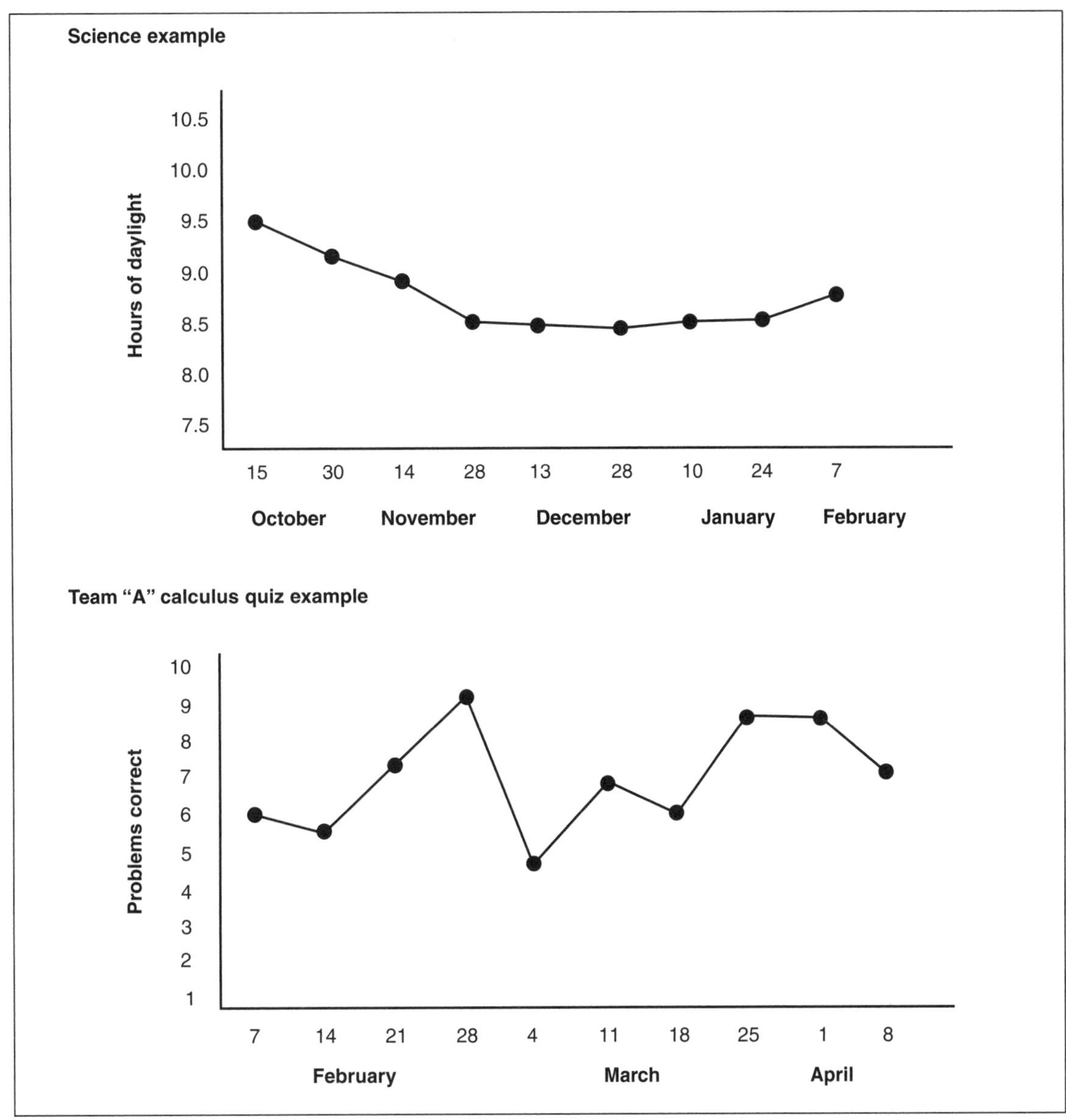

Percentage that meet/exceed grade level math requirements

Grade 8	Lielehai	2001	2002	2003	2004
40%	Hawaiian/part Hawaiian	10%	12%	13%	13%
30%	Asian-Pacific Islanders	39%	40%	41%	45%
13%	Caucasian	60%	62%	69%	70%
2%	Hispanic	60%	70%	80%	80%
15%	Black	25%	35%	42%	53%
70%	Free/reduced	30%	30%	30%	32%
30%	Pay lunch	58%	54%	65%	60%

Directions: Use the run chart and put all data on the same chart as you did in the previous exercise. Put all subgroups and all years on the same chart. Use different color markers for these data and include a legend.

Figure 3.4 Jane Smith's 8th grade state math proficiency results.

Next, let's look more closely at a different way to break down the results. Figure 3.5 shows comparative math and reading results for 2004 for several schools in the district.

2004 math results

School	Grade and number of students	Percent below	Percent approach	Percent meets	Percent exceeds
Elementary A	3 (41)	21	67	9	3
	5 (36)	12	69	17	2
Elementary B	3 (172)	32	58	10	0
	5 (169)	20	60	19	1
Elementary C	3 (41)	12	55	27	6
	5 (42)	17	60	23	0
Middle	8 (276)	22	50	24	4
High School	10 (180)	9	53	32	6

2004 reading results

School	Grade and number of students	Percent below	Percent approach	Percent meets	Percent exceeds
Elementary A	3 (42)	3	58	37	2
	5 (35)	3	49	48	0
Elementary B	3 (170)	15	51	32	2
	5 (164)	10	60	30	0
Elementary C	3 (40)	5	46	43	6
	5 (42)	8	41	45	6
Middle	8 (279)	15	44	40	1
High School	10 (188)	12	43	40	5

Directions: Use a histogram for these data. Chart the data from Figure 3.5 that is most appropriate for the grade or level you teach. Use a different color to signify each grade. Instructions for the histogram are on page 68.

These results are important for understanding just how many students are not meeting the standards. What is needed is the exact definition of "approaching." This is a clear opportunity teachers must seize.

Do teachers *know* what to change so the students in the "approaching" group can meet the standards?

These data are necessary for year-end analysis, but not sufficient to understand what midcourse corrections to make.

Figure 3.5 School comparisons: state math and reading proficiency results, 2004.

Histogram

What

A histogram is a snapshot, in bar graph form, of the distribution of data. In other words, the data are lined up according to frequency. It is a useful tool for helping groups see how powerful data in picture form can be and is often used in the popular press to make a point.

How

1. Determine the process or system to be studied.
2. Select the "classes" or subdivisions to display the data (for example, by grading scale 93–100; by weight: 75–90 pounds or 91–116 pounds; or by stanine scores on a standardized test).
3. Using data from a check sheet or other Quality tool, arrange it into the aforementioned class.
4. Draw the graph with an X axis (horizontal) and a Y axis (vertical). Each axis will be the same length.
5. Divide the X axis into the number of classes and label each.
6. Scale the Y axis from zero to the total number of data points in the class with the most frequency. Example: 10 students weigh 75–90 pounds. That is the most of any weight group. Scale the Y axis from 0–10.
7. Draw the graph.

Continued

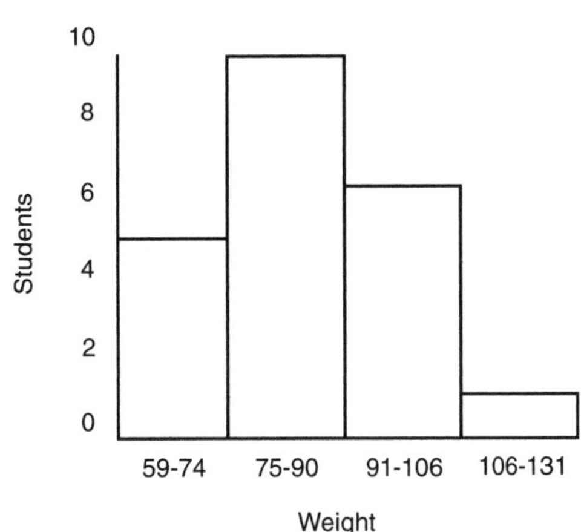

When

- It is important to see the frequency of distribution of the data.
- The group is studying statistics.
- There is a need to understand the amount of variation in any set of data.

Histogram

Example

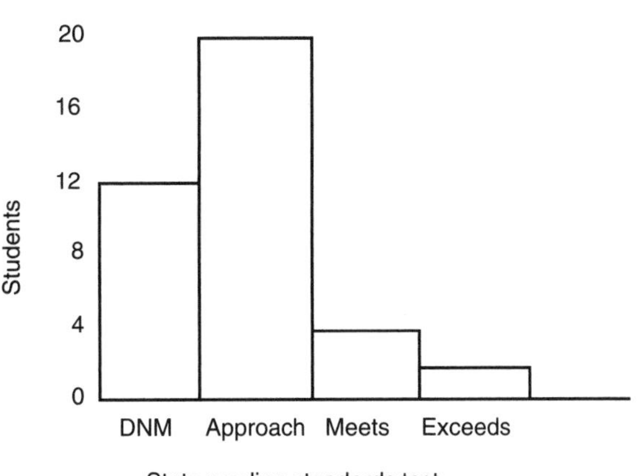

Chart interpretation

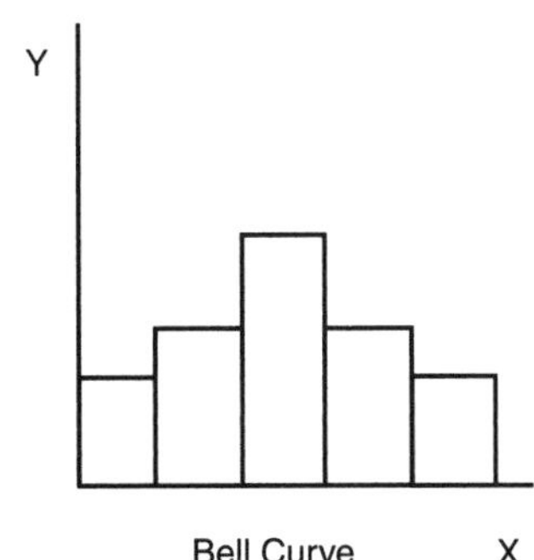

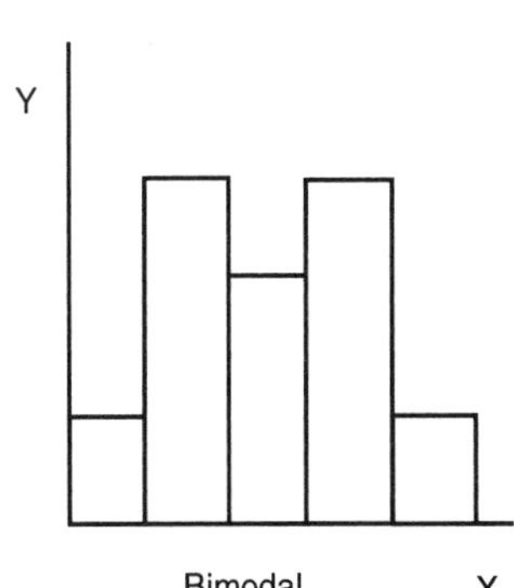

Continued

Continued

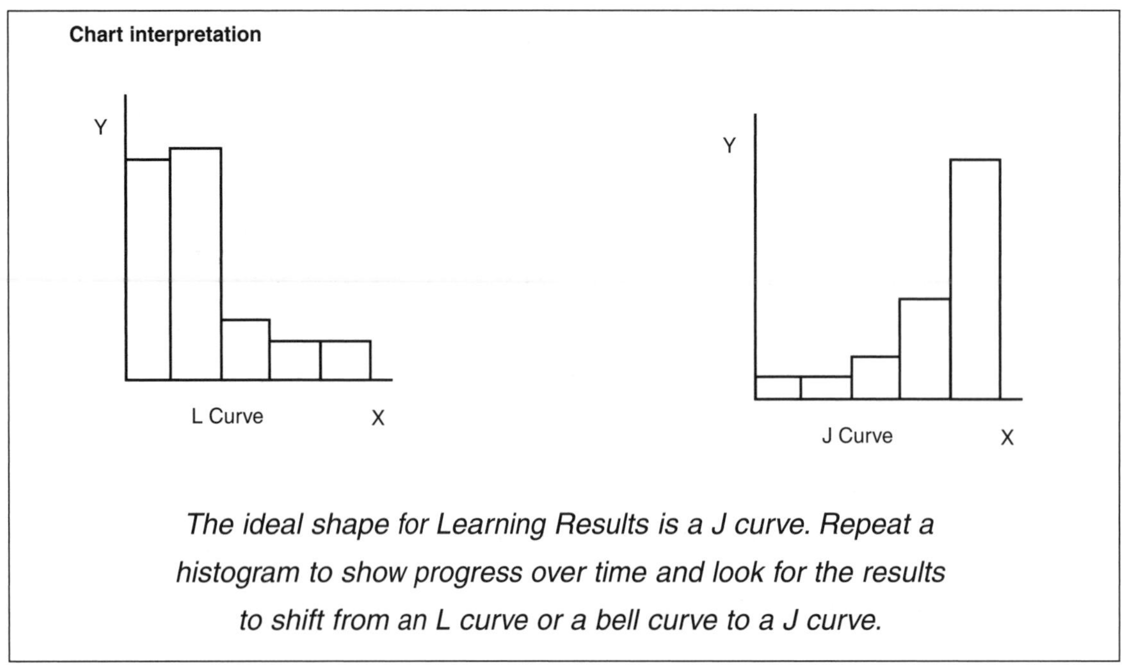

Chart interpretation
Y
L Curve
X
Y
J Curve
X
The ideal shape for Learning Results is a J curve. Repeat a histogram to show progress over time and look for the results to shift from an L curve or a bell curve to a J curve.

It is important to continue assessing the situation by looking at the results from different points of view. Continue to imagine you are Ms. Jane Smith. The results for your students by subgroup for the past two years are shown in Figure 3.6. Remember, once you have practiced by using this case study example, repeat each step, using data from your own classes.

Place the histograms side by side and review them along with the school data. What clues do you now have that you didn't have just by looking at the school data? What clues do you have that you didn't have just by looking at data for one year?

Continue working on this case study to see how to proceed. There's still a lot to learn.

Remember the two principles of a Baldrige-based quality classroom and apply them to yourself (facilitator of learning) as well as the students:

I am responsible for my own learning.

I am response-able to the success of the group.

The data previously examined was all results data. These are data collected at the end of the semester or school year. We have been looking at state test results because there is so much emphasis right now on high-stakes testing and the Annual Yearly Progress (AYP) required by the federal government based on a state formula to ensure that by 2014 all students will meet or exceed grade level standards. Other end results include any nationally standardized test or year-end or semester-end exam results.

Results data are an important part of the environmental scan, and review teachers must perform before each school year. Data analysis allows teachers to see the gaps and misalignment of the instructional process and methods with how much students learned.

Year	Subgroup	Number below	Number approach	Number meets	Number exceeds
2003	H/PH (15)	4	9	2	0
	Asian/PI (6)	1	2	2	1
	Caucasian (3)	0	1	1	1
	Hispanic (3)	1	2	0	0
	Black (5)	1	2	2	0
	F/R lunch (25)	6	15	4	0
	Pay lunch (7)	0	2	3	2
2004	H/PH (16)	8	6	2	0
	Asian/PI (8)	1	3	2	2
	Caucasian (6)	0	4	1	1
	Hispanic (1)	1	0	0	0
	Black (1)	0	0	1	0
	F/R lunch	10	11	3	1
	Pay lunch	1	2	3	1

These data are useful only if you pursue a deeper analysis. Here are some useful questions to ask:

- Is there a pattern with regard to the subgroups of students in my class and their success rates?
- Are the "footprints" (see Figures 3.7 and 3.8 below) made by these histograms similar?
- What do I know about the students and in particular what were their previous results? Is it possible to obtain data on these particular students? How might you do that?

These data and charts are *necessary but not sufficient* for you to know exactly what led to these results. It is important for you to follow up and learn as much as possible about learning styles of the ethnic subgroups. Then, review your lesson plans and decide whether or not you have addressed most, if not all, of the Multiple Intelligences (Figure 3.19 on page 93).

Directions: Use a histogram for these data. Place the data for each subgroup on a separate histogram, but place the histograms for each subgroup side by side. Label the charts accurately. See the example on page 68 for how to scale the histograms.

Figure 3.6 Ms. Smith's 8th grade class state math proficiency results for 2003–2004 (5 years in district, 4 years in this school).

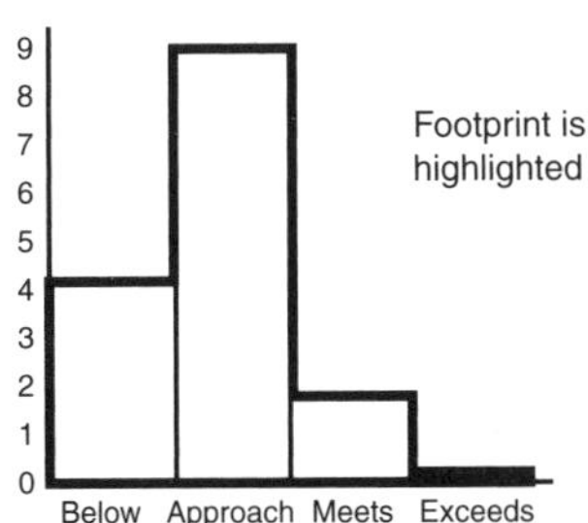

Figure 3.7 Footprint of 2003 state reading results: example.

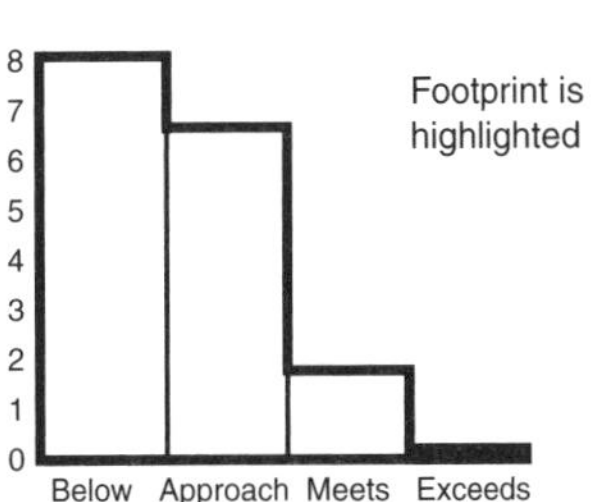

Figure 3.8 Footprint of 2004 state reading results: example.

Simply reviewing results data is too late to build in Quality for this student group but is invaluable when planning for the following year. Continue working through this case study.

PLAN Step 3: Analyze root cause (key opportunities to unlock the mysteries)

Analyze the previous year's lesson plans for the following:

- Alignment with the content standards.

  The International Center for Leadership in Education (ICLE) has done extensive work on analyzing the state standards and how each is aligned with its respective state competency test. Check www.icle.net for more information and specifically how to order the Curriculum Matrix Data. Dr. Robert Marzano, from the North Central Regional Education Laboratory, recognizes the problem, as does Dr. Willard Daggett, president of ICLE, in suggesting that the states have identified too many standards, making it difficult for any teacher to adequately address them all. Furthermore, while the states have a plethora of standards, they test significantly fewer. It's best to identify the absolutely essential standards, check to see if these are aligned with what is being tested in your state, and then make certain your lesson plans address these.

- Item analysis to identify student errors with how the concepts/standards were addressed in your lesson plans.
- Cross-reference student test scores by subgroup and the item analysis with the methods you used to teach the content standards.

Research "best practice" lesson plans from teachers who have had success with students like yours.

Here are some suggestions:

- Seek out the colleague within your district whose classes had the greatest success on the state tests.
- Meet with other grade-level teachers in your district to discover what approaches worked best with students in different subgroups.
- Other resources include (1) the local Phi Delta Kappa chapter, (2) any district or regional nationally board certified teachers, (3) other districts or schools within your state who've experienced the greatest success with any subgroup of students, (4) teachers in a Baldrige Award–winning school district.

Caution for the teacher: Avoid the temptation to believe that students in your classes are so unique that you cannot learn from others. If what you're doing is not working, it is foolish to assume the solution is that students need to try harder.

Conduct an environmental scan. Figure 3.9 is a tool that might help you understand the situation you may be faced with. It will help you anticipate the future and proactively prepare to meet the challenges.

Student body	**Current year**	**Next year**	**Projection for next 3 years**	
Percent with skills needed				
Special needs				
Limited English speaker				
Non-English speaker				
Free/reduced lunch				
Pay lunch				
Ethnic groups				
Enrollment in my class(es)				
Federal or state government; board policy or administrative changes				
Major changes in the district that could affect my assignment				

Figure 3.9 Example: environmental scan.

Understand process capability. Are your classroom processes capable of yielding the desired results? Every year (or semester) you work with a different set of students. Therefore, it is natural for teachers to cry "foul" when districts hold them accountable for student learning results. This, however, represents another key opportunity. A teacher dedicated to BBQ would want to know and, in fact, has a need to know, whether or not his/her system is capable of improved student learning results. Although there is a statistical formula you can use to determine whether your key processes are capable of reaching the standards you set, you can deduce this from looking at the results of your classes over time on any normed test.

One problem is that the states are mostly still unsettled as to what test they give and what grades or subjects are tested, and they frequently change the "cut" score for no apparent reason. If this is the situation in which you find yourself, a better approach (and a workable one) is to study the item analyses of *your* students from at least the previous three years. It is even better if you have access to this information from the previous five years. If the analyses provide demographic information about each student, that will allow you to chunk students from each subgroup. This will give you a more focused and accurate picture of what happens in your classroom. To assure yourself you are not biased and to ensure accuracy, place the data as shown in Figure 3.10.

Example: 3rd Grade

Reading	**Skill analyzed**	**Percent in 6th stanine or above**				
	Vocabulary	2000	2001	2002	2003	2004
Whole class						
Free/reduced lunch						
Male						

Continued

Figure 3.10 Example of a tool to assess previous success by subgroup.

Continued

Asian/Pacific Islanders						
Black						
Caucasian						
Hispanic						
Native American						
ESOL						
IEP students						

Figure 3.10 Example of a tool to assess previous success by subgroup.

Use a run chart with these data, and put all data on the same chart to see trends. If students from one or more subgroup consistently do not perform very well on any skill, you immediately learn that the current system is not capable of yielding better results. A BBQ teacher always sees data as a "gift" and uses them to improve processes.

About innovation.

Another of the Baldrige core values is *managing for innovation.* How do you balance systematic improvements using PDSA and a need for innovation that allows for breakthrough improvement? You need to give this serious consideration. It is appropriate to consider benchmarking another teacher from your school district or others, if the process or system under study is *not* capable of yielding the desired results or the *process or system under study has not undergone change in the last five to 10 years.* For instance, if you noticed a trend that few students in your classes from a specific ethnic group perform adequately in one area of the test, you might want to plan for innovation instead of using PDSA (at least when preparing for the beginning fall classes).

The Baldrige program defines innovation as "the adoption of an idea, process, technology, or product that is either new or new to its proposed application" (2005 Malcolm Baldrige National Quality Award Education criteria, page 35). You can benchmark other teachers within your district or neighboring districts that succeed with similar types of students by observing and/or discussing the types of activities they use. From the Baldrige perspective, benchmarking means "best practice." Best practice is:

- A superior method or innovative practice that contributes to superior performance
- A strength that fills an improvement opportunity (a gap) in your organization
- Generally defined by external, expert reviews with superior results that are breakthroughs in effectiveness and efficiency
- A source of high satisfaction ratings among students and stakeholders

Figure 3.11 describes the intestinal fortitude benchmarking requires. Don't forget that every situation is unique. It most likely will require you to modify the approach you are

Figure 3.11 Requirements of the benchmarking process.

benchmarking to suit the situation you have as defined by the Profile you completed in Chapter 1. If there was a "magic" approach in which one size fit every classroom in every school in this country, wouldn't everyone flock to buy it or copy it? Do not let this admonition deter you from benchmarking others. Just remember, use caution. We have much to learn from one another, and there is no need to continue to reinvent the wheel—or to continue banging our heads:

> Here is Edward Bear, coming downstairs now, bump, bump, bump, on the back of his head, behind Christopher Robin. It is, as far as he knows, the only way of coming downstairs, but sometimes, he feels that there really is another way . . . if only he could stop bumping for a moment and think of it.
>
> *Winnie-the-Pooh*
> A. A. Milne

PLAN Step 4: Write an improvement theory

Directions: Based on all that you've learned in your analysis and through the environmental scan you just completed, how will you change your lesson plans to improve student performance results? Write an Improvement Theory as an if/then statement.

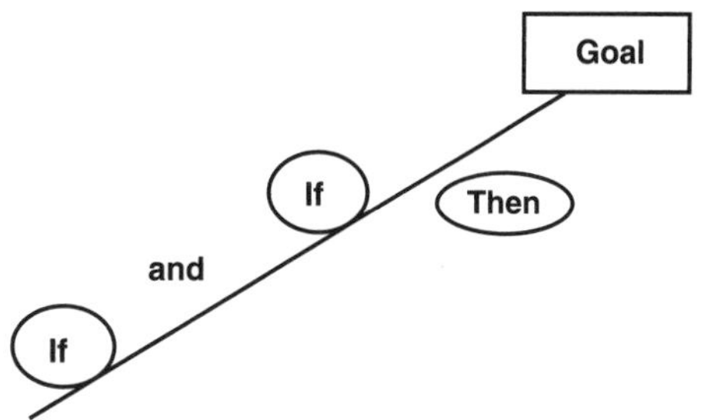

Example: If my lessons are aligned more precisely with the essential standards and I expand the learning activities to include the use of body/kinesthetic and musical/rhythmic intelligences, then students will achieve greater learning gains.

How will the success of the improvement theory be measured?

In-process (leading indicators are predictors of future success)

- Number of aligned lessons
- Number of body/kinesthetic and musical/rhythmic activities per week
- Quiz results—weekly

Results (lagging indicators)

- End-of-year or semester student learning results

DO Step 5: Try out the improvement theory

Collect data. Observe the process and how the students respond. Take notice of cycle time for mastering the skills.

STUDY Step 6: Did the improvement theory work? Did the improvement negatively impact the students?

Analyze the results and compare them with data used during Step 2 of Plan. Did the improvement theory yield better results? Even if the results were better, if students suffered any negative effects from the improvements to the system, these will have to be studied and eliminated before standardizing any system change.

ACT Step 7: Will you standardize the improvements?

Based on the year-end results, a BBQ teacher will decide whether to continue with the changes that were made the previous year in response to data analysis. If the results have improved but still don't reach the expected goal, there is more room for improvement and these would be identified based on an analysis of the new data. This is a PDSA cycle for strategic planning and a way to build in quality in the first place.

Use a Formal Plan-Do-Study-Act Cycle for Improving Instruction

Perhaps now you can begin to appreciate the absolute need to collect and analyze *in-process* (formative) data to make midcourse corrections to ensure more students gain the necessary skills. Effective use of in-process measures (leading indicators) holds the key to predicting future success. These are data that are used by leaders and workers (students) to measure the day-to-day effectiveness and efficiency of key classroom processes. Now, it is important to practice a full PDSA cycle for improving instruction. In Chapter 5, we will show you a more informal approach to PDSA, but for now, practice using the tools and learn the process. Practice the tools and how they flow together in a PDSA by doing the activities associated with this case study: *Hoping versus Knowing the Students Are Learning.*

PLAN Step 1: Define the problem (Figure 3.12)

Mr. Tryhard, a highly respected teacher, was concerned that his students were not learning at the rate required for them to achieve most of the district and state requirements. He had worried about this from the first day of school, when he got his class list. He had a total of 28 students: 17 boys and 11 girls. Of these, 10 were receiving some type of special services for learning needs, two were borderline emotionally disturbed, and three were overage for their class. Of the 28 students, six were mostly quiet and shy, and they were from

Figure 3.12 Plan: step 1.

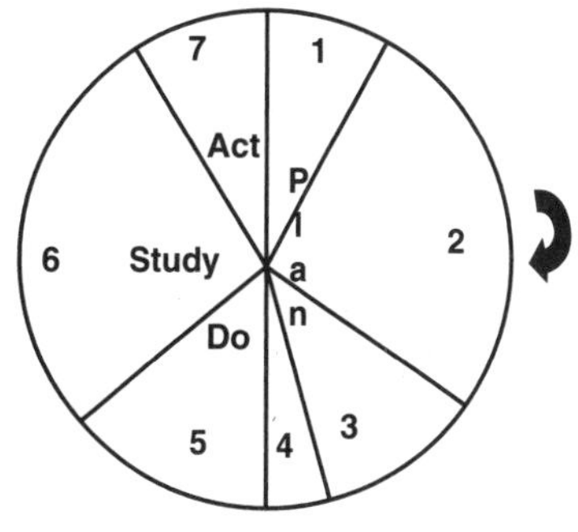

Figure 3.13 Plan: step 2.

non-English-speaking immigrant families from five countries. Six students were gifted. Oh yes, 19 students receive free lunch. Mr. Tryhard had a headache just thinking about how he could manage to encourage and motivate all these children and facilitate their learning, let alone reach the district's student performance expectations. It was about mid-September when Mr. Tryhard decided he needed to do something to get more students interested in learning.

Figure 3.14, a page in Mr. Tryhard's grade book, revealed the following information. (For confidentiality reasons student names are not used.) Weekly quizzes consisted of 10 items. The unit test was worth a total of 30 points.

PLAN Step 2: Assess the current situation (Figure 3.13)

Instructions for the line graph and scatter diagram are provided on pages 81 and 83. Instructions for the run chart and histogram are located on pages 66 and 68.

Directions: Analyze the data, using these different perspectives. If you are reading this as part of a training group, divide into small teams to analyze the data. Be certain to label all charts to indicate the data being analyzed.

1. Using method 2, make a **line graph** from the quiz data. Graph all four weekly quizzes for the entire class. Scale the chart from 0 to 10 (number of quiz items).
2. Make another **line graph** (method 2) for all quizzes for only the free-lunch students. Place this chart beside your first. Label the chart. Color code and segment results by gender. **Draw five lines on the chart as we'll be adding data to this later.**

Continued on page 79

Mr. Tryhard's grade book

Student	Quiz grades				Homework										Attendance															Unit test
1 (F,G)	7	6	8	10	•	•	•	•	•	•	•	•	•	•																20
2 (F, N)	4	5	9	9	•	•		•		•	•	•		•		a			a	a					a			a		10
3 (F, S)	2	6	7	8	•	•		•		•	•			•																13
4 (F, G)	8	8	9	8	•		•	•			•	•																		20
5 (S)	5	4	7	7	•	•	•	•	•	•	•	•		•																21
6 (F, S)	2	6	7	9	•			•		•		•	•	•																20
7 (F, N)	2	2	6	7	•	•	•	•		•	•	•		•		a	a	a				a	a							8
8	6	7	8	10	•	•				•	•		•	•																22
9 (G)	3	9	10	10	•	•																								24
10 (F)	8	5	9	8				•		•	•	•		•																25
11 (S)	5	7	7	8	•	•		•		•		•	•	•																21
12 (F, S)	4	6	8	7	•	•	•	•		•		•																		25
13 (F, S)	2	6	8	9	•	•	•	•	•	•	•	•	•	•																13
14 (N)	2	6	7	7	•				•			•		•					a					a			a	a	a	7
15 (F, S)	5	4	9	8	•	•	•	•		•	•	•		•																9
16 (F, G)	5	9	6	6	•		•				•		•																	25
17 (F)	8	8	10	9	•	•	•	•		•	•	•		•																28
18 (G)	9	9	9	10				•		•				•		a											a			27
19 (F, N)	2	6	10	10	•	•	•	•	•	•	•	•		•																14
20 (S)	5	4	7	7	•		•	•			•	•																		14
21 (F, N)	3	2	9	8	•	•	•	•		•	•	•		•					a	a		a	a					a		10
22 (F, S)	2	6	7	7	•	•	•	•	•	•	•	•	•	•																15
23 (F, N)	1	2	7	6	•			•			•			•																5
24 (F, S)	3	6	8	6	•	•	•	•		•	•	•	•	•					a											12
25 (F,G)	5	6	10	9	•	•		•		•	•	•					a		a				a					a	a	26
26	8	8	9	10	•	•	•	•	•	•	•	•	•	•																19
27	2	6	10	9				•		•		•		•	a	a	a	a		a	a				a			a	a	18
28 (F)	8	6	9	9	•	•		•		•			•																	15

Key: F = Free lunch; G = Gifted; N = Non-English speaking family; S = Special ed (IEP); **Bold = Girls**

Figure 3.14 Grade book example.

Continued from page 77

3. Make a **scatter diagram** of absences (independent variable—influencing) and unit test grade (dependent variable—effect). Place "absences" on the horizontal axis and unit grades along the vertical axis. Make certain both axes are of equal length.
4. Make a **scatter diagram** of homework (independent variable—influencing) and unit test grade (dependent variable—responding). Place "homework" on the horizontal axis and unit grades along the vertical axis. Make certain both axes are of equal length.
5. Make two **histograms** of the unit grades by free lunch and non-free-lunch. Divide the data into "classes" of 5 points (0–5, 6–10, 11–15, and so on) and use this across the horizontal axis. Scale the vertical axis from 0 to the highest number of data points from all the classes. Segment the free-lunch data by special needs, gifted, gender, and non–English-speaking families and color code it on the chart. Use the same color coding system for the non-free-lunch chart.
6. Make a **run chart** of the homework data. The horizontal axis should be divided into 20. **(You will be adding more data to this chart later.)** The vertical axis will be scaled from 0 to 28 (total number of students). Add up the totals for homework turned in for each day, and put these data on the run chart.
7. Make a **run chart** of attendance. The horizontal axis should be able to accommodate 15 data points. Scale the vertical axis from 0 to 28 (total number of students in the class). Add the totals for each day and use this number for the run chart.
8. Make a **scatter diagram** of the last quiz and unit test results. Color code the dots and segment the data by gender. The vertical axis will be unit grades (responding or dependent variable) and will be scaled from 0 to 30. The horizontal axis will be the third quiz data (influencing or independent variable) and will be scaled from 0 to 10. Make certain both axes are about the same length.

What situation does Mr. Tryhard find himself in?

What do we know now that we didn't know before analyzing the data?

What might we still need to analyze and learn about? What new information would this provide?

How do you know how much of these results are because students lack:

- Knowledge?
- Interest?
- Ability?

Line Graph

What

A line graph gives a vertical picture of the bandwidth of variation in any process. There are several types of line graphs. We will share the two most frequently used types. First is the line graph depicting the total score for the class on any measure; the second type displays individual student scores along the line.

How

1. State what is to be measured at the top of the page.
2. Draw a vertical axis to accommodate the amount of data.
3. Draw a horizontal axis extending from the bottom of the vertical axis and off to the right, long enough to accommodate at least nine data points.
4. Draw evenly spaced vertical lines up from the horizontal axis all across the page. (There should be one line for each data point you intend to collect.)
5. Label the horizontal axis "Time." Each vertical line coming up from it will be labeled with a date. (It is best to use one chart per marking period or for one semester. Each vertical line would represent a week.)
6. Label the vertical axis as follows: Chart Type Method1: Total number correct for the class; Chart Type Method 2: Correct responses per individual.
7. Scale the vertical axis as follows: Chart Type Method 1: Number of items tested per week times the number of students in the class. (Example: 10 items per week X 20 students enrolled in the class, or 200. The vertical axis would be scaled from 0 to 200.)

Method 1 line graph: class progress

Subject ____________ **Period** ____________

What is being studied ____________ **Class goal** ____________

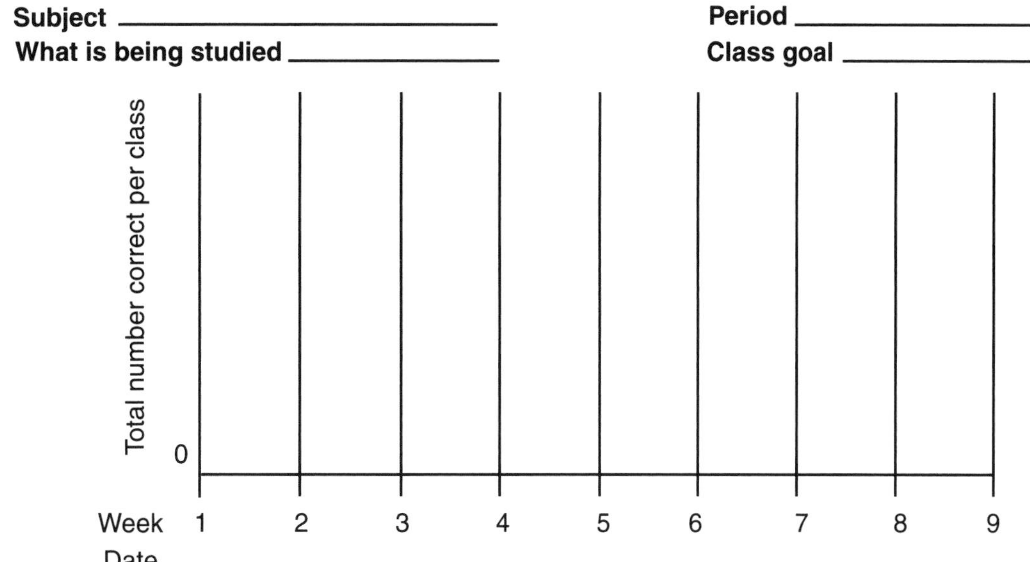

When

Use this tool when you want to watch class progress on any critical indicator (process measure) toward mastery of any content. Method 2 provides you with the bandwidth of variation within the class and allows you to share with parents and students how they are doing relative to the class as a whole.

Continued

Continued

Examples

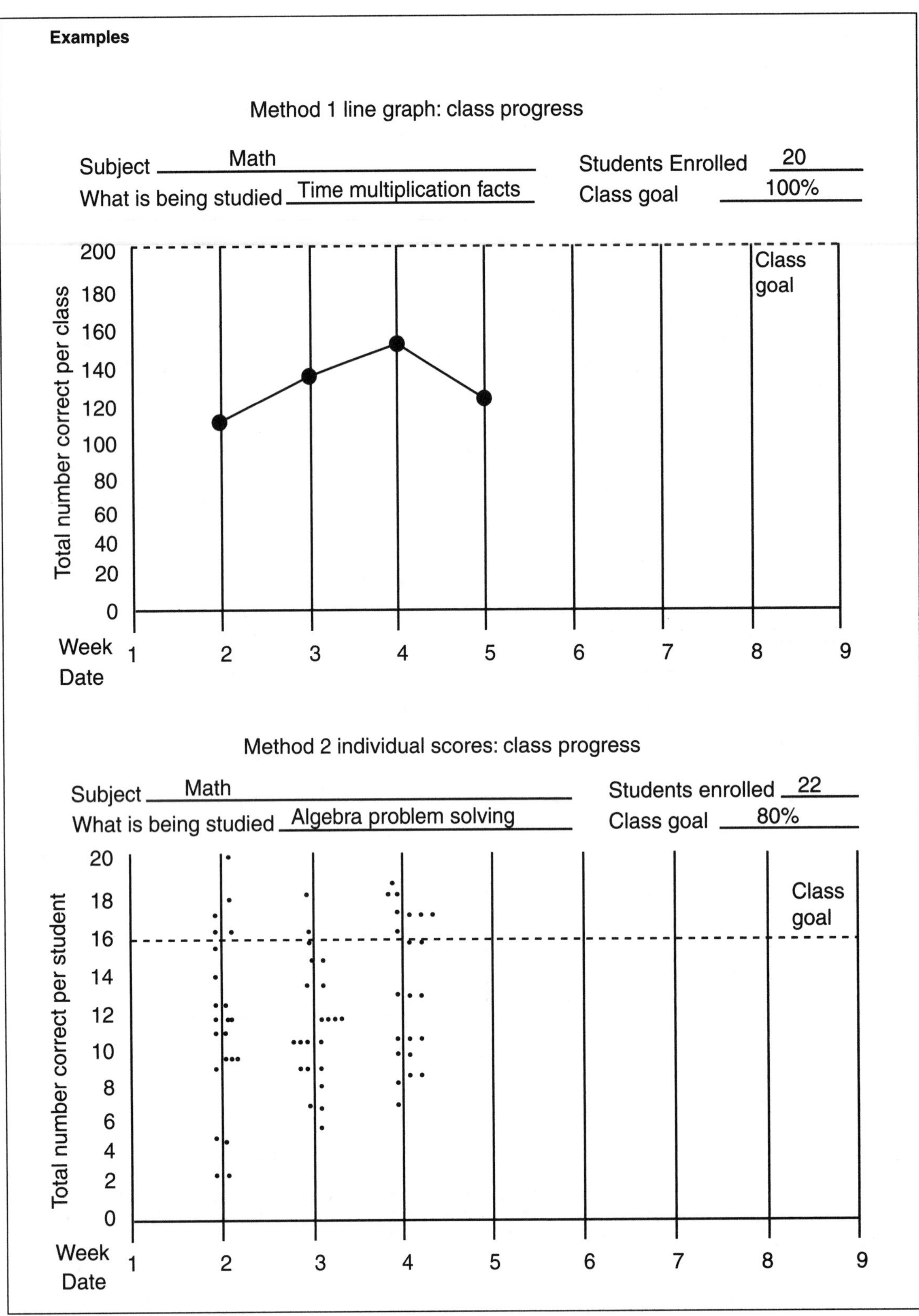

Scatter Diagram

What

A scatter diagram is a tool that can provide insight into a theory about whether a relationship exists between two factors. Care must be taken not to assume any correlation as absolute fact; however, one can draw inferences about the strength of the correlation between two pieces of data.

How

1. Determine the dependent responding variable to study. This is the factor believed to be affected by another factor, which is called the independent influencing variable.
2. Collect data on both factors over a period of time that provides enough data points to show a pattern. (We suggest a minimum of 20 data points.)
3. Both sets of data must be collected simultaneously, such as attendance and weekly quiz grades, or the number of laps swum in practice and timed swims.
4. Draw the diagram using a vertical and horizontal axis of the same length.
5. Place the dependent variable on the vertical axis. Scale the chart appropriately.
6. Place the independent variable on the horizontal axis and scale it appropriately.
7. Using the two data points, enter each point at the intersection of the dependent and independent variables. Draw a circle around a data point when there are duplicates, as shown in the example.
8. Continue entering data until finished as shown in the following table.

Student	Attendance	Quiz grade	Student	Attendance	Quiz grade
1	4	7	11	3	5
2	3	5	12	2	8
3	5	9	13	5	10
4	2	3	14	5	7
5	5	8	15	4	9
6	2	2	16	3	6
7	3	5	17	5	8
8	5	9	18	4	10
9	5	10	19	4	7
10	4	10	20	3	8

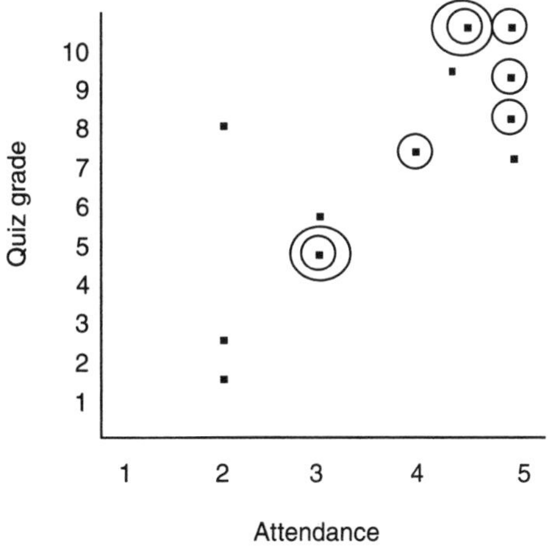

Continued

Continued

When

Use this tool to determine whether there is a relationship between two factors.

Chart interpretation

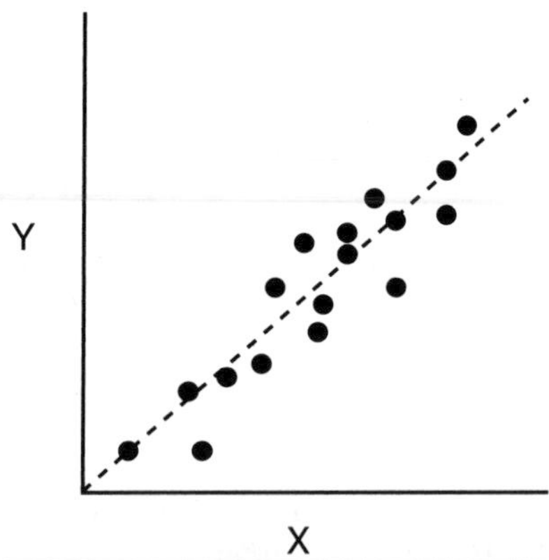

Positive correlation—An increase in Y may depend on an increase in X. If X is controlled, Y might be controlled. Note how close the data are to the line of central tendency.

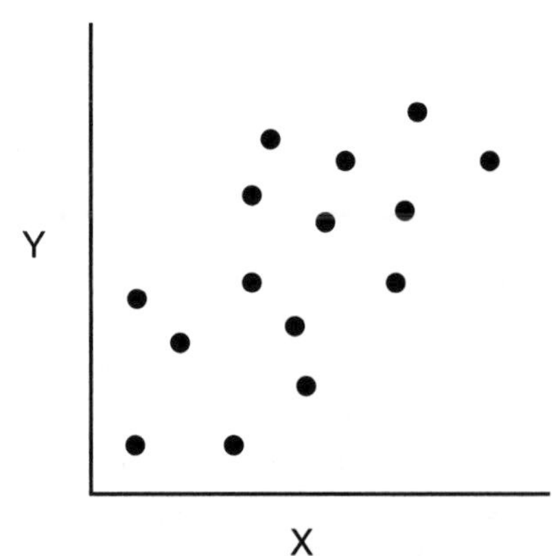

Possible positive correlation—If X is increased, Y may also increase somewhat. It is not possible to make strong inferences from these data.

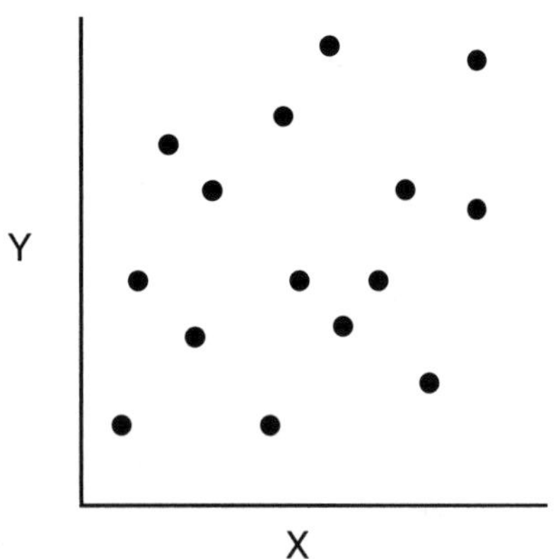

No correlation—Y may be dependent on another variable.

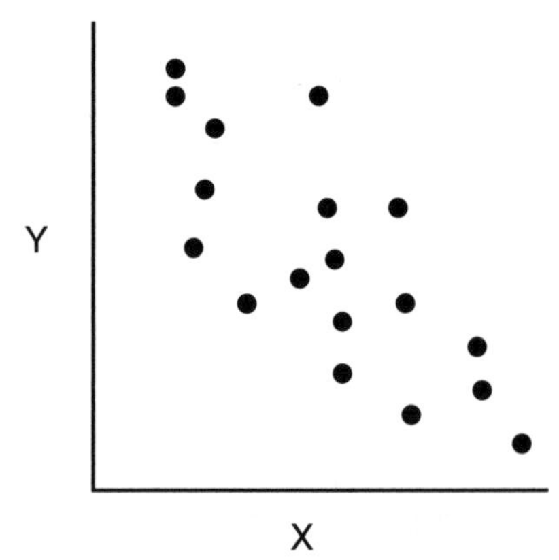

Possible negative correlation—An increase in X may cause a tendency for a decrease in Y.

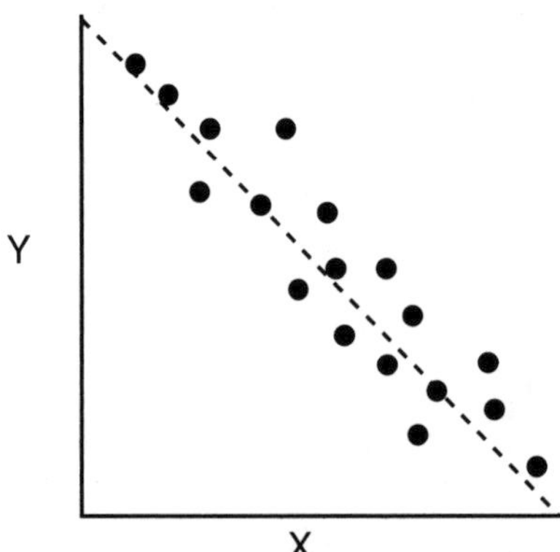

Negative correlation—An increase in X may cause a decrease in Y. As with the positive correlation, X may be controlled instead of Y. Note how close the data are to the line of central tendency.

Mr. Tryhard and you have come to the realization that you still don't know enough to be certain what to change to ensure more student success. It is necessary to use an item analysis to understand student errors on weekly quizzes. It's best to do this every week, but for the purposes of this example, in Figure 3.15 we're combining the error data for the first two quizzes from Mr. Tryhard's grade book on page 78.

Name	Addition	Subtraction	Multiplication	Borrowing	Carrying over
1 (F,G)		III	II	II	
2 (F, N)		IIIII	II	III	I
3 (F, S)	II	IIII	I	III	II
4 (F, G)		II	II		
5 (S)		IIII	I	III	III
6 (F, S)	III	III	I	III	II
7 (F, N)	I	IIIII	IIII	III	III
8	I	III	I	II	
9 (G)		IIII	I	II	I
10 (F)		IIII		III	
11 (S)		III	III	I	I
12 (F, S)		IIII	III	I	II
13 (F, S)	I	IIIII	III	II	I
14 (N)		IIII	III	II	III
15 (F, S)	I	III	IIII	II	I
16 (F, G)	I		IIII	I	
17 (F)		II	I	I	
18 (G)			II		
19 (F, N)	II	IIII	I	III	II
20 (S)	I	IIIII	II	II	I
21 (F, N)	II	III			
22 (F, S)	I	IIII	II	III	I
23 (F, N)		IIIIII	III	IIII	IIII
24 (F, S)	I	III	II	III	II
25 (F,G)	II	IIIII	I	I	
26		II	II		
27	II	IIII	III	II	I
28 (F)	I		IIII		
Total	22	94	62	52	29
Percentage	9%	36%	24%	20%	11%
Cum. %	100%	36%	60%	80%	91%

Finally, you have some clues about what instructional improvements are required. However, keep in mind, this is just another clue. You still don't have enough information to be certain what changes need to be made. We know there are numerous other error types a math teacher would use, but this is just an example. When doing this, use all the types of errors students made.

The beauty of nongraded quizzes is that students can chart their own errors. They will be honest because no harm will come to them for honesty. It is also understood that the purpose of these quizzes is to inform you how to improve the instructional process and not to punish students.

The eagerness that anyone brings to a learning environment is directly related to the stress and discomfort one feels. Eliminating grades on quizzes can be a major step toward eliminating unnecessary tension.

Directions: Put these data into a Pareto chart. Carefully review the Pareto chart instructions on page 86 before starting.

Figure 3.15 Math errors by type.

By now you have assessed the current situation, insofar as you know it, and the Pareto chart has indicated where to start the improvement efforts. Without a Pareto chart analysis, you may have made false assumptions about the problem that kept students from meeting the math goals.

Note to teachers: *In addition to analyzing hard data, you might also consider analyzing the following:*

1. *The arrangement used for learning activities.*
   a. *Classroom organization (rows of desks, tables, and so on).*
   b. *Individual or group activity (partners or cooperative learning).*
   c. *Silent or inquiry methods used.*
   d. *Active or passive learning activities used—how many of each?*
2. *Which of the multiple intelligences (MI) did each learning activity address? (See MI chart on page 93.)*
3. *The approach used to assess learning (timed quiz, mixture of word or numeric problems, and so on).*
4. *Feedback provided by students to improve the instructional process.*

Pareto Chart

What

A Pareto chart is a bar graph that displays the data from "most" to "least." It separates the vital few items or activities that contribute to a problem from the trivial many. It provides a starting point for continuous improvement projects.

How

Steps to creating a Pareto chart are:

1. Determine the data to be collected, taking into account the significance of things such as time of day, place of occurrence, and gender. Operationally define the data to be collected.
2. Determine what period of time the data are to be collected.
3. Determine who is in the best position to collect the data.
4. Use a check sheet and collect the data for the specified length of time.
5. Organize the data categories in descending order.
6. Draw the chart by drawing three equal lines to form a "U" shape.
7. Scale the chart by adding up the total of all data combined. On the left vertical axis, scale the chart from zero at the bottom to the total number of data points (for example, total errors of all types) at the top.
8. On the right vertical axis, scale the chart in percentages, noting 25%, 50%, 75%, and 100%.
9. Divide the horizontal axis into equal parts to match the number of categories of data collected.
10. Look at the data for each category and insert the categories in descending order from left to right, along the horizontal axis.
11. Draw the bar for each category.

Continued

12. Place a dot at the upper right-hand corner of the bar for the first category. Imagine you will stack the next "bar" on top and total both to calculate the cumulative percentage. Place a dot at the "imagined" right-hand corner where the second category would extend.
13. Continue to do this for all categories of data. Connect the dots, which will add up to 100%.
14. Interpret the chart by looking for causes that add up to approximately 70–80% of the total. (Pareto's Law says that 80% of the problems are caused by 20% of the symptoms.)
15. Begin the improvement plan by focusing on one of the most significant problems.

Example: Tardy to first period

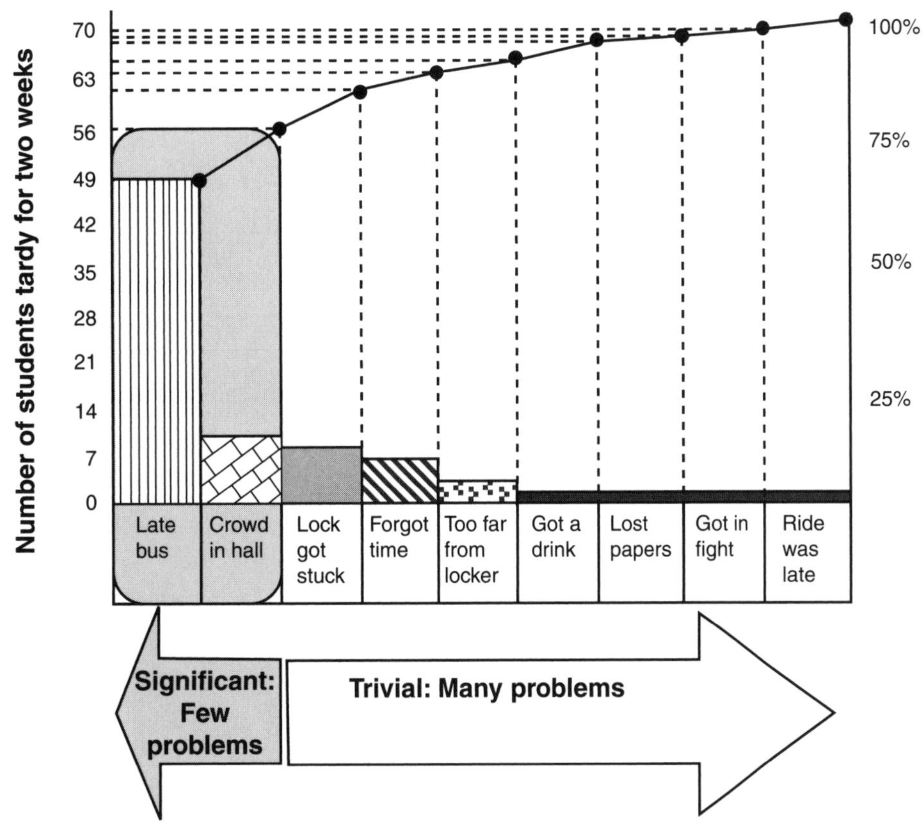

When

- It is important to determine the most significant cause of a problem.
- It is important to approach the problem in a focused way, getting the biggest improvement with your efforts.
- You want to observe how the improvement efforts have affected the issue.

Continued

Continued

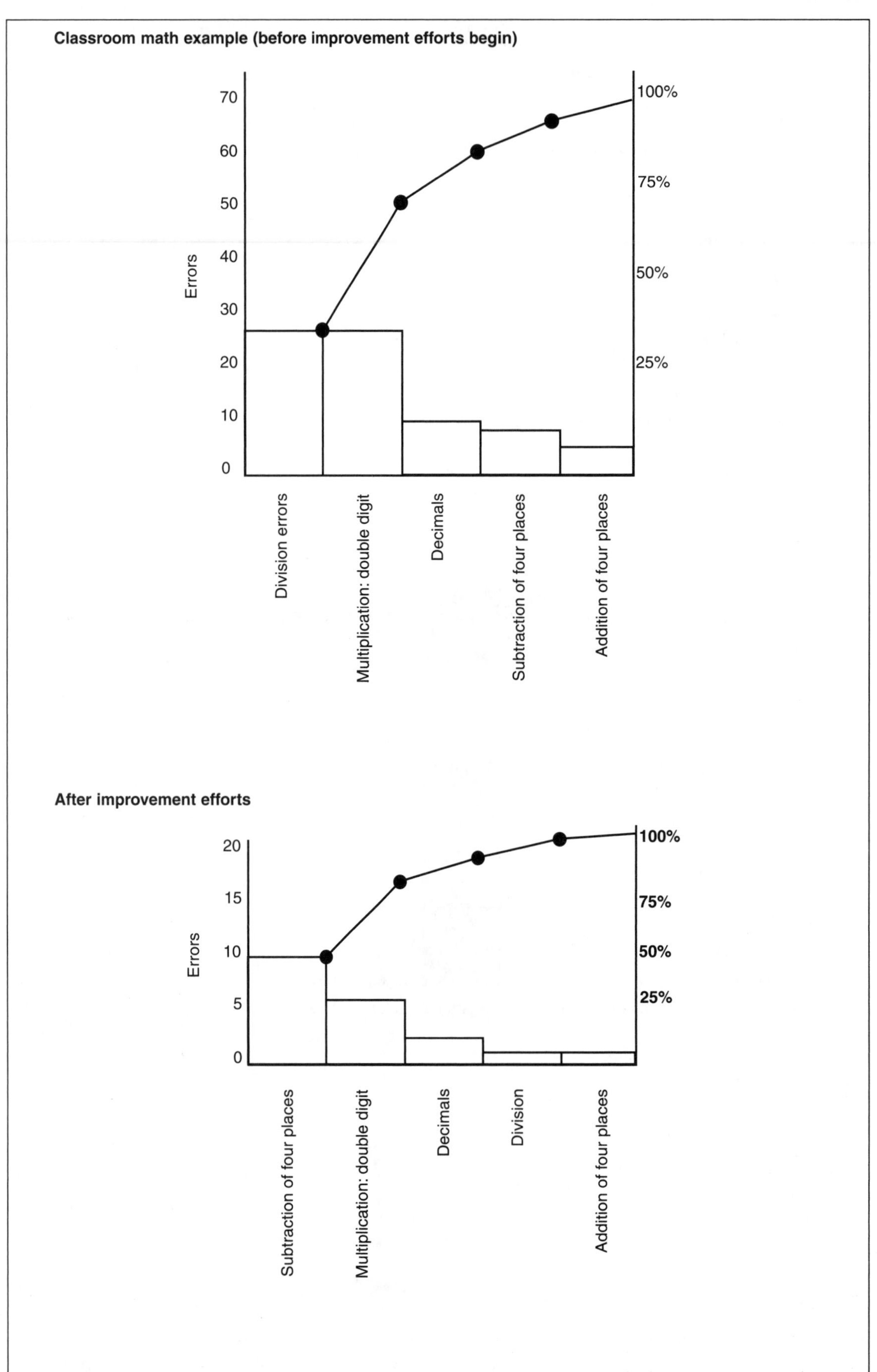
Classroom math example (before improvement efforts begin)
Errors
70
60
50
40
30
20
10
0
100%
75%
50%
25%
Division errors
Multiplication: double digit
Decimals
Subtraction of four places
Addition of four places
After improvement efforts
Errors
20
15
10
5
0
100%
75%
50%
25%
Subtraction of four places
Multiplication: double digit
Decimals
Division
Addition of four places

PLAN Step 3: Analyze root cause (Figure 3.16)

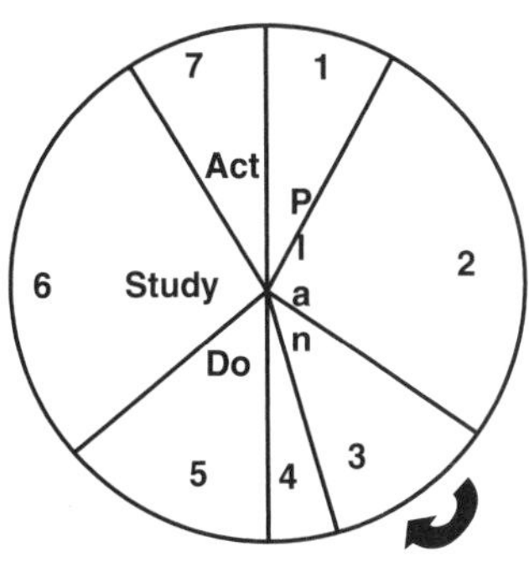

Figure 3.16 Plan: step 3.

Directions: It is difficult to do this without at least one other person. We will assume you can find a group to participate in a role play experience to analyze the root cause of the problem of why so many students are not learning the required math operations. Designate one member to be Mr. Tryhard and the others will be students in the class. Use the cause-effect diagram for this activity. Directions for this tool are on page 90. Label the major bones as follows: people, instructional process, materials, and classroom organization.

Those who are designated as students must assume roles of special needs, gifted, non-English-speakers, free lunch, or non–free lunch, and identify themselves as a boy or girl. All your responses should be in the voice of the student you represent. Be specific with your responses.

Mr. Tryhard will facilitate the process and make sure that everyone gets involved (Figure 3.17 on the next page). Only one person can speak at a time, and there can be no discussion about the issues being identified.

Once all the ideas are on the chart, Mr. Tryhard will clarify each one—or seek clarification from the student identifying the issue. Any that relate to things that cannot be changed or influenced by Mr. Tryhard and/or the class are not included in the voting process. (It is not possible to "fix" parents, for example, or move to a bigger classroom, so these are things that are out of the circle of influence for Mr. Tryhard and his students.)

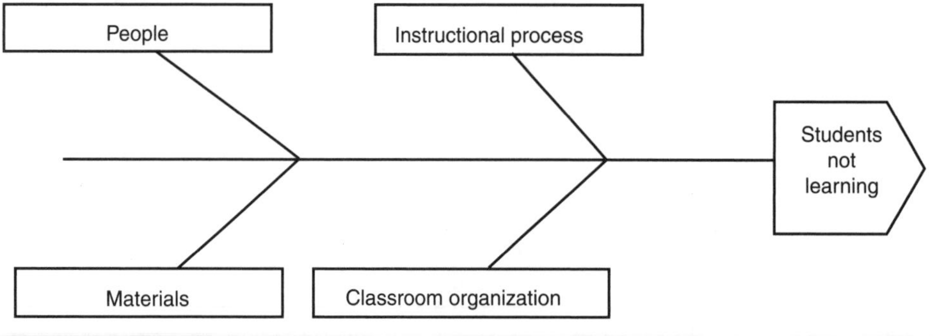

Figure 3.17 Cause-effect diagram.

Cause-Effect Diagram

What

The cause-effect diagram (Figure 3.17 above) is also known as an Ishikawa diagram (named for Professor Kaoru Ishikawa who developed the tool). It is a picture of elements of a system or process that contribute to a problem.

How

1. Draw a horizontal line, which is the center line.
2. At the right-hand edge of the center line, draw a rectangle, oval, or triangle. This will be the "head" of the diagram.
3. Write the effect of the problem in the head.
4. On each side of the center line, evenly spaced, draw two diagonal lines moving away from the head. Each of these represents a major category of causal factors.
5. At the end of each major causal factor line, draw a box. Label each as one of the major causal factors. It is possible to have more than four, but four is the norm.
6. Brainstorm specific factors relating to each of the major causal lines. The group may decide to write each idea on a Post-it note and place the notes on the line. Individuals may go to the chart and write their ideas at any time on the correct bone, or one person can be designated the writer while each major causal line is discussed separately. (Keep in mind, this is a brainstorming activity and the group is seeking to discover the root cause of a problem. Record all ideas as valid.)
7. If a cause has other underlying causes, these are recorded as subcauses and placed on a short line drawn horizontally off the major causal line. Sub-sub-causes may also be drawn underneath each subcause. The deeper the team gets into each cause, the greater the chances for discovering the true root cause.
8. Continue brainstorming until all ideas are on the diagram.

When

- Use this tool when studying a process or system problem.
- Many people are involved in the process and the issue is unclear.
- To brainstorm the root cause of current events, historical events, or the plot of a novel.

Directions: Multivote on the number one issue affecting student learning. See the instructions for multivoting on page 41. Each team member should get four votes. As a team, assign a point value for each different color of dot to reduce the possibility of more than one cause receiving the same weight. (For example, red = 7 points, blue = 5 points, and so on). Point values are always uneven numbers.

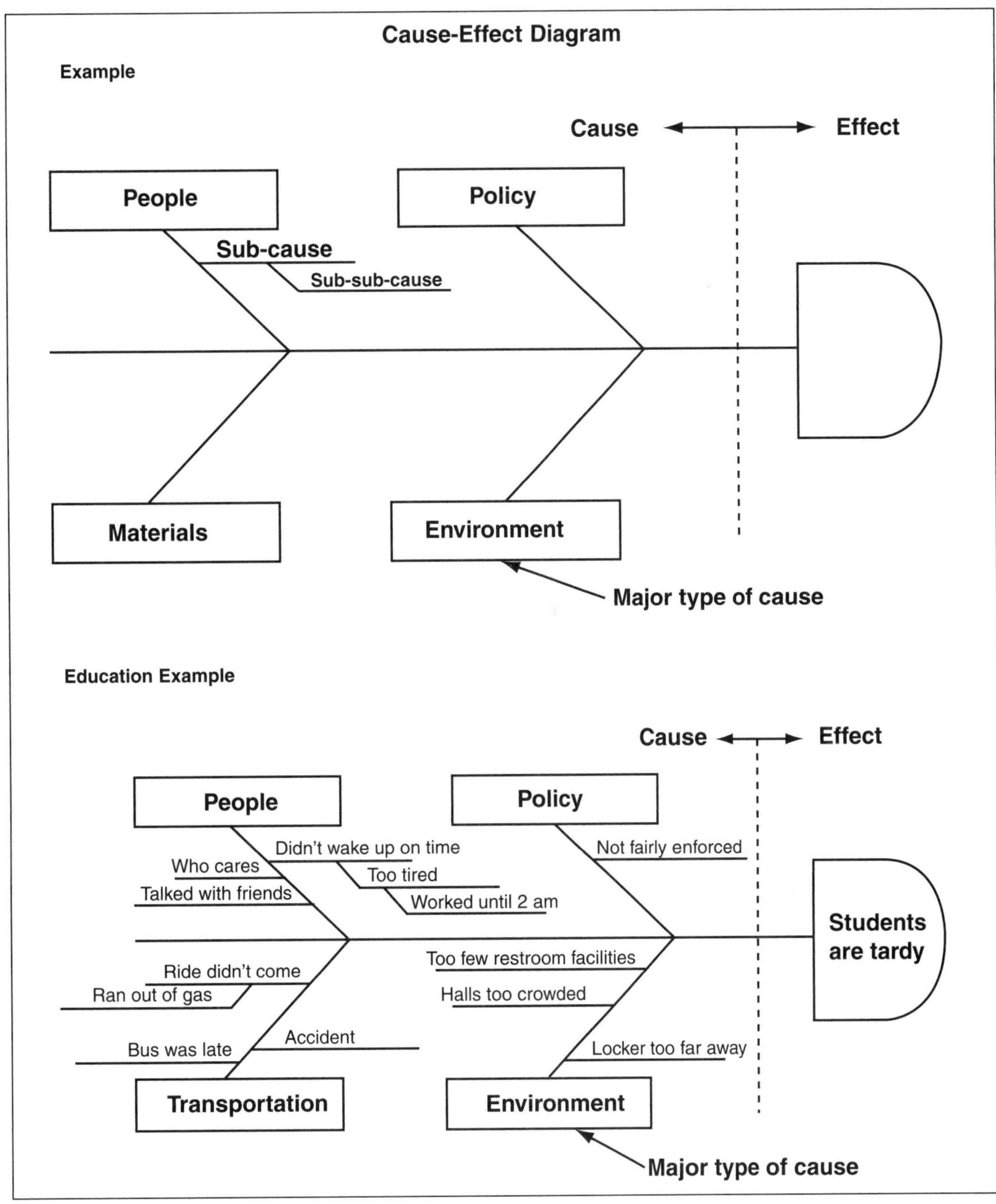

Mr. Tryhard will ask everyone to take a few moments to reflect on all the issues identified. At the table, decide where you will put your dots. If you feel strongly about one issue, you can put more than one dot on it. Add the points for each item and circle the No. 1 root cause of "students not learning."

> *As a general guiding principle, when multivoting, you want to ask students to make up their minds while at their desks. This eliminates much of the copycat*

Continued

Continued

effect. If you turn the cause-effect diagram around, or work from the back of the class and ask one student at a time to vote, you can eliminate much of the pressure students might feel from the more vocal, assertive students. These safeguards will provide you with more reliable results.

PLAN Step 4: Write an improvement theory (Figure 3.18)

Most students have never been asked to help resolve a classroom problem, but ignoring them is foolhardy as they are workers in the classroom system and therefore in the best position to help. Brainstorm a list of ideas that, if implemented, would directly improve the situation and more students would learn. Assume the role you've been given as a student or Mr. Tryhard. Review the Multiple Intelligences Toolbox (Figure 3.19) on page 93 for ideas to start the brainstorming. Give the students one or two ideas; then step back and listen and observe.

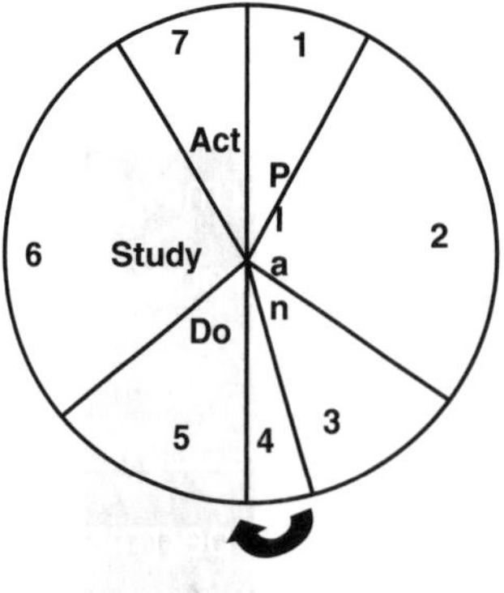

Figure 3.18 Plan: step 4.

Think first about your math lessons and which of the multiple intelligences you include in the activities. If your activities do not include a combination of kinesthetic, visual/spatial, and musical/rhythmic, you might want to share one of these as your suggestions. In fact, it is the combination of these three intelligences that seems to anchor learning for most students.

The only "rule" is that the ideas cannot be for external rewards (for example, stickers or parties). There can be no arguments, and all ideas will be posted. If someone wishes to expand someone else's idea, they need permission from the individual making the suggestion. The individual acting as Mr. Tryhard will facilitate the discussion and write the ideas on a flip chart. After all the ideas have been listed, the team will again multivote to select the two ideas that will be most effective in helping students meet the goals. Before voting, Mr. Tryhard will review all the ideas with the group to ensure common understanding.

Verbal/linguistic	Logical/mathematical	Visual/spatial	Body/kinesthetic
Reading Vocabulary Formal speech Journal/diary writing Creative writing Poetry Verbal debate Impromptu speaking Humor/jokes Storytelling	Abstract symbols Formulas Outlining Graphic organizers Number sequences Calculation Deciphering codes Forcing relationships Syllogisms Problem solving Pattern games	Guided imagery Active imagination Color schemes Patterns/designs Painting Drawing Mind-mapping Pretending Sculpture Pictures	Folk/creative dance Role playing Physical gestures Drama Martial arts Body language Physical exercise Mime Inventing Sports/games
Musical/rhythmic	**Interpersonal**	**Intrapersonal**	**Naturalist**
Rhythmic patterns Vocal sounds/tones Music composition and creation Percussion—vibrations Humming Environmental sounds Instrumental sounds Singing Chants Tonal patterns Music performance	Giving feedback Intuiting other's feelings Cooperative learning strategies Person-to-person communication Empathy practices Division of labor Collaboration skills Receiving feedback Sensing others' motives Group projects	Silent reflection methods Metacognition techniques Thinking strategies Emotional processing "Know thyself" procedures Mindfulness practices Focusing and concentration skills Higher-order reasoning Complex guided imagery "Centering" practices	Field trips Bird watching Observing nests Planting Photographing Nature walks Forecasting weather Star gazing Categorizing rocks Ecology studies Shell collecting Identifying plants Collecting insects

Figure 3.19 Multiple intelligences toolbox.
Modified from David Lazear, *Seven Ways of Teaching: The Artistry of Teaching with Multiple Intelligences,* Skylight Publishing, 1991.

Directions: Use these formal brainstorming rules to capture ideas to eliminate the root cause. Go around the group at least three times, in order, to gain ideas from all team members. "Yeah-buts" are not allowed. (A yeah-but is when an individual responds to another's suggestion with, "Yeah, but we tried that and it didn't work.") Ask permission from the original source to embellish or add on to a previous suggestion. List all suggestions on the flip chart.

Multivote to establish the approach the team (class) will use to resolve the problem and meet the learning goals. Write your improvement theory as an if/then statement.

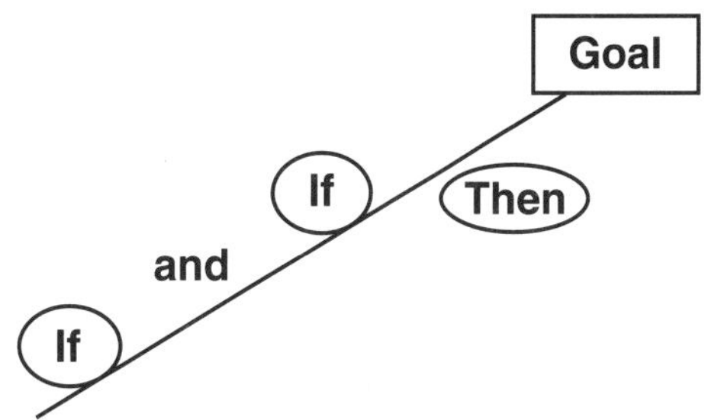

Example: *If* we work together as buddies, and use math challenge cards, *then* more students will master subtraction and there will be fewer errors.

How will the success of the improvement theory be measured?

In-process (leading indicators are predictors of future success):

- Frequency of buddy approach
- Number of minutes using math challenge cards per day
- Weekly quiz results

Results (lagging indicators):

- Student learning results on unit and semester or year-end assessment

DO Step 5: Try out the improvement theory (Figure 3.20)

As we have said before, *students do not decide what they will learn,* but they certainly can help decide *how they want to learn.* This concept is central to having more students meet or exceed the state standards, so lesson plans need to be robust to include multiple intelligences and differentiated instruction but also flexible so that teachers can make midcourse corrections to meet all students' needs. This is where student feedback can play a pivotal role, provided the teacher is willing to take the necessary risks to test out students' suggestions. Actually *there is no risk at all if the teacher's methods are not working for all the students.* Helpful tools are fast feedback and plus/delta, and directions can be found on pages 156 and 159.

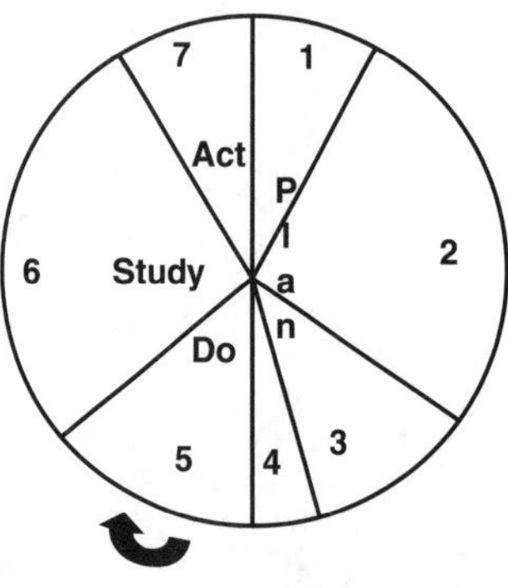

Figure 3.20 Do: step 5.

During the stage where the improvement theory is tested, be certain to collect data according to this case study example and in concert with the improvement suggestions. If you have a theory and then don't follow the plan, you will surely get mixed results and not be able to prove or disprove you understood root cause.

In this case, weekly quiz data are collected. A recommended approach for standardizing any data collection method is a check sheet. This tool and all the others can be used by students, which empowers them further to become part of the solution to classroom system problems (Figure 3.21). Directions for check sheets are on page 96.

Class: **4th grade**		What is being studied: **Math errors by type**			
Where: **Room 216**		Operational definition: **Specific errors made on all quiz problems**			
When: **10/11 and 10/18**		Number of quiz problems: **10 per week**			
Name	Addition	Subtraction	Multiplication	Borrowing	Carrying over
1 (F,G)			II		
2 (F, N)			I		I
3 (F, S)		I	II	II	
4 (F, G)	I		II		
5 (S)			III	I	II
6 (F, S)	I		III		
7 (F, N)	I	III		III	
8	I			I	
9 (G)					
10 (F)			I	I	I
11 (S)			III	I	I
12 (F, S)			I	II	II
13 (F, S)	I		II		
14 (N)	I		III		II
15 (F, S)	II				I
16 (F, G)	I		IIII		II
17 (F)			I		
18 (G)			I		
19 (F, N)					
20 (S)		I	I	II	II
21 (F, N)			III		
22 (F, S)		I	II	I	II
23 (F, N)			IIII		III
24 (F, S)	I		II	I	II
25 (F,G)			I		
26	I				
27	I				
28 (F)			II		
Total	12	6	45	15	21
Percentage	12%	6%	46%	15%	21%
Cum. %	94%	100%	46%	82%	67%

Key: F = Free lunch; G = Gifted; N = Non-English speaking family; S = Special ed (IEP); **Bold = Girls**

Figure 3.21 Mr. Tryhard's check sheet for math errors by type for quizzes 3 and 4 (from gradebook on page 78).

Check Sheet

What

A check sheet is a data collection chart. It is used to determine how often certain events occur. It always precedes a control chart and is helpful when creating Pareto charts.

How

1. Determine the data to collect and operationally define each.
2. Select a data collection plan based on the following:
   - Is time of day an issue?
   - Is the place where the event occurs significant?
   - Is the day of the week likely to make a difference?
   - Are there defining characteristics that need to be considered (for example, grade level, age, gender, and ethnicity)?
   - Who will collect the data?
   - How often will it be collected?
   - For what length of time will data be collected?
3. Design a form with all the factors from your data collection plan.
4. Select a small practice group to use the form to assess ease of use. If necessary, revise the form.
5. Educate all who will collect data on the use of the form and the operational definitions for each type of data to be collected.
6. Put a hash mark on the sheet whenever an occurrence happens.
7. At the end of the data collection period, total each type of occurrence and grand total all occurrences.

When

Use a check sheet when

- You are collecting data on a process over time.
- You want to gain a clearer picture of defects over time.
- You want to determine where and at what time most events occur.

Example

Name: *Mr. Tom Jones*					**What is being studied:** *Tardies*						
Where: *'B' Wing*	**Operational Definition:** *Students in the hall after the bell stops ringing.*										
Time collected: *8:10 am*						**Dates collected:** *October 1–15, 2002*					
OCTOBER											
Day of Week	**1**	**2**	**3**	**4**	**5**	**8**	**9**	**10**	**11**	**12**	**15**	**Ttl**
Monday	//					///						**5**
Tuesday		//					/					**3**
Wednesday			////									**4**
Thursday	/			/					//			**4**
Friday					~~////~~	//					///	**10**
TOTAL	**3**	**2**	**4**	**1**	**5**	**5**	**1**	**0**	**2**	**0**	**3**	**26**

Continued

Continued

Example

Name: *Ms. Alpha Bet*						**What is being studied:** *Punctuation Errors*						
Where: *Room 23*	**Operational Definition:** *See error type listed below*											
Time collected: *3rd period—English 1*							**Dates collected:** *November 3–17, 2002*					
						NOVEMBER						
Errors	**3**	**4**	**5**	**6**	**7**	**10**	**11**	**12**	**13**	**14**	**17**	**Ttl**
Missing quotation marks	~~////~~ ~~////~~	~~////~~		////		///		///		///	//	**30**
Incorrect use of commas	~~////~~	///	~~////~~ ~~////~~	///	~~////~~		/	///	~~////~~ ~~////~~	~~////~~	//	**47**
Incorrect use of semi-colons	////	~~////~~ ~~////~~ //	////			///		~~////~~ ///	~~////~~	//	////	**42**
Incorrect capitalization		///	////	/	////	///		//	//	////	/	**24**
Incorrect ending mark	///	////			~~////~~ ///	////		///		//	///	**27**
TOTAL	**22**	**27**	**18**	**8**	**17**	**13**	**1**	**19**	**17**	**16**	**12**	**170**

STUDY Step 6: What happened? Did the improvement theory work? (Figure 3.22)

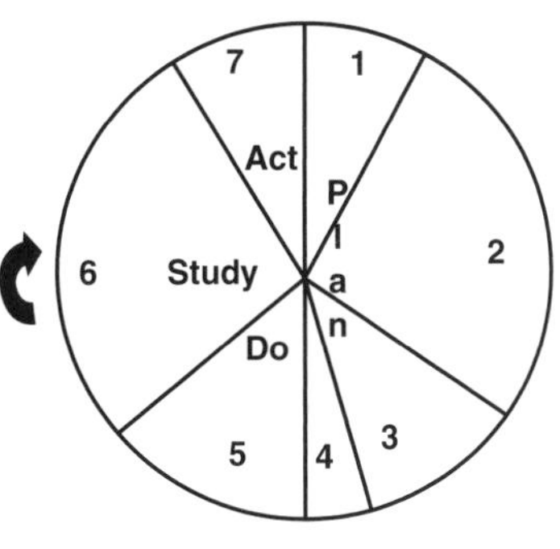

Figure 3.22 Study: step 6.

Directions: Look at the results from several perspectives to gain greater understanding of what happened.

- **Post the improvement theory data on a Pareto chart.**
  Place the pre- and post-Pareto charts next to each other. Did the improvement theory eliminate subtraction errors? Do the "borrowing" errors have any relationship to subtraction?
- **Histogram gender results.** Use the types of errors to represent each class of data. Does looking at the results from different perspectives

Continued

Continued

- **Use a bar graph to display** the results by free/reduced lunch and pay lunch. Put the pre- and post-intervention data for both groups on the same chart.

What inferences can you make by looking at the data from more than one perspective?

Look carefully at each individual's pre- and post-intervention results. If you were this teacher, identify the next steps you would take and explain why. (Hint: Use the students as helpers.) What other data would you collect and analyze to get to the bottom of why so many students are not learning the necessary math skills?

ACT Step 7: Make a decision—standardize, improve, or abandon the process (Figure 3.23)

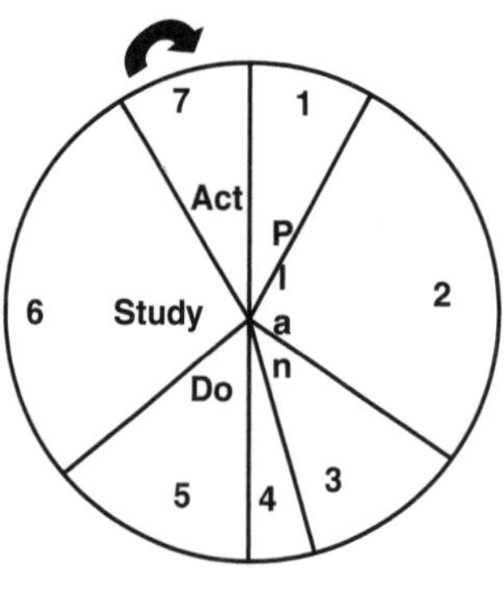

Figure 3.23 Act: step 7.

Improve

If the number of subtraction errors had not significantly been reduced, it probably means that the true root cause was not understood. This would require you to go back to the cause-effect diagram and again engage students in identifying the root cause, followed by a new improvement theory with different action plans.

In this case study, subtraction errors practically disappeared and only four students made any errors. If you look at the results for student 7, you'll see that she seems to have the most difficulty with subtraction and borrowing. This would now be considered "special cause" and student 7 would no doubt benefit from one-on-one help with the teacher and/or another student.

Standardize

In this case the results were impressive. You'd want to continue with the actions taken to resolve the problem, and that means to standardize the improvements. Students have helped you solve the perplexing questions about how they learn best. The questions to ask are: "Does this new process add value to student learning?" "Is this approach something that I can incorporate into my other lessons?" "If I did, would it help improve student learning?"

Every process breaks down over time, and it is important to hold the gains so the original problem does not resurface. You'll need to decide what data will be collected and how often to retest to ascertain student retention. This may be accomplished by adding a few questions covering the original material to subsequent unit tests.

Abandon

If the number of errors increased, you have a serious issue. This would mean that your improvements did not add value. In such an instance, the best advice is to abandon the suggested solutions. Buddies may not work. They may impede student learning, especially if students are unable to stay on task. In such a scenario, it is not that students didn't address the root cause; it is that the improvement theory didn't work.

Summary

In this chapter we have "chunked" a huge amount of information. As noted, there is an example of a more informal PDSA in Chapter 5. For now, you have practiced the basics of the Plan-Do-Study-Act cycle improvement process and learned some tools. You have also examined the importance of data analysis and of looking at data from more than one perspective. You may, at first, be uncomfortable until you become familiar with in-process measures and the tools used to analyze the data versus relying on outcomes measures. Be patient and take *all* the time you need to learn. Do not get discouraged. Again, stay the course. You are learning!

Reflections

4

PLAN FOR QUALITY IN KEY CLASSROOM PROCESSES

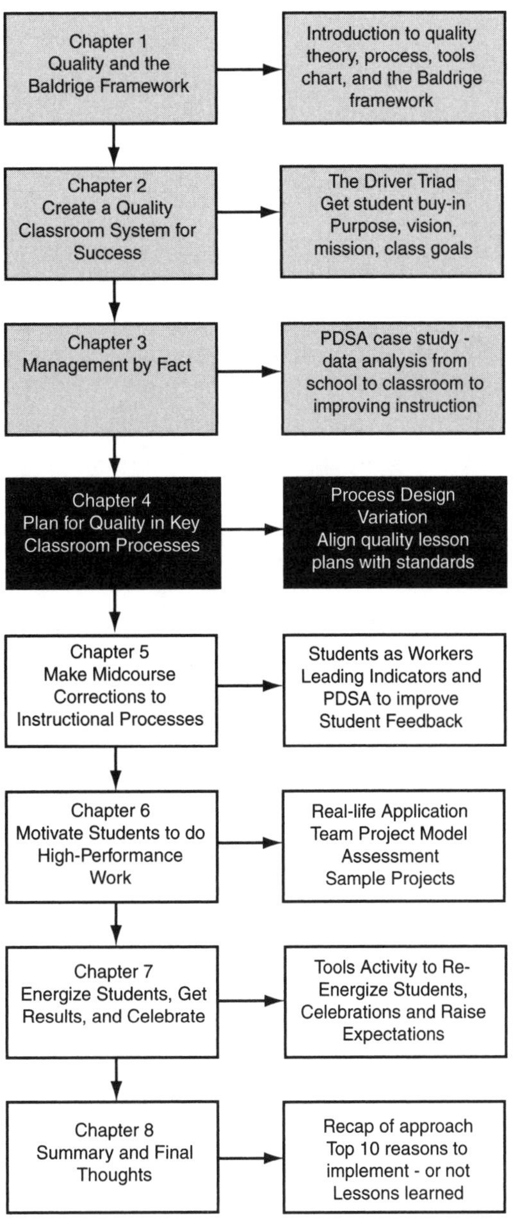

Conversation with the Teacher

Dr. Joseph Juran, another Quality guru, joins Dr. W. Edwards Deming in the belief that planning is of the greatest importance in reaching organizational goals with little rework. A key part of planning is to involve customers by seeking feedback from them about products and services. It also requires leaders to be willing to make midcourse corrections when it becomes evident that current processes are not effective or efficient. In other words, when processes yield too many defects, a lot of rework is required and the results are wasted resources (time, money, and people).

Most educators agree that there is not enough time in a school day to meet all the demands placed on them by policy makers and state and federal government regulations. They frequently cite lack of time as the reason for not being able to create a Baldrige-based Quality classroom. Time is definitely an issue—we all have the same amount, 24 hours in a day. It is a valuable resource that cannot afford to be wasted.

About how much instructional time is lost when your attention is diverted because of transitions, interruptions, or discipline problems? The most typical response received from this question of teachers we've trained around the country is roughly one hour of time lost every day. Since most school districts operate on a 180-day school year, 180 hours lost equals 30 school days. Divide this number into five-day weeks and you have a net loss of six weeks of school. It would be of great concern if this were the whole story, but you must also think about how much time you spend reteaching every year. With this information, is it any wonder that many students do not meet or exceed grade level standards? The facts are that today expectations are higher, stakes are higher, and there are no guarantees that "business as usual" in education will be allowed to go on much longer.

There are many reasons why educators need to change. Among the most significant are the economic consequences of not doing the job right the first time and the need to have an educated citizenry to preserve our democracy. Funding is a problem at the local and state levels, yet governments (state and federal) continue to add mandates, many of them unfunded, and this situation is not likely to dramatically change soon. If educators have any hope of meeting the expectations, the traditional way of doing business must change. We know that adding programs, adopting new textbooks, and buying more software and hardware while neither analyzing nor improving the system will not lead to sustained, improved results.

Further, most teachers we know are deeply concerned about the wide range of variation in student work. If you think about it, the range for "acceptable work" can vary from 100% correct to 60% correct. Teachers who are knowledgeable about the Quality process do not accept sloppy, incorrect student work, but instead build in processes that support high-performance work. Variation causes rework. How much time do you spend reteaching because students don't get it right the first time?

In this chapter you will learn:

- How to design the instructional process to reduce rework and improve effectiveness and efficiency
- How to reduce variation in completed student work
- How to design key classroom management processes to improve efficiency
- Some feedback tools to help make midcourse corrections

Instructional Process Design

Process Management (Category 6) is about how work gets done in the classroom. The way key classroom processes (Figure 1.6) are designed and used contributes immensely to the results. In the classroom, teachers are partners with students, and how the workers carry out the key processes is the other part of the puzzle. Figure 4.1 shows how process management is linked with the student as worker focus to form the *work core* that leads to results. When results don't meet expectations, look carefully at your design of key processes. They may not be capable of producing the desired results.

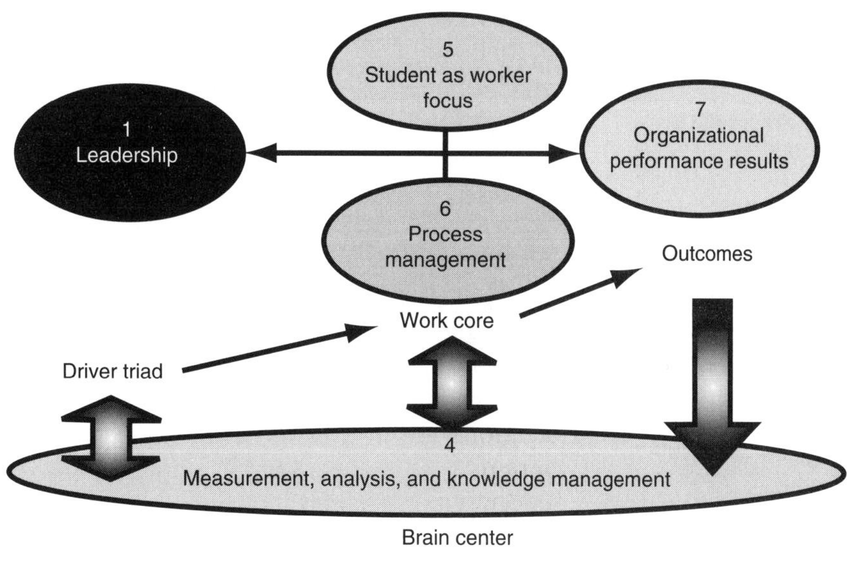

Figure 4.1 Focus on process management.

Every process yields a product. What is the product of education? This is a hot-button issue for some teachers who claim that because "we don't produce widgets" we cannot apply a business model to education. This is, of course, faulty thinking. Before proceeding, let's make sure we all share a common definition of the "product of education."

The product of education is the total of all skills + abilities + knowledge + wisdom that students have when they leave your class, grade, or school.

Because products are the result of actions taken during any process, it behooves every teacher to design an effective and efficient instructional process. The following are essential to instructional process design:

- Know the purpose and desired result.
- Keep in mind the process customers (*all* students and the next-teacher-in-line).
- Review the process requirements—the requirements of the district, state, or federal government (examples: curriculum, meet/exceed grade level standards, and so on).
- Determine the necessary steps to achieve the desired result.
- Determine supplies and materials to be used.
- Establish Quality Factors (essential elements that must be present in the product of any learning activity).
- Create the measurement system and decide on assessments.
- Determine how the process will be analyzed and improved.

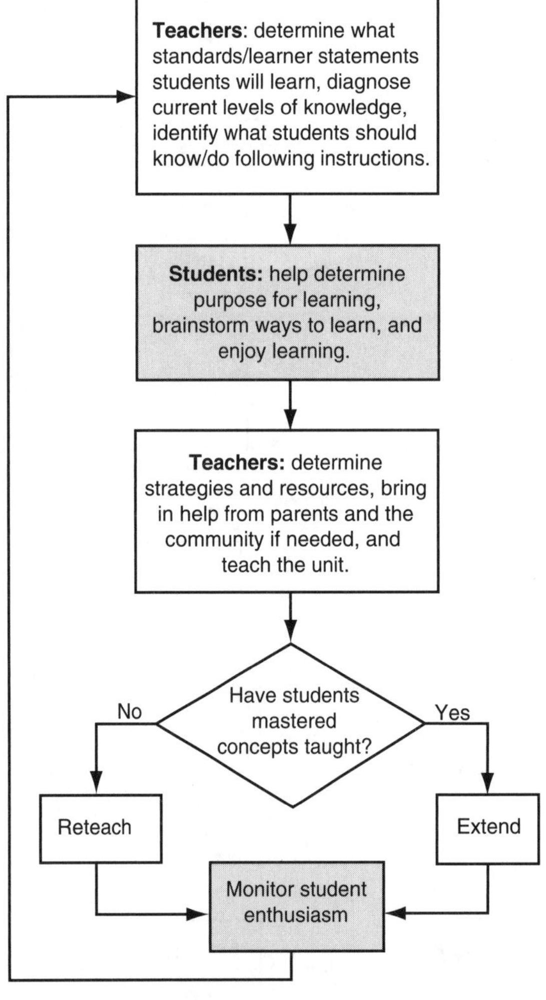

Figure 4.2 CCSD-15 instructional process flow chart.

Often we are not aware of all the steps involved in a process, so it helps to have a picture, which is the purpose of a flow chart. Instructional flow charts used by Community Consolidated School District 15 (D15), in Palatine, Illinois, are shown in Figures 4.2 and 4.3. This district won the Malcolm Baldrige National Quality Award for Performance Excellence in 2003. As early as 1999, D15, a K–8 district, had results above the national average on the Iowa Test of Basic Skills (ITBS), but they did not meet the school board's student performance targets. The board's expectation and target was/is that 90% of all students enrolled in the district for a year or more will meet or exceed grade-level standards on the Illinois state test and any nationally normed test. To meet this target, the district realized that many students who speak limited or no English and those with special needs would need to meet the Board's target also. D15 dedicated many resources (for example, added professional development, adopted new textbooks, improved the technology hardware and software) to this effort, but without system change it was unable to break the barrier and move enough students into the meets/exceeds category.

Around 2001 the administration realized that it had to standardize the instructional process and that to reach the 90% target it would need to engage students as part of this process. Figures 4.2 and 4.3 are the improved instructional processes used by D15. The

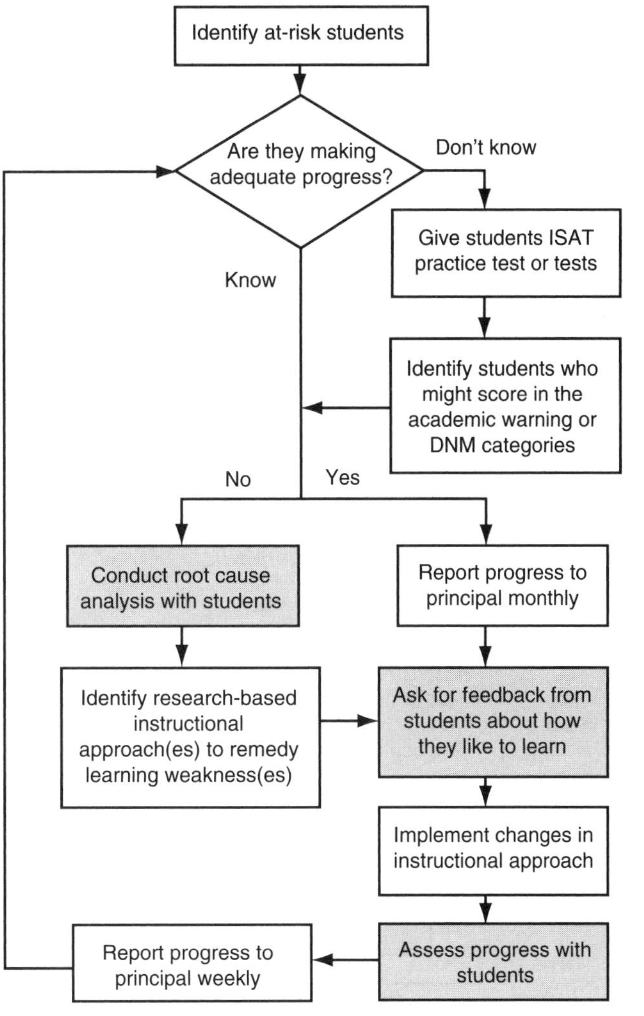

Figure 4.3 CCSD-15 at-risk process flow chart.

emphasis is the author's. D15 identifies at-risk students as those scoring below the fifth stanine on the Illinois state standards test or the ITBS. Once this approach was fully deployed throughout the district, major improvement in learning results became evident. Although this district has not closed the achievement gap entirely, it is well on the way.

Directions: Identify the differences between your instructional process and D15's. Identify the differences between the way you and/or your school addresses the needs of identified at-risk students and D15's way.

Directions: Draw a flow chart of your instructional process. Start with the step immediately after lesson planning. End with the last thing you do before going on to the next lesson. Use a marker to note the place where steps might be added or circle the steps that may need to be reconsidered in order that more students can be successful. Flow chart instructions are on page 107.

Flow Chart

What

A flow chart is a picture of a process. There are three types of flow charts:

- Process flow charts show only the process steps.
- Deployment flow charts show process steps and who's responsible for each.
- Deployment/time flow charts add the anticipated timeline to the chart.

Flow charts can be either complex, showing every small detail of each step of the process, or not as complex, showing only the major steps. When a team selects a less complex approach, care must be taken to ensure that everyone understands the smaller tasks behind each major process step.

How

1. Determine the process start and stop points.
2. List all the steps in the process. (It is recommended that this be done using Post-it notes or on a separate piece of paper.)
3. Put the steps in proper sequence.
4. Determine the nature of each step; that is, is it a task or a decision; must a report or form be completed?
5. Use the universal flow chart symbols on the following page to draw the chart.
6. Connect each step with an arrow.
7. If a decision is required, state the question so that it yields a "yes" or "no" response. If the answer is "yes," draw a straight arrow to the next step. If the answer is "no," decide what step must be looped back to in order to resolve the issue.
8. When there are multiple tasks behind a key task, draw shadow boxes to indicate the other tasks.

When

- Use flow charts when devising a new process.
- When you desire to study the effectiveness or efficiency of an existing process.
- For use when training new employees or new students.
- When a "picture" would help everyone involved realize the interdependency of individuals and/or departments to accomplish a complex task.

Flow Chart

The universal symbols

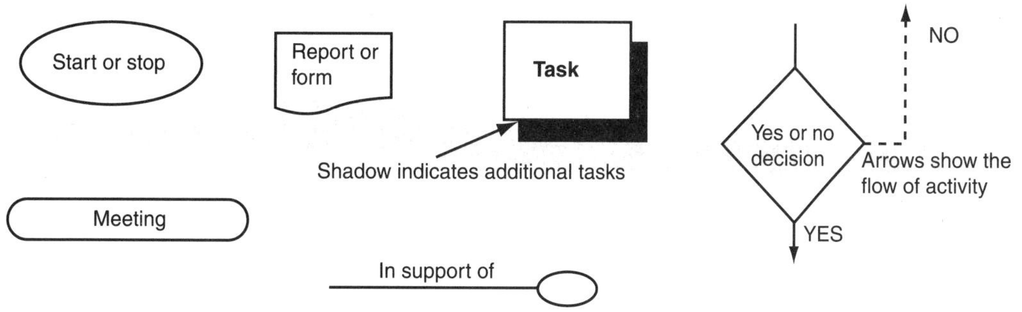

Start or stop

Report or form

Task

Shadow indicates additional tasks

Yes or no decision

NO

YES

Arrows show the flow of activity

Meeting

In support of

Continued

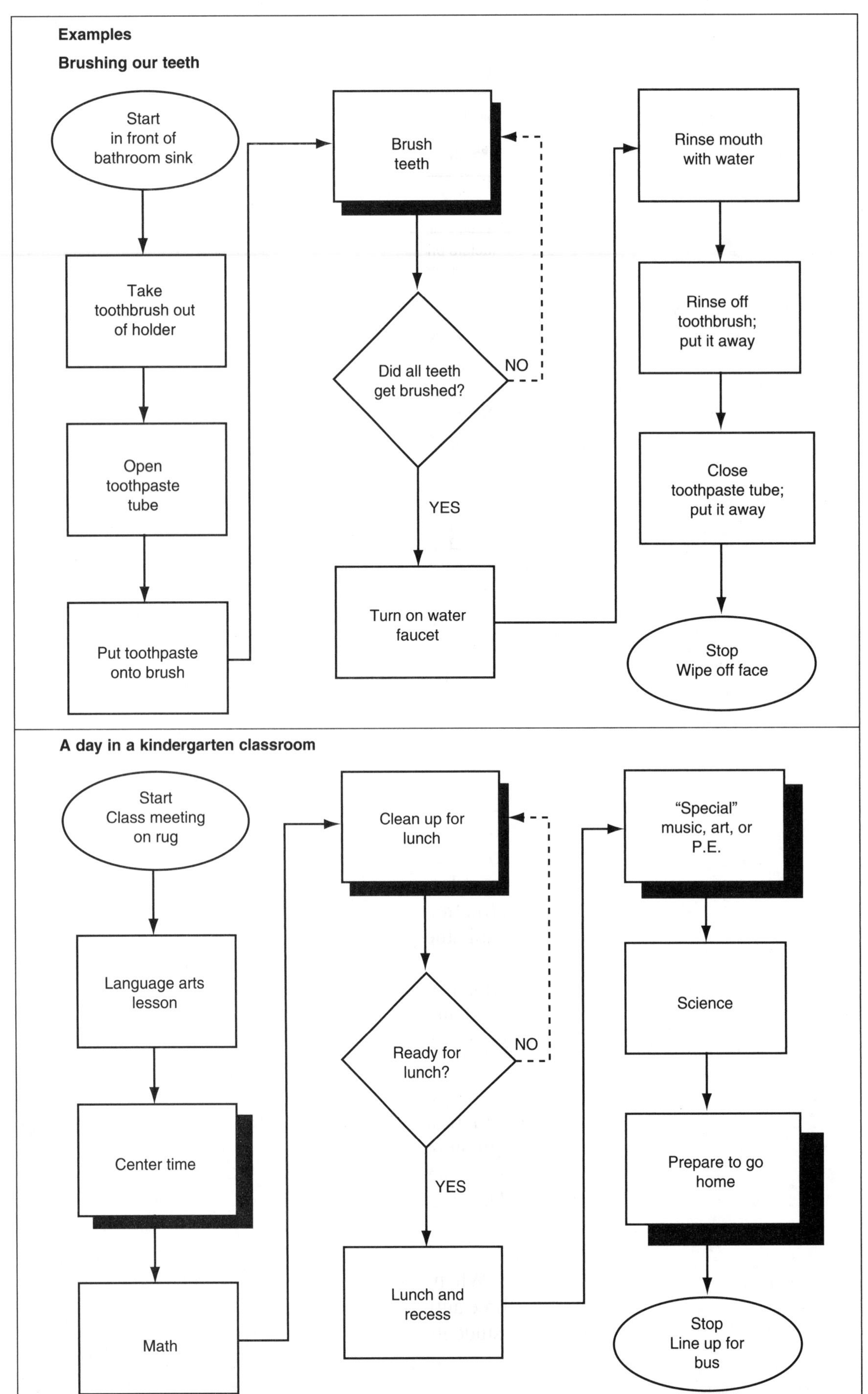
Examples
Brushing our teeth
Start
in front of
bathroom sink
Take
toothbrush out
of holder
Open
toothpaste
tube
Put toothpaste
onto brush
Brush
teeth
Did all teeth
get brushed?
NO
YES
Turn on water
faucet
Rinse mouth
with water
Rinse off
toothbrush;
put it away
Close
toothpaste tube;
put it away
Stop
Wipe off face
A day in a kindergarten classroom
Start
Class meeting
on rug
Language arts
lesson
Center time
Math
Clean up for
lunch
Ready for
lunch?
NO
YES
Lunch and
recess
"Special"
music, art, or
P.E.
Science
Prepare to go
home
Stop
Line up for
bus

Continued

Continued

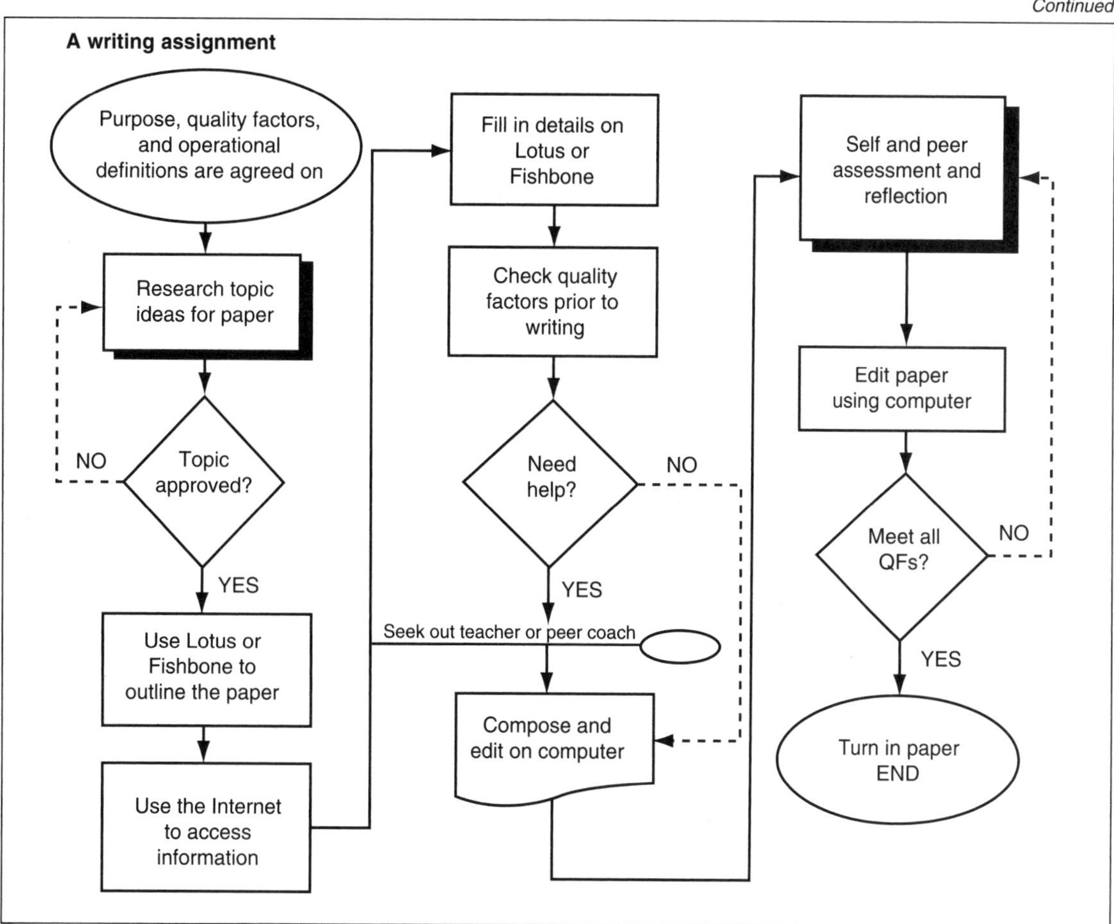

Align Lessons with Standards

As we have said, students do not decide *what they will learn,* as those decisions are left to policy makers, administrators, curriculum committees, and other key stakeholders. But, students certainly can help decide *how they want to learn* any content. This concept is central to their meeting or exceeding state standards, so weekly and daily lesson plans need to be robust and include differentiated instruction, but also flexible enough to allow teachers to make midcourse corrections to meet all students' needs.

Though you must align the instructional process with the intended outcome, there is still a great deal of flexibility in *how* students learn. The "how" relates to work systems (group or individual), multiple intelligences, how instruction is differentiated, and which learning activities will be used.

Design an effective and efficient instructional process by considering the following and checking the reference to process design steps over the next few pages. Figure 4.4 is an example of an instructional design process used by Hubert Minn, social studies teacher at Wahiawa Middle School in Wahiawa, Hawaii. His unit and lesson plans (Figures 4.5, 4.6, and 4.7) can be found on pages 110–112.

Another example comes from Ohio. When teaching physiology to her fifth-grade class (30 students—eight learning disabled, three autistic, and two emotionally disturbed students, along with gifted and regular education students), she asked the students how they wanted to

Design steps
1. Purpose: desired result
2. Process customers (all students and next-teacher-in-line)
3. Requirements (district, state, federal government, next-teacher-in-line)
4. Steps (flow)
5. Supplies/materials
6. Quality factors
7. Measurement system assessments
8. Process analysis (improved)

Figure 4.4 Instructional process design steps.

GLO	Baldrige-based quality classrooms
• The ability to be responsible for one's own learning	• Principle: I am responsible for my own learning. • Individual purpose, vision, mission and goals • Use of PDSA to solve personal problems • Keeping personal data charts • Knowledge of levels of learning and the ability to identify the level achieved
• The understanding that it is essential for human beings to work together.	• Principle: I am response-able to the success of the group. • PDSA for problems in the classroom or in other settings • Class purpose, vision, mission, and class goals • Team projects • Quality tools
• The ability to be involved in complex thinking and problem solving.	• Plan-Do-Study-Act for classroom/instructional system improvement • Team projects • Feedback in a Q classroom • Data-driven decision making • Data collection methods • Quality tools
• The ability to recognize and produce quality performance and quality products	• Quality factors • Operational definitions • Setting individual, team, or class goals • Quality features: raising the expectations over time • Individual and group data collection: peer and self-assessment for quality factors

Figure 4.5 Ways BBQ classrooms address the Hawaii General Learner Outcomes (GLO).

learn about the digestive system. After some brainstorming, the class decided to work in teams and, using household materials, create a "working" digestive system. Each group was responsible for making a presentation, demonstrating its system and knowing all the body parts as well as their functions. All students were actively engaged, and on the test at the end of the week, all scored 100%. Many told their parents that it was the most fun they'd ever had learning. At the end of the marking period (four weeks later), the teacher designed a different assessment instrument and retested the class on the digestive system. Once again every student scored 100%. It is doubtful this would have occurred in a traditional classroom.

You've probably guessed that we're passionate about the need to engage students as copartners in their own education. Without student input into the process, you can never be certain what causes the results. Hubert Minn of Hawaii, and many other teachers have discovered that giving students the opportunity to provide input into how they like to learn tremendously increases enthusiasm and "buy-in." Best of all, teachers who have implemented these approaches uniformly tell us that learning results dramatically improve.

Hawaii state standards focus on learning matrix

Name: Hubert Minn

Content area standards Social studies

Lesson	Date	(3) Standards	(3) GLO	(7) Assessment	Date	Quality?	
						Cognitive	Social skills
Essential quality behavior	8/1	B4	1, 3	Observation/quiz	8/5	Yes	Yes
Purpose/mission statements	8/2	B4	1, 3	Observation	8/5	Yes	Yes
Quality factors op-definitions	8/4		2, 4	Observation, quiz	8/5	Yes	Yes
Father's Day exercise	8/7		2, 3	Observation/quiz	8/7	Yes	Yes
TQL stages	8/8		2	Quiz	8/9	Not yet	Yes
Lotus matrix Hawaiian culture	8/10	A1	1, 2, 3	Lotus w QF	8/12	Yes	Yes
Early Hawaii chapter 4	8/16	A1	1, 2, 3	Report and Quiz	8/20	Yes	Yes
Hawaiian culture #1	8/21	A1 C2 A3	1, 2, 3, 4	Quality factors Exams	9/1	Yes	Yes
Hawaiian royal history	9/6	A1 D1 C2	1, 2	Reading Quiz Observation	9/12	Yes	Yes

Hawaii content and performance standards

A1 **History** *Change, continuity, causality*
Benchmarks: Identify possible causal relationships in historical chronologies; offer fact-based explanations for change and continuity in history.

B4 **Political science, civics** *Citizenship, participation*
Benchmarks: Explain the significance of citizenship and participate responsibly for the common good; for example, select and study an issue or problem and plan and implement a civic action.

C2 **Cultural anthropology** *Cultural diversity and unity*
Benchmarks: Explain conditions and motivations that contribute to conflict, cooperation, and interdependence among different individuals, groups and/or nations, and suggest alternative "win-win" solutions to persistent contemporary and emerging global issues.

D1 **Geography** *World in spatial terms*
Benchmarks: Interpret and construct geographic representations to explain human and physical distributions and patterns.

Figure 4.6 Example: standards-based unit plan.

HAWAIIAN CULTURE MAGIC JOURNEY

RM A-10 8/21/00 LESSON #1

(1) Purpose: **Content standards A1—6/8 (1)**
Employ chronology to understand change and/or continuity and cause and/or effect in history.
History of the Hawaiian kingdom/Hawaiian culture
Content standards A3—6/8 (1)
Understand culture as a system of beliefs, knowledge, practices shared by a group.

(1) Mission: By working together cooperatively and meeting our quality factors we will reach our goals.

(1) Goals:

1. 100% participation by students
2. Class average for exam is above 90%
3. All students reach quality—social/academic
4. Meet the state standards

(6) Quality factors	Operational definition
Cooperate	Help your group be successful in what they are trying to accomplish. Don't argue or put people down. Use social skills evaluation daily.
Reach Learning Level 4 (Bloom's Taxonomy)	Able to recall information Understand cause and effect Analyze errors and then create improvement
Plan-Do-Study-Act	Take assessment of group test data and average the group scores **Plan**—How you intend for the group to all pass at a rate of 90% on the next exam (e.g., group learning the answers together by reading, listening to lectures, taking notes, testing each other) **Do**—Test again and then **Study**—Scores (Did the score for your group improve?) **Act**—How can you improve even more?
Reach Learning Level 5	Create an individual lotus diagram of Hawaiian culture information learned from exam and PDSA plan

(4) Lesson plan flow chart

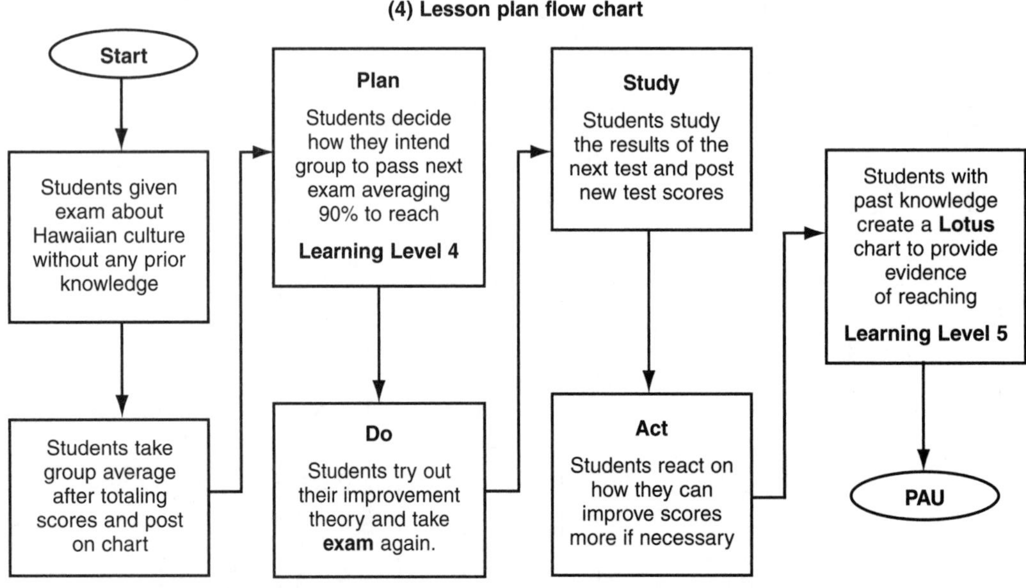

Figure 4.7 BBQ aligned lesson plan.

Improve Efficiency and Effectiveness of the Instructional Process

Variation

As shown in Chapter 1, Figures 1.7, 1.8, and 1.9, every process exhibits some variation. Dr. Deming implored us all to understand variation and its causes before making any system change. Far too frequently, educators, who pride themselves on taking action, fail to understand the variation of results and often end up tinkering with the system, frequently making matters worse. Figure 4.8 provides a *very* abbreviated lesson on variation. For more information about variation, we recommend Dr. W. Edwards Deming, *The New Economics for Industry, Government, Education,* MIT Center for Advanced Engineering Study, 1993. Another resource, which provides the statistical formulas and explanations about control charts, is *The Six Sigma Memory Jogger II,* GOAL/QPC, 2002. Keep in mind, the goal of a BBQ classroom is to reduce the amount (bandwidth) of variation.

Set Specifications and Reduce Variation in Student Work

Have you ever wondered why there is such variation in completed assignments after you've given everyone the same instructions? Instructions that may seem clear to teachers are often ambiguous or not clearly defined for all students and unfortunately, some students do not feel comfortable asking for clarification. (If this describes your classroom, it is necessary to understand what has driven fear into the classroom.) Or, do you wonder

Types of variation

Common cause variation	Special cause variation
Results from system problems and can only be eliminated by changing the system. Example: The average number of students coming to first period class after the bell rings is 6. (Teacher is frequently late and doesn't take roll until the end of the period.)	Results from unpredictable and sporadic circumstances; not due to system problems but must be eliminated or addressed before changing the system. Example: A spike in tardiness to class on a specific date. (A traffic accident resulted in six of 10 buses arriving late for school.)

What it looks like

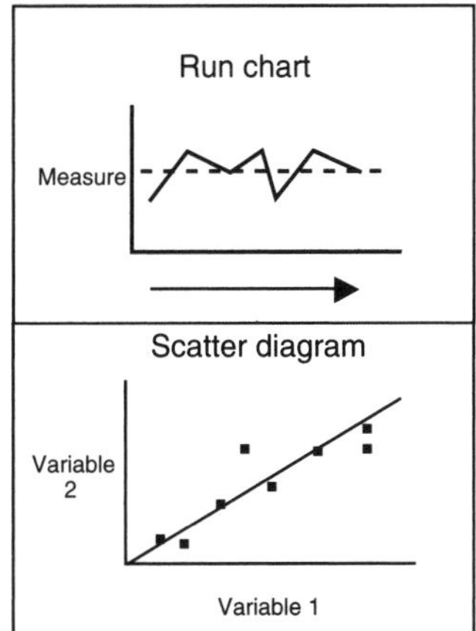

What it looks like

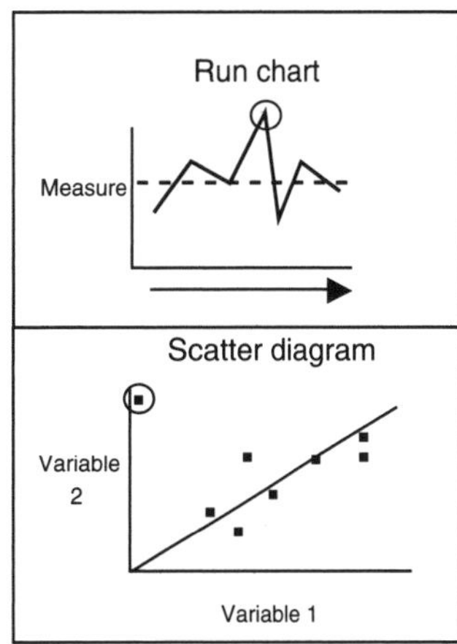

Figure 4.8 Examples of common and special cause variation.

why some students don't seem to care about the work they turn in? Perhaps it is because when previous assignments were returned, students realized certain things went unnoticed and were therefore not considered important enough to remember. *The cumulative effect of this over time lends less credibility to the need for giving careful attention to work before it is turned in to the teacher.*

> *For example, a teacher might say, "Students, your book reports will be due on Monday. Remember to write your report in paragraph form and use proper punctuation and include everything you have learned about good book reports."*

Immediately, this teacher has invited trouble. In this example, one cannot assume that all students can or will interpret the definition of "good book reports" exactly the same way. While all processes contain some variation, it increases when there is no clear, concise definition of Quality work. To reduce the variation and to ensure that more students meet the learning goals, it is necessary to help students define Quality in schoolwork, in their lives, and in their choices. Without ever thinking about what Quality means, many students go through life with vague ideas and few discriminating habits. Quality Factors and operational definitions set specifications and help reduce variation in students' work. The following activity is designed to begin the discussion of Quality.

Quality Factors and Quality Features

Quality Factors are *the absolute essential elements of a product or service*. They are the *wow* factors, or the standard way to measure excellence of a product or service. (They are the specifications.) Quality Factors are determined by the customers—people who use the product or service—and therefore Quality Factors frequently change as expectations increase.

It is imperative for all of us to be concerned that students understand Quality work. The most salient reasons are these:

- Too many students graduate without minimal skills to succeed in the workforce or in postsecondary education.
- The extraordinary high cost of rework and "educational scrap" drains instructional budgets, teachers' energy, and students' enthusiasm for learning.
- Unless all students understand what Quality work is, they will be inadequately prepared to meet the challenges of their adult life.
- Students who can define and understand Quality work are more discriminating about other areas in their lives.

In contrast to Quality Factors, students must understand Quality Features. Quality Features are *nonessential elements of a product or service that delight the customer,* going beyond meeting customer needs and expectations. You must understand that today's Quality Features are tomorrow's Quality Factors. For example, think about the changes in audio systems in automobiles since the 1930s. Radios used to be available only as an upgrade or in luxury cars. With increased customer demand, radios became standard equipment in all automobiles, thus turning the radio into a Quality Factor. Next came the demand for tape players, and now we have CD players as standard equipment in many automobiles.

Another example comes from the world of figure skating. Think about all the changes in complexity of programs the figure skating champions have performed over time. At first, champions did spirals, balance figures, and a few simple jumps. Now, triple or quadruple jump combinations, fancy footwork, and spirals in many positions are all required to become a champion. Thus, the expectations of the standards (jumps, spirals, footwork, and so on) have been greatly ratcheted up over the years, and we expect champion figure skaters to have a much higher skill level now. How does it happen? If one skater takes a risk and creates a new or more difficult element that delights the judges, the other skaters realize the bar has been raised and expectations become higher for them all.

ACTIVITY: *Define Quality*

Teacher prep work:

- Gather materials.
- Select three varieties of apples (one set of apples for each group of students), with as few outward defects as possible (bruises, punctures, and so on). We generally use Red Delicious, Fuji, and Granny Smith apples because they are very different in color, taste, and sweetness, but you can use any product with which all students are familiar. Food seems to work out well for this activity, but we know some teachers have used bubble gum and pencils. Just avoid using any product that would discriminate against students of different cultures or lower socioeconomic status.
- Napkins, one per person.
- Small paper plates (mark each plate with an "A," "B," or "C"). Each table will have one set (A, B , and C) of plates.
- Decide which variety of apple will be A, B, and C. Organize the apples on the plates; for example, all Red Delicious will be A, all Fuji will be B, and so on.
- A plastic knife on each table (if you are uncomfortable having students cut the apples, you can cut all the apples).
- Make a transparency of a Data Collection Plan (DCP)—Figure 4.9—template.
- Pass out a copy of the Data Collection Form (DCF)—Figure 4.10—for each student.

Steps:

1. Explain to the students that for this activity they will be quality inspectors, an important scientific job. Their task is to discover the *wow* or Quality Factors (QFs) for an eating apple and to test each apple to see if it meets expectations. Remind students that the QFs for an eating apple are different than those for apples used in baking, for example.

Data collection plan to be completed by the teacher

Quality factor	Operational definition	How measured?	When?	By whom?
Example: *Juicy*	*Example:* *Juice is visible on plate immediately after apple is cut.*	*Example:* *Visual test*	*Example:* *Immediately after cutting apple*	*Example:* *Everyone on the team will do the test.* *The team leader or aide or teacher will cut the apple.*

Figure 4.9 Sample data collection plan.

Data collection form to be completed by students

Name: *Suze* **Date:** 9/12/05

Quality factor	Operational definition	How measured?	When?	Sample A	Sample B	Sample C
Example: Juicy	*Example: Juice is visible on plate immediately after apple is cut.*	*Example: Visual test*	*Example: Juicy*	*Q*	–	–

Figure 4.10 Sample data collection form.

2. Ask the students to go back into their memory and visualize the *best* eating apple they've ever had. Visualizing helps get the senses into play to articulate Quality Factors.
3. Write down all brainstormed student suggestions on the flip chart or board.
4. After all ideas are exhausted, review the list and ask, "Are there any ideas on this list that may not be *absolutely essential* characteristics of the *best* eating apple?
5. Eliminate those that the class agrees are not absolutely essential, but remind the students that these qualities are individual preferences and, therefore, are Quality Features that delight them, making them important but not essential to a wow eating apple. An example might be *shiny* or *caramel dipped.*
6. Ask, "Can any of the remaining ideas be combined?" If so, put them together.
7. Explain that for the purposes of this experiment, the group should consider only three Quality Factors. Also explain that you've selected three varieties of apples, and so that eliminates taste and color from becoming Quality Factors. Taste is a factor (sugar content) for the wholesale buyer and does affect the amount of money paid to a grower, but this class doesn't have the capability of measuring sugar content. Therefore, for our purposes, taste (sweet or sour) becomes a quality feature. The same goes for color, which is important when the buyers set the price to the growers.
8. Explain the necessity of establishing a Data Collection Plan. (See the Data Collection Plan on page 116 and make it into a transparency.) DCPs answer key questions about what the Quality Factors are, how they will be measured, and what data is to be collected. *The teacher completes the DCP*. Have the class operationally define each of the Quality Factors and completely fill in the DCP as shown in Figure 4.9.
9. Ask students to take out the Data Collection Form (Figure 4.10). As a class, decide which of the three Quality Factor tests need to be done first, second, and third. The type of test (visual, tactile, audio, and so on) and what is being measured determine the order of tests. Students individually fill in the quality factors in the order each will be tested.
10. Each student completes his or her Data Collection Form, paying close attention to the agreed-upon operational definitions for each Quality Factor.
11. Give the students 10 minutes to perform each quality test individually and to chart the data. Each apple is to be judged independently from the others and only as to whether or not it meets each Quality Factor—based *solely* on the Operational Definition. Students should mark a "Q" if it meets the operational definition or "—" if it does not. Do this for each apple and each Quality Factor.
12. Allow five minutes for teams to come to consensus on each Quality Factor for each variety of apple.

Debrief with these questions:

- How many teams had complete agreement before the team discussion? *Variation* in the results of team members depends on the completeness and clarity of the

Operational Definitions. (This is one significant cause of variation in student work.)

- What were the benefits to having you [students] determine the Quality Factors?
- What are the insights you have gained about the differences between Quality Factors and Features?

> *Note to teachers: Assess products of learning activities based on Quality Factors,* not *Quality Features. Quality Features, if agreed upon by the class, may become Quality Factors for the next learning product. In this way, the Quality of what students produce continuously increases over time.*

The customer defines quality, and this is a central reason to engage students in determining Quality Factors. The students are customers in the classroom. By being engaged in this manner, students are active rather than passive and further embody the two principles: *I am responsible for my own learning* and *I am response-able to the success of the group.* This type of activity requires students to think critically about what quality is and to be precise in their thinking. By-products of this type of thinking spread to their personal lives, and we have heard stories of students teaching their parents about quality when they go to the grocery store. It is a great way to get parents involved in discussions about quality and quality work.

Teachers play a customer role too and represent the needs/expectations of customers not present, such as the next-teacher-in-line and the district. When it comes to learning activities, teachers must also participate in establishing Quality Factors, especially when students don't always come up with what the teacher knows is expected. (More on this in Chapter 8.) **Helpful tips:**

- Guide the discussion along when students define Quality Factors to avoid getting bogged down in the activity.
- Always use a product with which the students are familiar.
- Avoid using "class specific" products such as designer clothing or athletic shoes.
- Use a product in which many students would be interested. Older students may be more concerned about cars or trucks, CD players, or video games, but be careful when choosing one of these products.
- You may need to come back and use a similar activity just to remind students to more clearly define quality.
- Make the leap to the curriculum quickly so the lessons learned with the apples are not lost on students. See the next section for more on this.

Establish Quality Factors (Specifications) for the Assignment and Reduce Variation

Like all states, Hawaii uses a rubric to assess students' abilities to meet writing standards. The rubric uses a five-point scale with these five dimensions: meaning, voice, clarity, design, and conventions. We submit that teachers may want to change the way they approach writing and the expectations for all students as the school year progresses. For example, "voice" is defined in the HCPS II State Assessment Teacher's Guide (2003) as shown in Figure 4.11 on the opposite page. You can see the requirements for Grades 3 and 5 with the progression from level 3 to 5 for Grades 8 and 10.

It doesn't matter how your state has defined the writing dimensions, what matters is how you guide students to raise expectations over the course of a school year. We highly recommend beginning the school year with the expectation that all students will write at a score point of three; then quickly raise the bar to score-point five for all students. Impossible, you say? Perhaps in a traditional classroom, but how can you be sure? Teachers in a Baldrige-based quality classroom will have a much greater chance of having more, if not all students reach the highest levels. On the following pages, we provide a suggestion and example.

Example: Goal (Language Arts) *Write to communicate for a variety of purposes and audiences.*

Duty of teacher
1. Identify the state standards to be addressed: Example: Compose a well-organized and coherent writing for specific purposes and audiences. 2. Establish the purpose of the assignment: Example: To write an expository essay. 3. Determine the assignment: Example: Write a story about people close to you. 4. Determine the Quality Factors: See the following example.
Duty of teacher and students together
Determine, through a brainstorming process, the operational definitions for each of the standards to be addressed.

These fifth-grade students helped determine the Quality Factors and the operational definitions of this class, as shown in Figure 4.12 on page 122. We have included only a partial list to demonstrate how students helped and came up with definitions in their language. This process took out the guesswork and allowed every student to know precisely what was expected. When finished, each student self-assessed his or her writing and then asked a buddy to be their quality coach and peer assessor.

The peer assessors gave coaching tips to explain what needed to improve to meet the Quality Factors. Students then had an opportunity to edit their work before turning it in. The result was remarkably improved writing, the teacher was less stressed from having to grade every paper, and every student felt empowered.

In a Baldrige-based quality classroom, the peer assessment process is considered very important and students are expected to take it seriously. This relates to the principle of "I am response-able to the success of the group." It is not only the accomplished students who participate in this coaching process, but everyone. As a result, the skill level of the entire class improves each writing cycle. Teacher, acting as facilitator, constantly moves around the class and easily can see when individual, group, or whole-class direct instruction is required.

We suggest that schools and grade-level teams adopt a standardized "best practice" writing process and expectations. Students, regardless of the class, should be held to the

HCPS II state assessment writing rubric (2003)

Dimension		Score point 1	Score point 2	Score point 3	Score point 4	Score point 5
Voice The imprint of the writer; the reader has a sense of a writer behind the words; writing shows conviction, caring, and/or engages the reader.	Grades 3 and 5	• The writing sounds wooden or mechanical. • The writing seems anonymous with no sense that any particular individual wrote it. • The writer appears detached or indifferent to the reader; there is no sense that the writer cares about or is interested in the topic.	• The response may demonstrate some attempt at life or movement. • The reader may at times catch a brief glimpse of the writer as an individual. • The writer may sometimes show an attempt to demonstrate engagement with the topic but such attempts may be superficial or flawed.	• The writing has some life to it, generally pleasing with safe generalities. • The reader senses a writer behind the words, but the writer seems half-hidden. • The writing appears lukewarm or half-hearted, but now and then conviction or caring comes through.	• Writing demonstrates spark but no flame. • Writer takes calculated risk of exposing himself/herself to personalize the writing. • Writing shows sincerity and honesty but is tempered with caution.	• The writer speaks to or captures the reader; it is lively or earnest. • The reader senses a particular writer behind the words. • The writing appears to say what the writer honestly thinks or feels. Conviction or caring is evident.
	Grades 8 and 10	• Writing has some life to it; generally pleasing with safe generalities. • The reader senses a writer behind the words, but the writer seems half-hidden. • The writing appears lukewarm or half-hearted, but now and then conviction or caring comes through.	• The writer demonstrates spark, but no flame. • Writer takes risk of exposing himself/herself to personalize the writing. • Writing shows sincerity and honesty but is tempered with caution.	• The writing speaks to or captures the reader; it is lively or earnest. • The reader senses a particular writer (not person) behind the words. • The writing appears to say what the writer honestly thinks or feels. Conviction or caring is evident.	• The writing has life and movement. • The reader senses only this individual writer could have produced this writing. • In general, the writing is captivating and convincing.	• The writing establishes a strong interaction with the reader compelling the reader to pay attention. • The writing is easily, readily linked to the writer and is very much his/her own. • There is a strong sense of the writer's conviction and caring in the writing.

Grades 3–5 Level 5 →

- The writer speaks to or captures the reader; it is lively or earnest.
- The reader senses a particular writer behind the words.
- The writing appears to say what the writer honestly thinks or feels. Conviction or caring is evident

Becomes → **Grades 8–10 Level 3** (Required in fall) →

- The writer speaks to or captures the reader; it is lively or earnest.
- The reader senses a particular writer behind the words.
- The writing appears to say what the writer honestly thinks or feels. Conviction or caring is evident

Becomes → **Grades 8–10 Level 5** (Expected by spring) →

- The writing establishes a strong interaction with the reader compelling the reader to pay attention.
- The writing is easily, readily linked to the writer and is very much his/her own.
- There is a strong sense of the writer's conviction and caring in the writing.

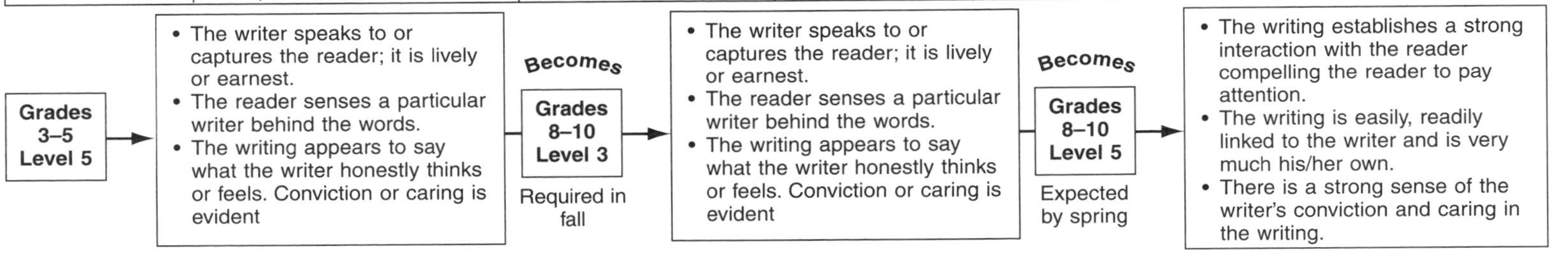

Figure 4.11 Expectation for progression of writing skills for a class.
Rubric reprinted with permission from Hawaii Department of Education.

Quality factor	Operational definition	Q? NY?	Coaching tips
Explains or describes the topic	At least 3 valid points.		
Length	5 paragraphs		
Paragraphs	All: topic sentence		
	All: supporting details		
	#1 Introduces the topic and intent of entire essay		
	#2–4 Relate to and elaborate upon the introduction		
	#5 Conclusion: summarizing points		
Grammar usage and mechanics	Spelling		
No errors	Subject-verb agreement		
	Punctuation		
	Capitalization		
	Parts of speech		
	Sentence fragments		
	Run-on sentences		
Neatness	No smudges or erasures		
	No wrinkles		

Figure 4.12 Example of Quality Factors sheet with operational definitions.

same writing standards and expectations. If every teacher expected the same degree of expertise in writing, students would learn, variation would vastly decrease, and, we submit, many more students would reach the highest level. This expectation is not just to satisfy state requirements. Writing is an important life skill and vital for anyone entering the job market. It is time to set the bar high for all students and help them reach it.

ACTIVITY: *Teach Students to Reflect on Their Own Work and the Work of Their Peers*

Steps:

1. Put one of the work samples (see the examples on the next page) on the overhead projector and draw everyone's attention to the first Quality Factor. Ask the students to reflect on the sample and determine whether or not the Quality Factor is visible. Ask for a volunteer to come and point out where the QF is in the document. If it is not there, describe the problem and what needs to be done to meet that particular QF.
2. Repeat this with the other work samples, different student volunteers, and other QFs.
3. Put another sample on the projector and ask the students to rate it for each QF. If the sample meets any QF, students can make a "Q" in the appropriate box. If it does not, write "NY" ("not yet") in the box and provide coaching tips.
4. For each learning activity, have students reflect on their own work for Quality and if any QFs are missing, revise the work. Before turning any work in, ask students to give their papers to another student for peer assessment and coaching.

Example 1—Second Grade
(This sample has been reprinted exactly as the anonymous student author wrote it.)

My Sassy Sister

I have a sassy sister. She yells at me so loud
by ears come off. She bosses me around and I
hate it because, she declares "You don't do anything around
the house." But I clean the house every Wednesday. What
else does she want me to do? She thinks she own
my mom's house. But she is not paying the t.V. bill,
the phone bill, the water bill, and the electric bill. Man I hate
my sister. When we both disagree on somthing we fight and talk
back like this "Am I talking to you, No!" I reply. She grumbled. "Did
I say anything, No!" Then she teases me and say JenniferPest
the door." You see my last name is Pescador. I cry and slam my door
behind me because I'm mad. Man I really hate my sister but if I
get in trouble she will always be by my side so I guess she isn't
bad after all.

Example 2—Third Grade
(This sample has been reprinted exactly as the anonymous student author wrote it.)

Friends

A friend is someone who is there for you and cares about what
you do. Some people even have friends to help them do things like homework.
I have friends so I won't get lonely or sad. A friend is a very special person.
Sometimes they are friends you go to birthdays or sleepovers. Friends are people
you can tell anything that you can't tell others. Sometimes you can tell them
things you can't tell your family like if you got a bad grade in school.

Friends are people that are special to you. Sometimes people get there friends
to do chores for them. But sometimes you just have to let them go and not bother
with them. Or like myself I just ignore them to get more work done,
but sometimes you need them to help you.

The kinds of friends you would like is friends like Mohala, Krystal, Elizabeth
and Lehua. You would like that kind of friend because they all have a sense
of humor. They all are this type of friend.

Following are some helpful tips:

- Avoid overwhelming students in the beginning of the year with too many Quality Factors. Begin small and add more with each assignment. Soon the students will uniformly be achieving more than ever before.
- Teach reflection skills often in the beginning and especially when the Quality Factors are ratcheted up, as this means there is a higher level of specifications to which students are going to be held. (See the example from Candace Smith in Chapter 8.)

Tools to Analyze the Instructional Process

On the next several pages are instructions for four tools. *How Helpful Were These Resources,* is a student satisfaction tool. Resources can be a major barrier to student success, and as you know now, there is no other way to be certain anything is working unless you ask the students. A *Force Field Analysis* is a powerful tool for individual students or the class to assess what drives or keeps them from achieving any goal. The *Affinity Diagram* and *Relations Digraph* are most powerfully used in tandem, although it is not essential to do so. These tools are great for analyzing the effectiveness of any classroom process, including the instructional process. Templates of all these tools can be found in Appendix D.

How Helpful Were These Resources?

As part of the debriefing after each instructional unit, obtain feedback from students about the usefulness of the resources that were used (Figure 4.13). Students can tabulate the results, make a histogram of the results, and assist the teacher in understanding issues surrounding the use of the resources. For instance, the students may report that they find the lectures to be a waste of time. The teacher may feel that it is one of the best ways to deliver certain material to the students. In such a case, the teacher will want to ask the students what made them feel the lecture is a waste of time. Perhaps the lectures are too long or the teacher uses language that is too difficult to understand.

> *"How Helpful Were These Resources?" is one tool that you cannot duplicate as shown: teachers have shared with us that their students evaluated resources never used. A generic template is provided in Appendix D.*

How helpful were these resources?

Class: Year: Project or unit: Date:

Rating scale:
E = Excellent; couldn't have done without it.
G = Good; was a big help.
O = Okay; wasn't that much help.
W = Waste of time; was no help whatsoever.

Please rate each of the following resources on how much it helped during this learning experience.

	E	G	O	W
Lecture				
Textbook				
Library books				
CD				
Computer—software				
Computer—Internet				
Video				
Class discussion				
Field trip				
Articles				
Newspaper				
Outside experts				

Figure 4.13 Example of How Helpful Were These Resources? tool.

Force Field Analysis

What

A Force Field Analysis is a planning tool that encourages team or group discussion about the driving and restraining forces that affect goal attainment. The object is to reduce or eliminate the restraining forces rather than focus on the driving forces.

How

1. Draw a horizontal line about four inches from the top of a piece of flip chart paper. Write the goal statement in this area.
2. In the center of the paper, just under the goal statement, draw a vertical line to the bottom of the paper.
3. Draw a horizontal line approximately three inches down. In the rectangle on the upper left, draw a large "+" sign. These are the driving forces.
4. Draw a large "−" sign in the space on the right of the vertical line. These are the restraining forces.
5. Explain that the object of this is to identify all the positive and negative forces that will affect goal attainment.
6. Ask the question: What things might make it easier to reach the goal? Write these in the "+" column and draw an arrow from each to the center line.
7. Next, ask: What are the things that might make it more difficult to reach the goal? These might be distractions or actual impediments such as lack of knowledge. Write the responses in the "−" column with an arrow drawn to the center line.
8. Prioritize the driving and restraining forces.
9. When all driving and restraining forces are identified and prioritized, make a list of the actions necessary to achieve the goal.

When

- If the class, an individual, or a team is having difficulty.
- In an individual counseling session or student/parent conference setting.
- Before beginning a major project.
- If the focus is lost and the team, class, or individuals are not making progress.

Example

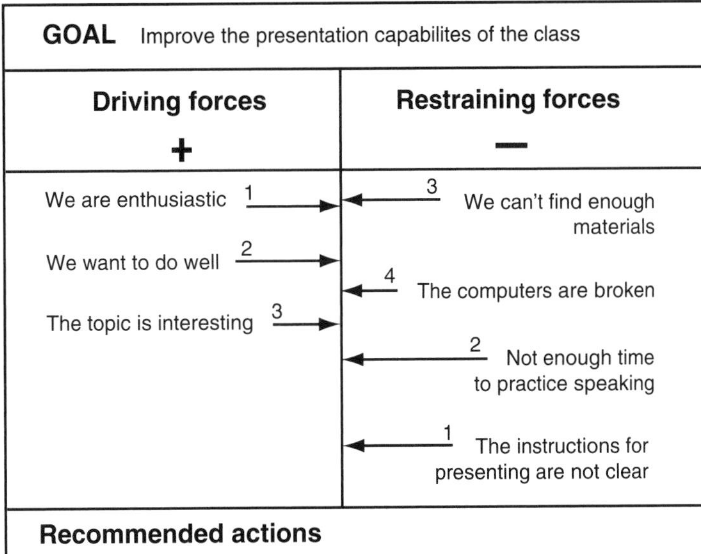

GOAL Improve the presentation capabilites of the class
Driving forces
+
Restraining forces
—
We are enthusiastic 1
We want to do well 2
The topic is interesting 3
3 We can't find enough materials
4 The computers are broken
2 Not enough time to practice speaking
1 The instructions for presenting are not clear
Recommended actions
1. Teacher will explain criteria and we'll set operational definitions. (1)
2. We will collaborate to set aside time to practice daily for one week. (2)
3. Miss Jones will research more materials and give us a list by Monday. (3)
4. Miss Jones will complete a work order to have the computers fixed. (4)
5. Miss Jones will work with Mr. Boone to trade classrooms twice a week to use his computers. (4)

Continued

Continued

Counseling Example

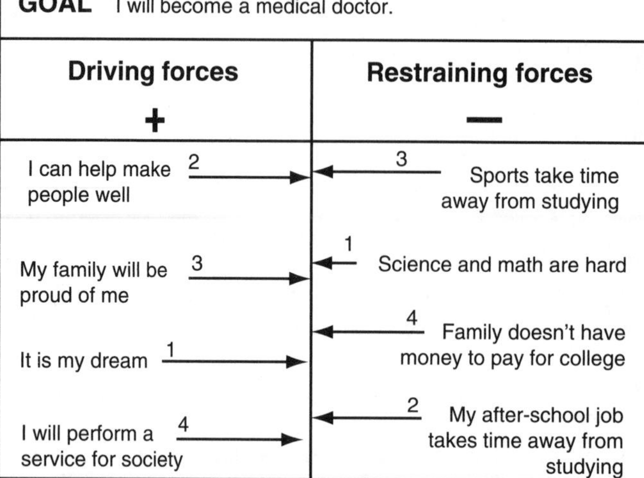

GOAL I will become a medical doctor.
Driving forces
+
Restraining forces
—
I can help make people well 2
3 Sports take time away from studying
My family will be proud of me 3
1 Science and math are hard
4 Family doesn't have money to pay for college
It is my dream 1
2 My after-school job takes time away from studying
I will perform a service for society 4

Recommended actions

1. I will get a study buddy tutor to help me with science and math. (1)
2. I will work fewer hours and set up a planned study time. (2)
3. I will concentrate on football and drop baseball. (3)
4. Mrs. Lark will explore scholarship opportunities for me. (4)
5. I will work hard to win a scholarship and bring my GPA to over 3.5. (4)

Affinity Diagram

What

An Affinity Diagram is a silent brainstorming tool that allows groups to identify and organize large quantities of information or ideas in a short time.

How

1. Clearly state the topic and write it down for all to see.
2. Pass out a half-dozen 3x3-inch Post-it notes or index cards to each group member (more if available).
3. Each person will write one idea per note until he or she has run out of ideas or the allotted time has passed. *This is to be done silently.*
4. When finished, each person places his or her ideas on the board or in the middle of the table for all to see.
5. *Silently,* the group begins moving "like" ideas into categories. Generally, groups put like ideas into columns.
6. Individuals may continue moving cards from one grouping to another until everyone is satisfied. Ideas that don't seem to "fit" any category can be placed into a miscellaneous one. Individuals can ask for clarification about the meaning of any idea they are unclear about.
7. The group as a whole will determine titles or "headers" for each category. Headers ought to be noun/verb phrases for greater understanding and clarification.
8. Each agreed-upon header is written on a Post-it note of a distinguishing color and placed at the top of its respective column. To complete the Affinity Diagram, each group of ideas is enclosed in a rectangle.

When

- One or more individuals in the group are very assertive and others are quiet and shy.
- It is important to learn what individuals' ideas or thoughts are about a complex topic.
- You want to know how much students know about a topic.
- The class is studying categorization or classification.

Example

Topic: What are the elements of a successful field trip?

Permission slips Adults to help Cooperation from everybody Lunch or snacks
Learn a lot Go to a fun place Admission money Nice weather Ask questions
Good manners Friendly bus driver Buy candy See interesting stuff
Don't climb on stuff without permission Don't fight Be good listeners

What are the elements of a successful field trip?

Things to Remember	We wish for	We want	Help we need!
Permission slips Admission money Ask questions Be good listeners Don't fight Buddy System Good manners Don't climb on stuff without permission Lunch or snacks	Nice weather	See interesting stuff Go to a fun place Learn a lot	Adults to help Friendly bus driver Cooperation from everybody

Other Educational Topic Ideas

- Characteristics of a Quality student
- Things that fly
- Modes of transportation
- What do you know about your state
- What keeps students from doing homework
- Animals with four legs
- Characteristics of the major characters of a novel

Relations Digraph

What

The Relations Digraph is a planning tool that shows the relationship between any two factors of an issue. The purpose is to identify and study the cause and effect between factors of a problem. Root causes are those that primarily influence other factors. Root effects are factors that are primarily influenced by other factors. This tool is most often used in conjunction with the Affinity Diagram.

How

The steps to creating a Relations Digraph are:

1. Place the central issue or problem in the center of a large piece of paper. Circle it.
2. Place the "headers" of the previously completed Affinity Diagram around the outside perimeter of the paper. Draw a rectangle around each "header."
3. Analyze the relationships between headers by asking the question: "Does this issue influence this one, or is it influenced by the other?"
4. Allow the team time to discuss the potential relationship, but do not get hung up on semantics. Make every attempt to reach consensus on the nature of the relationship.
5. Draw an arrow from the "influencing" header to the "affected" header.
6. Move systematically around the diagram until each header has been examined by each of the others.
7. If a relationship exists, an arrow must be drawn between the two headers. *Do not draw a line between two headers unless a relationship exists.*
8. When all the headers have been considered and all arrows are drawn, count the number of arrows going out of each header. Place the total for each inside the header box.
9. Count all arrows coming into each header and place that number in the header box. (Example: 6 arrows coming in and 3 arrows going out would be shown as 6:3.)
10. The header with the most arrows coming in is the *root effect.* The header with the most arrows going out is the root cause.
11. If there is a tie for the root cause, look at the two headers and compare them again.

When

- Use this tool when it is important to understand where to begin an improvement project.
- When it is necessary to gain greater understanding of the cause/effect of a complex content related issue.
- When planning a major project that may have ramifications throughout the school and/or class.

Example

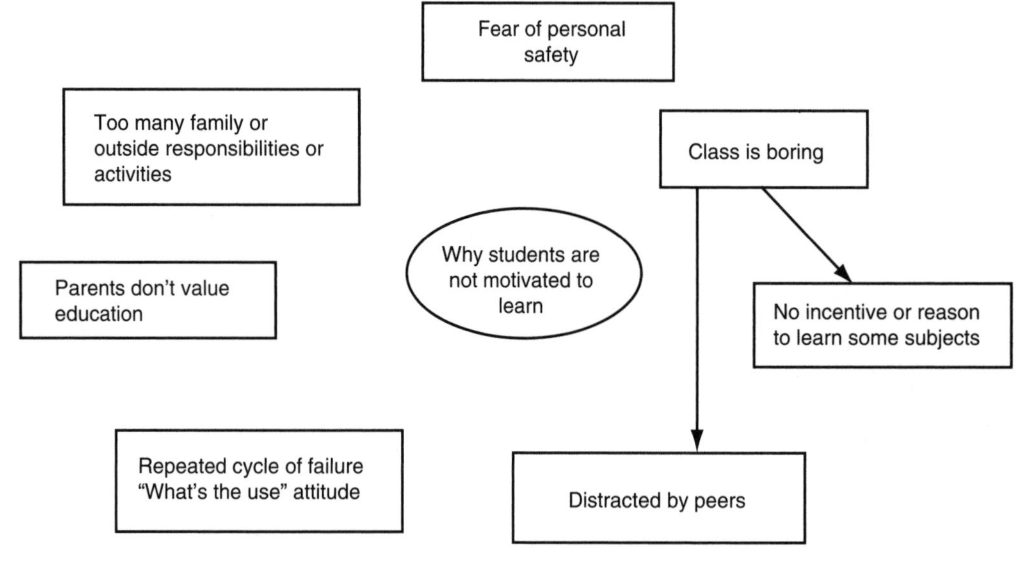

Continued

Continued

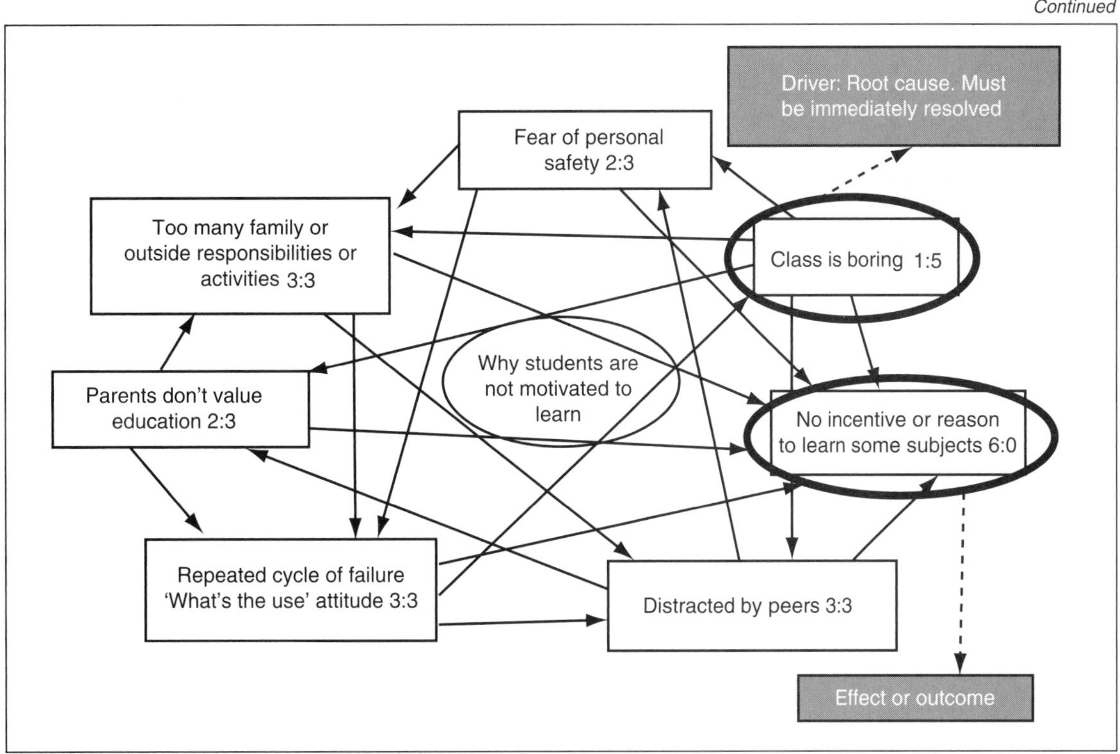

Design of Noninstructional Classroom Processes

Remember in Chapter 2, we discussed Rules versus Procedures? It is time to take another look at procedures, which is another name for a process. Remember, *a process is a series of steps taken to achieve a task.* Examples of classroom procedures include start of class, homework, transition from one activity to another, permission to use the lavatory, and make-up tests. When a standardized process is not used, there is great variation in the activities' effectiveness and efficiency. The object here is to improve both. Effective processes yield the desired results. Efficient processes yield the desired results in a shorter amount of time. Your goal ought to be to design classroom management processes such that are both effective and efficient. Time spent on the design of these processes will reduce wasted time and therefore ultimately yield more instructional time.

Notice that in Figure 4.14 we have highlighted Student as Worker Focus (Category 5) as well as Process Management (Category 6). This is because students are workers in the system traditionally designed by teachers, but in a Baldrige-based quality classroom they become partners with teachers to help improve the key classroom processes.

Each key classroom process can be flowcharted. Figure 4.15 provides some suggestions for noninstructional processes. Practice making a flow chart of one noninstructional process on page 132. The design of noninstructional processes contains the same essential components as the instructional design process, but they are stated somewhat differently. Following is our recommended approach, but this, like everything is this book, ought to be viewed in the context you described when completing your profile in Chapter 1.

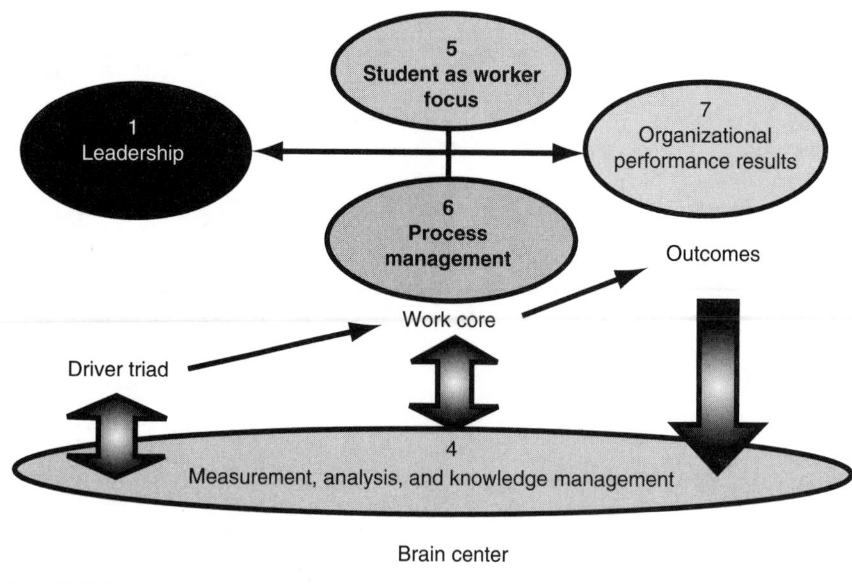

Figure 4.14 Link between Work Core and results.

Directions: Complete the following chart for one noninstructional process.

One Approach to Designing Noninstructional Processes

Process	Requirements	Success measure(s)	Quality standards	Control strategies what, who, how often
Example Start of Class	• Minimize lost instructional time • Start the day on a positive note	• Time it takes for all students to be ready to learn	• 10 seconds or less after bell rings • Students receive training on process	• Flow chart posted in room • Timed by teacher or designee each day for 1 month; thereafter 2 times a week for 2 months • Run chart of time posted in class
Complete this chart for one noninstructional classroom process				
Process	**Requirements**	**Success measure(s)**	**Quality standards**	**Control strategies what, who, how often**

Pre-K, kindergarten SPED (contained)	Elementary grades	Middle or high school
School day Lavatory use Transitions to recess, special classes End of day process Transition from one subject to another Moving through school to cafeteria or playground	School day Transitions to recess, special classes End-of-day process Transition from one subject to another Moving through school to cafeteria or playground Homework Lunch selection/payments for field trips, etc. Make-up work or tests due to absence	Start of class End of class process Homework Make-up work or tests due to absence Attendance and tardy
Other	**Other**	**Other**
Physical education	**Music**	**Art**
Start of class End of class Safety procedures Getting/putting away equipment Attendance and tardy	Start of class Transition back to class (elementary) End of class (middle/high school) Getting out and putting away music Handling of instruments Attendance and tardy	Start of class End of class Getting out and putting away supplies Safety procedures Cleaning up work area Attendance and tardy
Other	**Other**	**Other**
Shop	**Lab classes**	**Media centers/labs**
Start of class End of class Safety procedures Getting/putting away materials Attendance and tardy Getting/putting away supplies and equipment Project work Make-up work due to absences	Safety procedures Getting/putting away equipment Setting up experiments Attendance and tardy Make-up work due to absences	Safety procedures Getting/putting away materials Turning on/off computers Saving files and projects Checking out books, software, videos, etc.
Other	**Other**	**Other**

Figure 4.15 Examples of noninstructional classroom processes.

Directions: Flow chart one noninstructional process for your class.

ACTIVITY: ***Reduce transition time in an early learner classroom.***

The following is an example of one way to reduce transition times in a pre-K, kindergarten, or first-grade class. Create and hang process flow charts to optimize instructional time and minimize classroom management problems.

Materials needed:

- Heavyweight poster board in several colors
- Paper clips
- Lightweight ribbon
- Markers
- Brass brackets (optional)
- Scissors
- Ruler
- Paper clock faces (optional)

Steps:

1. Draw each process step on different colored sheets of heavy poster board. The optimal size is no larger than 12 inches long; otherwise, the poster board may not support its weight.
2. Arrange the steps in correct order.
3. Open the paper clips to create an "S" hook and puncture a hole in the top and bottom of each poster board step.
4. Thread the "S" hook through one hole and close it; then thread the bottom half through the next process step. Close the ends.
5. Continue hooking process steps together.
6. If there is a feedback loop, gently thread a piece of ribbon through the side of the decision diamond and back to the step that indicates where to regroup. Gently tie the ribbon on the edge of that step.
7. Poke a hole in the first process step with a heavy paper clip and use that to hang the flow chart in the classroom.

To help nonreaders:

1. Color-code the process steps with the activity. For example, yellow indicates reading, orange indicates math, green indicates recess, and so on.
2. To help students become self-directed, glue a small round clock face to each side of the process step. Use brackets to "set the clock" for start and stop times.

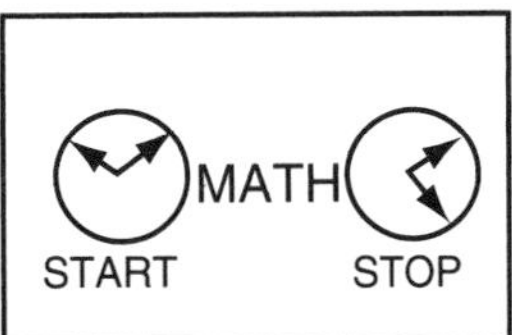

3. Hook the steps together as described, using paper clips.
4. Take photos and/or draw pictures of the activity on the poster board at each step.

Helpful tips:

- Use one Post-it note per process step and arrange the steps in correct order before finalizing the flow chart.
- Ask the students to move through the process steps as they are arranged to make certain no steps are left out and that the order makes sense.
- When everyone agrees on the process, have each student copy it, post it prominently in the room, and measure as noted in your design.
- Chart the results.
- After the first month, review the results to see if this process is meeting requirements and working as designed. If it is, continue to measure and monitor. If not, then follow these directions:
  - Circle the "sticky points"—those that cause the process to break down.
  - Work with students to analyze the root cause of the problem.
  - Come up with improvement ideas; select one and redraw the process flow chart.
  - Measure and monitor the new "best practice" process and regularly review the results.

Figure 4.16 provides you with a graphical picture of what's involved in planning to build quality into your processes. Once you've established the process, it becomes necessary to rotate Plan-Do-Study-Act if you hope to remove barriers and gain performance excellence.

Summary

This chapter has focused on designing effective and efficient instructional processes for your students. You can avoid rework by using Quality Factors and operational definitions and understanding the importance of feedback tools that allow you to make midcourse corrections. Capturing student feedback on satisfaction is necessary but not sufficient to ensure the instructional process is improved to yield better results. Students may feel satisfied, but if the results are not better, the process is still not effective.

As you reflect on your learning, gain courage from the fact that now, more than ever, educators need to become role models for change. This is important because children who begin school today will have to change careers at least seven times during their working lifespan. Every day we read about jobs lost and new career fields opening up, but these require people to shift gears and learn new skills. For those who won't change, the future is bleak.

You have learned how to design noninstructional processes to reduce wasted time, thus making your system more efficient and allowing more instructional time. Teachers around the country who use this model tell us consistently that for every minute spent learning and teaching their students about Quality, they gain 10 minutes of instructional time. Yes, there is additional time spent upfront learning the process, but the payoff at the end is well worth it.

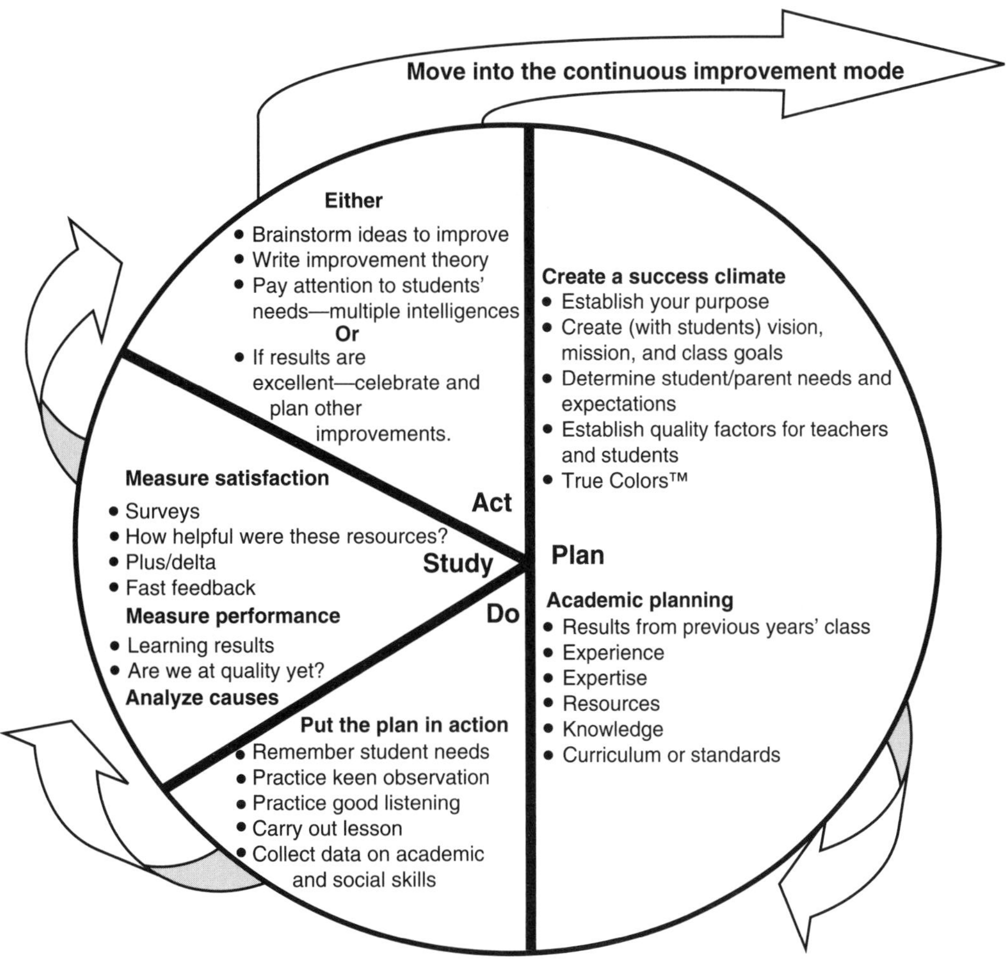
Move into the continuous improvement mode
Either
• Brainstorm ideas to improve
• Write improvement theory
• Pay attention to students' needs—multiple intelligences
Or
• If results are excellent—celebrate and plan other improvements.
Act
Create a success climate
• Establish your purpose
• Create (with students) vision, mission, and class goals
• Determine student/parent needs and expectations
• Establish quality factors for teachers and students
• True Colors™
Plan
Academic planning
• Results from previous years' class
• Experience
• Expertise
• Resources
• Knowledge
• Curriculum or standards
Measure satisfaction
• Surveys
• How helpful were these resources?
• Plus/delta
• Fast feedback
Measure performance
• Learning results
• Are we at quality yet?
Analyze causes
Study
Do
Put the plan in action
• Remember student needs
• Practice keen observation
• Practice good listening
• Carry out lesson
• Collect data on academic and social skills

Figure 4.16 PDSA cycle to build in quality.

Reflections

5

MAKE MIDCOURSE CORRECTIONS TO INSTRUCTIONAL PROCESSES

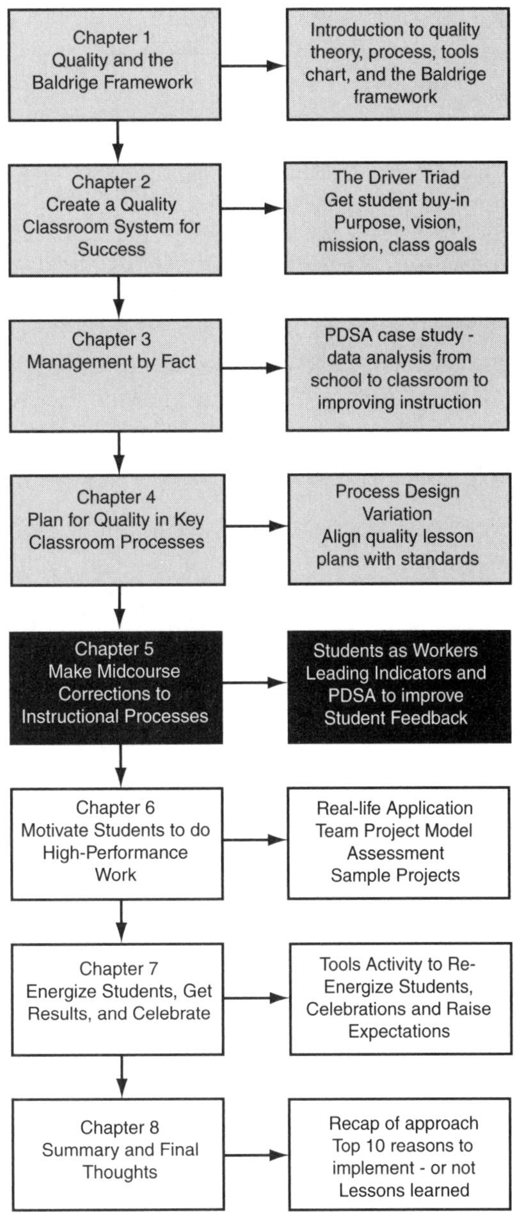

Conversation with the Teacher

Perhaps you are concerned that going through the formal Plan-Do-Study-Act cycle as described in Chapter 2 is overwhelming and not feasible for you on a regular basis, especially because you have a curriculum to cover and worry about the amount of time it takes away from instruction. It is not unusual to have these feelings, but in this chapter we pose a more informal approach that is literally going to save you instructional time and not overwhelm you or the students. In fact, this approach uses a different set of leading indicators to help you predict better end results, taking much of the worry out of whether or not your students will gain the skills they need for success. Of course, you have to be brave and make the decision to follow the plan on a regular basis regardless of the curriculum.

It concerns us that so many teachers feel they have to shoulder the burden of getting the students from here to there by themselves and so they rely heavily on the textbook companies, which put together nice, neat packages that include books, test questions, activities, and often software and transparencies "guaranteed to work." In fact, "canned," structured curricular programs sometimes lead teachers to feel disempowered to do anything but follow the script. After all, the textbook companies guarantee results if you follow the steps. Teachers cannot expect a textbook program to do all the work, just as students cannot expect teachers to do all the work. This is not an indictment of such programs, because they do work for some students. However, we firmly believe that unless teachers engage in systems thinking and make changes based on data and feedback from students, some students will always be left behind.

System change involves doing things differently; Baldrige-based quality classrooms are not scripted. Personal and organizational learning is never neat or simple and sometimes not even comfortable. Yet, the lives of our students depend on the quality of the educational experience they have, and that means we have a moral obligation to every child to let go of the need for control and engage them as copartners in this venture. As you may have guessed, it starts with you, the leader.

This chapter is all about change. We have made it as practical and simple as possible, and we believe, based on the experiences of teachers who have implemented this approach, that you have almost nothing to lose and everything to gain.

In this chapter you will learn:

- To identify key predictors (leading indicators) of success in your content area
- To use student feedback to change instructional processes
- To measure and chart class progress and get students to help make changes to the instructional process so they can succeed
- To wrap the class vision, goals, and principles of a Quality classroom around an informal Plan-Do-Study-Act cycle

Students as Workers in Learning-Centered Classrooms

Figure 5.1 reminds us that students are workers in the classroom. They are the ones who must thrive and produce in the system traditionally created by their teachers. It is interesting to note, but not unusual, that systems are created initially to reflect the philosophy and comfort level of the leader. As time goes on, typically leaders add more requirements or delete things that they perceive to be non–value added. If you had any doubt, think about the contract your bargaining unit has with the district. When every contractual detail is dictated, it makes you, the worker, feel disempowered. It can even change your mind-set about your work and working relationships. You know how it feels. Creative energy is often lost, and for many teachers what may have once been a calling is now considered a job. Can you imagine how students feel when the system in which they must work and function operates within a similar paradigm, especially when more rules are added in response to the actions of a few?

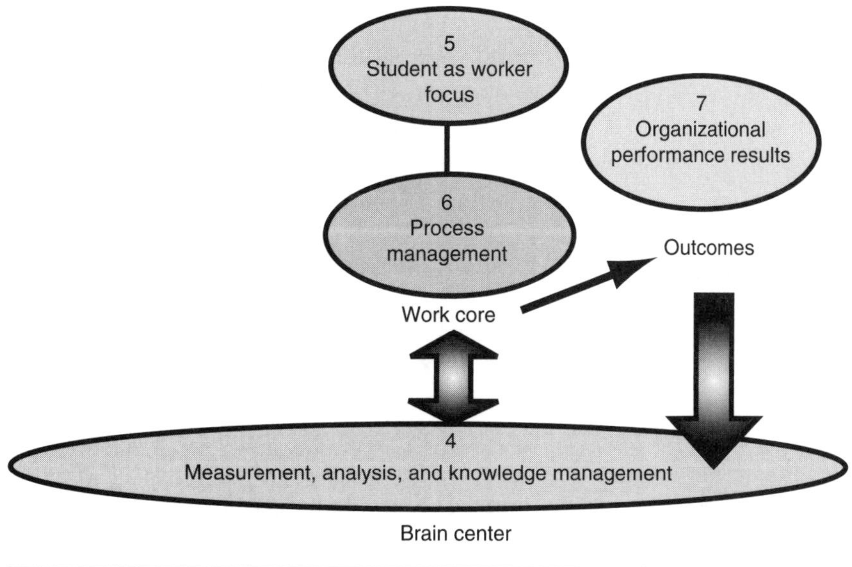

Figure 5.1 Brain center informs the Work Core to produce results.

Teachers sometimes don't realize that what they want and need are the same things that students want and need to thrive in school. As Dr. William Glasser, psychiatrist and author of *The Quality School*, points out, five basic human needs form the basis for all behavior. They are love/belonging, freedom, fun, power, and survival.

Directions: Think about your classroom system. In what ways have you organized the classroom to provide students with all these needs? Does it matter? In what ways have you altered your classroom system (review the classroom system diagram in Chapter 1) over the past few years to accommodate diverse student needs? Complete the chart.

The five basic human needs				
Love/belonging	**Freedom**	**Fun**	**Power**	**Survival**
Example: We celebrate birthdays.	Example: Students can choose the centers they want to go to first.	Example: We have 5 minutes of free discussion on Fridays.	Example: Students share leadership roles.	Example: I do not allow bullying among students.

Learning Styles and Closing the Achievement Gap

We all know about the achievement gap between students from ethnically diverse backgrounds and lower socioeconomic families and students who come from higher socioeconomic families. It should come as no surprise that BBQ classrooms confront this issue immediately through creating a climate for success as described in Chapter 2. Teachers in BBQ classrooms also address these issues directly by (1) analyzing results from previous and current classes by subgroup and (2) seeking feedback from students to make midcourse corrections in the instructional process. It is the latter that provides teachers the most hope for predicting the learning success of students.

We all have our own learning styles or our own strategies for learning that govern how we approach new projects, how we increase our capabilities, and whether we find it difficult or easy to work in a team situation. Getting a good mix of learning styles can be critical to individual and class long-term success. As a teacher-leader, you too have a preferred teaching style, and as noted earlier, most teachers set up their classroom system in their preferred teaching style. Fortunately, most schools have provided staff development over the last several decades that help teachers be aware of the different learning styles of their students, but how *individual* learning styles are accommodated in the classroom may not be fully understood.

For example, the different cultures that are represented across America in today's classroom might include children with ethnic backgrounds of African American, Hispanic, Native American, or Asian–Pacific Islander. Florida schools are seeing large numbers of students arrive from Central America and the Caribbean, and Wisconsin schools are receiving large numbers of Hmong students. Each of these cultures influences how children learn. Ronald Takaki, author of *A Different Mirror: A History of Multicultural America* (Little, Brown, 1993) points out that most of today's immigrants come from Asia and Latin America. In fact, over 80% of all immigrants have been arriving from these two regions, adding to America's racial diversity—a reality charged with consequences for our nation's workforce. These statistics are still holding through 2004.

The necessity of addressing these cultural differences is no more apparent than in the high school graduation rates for Hispanics, which are at about 65%. The U.S. Census Bureau predicts that by 2010,

Hispanics will be the majority minority and will soon be the majority of all Americans. Teachers *must* pay attention to these data. Research done by Darlene Fierro ("Is There A Difference in Learning Style Among Cultures?", ERIC, 1997) indicates that although learning styles are innate, they also reflect the cultural values and norms. This research supports the suggestion that most Hispanics and many other cultural groups learn best by body/kinesthetic and musical/rhythmic approaches. This is a key opportunity for BBQ teachers that cannot be ignored. All children and youth deserve and have a right to a share of the American dream, yet without an adequate education, it is highly unlikely to happen. BBQ classrooms can lead the change and make certain that the learning needs of every student are met.

Bette Wilson, recently retired director of the Multi-Cultural Education Department and Resource Center of Oak Park Public Schools in Oak Park, Illinois, points out that teachers must discover for themselves the cultural barriers that may keep all students from learning. She says, for example, that although many African American children tend to learn kinesthetically and visually, others may have a different learning style. The only way to find out is to ask, "How would you like to learn? What suggestions do you have for ways to learn this material that would be 'fun and interesting' so that we could all learn faster and we'd be able to remember?"

> *Caution to teachers: If you aren't prepared to make changes based on student feedback, don't ask.*
>
> *All students need to be heard. This is why a systematic process is necessary.*

It should not surprise anyone that students with learning styles most similar to a teacher's preferred teaching style are typically the most successful. It is for this very reason that BBQ teachers realize the absolute need to get feedback from *all* students. Those who act out, those with limited English skills, those with learning disabilities all have needs that may not be met by the current instructional approach.

The WIIFM (what's in it for me?) for teachers:

- Fewer discipline issues
- More students on-task
- Excitement as lightbulbs go off in students' heads
- Learning results improve, creating *less rework and stress*

The WIIFM for students is:

- Learning becomes fun
- Learning has more meaning
- Success breeds success
- Ultimately, with repeated cycles of success, self-esteem rises

OPPORTUNITY Teachers in urban, suburban, and rural settings must also face the realities of children in the classroom who come from poverty. Forty-plus years ago Michael Harrington exposed the unpleasant facts of poverty in the United States in his book *The Other America.* The scandal persists, making the book as significant now as it was on the day of its publication. Too often educators shake their heads, saying, "It all begins in the home. We simply can't teach those kids." Your classroom may represent the only safe and "normal" place for some children. You have the key opportunity to reach out and offer the American dream in spite of the home circumstances, whatever they may be. Research has proven over the years that if a child has only two adults throughout the years of school who believe in the child when the child doesn't believe in himself or herself, success can follow. Never underestimate the ability of a child to flourish when his/her learning needs are met in school.

Wilson recommends that you consider the following strategies in a diverse classroom:

- The teacher's perceptions of these students have the greatest influence on their performance. *(See "inputs" on the Classroom System Diagram in Chapter 1.)*
- Teachers need to take steps to learn and understand the diverse cultures in their classroom and integrate a part of the culture into the curriculum. *(See Chapter 2.)*
- Active learning and team activities are successful with all students whereas classrooms with a great deal of "sitting time" may pose a problem. *(See suggestions in this chapter and Chapter 6.)*
- Appreciate the culture-specific vernacular English (that is, Ebonics or pidgin English); at the same time help these students achieve the standards, through the establishment of Quality Factors for writing and speaking English. Celebrate all cultures while emphasizing the need for excellent speaking, writing, and reading skills in English. The future belongs to those who can communicate in standard English. *(See Chapter 4.)*

Directions: Reflect upon the following and jot down your honest responses as you model the two principles of a BBQ classroom (*I am response-able for the success of the group, which translates to my responsiblity for my own learning.*)

Challenge your own perceptions about race, gender, culture, and so on. How do these perceptions play out in the learning experiences you provide students?

____

____

____

____

____

____

Think of a student in your classroom who is having difficulty learning. Reframe your perceptions of that student's behavior or attitude.

____

____

____

Don't ask, "How smart is this child?" Instead ask, "How is this child smart?" Listen and learn from the responses each child makes to the question you pose about how they want to learn.

____

____

____

Find "it." ("It" is that special something that lives in every child.) Listen, observe, and learn from each student's behavior, questions, and participation in learning activities.

____

____

____

Help the child see himself or herself in the future. As we stated earlier, the number one issue for at-risk students is "no hope for the future."

____

____

____

If you need resources for some excellent learning style inventories, we can refer you to The Learning Style Inventory developed by David Kolb (see his website). This simple, 12-question inventory asks you to describe your learning habits directly and is recommended in Peter Senge's *The Fifth Discipline Field Book* (see Recommended Reading). Our favorite for the classroom is True Colors™ (see Interesting Programs in the Recommended Reading list). This is an adaptation of the Meyers-Briggs. It is a simple way for students and teachers to identify their predominant personality or character traits that affect all behavior and also gives teachers insights into how students learn. This is also a fun and insightful way for students and teachers to learn more about each other. The Multiple Intelligences Tool Box on page 93 in Chapter 3 is an excellent way to address varied learning styles in your classroom.

Work Systems

Student as Worker (Baldrige Category 5) asks how students in your class are organized to do their work. In what ways do you expect and allow students to model the two principles of a Baldrige-based quality classroom? These principles go to the heart of student involvement and internal motivation. They are also directly related to the human needs of freedom, power, love/belonging, survival, and even fun. The point is that you can encourage these two principles by the way you organize the classroom. This describes the work core (Figure 5.2).

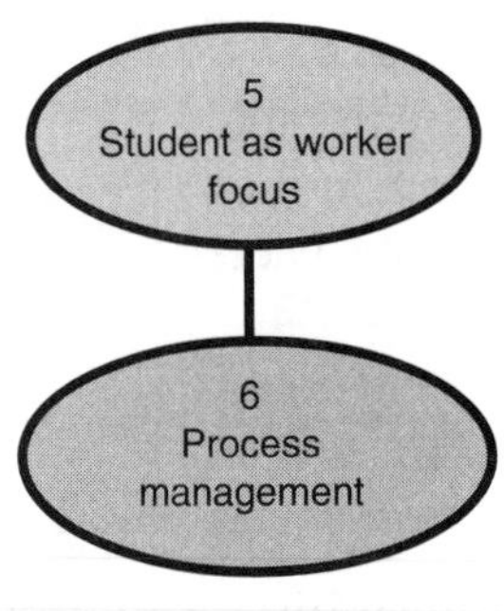

Figure 5.2 The Work Core.

Is there a balance of how students are organized, and are they sometimes in groups, sometimes required to work independently? Work systems should align with the class vision and mission. There is a legitimate expectation that class goals will be met because of the alignment and integration of all aspects of the class.

I am responsible for my own learning.

I am response-able to the success of the group.

For example, survival into adulthood requires students to learn leadership skills, work successfully and productively with diverse groups to complete projects, begin and finish independent projects, and do all this within a given amount of time. Additionally, students must learn how to analyze situations and problems and come up with solutions that resolve/dissolve problems. They need to be able to apply these lessons to their daily lives and they need to practice working in these ways from kindergarten through the rest of their schooling.

Directions: Review the following examples of classroom work systems. Write in the approximate percentage of time your class resembles these descriptors on the chart. Are your work systems reflective of a teacher orientation or a facilitator of learning orientation?

- ☐ Individual desks are in neat rows. Students do most work at their desks independently, engage in class discussion, and participate in an occasional group activity.
- ☐ The class is arranged with tables for four to six students. Students do some independent work but are free to help each other some of the time. Cooperative learning group activities are used some of the time.
- ☐ The class is fluid with tables, but tables can be moved to suit the activity underway. There is a mixture of independent work and group work.

Continued

Continued

☐	• The classroom is fluid with tables. Student groups are free to work in the media center, in the computer lab, in the classroom, and sometimes in the hall to accomplish team tasks. Everyone knows and respects the expected behaviors, and it is rare for the teacher to get complaints about his/her students from others in the building. Students are self-starters. They do not need the teacher to start working.
☐	• Students all have responsibilities to teach and/or tutor younger students who are struggling readers, writers, or mathematicians. This includes those who may struggle themselves. By having the responsibility for teaching other, younger students, everyone improves. The older students are responsible for selecting appropriate reading materials and coming up with lesson plans and vocabulary lists for the younger students they teach. Bonds between older and younger students are formed. Respect grows and everyone benefits.
☐	• Students organize and carry out community service projects that are important to citizen groups and the community. This is a requirement at each grade level starting in first grade.

Learning-Centered Education

In the 2004 Baldrige Education Criteria booklet, a learning-centered education is described this way: "In order to develop the fullest potential of all students, education organizations need to afford them opportunities to pursue a variety of avenues to success. Learning-centered education supports this goal by placing the focus of education on learning and the real needs of students. . . . Most analysts conclude that to prepare students for this work environment, education organizations of all types need to focus more on students' active learning and on the development of problem-solving skills. . . . Key characteristics of learning-centered education include the following:

- High developmental expectations and standards are set for all students.
- Faculty understand that students may learn in different ways and at different rates.
- A primary emphasis on active learning is provided.
- Formative assessment is used to measure learning early in the learning process and to tailor learning experiences to individual needs and learning styles.
- Summative assessment is used to measure progress against key, relevant, external standards and norms regarding what students should know and should be able to do.
- Students and families are assisted in using self-assessment to chart progress and to clarify goals and gaps.
- There is a focus on key transitions such as school-to-school and school-to-work.

Transform the Instructional Process to Reach the Vision and Goals

We have already established that students are workers in the classroom and that those closest to the work are in the best position to provide improvement suggestions. Instruction is the most critical key process in any classroom, yet many teachers resist the idea of asking students to help identify problems, let alone make suggestions for improving his/her instructional approach. It's ironic that educators value and "teach" critical thinking skills but may resist when it comes to improving the classroom. This may be one of the greatest barriers facing students, yet many teachers fear anarchy and resist facing the truth. We (teachers) do *not* know all the answers about why students aren't learning. We make many assumptions, spend a great deal of time crafting unit and lesson plans, and then are disappointed or frustrated if/when all the students don't show enthusiasm for learning. That is precisely the point. Teachers have typically done most of the work, while students expect teachers to "learn me." That is, students are passive and expect teachers to open their skulls and pour in all knowledge.

This has to change for several reasons. One, we cannot afford teachers burning out and leaving the profession. Two, students cannot afford to go through the first 16 or so years of their lives with others making nearly all decisions for them. Inevitably this leads to teenagers who are unable to handle real-life problems and who make poor choices that often lead to disastrous results. Figure 5.3 reveals how the balance of power shifts from a traditional classroom to a BBQ classroom.

Traditional	BBQ
Teacher is the all-knowing expert, sets all rules, plans, directs, and evaluates students. There is one-way communication with students and parents. Teacher makes all the decisions.	Teacher brings expertise on standards, subject area knowledge, and assessment and practices two-way communication and leadership. Teacher engages students to help make decisions about things that most affect them.
Students are passive learners. Some are reluctant; some are disengaged. Many students take no pride in workmanship and don't care much about what kind of work they do or how much they learn.	Students are active learners and engaged in helping each other and the teacher improve the learning activities so they can learn. Many students take great pride in workmanship and care about learning because it is tied to real-life situations.

Figure 5.3 Balance of power shift.

Begin with the end in mind and become comfortable with letting go of the need to control every aspect of the classroom. *The only exception to this is where student safety is concerned. Never, ever compromise student safety. If a student acts out in a violent way, immediately act to protect the other students. It is not time to collect data for problem solving. After the incident has been addressed, however, go back and analyze what caused the situation to happen in the first place. Always be prepared to ask, "Is there a system problem here?"*

OPPORTUNITY

We remind you that we said to make decisions about *how* students will learn, not *what* they will learn. School districts generally decide the *what* question, but teachers are generally given wide latitude and through lesson planning make most decisions about *how* students learn. This is another key opportunity that often makes the difference between how much is learned, who learns, who is actively engaged, and whether any students are left behind.

Success in unlocking the mystery of why so many students are not fully engaged in learning is what makes the difference in being able to predict how well students will perform on any district, state, or national test, and more importantly how easily they are able to apply their knowledge to different situations. With high-stakes testing a reality in our schools, teachers often feel too stressed to step back and let students assist them in understanding their needs and interests. The sad thing is that this stress keeps teachers from feeling free to take risks that require engaging students in determining *how* they will learn, yet this is exactly what is needed.

When schools and school districts require teachers to provide lockstep weekly lesson plans and unit plans, they rob teachers of the opportunity to make midcourse corrections based on feedback from students. This is a pity because such feedback is essential to student and teacher success.

Leading Indicators as Key Predictors of Success

Now is the time to identify the leading indicators (key predictors of success) for your content. For example, the leading indicators of reading are phonemic awareness, phonemes, vocabulary, comprehension, and fluency. In fact, a leading indicator of any subject is vocabulary. That is, we could predict greater student success if students knew and understood the meaning of all key vocabulary words for any content. It doesn't matter what you teach!

OPPORTUNITY

Another of the key opportunities is to establish a plan to regularly measure at least one leading indicator per subject or course taught. Since vocabulary is one of the leading, if not the most indicative key predictors of success in any content area, we suggest that you identify the 100 most important words that would give students an understanding of the concepts they must know when they leave your class. For kindergarten and first-grade teachers, the Dolch sight words would be helpful. For elementary and middle school teachers, there are the 1000 most frequently used words in the English language, for example (see these websites listed among the references). While mastery of vocabulary will not guarantee success in application of any subject, without this knowledge, you can be sure of failure. Students who do not understand math vocabulary, for example, will not be able to solve word problems and you know already the high the cost of rework each year because students come to class without basic knowledge.

Directions: Use the chart on page 148 to list the 100 most important words for your subject area. You can define them later, once the list is completed. (Elementary teachers begin by identifying words for one subject.)

In our training sessions, we use a book by Boye De Mente, *Instant Japanese: Everything You Need in 100 Key Words* (Tuttle, 2003), to make this point. Quoting the author, "This handy guide is designed to show how a very small vocabulary is enough to quickly and fluently communicate over 1,000 ideas in Japanese." English is not that simple, but this example does make a powerful statement of the importance of vocabulary and its use as a leading indicator of future success.

Our Recommended Approach—PDSA for Agility in the Instructional Process to Predict Success

Before school or the new semester starts, prepare several quiz formats for each problem, word, or concept. This will take time, but it will be invaluable as the semester and year progress. For example, you might have three formats for each numbered item—(a) define the word, (b) spell the word, and (c) multiple choice from different definitions. Then, as the school year progresses, you'll already have the quizzes prepared.

During the first day of school, pass this numbered vocabulary list out to students, along with definitions, and provide a list for parents as well. On a large piece of poster board, write the numbered list and post it prominently in the classroom, but it in a way that the list can be turned over on quiz days. Use this list to guide your instruction for the semester or year.

Key vocabulary words ____________ (subject)

1.	26.	51.	76.
2.	27.	52.	77.
3.	28.	53.	78.
4.	29.	54.	79.
5.	30.	55.	80.
6.	31.	56.	81.
7.	32.	57.	82.
8.	33.	58.	83.
9.	34.	59.	84.
10.	35.	60.	85.
11.	36.	61.	86.
12.	37.	62.	87.
13.	38.	63.	88.
14.	39.	64.	89.
15.	40.	65.	90.
16.	41.	66.	91.
17.	42.	67.	92.
18.	43.	68.	93.
19.	44.	69.	94.
20.	45.	70.	95.
21.	46.	71.	96.
22.	47.	72.	97.
23.	48.	73.	98.
24.	49.	74.	99.
25.	50.	75.	100.

Each week, you'll quiz the students on *a random sample of the square root* of the list. You may decide you want to chunk the list into things to be learned each marking period. For example, if you don't chunk the list, each weekly quiz would be 10 items. This is the square root of 100. You may choose to chunk the words by marking period, which would mean lesson plans focus on learning those words and concepts associated with them. If you chunk the list into four marking periods, each with 25 words, then you'd be quizzing five items the first marking period, seven the second marking period (includes the first 50 words), and so on.

Determine what day and time to give the quiz and stick to that decision. If there is no school scheduled for quiz day, or if an assembly is planned, then there is no quiz for that week. Avoid the temptation to alter either day or time of the quiz. Remember, this is not a quiz students can study for because it is a random sample of the items. Instead, you are seeking information about the effectiveness of your instructional approach(es). It is *not* a shame-and-blame activity!

Plan Review the Plan section of Figure 5.4 for information needed to plan daily lessons and don't forget to include all that you have already learned about your students in your planning.

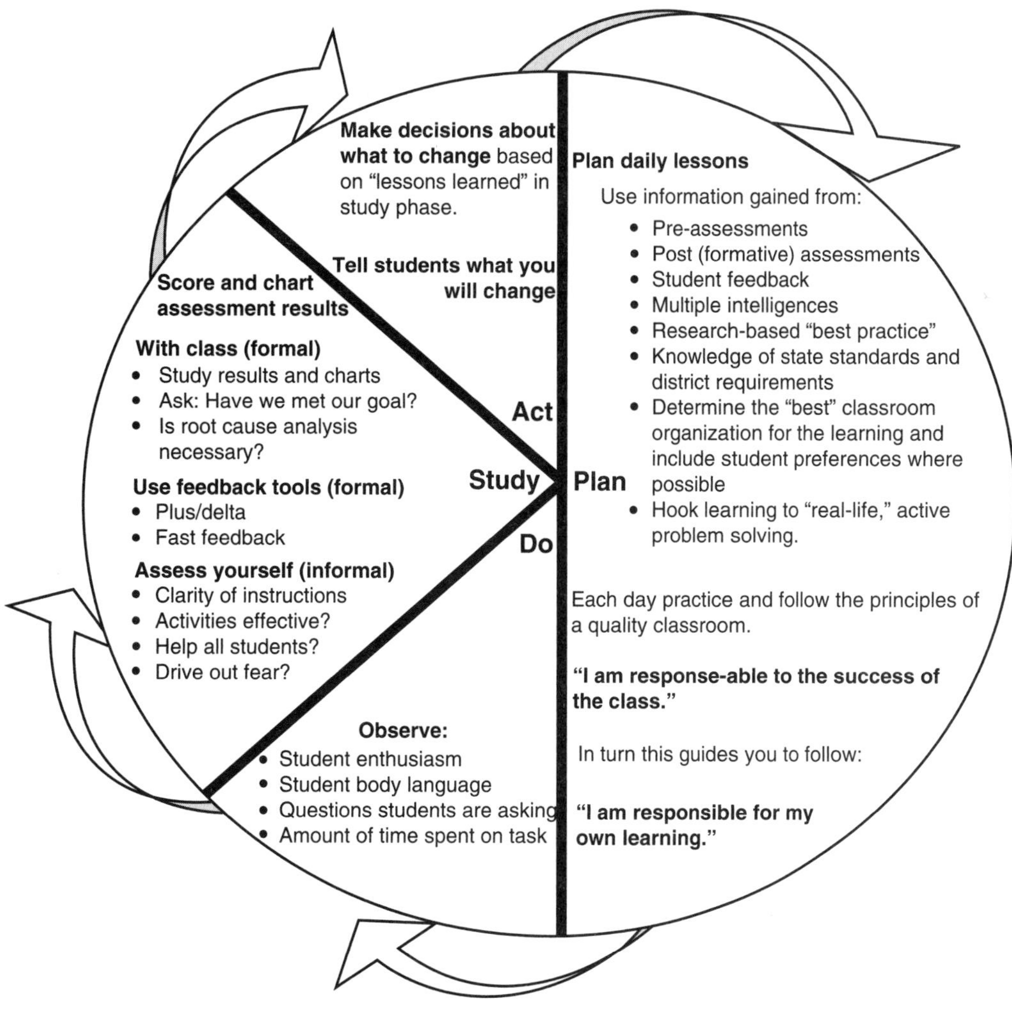

Figure 5.4 Informal PDSA for day-to-day operations.

Do

Carry out the lesson as planned. Observe how engaged students are and their enthusiasm for learning.

On quiz day, turn the numbered list over, and ask students to choose random numbers from a bag or hat with all the numbers in it. (Select different students each week, to ensure they do not accuse you of purposefully picking all the hard or easy ones. The numbers selected correspond to the words to be quizzed.) Mix the quiz format (from the original three previously developed) to reflect the different approaches used on the state standards test and/or other nationally normed tests. Be certain to note the date and format used for each item so as not to repeat the testing approach each time a certain word comes up. This is *not* teaching to the test, but helping students learn to respond to question formats with which they will be expected to become proficient.

Study

Ask students to exchange papers after the quiz and provide the correct answers. Peers, as coaches, are responsible for making corrections. When students receive their papers back, chart the data using a line graph and Method 2 as follows.

1. *Chart the results.* We suggest you make a large line graph on a piece of poster board or butcher paper and post it in the classroom. In the example, 10 items are tested each week (see Figure 5.5). Use Method 2, and follow the instructions for the line graph in Chapter 3, page 81.
2. *Check out the bandwidth of variation.* Remember the goal of BBQ classrooms is to improve effectiveness (how many have learned) and efficiency (how quickly) of all key processes, especially the instructional process. Review Figures 1.7 and 1.8 in Chapter 1. The bandwidth of variation in this example is from 2 to 10. In fact, 14 students scored 50% or below.

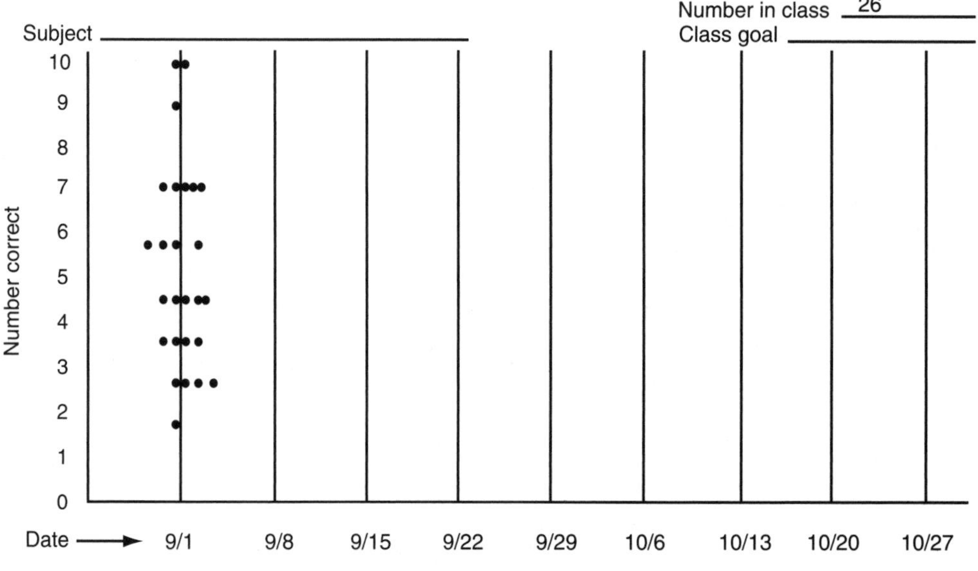

Figure 5.5 Line graph: weekly quiz grades for the class.

ACTIVITY: ***Use the same data and create a histogram.***

Directions: For your own information and to get a somewhat different view of the results, put these data into a histogram. Chunk the data from Figure 5.5 into these "classes" according to the number correct: one and two; three and four; five and six; seven and eight; nine and ten. See instructions for the histogram in Chapter 3, page 68.

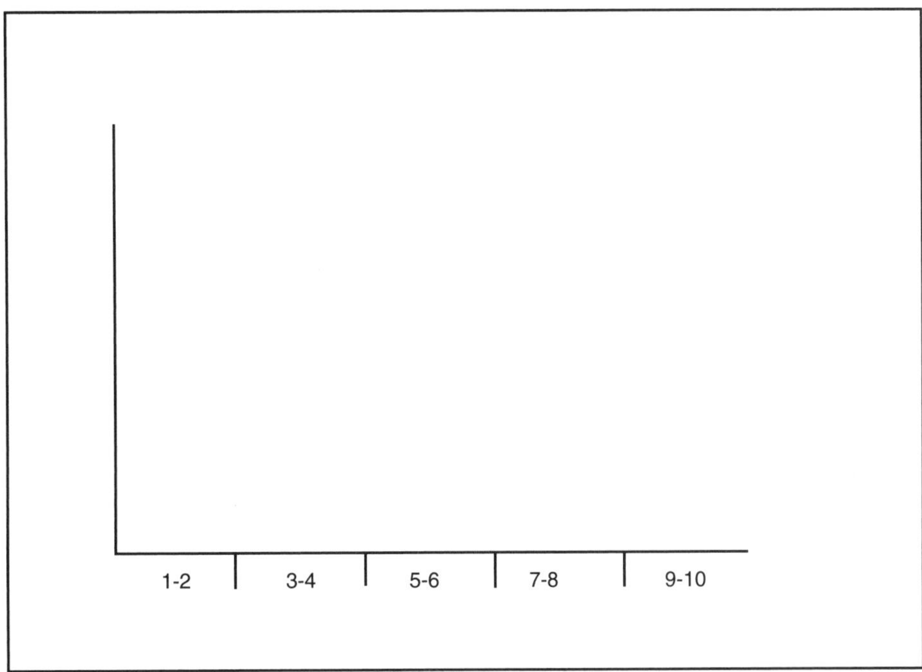

What do you see? Is this acceptable to you? This is the paradigm that must be broken if we are to succeed in eliminating the athletic model for education. A bell curve is not acceptable, as too many students will be left behind.

Teachers must remain optimistic and continuously instill hope into the class and maintain a firm belief that all students can meet the learning goals. Dr. Deming believed that faulty systems or processes cause 90% or more of all problems. It is not faulty students.

3. *Review results with students.* Ask, "Are we at quality yet?" (Meaning, have we met our class goal yet? See how important it is for you to have all students sign off on the goals? Without that step, some will not *care*.)

This is a key opportunity. Capture and use feedback from students about what kept them from learning as a routine part of postassessment to make changes and improve the instructional process.

4. *Remind students of the methods/approaches used during the previous week to learn the words.* Remember, you are only quizzing a random sample of the square root of the total. There may have been words that came up that had not been directly taught, but since you've given the students the list on the first week of school, have it posted in the room, and may have decided to chunk the list into topics covered during that marking period, all words can be fair game. Historical information regarding methods used to learn is very important and placing it on the chart is important to your improvement efforts. Take a look at Figure 5.6 below.

5. *Ask students to brainstorm how they would like to learn these words.* Once again, students may not be used to this approach and therefore may be reluctant at first to provide suggestions. This is your opportunity key. Review the Multiple Intelligences Toolbox on page 93 in Chapter 3. Often, when students don't learn, it is the result of a mismatch between teaching and learning styles.

If your students have trouble coming up with any ideas after 15–20 seconds, you might offer one suggestion from one of these three intelligences—body/kinesthetic, musical/rhythmic, or visual/spatial. It is the combination of these three in unison that allows students to learn more, learn faster, and remember it well. (The first realization I had of this premise is when my daughter took an art history class 15 years ago. Her teacher had the class create a song and choreograph a simple dance as he showed the slides of famous

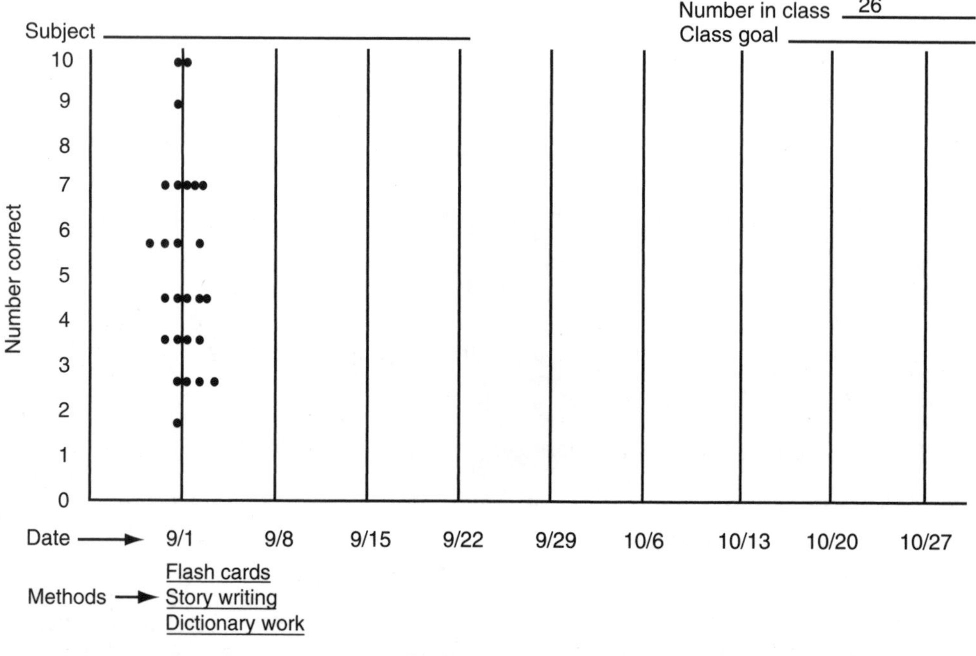

Figure 5.6 Line graph with historical information.

artists and examples of their work. Each day, the class sang and danced their way to learning art history. To this day she can still remember the song, dance, and artists, as well as key facts about their works.)

Write the brainstormed list on the board. Ask the class to multivote on the two approaches each feels will be *most beneficial to their learning* during the next week. See the instructions for multivoting in Chapter 2, page 41. Circle the top two responses.

> *Remember, this is not about you. It is about you being a facilitator of learning. It is about you being able to engage students as copartners, recognizing they are workers in the classroom system and therefore have many answers about why they cannot learn with the methods you have used. It is about having more students learn and therefore reach the learning goals set out by the class and required by the district or state.*

Act

6. *Commit to the improvement suggestions made by students.* Make a pact with the students that each day during the following week, they will have a portion of instructional time (say, 10 minutes) devoted to these two approaches. We are not suggesting you throw the baby out with the bath water and stop using all your methods. Instead, we ask you to make a commitment to listen, hear, and honor the students' requests. This approach accomplishes the following:
   - Builds trust between teacher and students.
   - Empowers students to have a say in the way they learn and therefore builds enthusiasm for learning and buy-in to the process.

ACTIVITY: What Does the Teacher Learn During This Process?

Directions: List all the ways this process benefits the teacher. As a facilitator of learning, and modeling the principle "I am response-able to the success of the class," what do you learn from using this process? How would you use the information gained beyond the two approaches the class votes to use the following week? Why is this important?

Rotate PDSA

7. *The following week, repeat the process, chart the new results, check to see if there has been any improvement, and again follow the approach of asking students what worked.* Be careful not to change approaches the students suggest on a whim. Make mental notes of all suggestions specific students make, as this gives you insights into how they learn. Incorporate these approaches into your teaching strategies even if the whole class has not voted to make them a priority. Under no circumstances would you continue to add new approaches without first taking some away; otherwise, there is no way to know which approaches work and which do not.
8. *After three weeks, if there is no significant improvement, it is not only important to seek feedback on how they would like to learn, but also to discover which of your methods is most helpful to the least helpful.* A more formal root-cause analysis may be required and you have to be willing to let go of methods that do not work.

> *Change for the sake of change equals tinkering with the system and will not yield sustained, improved results.*

Improve the Instructional Process for Conceptual Learning Activities

Here is one of the goals from the Japanese I class described on page 51 in Chapter 2:

We will prepare marketing materials in Japanese for products of U.S. companies.

For these types of learning experiences that embrace not only mastery of vocabulary, but also research, critical thinking skills, creativity, technology, writing and presentation skills, a different approach is required. Some teachers, like Jeff Burgard, a former science teacher in Redding, California, had his students create a rubric for what he called POWs (problems of the week). This was the approach used to cover all the key concepts students needed to learn. Other BBQ teachers, like Candace (Allen) Smith, a high school social studies teacher from Pueblo, Colorado, had students collaborate on defining Quality Factors (QFs) and then participate in evaluating the class's work. Candace's approach required students to continually raise the bar on expectations and this became a routine part of the evaluation process at the end of each assignment. Not only did QFs increase, but the operational definitions also became more precise. Students in her classes began to realize how unfairly they were evaluated when the operational definitions were not precise. You can read Candace's story on page 213 in Chapter 7.

Our preference is the Quality Factor approach over a static rubric because it sets the standard for everyone and does not allow students to squirm out of their responsibility to do high performance work. Of course, this approach works best if teachers allow students to go back, edit, or redo their work to make certain it meets the Quality Factors. In this way, all students can reach quality in their work and there are no winners and losers. Obviously, the decision about how often students can retake tests or refine products of learning activities is the teacher's, but you might consider negotiating this with students in the beginning and revisit that decision each marking period. The valuable lesson is, *teachers who refuse to accept schlock from their students get better work from all students and student learning improves.* Over time, those who previously got away with doing less than their best learn that it is better and easier to do it right the first time. This saves the students valuable time doing rework and saves the teacher valuable time from having to read and grade sloppy work. In the end, time saved means the teacher has more flexibility to extend the learning and celebrate success, as this surely indicates movement toward accomplishment of the goals and vision.

Useful Feedback Tools to Improve Instruction on a Daily or Weekly Basis

In addition to getting information from students about how they like to learn, it is necessary to seek more formal feedback systematically and regularly in-process to complete the PDSA cycle and make improvements to predict better results. The tools that measure perception most easily used in-process are the following:

- Fast Feedback
- Enthusiasm and Learning Chart
- Plus/Delta Chart

They are powerful tools to use and easy to learn, but be aware that use of the plus/delta chart in isolation may result in your responding to special cause rather than common cause variation. That is, you may be unaware of how many students have the same or similar issues reflected on the delta side of the chart. Likewise, you may be unaware of how many students agree with items on the plus side of the chart. It is never a good idea to make major changes based on limited data, such as that afforded by the plus/delta chart. However, this chart is made more powerful when used in combination with the Enthusiasm and Learning Chart, as shown in the example on page 158.

When you use the Enthusiasm and Learning Chart, you want most of the dots to be placed in the upper right quadrant on the chart. Some teachers suggest turning the chart around as students place their dots to reduce the halo effect or influence from one student to the others. Realize that this chart and the plus/delta chart are necessary but not sufficient to inform you about your system. Students may be very happy, and say they are learning a lot, but unless the results bear this out (hard data), you *must* go back to students for a root cause analysis. If this happens, you could combine the affinity diagram (to brainstorm causes) and then use the headers for a relations digraph learned in Chapter 4.

As we discussed in Chapter 4, every process exhibits some variation, and every process breaks down over time unless monitored regularly to hold the gains. For teachers, this means that once the instructional process is deemed effective and efficient as measured by student learning results and enthusiasm and satisfaction, there is a need to continue to collect data on the process regularly and systematically to monitor its continued effectiveness. Therefore, one approach to this is to use the Enthusiasm and Learning Chart throughout the school year. As soon as you see slippage and more dots going into the column "It was okay," as shown in Figure 5.7 on the next page, take action to understand why student enthusiasm is not being maintained. This does not require a formal root cause analysis at this point, but signals concern that continuing along the path without intervention may mean ultimately that students will not learn as much. (For instance, overuse of certain methods can and does lead to boredom.) At this point, you might go back to the brainstorm

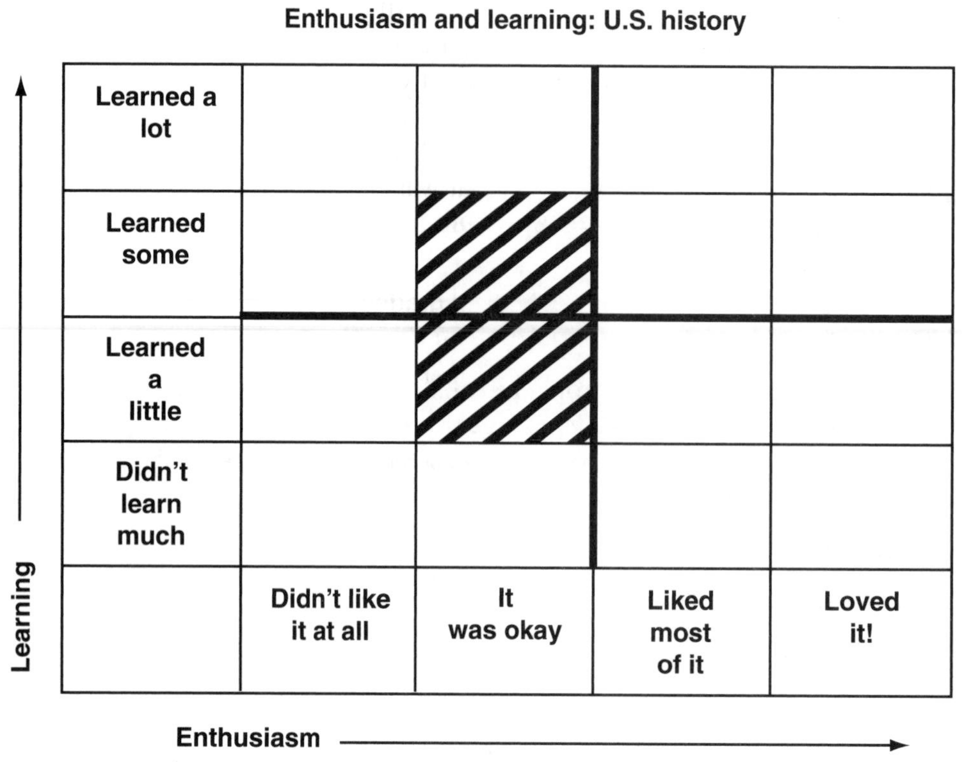

Enthusiasm and learning: U.S. history

Learning ↑				
Learned a lot				
Learned some				
Learned a little				
Didn't learn much				
	Didn't like it at all	It was okay	Liked most of it	Loved it!

Enthusiasm →

Figure 5.7 Example of undesirable pattern of data points.

activity we used earlier in this chapter as teachers can learn a great deal about student needs during that process. *When 10% or more of the class places their dot in the lower left quadrant, the issues must be addressed immediately. Teachers have everything to gain and almost nothing to lose by seeking help from students about how they like to learn.*

If you combine the Enthusiasm and Learning chart with a plus/delta chart, you gain actionable feedback (see the example on page 158–159). This makes both charts more valuable.

The benefit to this approach extends beyond learning to a reduction in discipline problems in the classroom. In fact, the more frequently you engage in these practices and respond to student feedback, the more trust levels will rise and students will demonstrate buy-in and commitment to the vision and goals. They will have a decreased need to act out or opt out. In the end, you will see a corresponding improvement in student learning results. These results will not be a fluke, but will be the direct result of process and system improvement. *This is the only way to get sustained improved results.* With so few instructional minutes in the school day/year, a teacher is wise to avail himself or herself of whatever timesavers are available.

Fast Feedback

Use fast feedback with older students. Begin by asking for their help and explain that this approach will consume no more than five seconds at the end of the class. Explain your desire to improve your teaching and how you need them to help. Put all the names into a box, bowl, or hat and each day select a random sample of the total in your class or a minimum of five names. These are the only students who will be completing the fast feedback form that day.

Prepare two or three questions that you think will give you information required to give insight into whether or not the students understood the material covered that day. Use the same items all semester, so word them generically to fit any content, but specific enough to give you actionable information. Daily collate the data and use a histogram to chart the responses to the questions and share it with the class the next day. If students respond with specific "muddy" points from the lesson (what was unclear), you know immediately what the start of the next day's lesson will be. Figure 5.8 is an example of the tool.

Fast feedback form: grades 3 and up

Instructions: Circle the number that best represents your thoughts on today's lesson.			
I understand the logic of today's problem or concept.			
1 Strongly agree	2 Agree	3 Somewhat disagree	4 Disagree
I could apply this logic (or concept) to another situation.			
1 Strongly agree	2 Agree	3 Somewhat disagree	4 Disagree
The "muddy" points about today's lesson were:			
The pace of this class is (circle one)	Too slow	Just right	Too fast
I'd like some additional help, please. (signed) ____________________			

Figure 5.8 Fast Feedback example.

Enthusiasm and Learning Chart

What

The Enthusiasm and Learning Chart gives feedback to the teacher about the relationship between student enthusiasm for learning and how much was learned. This provides an important means for teachers to gain input from students about what to change so they can learn more and enjoy it too.

How

The steps to creating an Enthusiasm and Learning Chart are:

1. Create a matrix like the one shown with the learning continuum along the left vertical and enthusiasm horizontally along the bottom.
2. At the end of each day, week, lesson, or unit, ask students to silently reflect on their learning and the activities they were engaged in to learn it.
3. Pass out colored dots or provide colored markers to the students. (If the chart is laminated, it can be used over and over throughout the school year.)
4. Each student will silently come to the chart—preferably without the teacher present to preserve anonymity—and put a dot or marker in the square that best represents his or her feelings about the classroom experience.

When

At the end of a day, week, lesson, or unit.

Continued

Continued

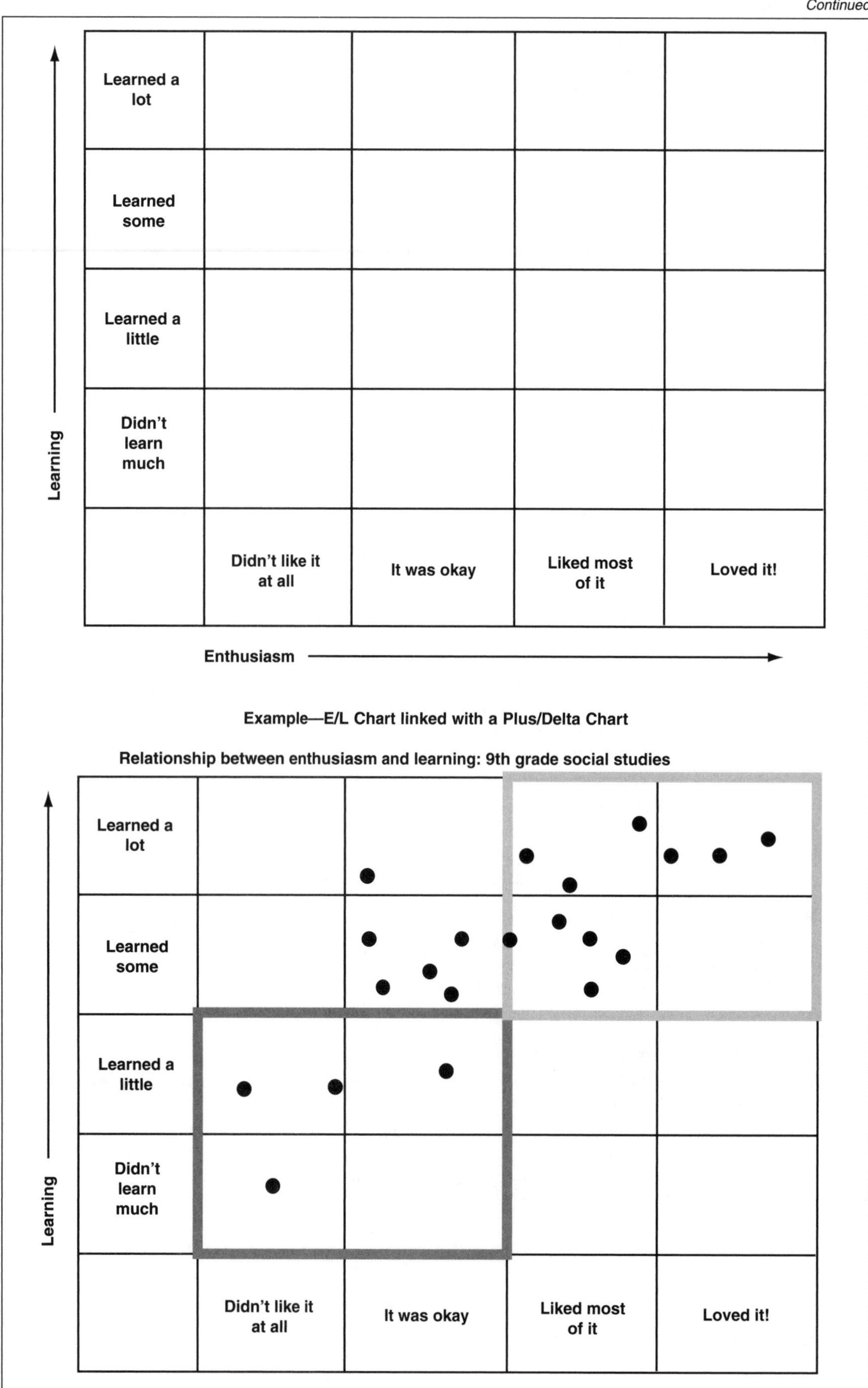
Learned a lot
Learned some
Learned a little
Didn't learn much
Didn't like it at all
It was okay
Liked most of it
Loved it!
Learning
Enthusiasm
Example—E/L Chart linked with a Plus/Delta Chart
Relationship between enthusiasm and learning: 9th grade social studies
Learned a lot
Learned some
Learned a little
Didn't learn much
Didn't like it at all
It was okay
Liked most of it
Loved it!
Learning
Enthusiasm

What helped you learn? What did you like? +	What kept you from learning? What is a better way to learn? Δ
I loved the experiments	I didn't feel like anyone listened to me
The way we were able to work with each other	Reading too hard
	Not enough time to finish everything
Neat video	Lectures were not interesting

Plus/Delta Chart

What

A Plus/Delta Chart is a simple feedback tool that can be used at the end of each day, unit, or after any lesson. It provides teachers, team leaders, and others with valuable information about how to improve.

How

1. Draw a vertical line in the middle of a piece of flip chart paper—or on the chalkboard.
2. Approximately 4 inches down from the top, draw a horizontal line across the paper.
3. In the upper left rectangle, draw a large "+" sign.
4. In the upper right rectangle, draw a large sign (the mathematical symbol for "change").
5. Explain your desire to gain feedback to improve the class, assignment, unit, test, meeting, and so forth.
6. *Wording is very important.* Say, "Please share with us what worked for you today; what was good about the day; perhaps an 'ah-ha' you had today; or maybe what you learned today. What was good about today?"
7. When all the good news is exhausted, go on with the deltas. "Please tell me what we can do differently tomorrow so we can all have a better day." Or, in the case of a Plus/Delta after a test you might say, "What could we do differently to prepare so that we could all do better on the test." Remind everyone this is about how to *change, and not what was done wrong.*
8. Give the group Post-it notes to write their comments. Ask them to write a "+" or at the top of the note and then one comment per note.
9. Or, write all ideas on the chart if the group is unable to write their own feedback.
10. Take each Delta into consideration for the following day, unit, and so forth. Let the students know how you've changed things in response to their requests for change. This will help build trust and student buy-in to the Quality effort.

When

- After completing any unit.
- The last three minutes at the end of the day.
- At least weekly in high school, at the end of each class period if operating on a block schedule.
- There is a need to determine issues students have after taking a test or completing a project.

Continued

Continued

Classroom Examples

Chorus—After the spring concert and listening to a tape of the performance

+	Δ
We enunciated well.	We need rhythm practice when we sing jazz and blues pieces.
The soprano solo was great.	The whole chorus can learn better ways to blend our voices.
The mood of the music came through.	We need to stop 'rustling' when we're not singing.
The audience was responsive.	Better breath control would help.
The melodies were carried well.	
The baritones hit 'that' note.	

Elementary class—at the end of the school day

+	Δ
We went outdoors for P.E.	We talk too much when we get excited.
The story lady was great.	Please don't yell at us.
We all know our times tables to 9 with no mistakes.	It takes too long to get ready for the buses.
Lunch was good today.	The way we choose who gets balls at recess is not fair.
We finished writing our stories.	The classroom is pretty dirty.
Getting our portfolios ready.	

Any class—after taking a practice standardized test

+	Δ
I finished all the items.	The time limit scares me and makes me 'freeze up'.
We all understood the math vocabulary words.	I get mixed up on the directions.
I liked the way we practiced word problems and also the problems with diagrams before taking this test. It helped.	We need to practice more often.

Summary

Again, we urge you to remain strong and resolute! We can picture you saying, "Who says data are a gift to the teacher! My head is swimming with line graphs and histograms!" If this resembles you at this moment, do not even think of giving up. Instead, step back and reflect on how much you have learned. If you have made it through Chapter 5, you have learned how to use student feedback, how to measure and chart class progress, and how to integrate the class vision, goals, and principles of a BBQ classroom. You are *using* the Plan-Do-Study-Act improvement cycle, and you are *changing* your classroom system. Now give yourself a pat on the back and move on to Chapter 6.

Reflections

6

MOTIVATE STUDENTS TO DO HIGH-PERFORMANCE WORK

Hook the Curriculum to Real-Life Team Problem-Solving Projects

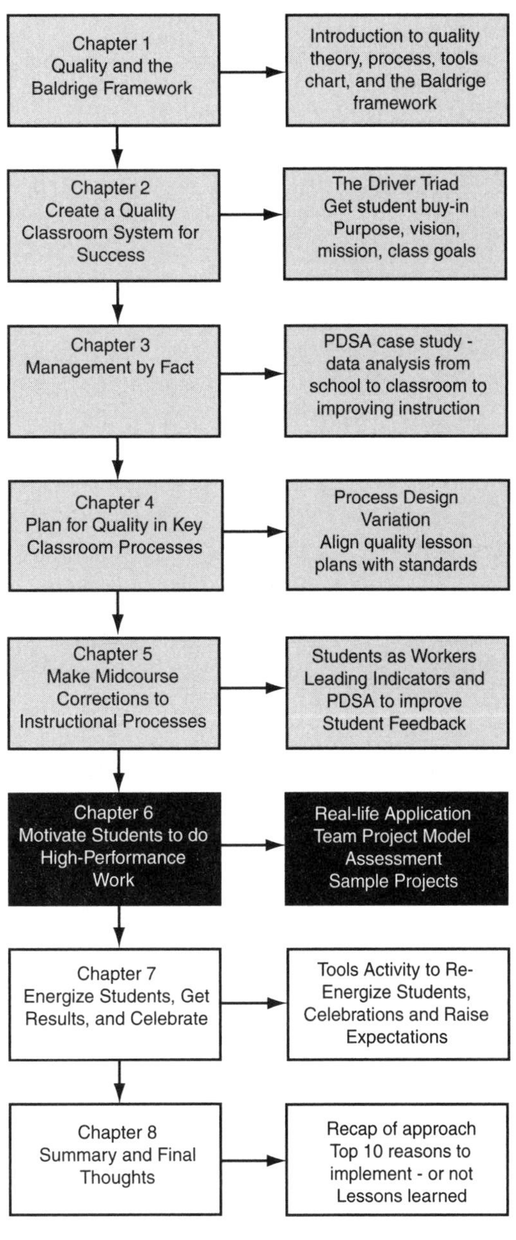

Conversation with the Teacher

It isn't easy to organize a series of learning activities that capture the imagination of all students, but it is important if we expect all students to meet the challenges of their adult life. For those the system has failed because they learn differently and at rates different from some of their peers, the road ahead will be very difficult. For these students, the school experience is painful, and after a while (say, third grade when many begin to opt out), who would willingly engage in an activity that hurts?

Add to this the fact that we (adults/educators) have no concrete conception of all the skills this generation will need to possess to be successful adults. So, how can we be certain that we are teaching the right things and that the curriculum is appropriate? In 1991, the U.S. Department of Labor published a significant report entitled "What Work Requires of Schools: A SCANS (Secretary's Commission on Achieving Necessary Skills) Report." It was a combined effort of the Departments of Labor and Education and of leaders from business, government, and education. We will share the SCANS skills in detail in this chapter because we believe they outline essential skills, many not adequately addressed by K–12 systems.

Aside from academic skills, SCANS emphasizes that successful graduates must be able to work with diverse groups of people to achieve complex tasks or projects. This concept goes beyond cooperative learning activities. It requires teachers to think about how students can be organized in different ways and learn how to self-organize and to self-manage a team to address real-life problems in their school, community, or the nation. It requires a holistic approach to learning. We hope that the silos of secondary education can be broken so students have an opportunity to experience true learning and not only "school" learning.

I was astonished several years ago as I listened to a group of high school social studies teachers share their department's Quality project. The goal was to increase the number of ninth-graders passing social studies because over the previous five years, 40% of all ninth-graders failed social studies, regardless of their teacher. To address the situation, the teachers brainstormed the causes of students' not learning and came up with "don't do homework and are disorganized" as the major causes. A survey of students revealed an overwhelming response: "Class is boring." The teachers came up with a list of approaches they thought might work so more students would pass and asked students to prioritize the list. Students said they wanted to work in teams and put a homework hotline near the bottom. The teachers then agreed to allow students to work once a semester in teams. They instituted and manned a homework hotline, gave students a short course on time management, and provided them with daily planners.

At the end of the semester, failure rate dropped from 40% to less than 15%. Teachers asked the students to rate the effectiveness of the interventions. Working in teams was the approach that all students felt helped them the most. Meanwhile, not one student called the homework hotline, although it was manned every day. So, what astonished me? The teachers dropped the team project work and continued the homework hotline! (No kidding, this is a true story. Go figure!)

In this chapter you will learn:

- The SCANS skills
- A model for Baldrige-based quality team projects
- Some examples of cross-curricular team projects suitable for most grade-level students

Value—Need for Team Projects

Sputnik shocked America into the realization that the Soviet Union had made great strides in science, mathematics, and technology. The United States government was concerned that these developments threatened its prominence as a super power. In response, President Kennedy stated his vision to land a man on the moon within a decade. He provided resources, gathered together the best and brightest people to create and run NASA, provided money to improve K–16 math and science instruction, and encouraged students to pursue scientific and engineering careers. He challenged NASA to achieve his vision. It was the nation's largest peace-time team effort ever, and national pride soared as we watched Neil Armstrong walk on the moon July 21, 1969.

The road to NASA's success, however, was not smooth. It required *teamwork at many different levels, constant evaluation of problems,* and a *willingness of leadership to listen* to others to achieve the goal. Lessons learned from analyzing data to discover root cause of problems seemed to be the key. This required the collective thinking of many scientists, computer analysts, and engineers. Equally important was their ability to work together, to communicate effectively with each other and to work well under highly stressful conditions.

Today, the implications for education go beyond those just mentioned as we are aware that many skilled and unskilled American jobs are being relocated to China, India, Mexico, South Korea, and other countries. Despite claims by some, the reason for outsourcing jobs is only partly due to lower wages. Another reason corporations have begun to outsource technical jobs is their view that educational systems abroad, for example, those in India and China, are superior to the American system. In the 1980s, when manufacturing jobs began to be lost to low-wage nations, American entrepreneurs established computer-related industries that provided high wage jobs to replace the lost manufacturing jobs. Today, we are faced with a similar situation; however, there are fewer engineers and scientists graduating from our nation's universities. Research and development of new products and solutions to current problems will be required if America is to survive as the global superpower.

At a UNESCO international conference in 2004 held in Gothenburg, Sweden, educators, scientists, government representatives, and people from nongovernmental organizations from around the world discussed global issues and made recommendations to ensure a better quality of life for all people. The central sustainability issues of access to education and health care, eradication of HIV/AIDS and other diseases, clean air and water, adequate sewage facilities, dependence on nonrenewable energy sources, violence, and an appreciation for diversity were constant themes of the conference. The issues are interdependent and all will require teams of diverse individuals to team up and work together to solve them. This is why UNESCO has identified the years 2005–2014 as the Decade of Education for Sustainable Development.

The need for education reform emerged as the core issue as all delegates agreed that without this, people, families, towns, countries, and regions will be unable to solve their problems or find new solutions to difficult problems. Throughout the conference, delegates suggested emphasizing the following: (1) fundamental skills, (2) communication and interpersonal skills, (3) math and science, (4) teamwork starting at an early age to engage in community improvement projects, and (5) reduction of violence/bullying through an appreciation for diversity and team projects that require students to work together.

Dr. Deming, the father of modern quality theory, realized the power of teams to solve problems and emphasized the necessity of engaging those involved in the process to lead the way in finding solutions to the problems of business, industry, healthcare, government, and education. There has never been a greater need to prepare students to be good problem solvers and entrepreneurs, as evidenced by the 2004 UNESCO conference.

Brain Research, Multiple Intelligences, and Teaming

Lessons from brain research teach us that the use of real-life, complex tasks that allow students to use the information and skills learned leads to greater long-term learning. This is especially true if those tasks resemble those that will be encountered in the real world. When real-life, complex tasks are combined with a team approach, students learn the interpersonal skills and team responsibilities useful in most careers. Additionally, many students become more energized and demonstrate an increase in self-esteem and pride when their team's work makes their community a better place to live. In some schools, this is called "service learning."

Beginning in early elementary school, teachers can hook the state standards and learning objectives to real-life situations, so students begin to develop interpersonal skills. It is particularly important for students to become better communicators and more tolerant of diversity. Cultural, socioeconomic, gender, and racial differences are four obvious influencers of communication styles. Less obvious may be differences of religion, sexual identity, and physical size (extremes of height or weight). Effective teachers seek out learning opportunities (hooked and aligned always with what students need to know and learn) that capitalize on broadening students' views and abilities to work with others—a key SCANS skill.

As we have learned from Dr. Howard Gardner, who has done the seminal work on how people learn, there are at least eight intelligences, or pathways people use to learn. Gardner suggests that American schools mostly address the logical/mathematical and verbal/linguistic intelligences and only occasionally encourage the use of the other intelligences. Learning opportunities that capitalize on several intelligences at once are the most powerful for advancing long-term learning. (See the Multiple Intelligences Toolbox on page 93 of Chapter 3.) Team projects designed with Quality Factors that include creativity and that require a product at the end (game, multimedia, music, presentation, newspaper, and so on) include many of the intelligences and address all the SCANS skills. By their nature, team projects expand students' interpersonal capabilities. It has been proven that when teachers expand the learning pathways, more students master the required skills.

The SCANS Skills

In 1991, the SCANS (Secretary's Commission on Achieving Necessary Skills) report identified the skills students would need to become employed in the 21st century (Figure 6.1).

<table>
<tr><th colspan="3">Foundation skills
Competent workers in the high-performance workplace need:</th></tr>
<tr><td>Basic skills:
• reading
• writing
• arithmetic
• speaking
• listening</td><td>Thinking skills:
• ability to learn
• to reason
• to think creatively
• to make decisions
• to solve problems</td><td>Personal qualities:
• individual responsibility
• self-esteem
• self-management
• sociability
• integrity</td></tr>
<tr><th colspan="3">Workplace competencies
Effective workers can productively use:</th></tr>
<tr><td>Resources:
Know how to allocate:
• Time
• Money
• Materials
• Space
• Staff</td><td>Interpersonal skills:
• Work on teams
• Teach others
• Serve customers
• Lead
• Negotiate
• Work well with culturally diverse people</td><td>Information:
• Acquire and evaluate data
• Organize and maintain files
• Interpret and communicate
• Use computers to process information</td></tr>
<tr><td colspan="2">Systems:
• Understand social, organizational, and technological systems
• Monitor and correct performance
• Design or improve systems</td><td>Technology:
• Select equipment and tools
• Apply technology to specific tasks
• Maintain and troubleshoot equipment</td></tr>
</table>

Figure 6.1 The Secretary's Commission on Achieving Necessary Skills (SCANS).

We believe it is possible to have high-performing teams of students solving real-life problems that are cross-curricular in nature, address the state standards, and meet the SCANS requirements, starting in grade 1. Imagine the pride in workmanship students feel when they model the two principles of a BBQ classroom: "I am responsible for my own learning" and "I am response-able to the success of the class."

How educators choose to include the SCANS skills in their classes is an individual decision; however, the need to do so systematically from grades 4 through 12 is vital to the success of all graduates. Figure 6.2 on the next page provides a glimpse of the paradigm shift away from a traditional education to one focused on SCANS. We suggest you compare the BBQ classroom model and our team project model to this chart.

Student as Worker and Team Development

To obtain the desired results, you must understand how this fits into the Baldrige framework. Team projects are a result of action plans developed during classroom strategic planning. They are one approach the teacher has identified to meet one or more learning goals, and therefore are an integral part of the Student as Worker Focus (Figure 6.3 on the next page). The Baldrige education criteria divide this category (Student as Worker Focus) into three parts: (1) work systems, (2) education and training, and (3) well-being and satisfaction. Team projects become the way students work together to learn and they represent a different work system than a more traditional approach.

When teachers educate students about the Team Project model described here, it becomes part of the students' education and training to do their jobs better and helps promote high-performance work. Student well-being is derived from the many ways teachers as leaders facilitate a new classroom culture of respect and civility as described in Chapter 2.

Traditional classrooms	SCANS classrooms
Instructor knows answers.	More than one solution may be viable.
Students routinely work alone.	Students routinely work with instructors, peers, and community members.
Instructors plan all activities.	Students and instructors plan and negotiate activities.
Instructors make all assessments.	Students routinely assess themselves.
Information is organized, evaluated, interpreted, and communicated to students by instructor.	Information is acquired, evaluated, organized, interpreted, and communicated by students to appropriate audience.
Organizing system of the classroom is simple: one instructor teaches 30 students.	Organizing systems are complex: instructor and students both reach out beyond school for additional information.
Reading, writing, and math are treated as separate disciplines; listening and speaking often are missing from curriculum.	Disciplines needed for problem solving are integrated; listening and speaking are fundamental parts of learning.
Thinking is usually theoretical and "academic."	Thinking involves problem solving, reasoning, and decision making.
Students are expected to conform to instructor's behavioral expectations; the instructor monitors integrity and honesty; student self-esteem is often poor.	Students are expected to be responsible, sociable, self-managing, and resourceful; integrity and honesty are monitored within the social context of the classroom; students are in charge of their own learning.

Figure 6.2 Comparison of traditional and SCANS classrooms.

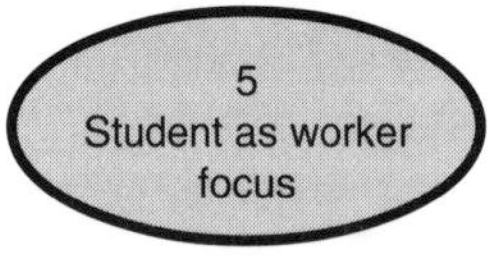

Figure 6.3 Category 5.

In addition, this team project model provides another approach to well-being and satisfaction. All of these factor into process management, which during team projects is turned over to students. They determine the answers to who, how, when, and what they will produce, based on collaboratively agreed-upon Quality Factors and a time frame for completion.

Unlike cooperative learning groups, team projects serve a different purpose. Students are not grouped into teams based on achievement (highly skilled paired with those of fewer skills); instead students may be grouped randomly, or by communication styles (a mixture is best), or perhaps by skills (detail person, creative person, skilled organizer, and so on).

There is no set way to organize students into teams. Hubert Minn, for example, often asks his middle school students to throw one of their shoes into a pile, and then he selects four shoes randomly. Students whose shoes are selected become a team for that project. While many students prefer to work with the same group all the time, we believe it is in everyone's best interest to change team membership for every project.

It is important to note that simply putting people together and giving them a task rarely results in a high performing team. This is true of teachers within a school, administrators within a district, and students within any classroom. Like clockwork, nearly every team moves through the four stages: forming, storming, norming, and performing (Figure 6.4 on the next page). On the following page you will find the stages of team development. When you see the word "class," mentally substitute the word "team." Proper planning ensures greater success, and you will see how the team project model we recommend can help students move beyond the storming phase. Also note how the interpersonal skills required by SCANS help lead to successful teams and completion of the project. Above all, do not assume that students have the skills necessary to become a high performing team without appropriate guidance and instruction.

Directions: Review the stages of classroom or team development by yourself. Think about your class. Read the "observables" for each stage. Make a preliminary judgment of the stage you think your class is at now, or how it ended the school year. How much time was spent in rework because of the stage your class is/was in? What could you have done (Hint: review the group and individual behaviors) to improve the situation and move the entire class to the high-performing stage earlier in the school year?

Stage 1: Forming Individual	Group	Observables
Why am I here? What's expected of me? How much influence will I have? How much am I willing to give?	What's the purpose of this class? What are we supposed to accomplish? What methods/procedures can we use? What should the class's code of conduct be?	Sporadic and uneven participation Strong personalities may try to take over Testing and false starts First agreements
Stage 2: Storming **Individual**	**Group**	**Observables**
Do I agree with the class purpose and am I committed to it? How do I feel about the power structure (teacher and/or student leaders) in the class and its effect on my personal freedom? What are the benefits and risks of sharing information and asking questions in this class?	How should the class deal with code of conduct violations? How should the class handle conflict when two or more persons can't get along? How can conflicts of purpose or methods be resolved? How is student leadership decided?	Personal power struggles and clashes Negative emotions and body language Lack of consensus seeking behavior Confusion/loss of interest/opting out Lack of progress Attack the student leaders and/or teacher
Stage 3: Norming **Individual**	**Group**	**Observables**
I have a sense of belonging to the class. I have a sense of personal accomplishment. I understand my role(s) and contribute effectively. I have freedom to be myself and express my ideas. I feel I can trust the class members and they can trust me.	A unified mission/purpose A healthy balance of power among student leaders Effective group procedures are practiced Sincere attempt to achieve consensus decisions Students and the teacher honor the code of conduct A "class" identity emerges High productivity	Consistently setting and achieving task milestones Students acknowledge and solicit the unique contributions of other students Class attacks problems, not each other Use of we, us, our; not I, me, you, mine Good communications Free participation Steady progress
Stage 4: Performing **Individual**	**Group**	**Observables**
Fun and exciting High feeling of trust and friendship with class members High personal commitment to the class Involvement with the class inspires my best	Creative use of existing resources True consensus decision making Very high level of mutual support Sense of pride in being part of the class and with classmates that extends beyond the class Internalized purpose and mission become a basis for action Optimal communication and exchange with "outside world"	Humor Smooth task and process flow within the class Flexibility and versatility Excited and animated participation Enthusiastic commitment to class decisions Lots of volunteering Pride in class accomplishments Open expressions of appreciation, recognition, and caring

Figure 6.4 Stages of classroom or team development. Modified from Hewlett-Packard's 4 stages of team building.

Team Projects

Before embarking on any team project, the teacher has important pre-work responsibilities. We have outlined these responsibilities below. The team project model we recommend follows the PDSA process, which means students have a structured approach within which to operate. At the same time, they learn self-organization and how to use PDSA and tools to produce a high quality product. On the next several pages you will see details of the 10-Step Team Project model appropriate for grades 6–12. Following the detailed model, we've included a matrix outlining all steps, tools, and outputs for early grades and intermediate grades on pages 173–177. Templates for all the charts are located in Appendix D.

Teacher's Responsibility—Pre-work for the First Team Project

1. Determine the purpose or aim of the assignment.
2. Decide which Quality Factors (essential elements) must be included in the final product based on identified competencies students need to know and be able to do by the end of the project. What standards will be addressed when students complete this project?
3. Coordinate with other English teachers and teachers from other academic disciplines to assure expectations for writing, math, and other disciplines are included if possible. This helps students realize the continuity of all subjects and expectations.
4. With the class, operationally define each Quality Factor to eliminate variation in the final products and also to improve each student's ability to succeed. Note: Final products may vary for each team, but the requirements (QFs) remain the same for all.
5. Determine the parameters within which the students will be allowed to operate. (For example, will they be able to have unlimited access to the computer lab? Media center? Where can they work?)
6. Determine the project time frame for completion and process checkpoints along the way.
7. Develop a list of potential resources to include Internet sites, media materials, experts, and so forth available to teams.
8. Make a decision about how students will be divided into teams.
9. When the teams are determined, facilitate the entire class in going through all the planning steps together. After explanations are complete, teams should use the tools and complete the work to produce the result described at each step. The tools become part of each team's storyboard presentation at the end of the project.

A 10-Step Model for Team Projects—Grades 6–12

PLAN—Team Organization

Step 1: Purpose—*What is the team's purpose for this project?*

Use any of the following tools:

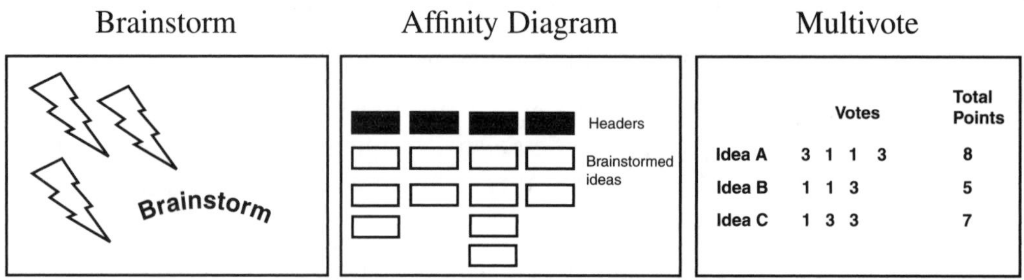

Product of this step: A written statement, signed by all members of the team, stating the team purpose and evidence of the tool(s) used to write the purpose.

Step 2: Mission—*How are you (as a small team) going to accomplish this purpose?*

Define the way you will work together as a team. What social skills will the team identify as critical to success? (Think about action verbs and phrases such as "accept responsibility," "help," "respect," and "come on time.")

Use any of the following tools:

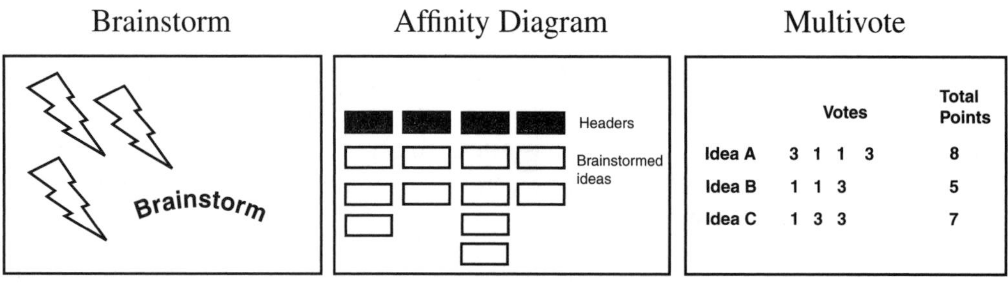

Products of this step: A **written mission statement,** signed by all members of the team that describes the way the team is committed to working together to achieve the purpose of the project and a **social/team skills matrix,** using the verbs from the mission statement (QFs for teamwork) and create a matrix with operational definitions for each QF. See Figures 6.5 and 6.6.

Team name: Sharks **Coach:** Celia

Project: Ecosystems of the Ocean **Date** Nov. 15

Team mission: *We will* ***participate*** *every day,* ***cooperate*** *with each other, take full* ***responsibility*** *for completing our work on time,* ***contribute*** *by helping each other and offering information, and take our* ***leadership*** *roles seriously. We'll maintain a good sense of humor.*

Quality factors

Name	Participation	Cooperation	Responsibility	Contribution	Leadership	Coaching tips
	Each day we will come to class on time and take an active role in learning and team decision-making.	We will get along with each other, and willingly help each other by answering questions and assisting with any and all tasks.	We will take full responsibility for all assigned tasks and complete them on time. If there are problems or questions, we will ask for help early enough to get the job done on time.	We will make suggestions, bring materials, add to the discussions, and challenge each other to think more clearly about the project.	We will take charge of the assigned tasks we have and get whatever supplies are necessary, arrange for meetings, and speak for the team when it is our turn to lead a portion of the project.	
Norman	NY	NY	NY	Y	NY	Please try to be happy and come ready to listen. I like you and the team needs your help.
Celia	Y	NY	NY	NY	Y	I need to be happier and more willing to listen to other suggestions.
Shari	NY	NY	Y	NY	Y	Please talk more in team meetings and offer more suggestions.
Thomas	Y	Y	NY	Y	NY	Please come to class with your assignments finished. If you need help, just ask us.

Has the QF, as stated in the operational definition, been met? Yes
Has the QF, as stated in the operational definition, not been met? Not yet

Figure 6.5 Example: team skills matrix.

Team name: ______________________ Coach: ______________________

Project: ______________________________________ Date ____________

Team mission:

Quality factors →

Names						

Has the QF, as stated in the operational definition, been met? Yes
Has the QF, as stated in the operational definition, not been met? Not yet

Figure 6.6 Sample: team skills matrix.

Step 3: Set expectations—*What are the Quality Factors for the project? What will the team need to learn about and what will the team's final product look like?*

The team will need to gain a clear understanding of what needs to be studied and the Quality Factors for successful completion of the project. (If a QF for creativity is required, teams might brainstorm and multivote to reach consensus on how the team project will demonstrate creativity.)

Now is a good time to introduce a new tool—the lotus diagram. It is a brainstorming tool that helps with planning and organization. Instructions for the lotus diagram are shown below, immediately after the Quality Factors for Learning Matrix.

Use the following tools:

Quality Factor Matrix | Lotus Diagram 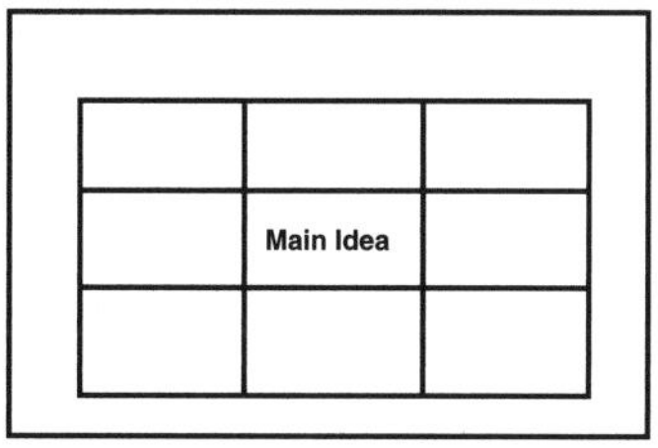 | Brainstorm/Multivote

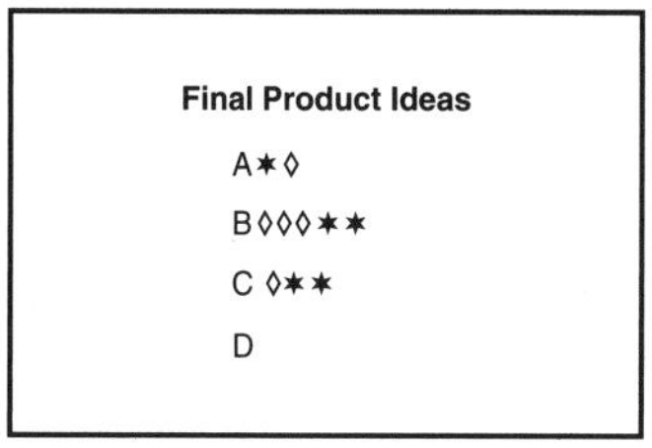

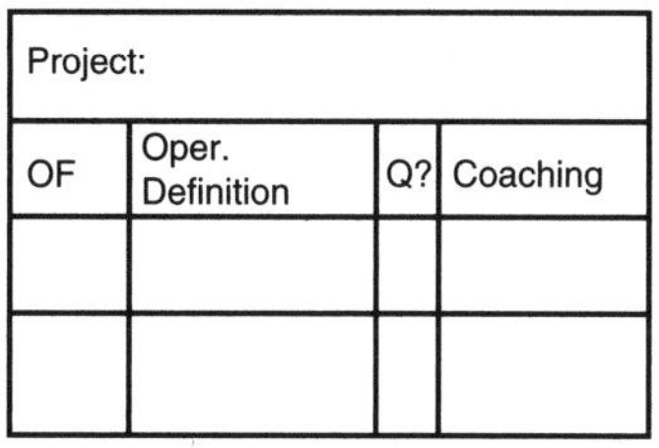 Project:			
OF	Oper. Definition	Q?	Coaching

	Main Idea	

Final Product Ideas

A∗◊
B◊◊◊∗∗
C ◊∗∗
D

Products of this step:

A completely filled out QF for Learning Matrix

A completed lotus diagram, with the project title in the center and areas of "need to know" in the surrounding boxes

A brainstormed list and determination of the final product (for example, multimedia presentation, newspaper, or game)

See Figures 6.7 and 6.8 on the following pages for the QF for Learning Matrix.

Quality factors	Operational definitions	Q? Not yet	Coaching tips
Written reports			
Grammar usage and mechanics	Spelling		
	Subject-verb agreement		
	Punctuation		
(no errors)	Capitalization		
	Parts of speech		
	Sentence fragments		
	Run-on sentences		
Paragraphs	Each: Topic sentence		
	All: At least three supporting details that all relate to the introduction or topic sentence		
Data collection and charts			
Sources	Data from three different sources		
Accurate	No errors in data		
Charts	No errors on charts		
	At least three types of charts or graphs		
	Proper labeling of all charts with titles		
Creativity			
Color	Use at least two or more colors		
Multimedia Audio Video Interactive	Select one or more of these modes for your presentation.		
Neatness (polish)			
	No wrinkles		
	No erasures		
	Use a word processor		
	No smudges		

Figure 6.7 Example: Quality Factors for learning matrix.

State standards included: ______________________________ Project due date: ______________

______________________________ Team members: ______________

Quality factors Written reports	Operational definitions	Q? Not yet	Coaching tips
Oral presentations			
Data collection and charts	Operational definitions	Q? Not yet	Coaching tips
Creativity			
Neatness (polish)			

Figure 6.8 Sample: Quality Factors for learning matrix.

Lotus Diagram

What

The lotus diagram is an analytical tool that can also be used for organization and brainstorming. It helps break down topics or information, which can then be prioritized for additional study.

How

The steps to creating a lotus diagram are:

1. Determine the topic to be studied.
2. Brainstorm ideas by using the Affinity Process (or simply generating ideas through a more traditional approach) and prioritize the ideas into major topics.
3. Use this template or create your own lotus diagram by folding a large piece of paper into thirds lengthwise and crease the folds. Open the paper and fold it again into thirds in the opposite direction and crease the folds. This yields nine smaller squares. Outline the center box with a marker. Fold the paper again into thirds lengthwise; then fold it into thirds one more time, making sure to crease the folds. Open the paper and fold it back into thirds horizontally and then fold the paper again into thirds. Crease all folds. Open the paper and you should have 81 squares.
4. Use a dark marker to draw lines on each fold.

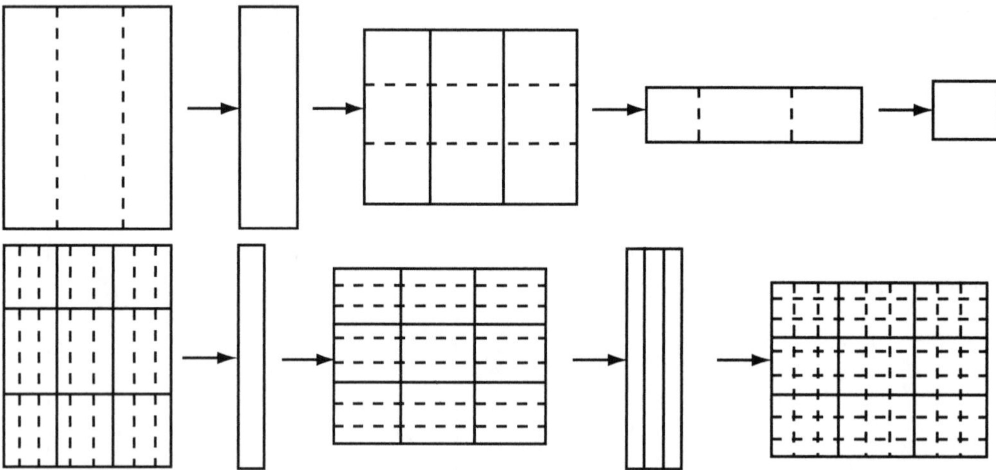

5. Place the Main Topic in the center rectangle of the lotus diagram. Beginning at the diagonal right outer rectangle, number each around the center from 1 to 8. (See the Georgia History example.)
6. Place each of the headers from the affinity diagram in a numbered rectangle around the center. These are the subtopics to study. Each one is then carried over to the corresponding center box of one of the outer rectangles. Number 1 moves to the upper right rectangle, 2 to the center right rectangle, and so forth clockwise around the center set of boxes.
7. Brainstorm information about each of the subtopics to study. (See the Elementary example.) Students can then research each of the ideas.

When

As a means to promote logical and creative thinking.

As a spatial and interactive activity.

As a means to engage all the students in analysis and brainstorming.

As a means to study for an upcoming unit test.

As a break from more traditional learning approaches.

As a means to address all learning styles.

Example

Topic: Georgia History

Students used the affinity process to brainstorm what they wanted to learn about.

Continued on next page

Continued

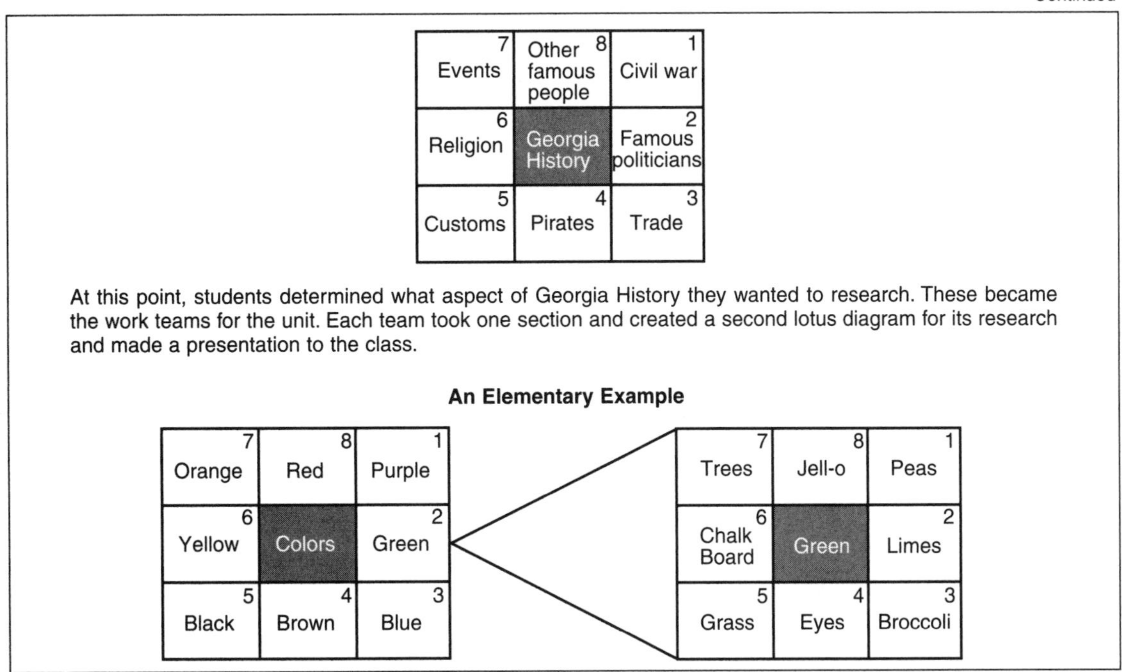

At this point, students determined what aspect of Georgia History they wanted to research. These became the work teams for the unit. Each team took one section and created a second lotus diagram for its research and made a presentation to the class.

An Elementary Example

Plan-Team Organization Continued

Step 4: Responsibilities—Who is responsible for taking charge of specific tasks related to the project?

In this step, the team will brainstorm and determine all the tasks required to complete the project. Use the just completed lotus diagram for clues about the different tasks involved, and reference the QF for Learning Matrix to make certain every aspect of the project has been carefully considered. Brainstorm a list of responsibilities.

Decide which team member(s) will take responsibility for coordinating each role. In addition, determine what needs to be done to ensure the entire project will come together on time and meet all QFs. Identify a Quality Inspector, who will take responsibility for assessing the project at each process checkpoint (the team may decide to share this role, with different members taking responsibility at different checkpoints), ensuring that team members receive adequate editing/coaching so project deadlines and specifications are met. One or more team members may be responsible for one or more aspects of the project, but one person should be assigned as project coordinator for each role.

Team members should be given the option of selecting the area in which they are most interested in working. Everyone on the team will be held accountable for meeting each of the core competencies assigned to this project and for learning the standards. (A test covering all standards embedded in the project is given at the completion of all projects.)

If a task isn't assigned to a specific person, there is a good chance it will not get done, causing the team problems in completing the project on time.

Lotus Example—What Will Be Studied About Transportation

Cruise ship	Aircraft carrier	Swimming	Throughbred race horse	(Picture)	Donkey	Motorcycle	Wagon	Car
Steamer	**Water** 7	Pontoon boat	Horse-drawn carriage	**Hoof** 8	Bull-riding	School bus	**Wheels** 1	Farm tractor
Surfing	Speed boat	Tubing	Horse-drawn sleigh	Horse	Oxen	In-line skates	Train	Truck
Jet shoes	Personal aircraft	Inter-planetary cars	**Water** 7	**Hoof** 8	**Wheels** 1	Propeller airplanes	Bi-Plane	WWII pigeon
Cars that drive themselves	**Future** 6	Space bus	**Future** 6	**Transporation**	**Wings** 2	Birds/insects	**Wings** 2	Jet airplane
Highway people-mover belts	Speed of light trains	Inter-glactic space ships	**Feet** 5	**Space** 4	**Paddle** 3	Angels/fairies	Jet fighter	Sky diver plane
Hopping	(picture)	Walking	Mars rover	Space walk	Space ship	Racing skiff	Duck	Canoe
Sliding	**Feet** 5	Running	Rocket	**Space** 4	Hot air balloon	Scuba diver flipper	**Paddle** 3	Kayak
Skipping	Leaping	Jumping	Space shuttle	Lunar module	Lunar lander	Row boat	Paddle boat	Paddle wheeler

Use either of the following tools:

Satellite Diagram

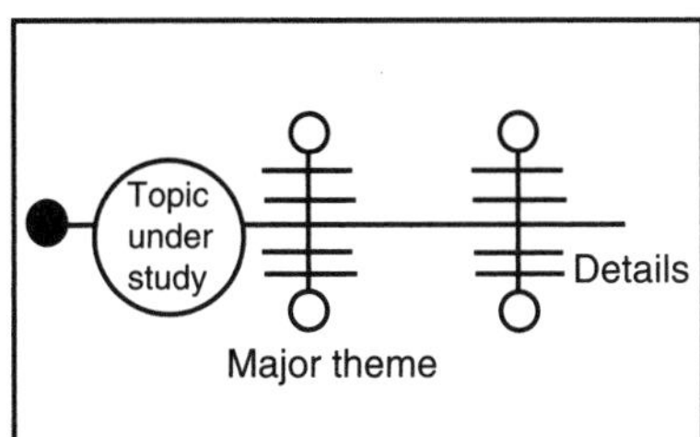

Affinity Diagram

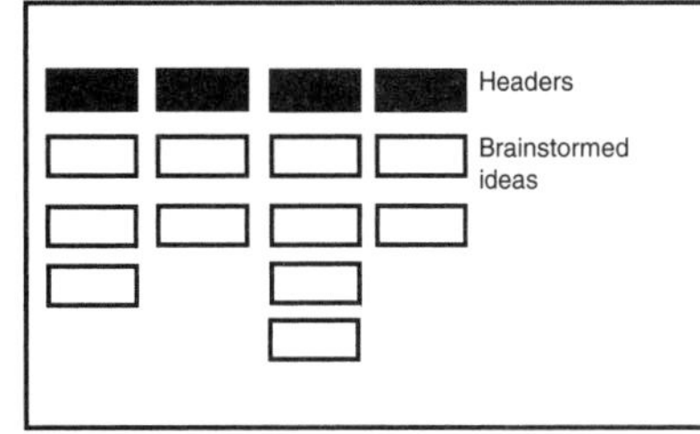

Place each person's name at the end of one of the "arms" of the satellite chart and/or as headers for the affinity diagram and, using the round robin approach, have each team member select a role until all roles are filled.

Instructions for the satellite diagram are on page 182.

Product of this step: A tool that shows specific tasks with each student's responsibilities.

Plan-Team Organization Continued

Step 5: Resources—What resources are available in the community and/or school to help in the project? (Examples: library, Internet, businesses, computer)

The teacher provides a list of potential resources but teams are encouraged to add others.

Use one of the following tools:

Brainstorm

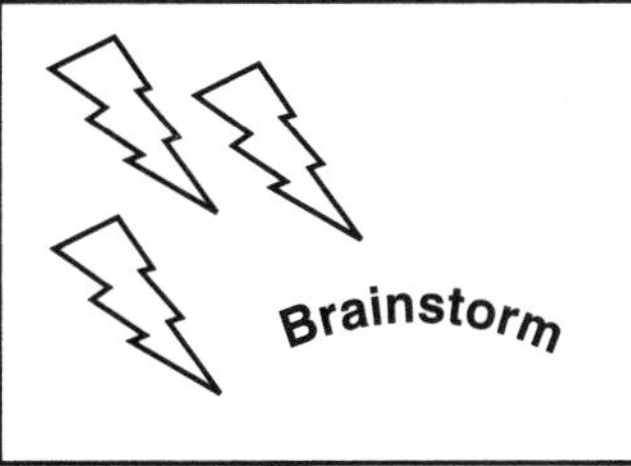

Affinity Diagram

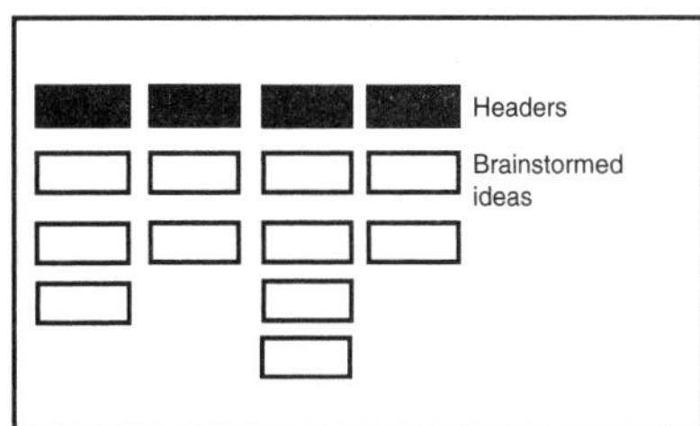

Product of this step: Teams members will have signed off on a list of resources to use for their project.

Satellite Diagram

What

A Satellite Diagram dissects content-related material, such as character analysis in a novel, elements of a story, parts of speech, multiplication tables or other math problems, or compare and contrast activities. It can also be used as a planning tool.

How

1. Draw a horizontal line, which is the center line.
2. At the far left-hand edge of the center line, draw a circle or oval. This will become the head of the satellite.
3. Write the topic under study in the head.
4. On each side of the center line, evenly spaced, draw two or more vertical lines as arms of the satellite. Each of these represents a major category of the topic under study. Label each arm with the general category under study.
5. Fill in as much detail on each arm as possible, either from memory, from brainstorming, or from reading or research.

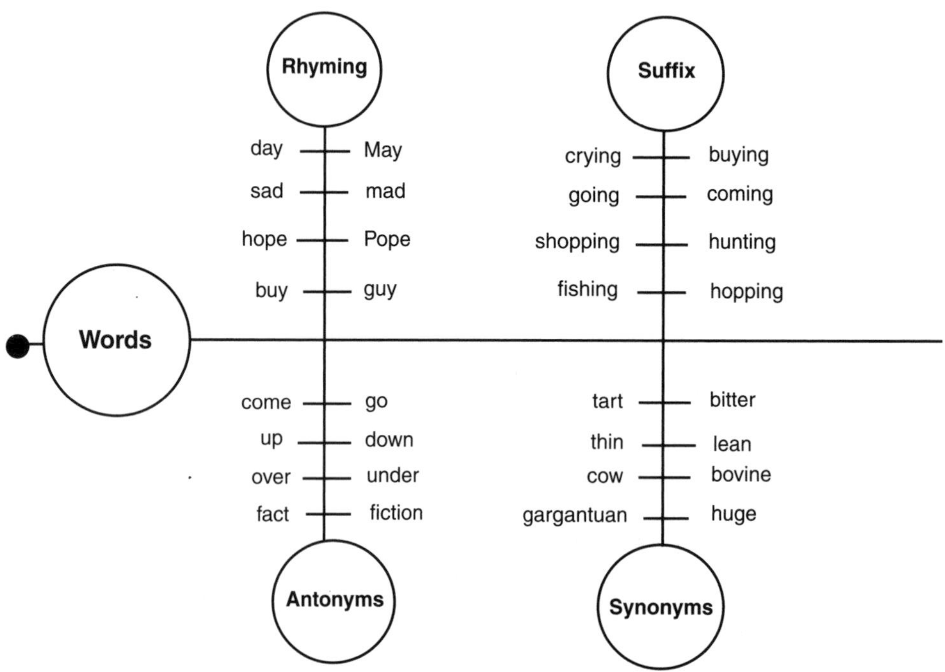

When

Use this tool when students could benefit from a graphic organizer, such as to study for a test or when learning new material;

- If some students are having trouble grasping certain concepts.
- As a means of engaging the visual intelligence.

Continued

Continued

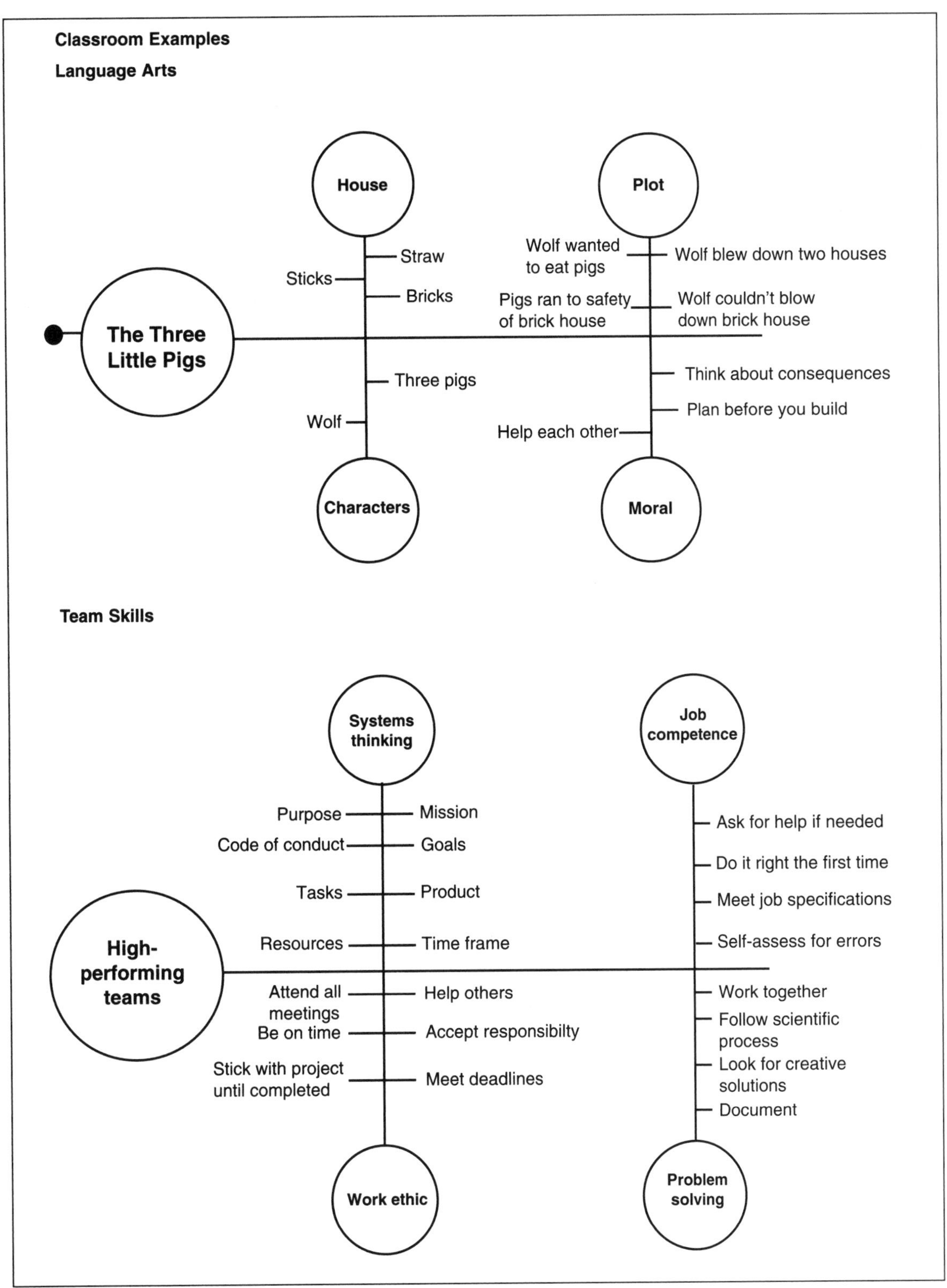

Classroom Examples
Language Arts
House
Plot
Straw
Sticks
Bricks
Wolf wanted to eat pigs
Wolf blew down two houses
Pigs ran to safety of brick house
Wolf couldn't blow down brick house
The Three Little Pigs
Three pigs
Wolf
Think about consequences
Plan before you build
Help each other
Characters
Moral
Team Skills
Systems thinking
Job competence
Purpose
Mission
Code of conduct
Goals
Tasks
Product
Resources
Time frame
Ask for help if needed
Do it right the first time
Meet job specifications
Self-assess for errors
High-performing teams
Attend all meetings
Help others
Be on time
Accept responsibilty
Stick with project until completed
Meet deadlines
Work together
Follow scientific process
Look for creative solutions
Document
Work ethic
Problem solving

Step 6: Manage the team process—How will work flow to meet the project deadlines and specifications?

The teacher provides the deadline for project completion and dates for critical process checks along the way. The team will determine how work will flow to meet all process checks and the final deadline for a Quality project. Instructions for the Gantt chart follow.

Use one of the following tools:

Flow Chart

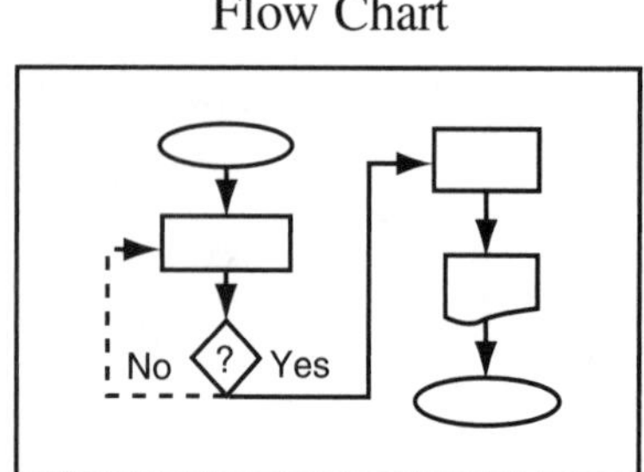

Gantt Chart

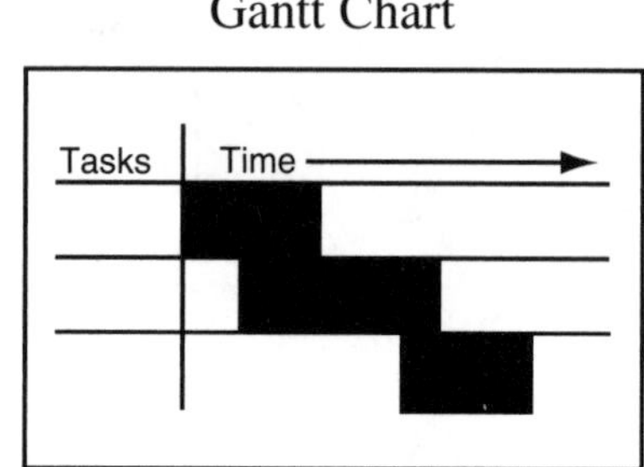

Product of this step: A flow chart or Gantt chart with tasks, responsibilities, start and finish times, and process checkpoint dates.

Gantt Chart

What

A Gantt chart is a picture of the timeline for completing a project. It shows the flow of the work and provides information about the start time and completion times for tasks within the project. A Gantt chart also shows who is responsible for seeing that each task is completed.

How

1. Make a list of all activities that must be accomplished to complete the project.
2. Review each activity to determine whether or not it requires some previous action or is otherwise integral to another activity.
3. Note where one activity is dependent on another, and list them in sequential order.
4. Determine the project completion date.
5. Determine the approximate amount of time it will take to complete each task.
6. Make certain that tasks that must be done in sequential order are properly planned with time allowed to complete all tasks. Individuals with responsibility for each task may need to negotiate shorter completion times and/or a there may need to be an adjustment to the date for project completion.
7. Avoid assigning to the same individual tasks that overlap in time.
8. Draw the chart. Determine how time will be displayed: days, weeks, months, and so on. Place the allotted time frame across the top of the chart. Along the left-hand side, list the activities in sequential order. On the far right-hand side of the chart, list the individual responsible for ensuring that each task is completed.
9. Post the chart so it is visible to everyone working on the project. Provide everyone on the team with a copy of the chart. Refer to the Gantt chart at every project update meeting. As situations arise that prevent certain activities from being completed on time, note what the problem is (this is an opportunity for process improvement) and if necessary, adjust the time frames for subsequent activities.

Continued

Continued

When

- It is desirable for all team members to see the project scope and sequence.
- As a means of keeping team members on-task.
- To teach students how to develop and use timelines.

Gantt Chart

Team project example—Charity spook house

TASK (What?)	DATE (When?)				October						Who?
	15	16	17	18	19	22	23	24	25	26	
Research other spook houses	X	X									Sue, Jose, and Josh
Research place for spook house	X	X									Tim, Tabetha, and Maria
Team meeting reports & decisions			X								Team
Plan the scary events in spook house & choose roles to play				X	X						Team
Process check					X						Teacher
Get materials for 'events'						X	X				Tim, Tabetha, Josh
Do art work to set the atmosphere					X	X	X				Maria, Sue, Jose
Use technology to make advertising posters and tickets					X						Tim, Josh
Sell tickets						X	X	X			Team
Set up spook house								X			Team
Open spook house									X	X	Team

Class example—Poetry journal class project

TASK	DATE *School Year 2004-05*						Who?
	JAN.	FEB.	MAR.	APR.	MAY	JUNE	
Establish guidelines for submission							Class
Submit poems to committee							All 10th graders
Select poems for submission							Journal team
Proofread selected poems							Proofing team
Design cover							Cover team
Journal layout & design							L & D team
Develop marketing/dates plan							Marketing team
Take copy to print shop							Mr. Harry
Take journal orders							Sales team
Distribute finished product							Class

Do—Learning

> Step 7: Process information—Team members conduct research and/or experiments to accomplish the necessary learning, achieve the aim of the project, and construct and complete the final product.

Teams move through the process, following their flow chart to complete the project, making sure all QFs for learning are achieved.

Use the following tool: QF for Learning Matrix

Project			
OF oper.	Definition	Q?	Coaching

Product of this step: When the project is turned in, a completed Matrix with an assessment of each QF and coaching tips from the team's Quality Inspector will be included. The final product is presented.

> Step 8: PDSA inside the project—How can the teams improve their work to meet all QFs?

At each process checkpoint, the Quality Inspector carefully reviews the team's work against the QFs, using the matrix. An error chart for the project is filled out, along with coaching tips. *Team members are responsible for learning, editing, and improving their work based on the feedback from their team's Quality Inspector* and by implementing the team's improvement theory. This occurs at each critical process checkpoint.

Use each of the following tools:

Process Check Assessment

Project:			
OF	Oper. definition	Q?	Coaching

Error Chart

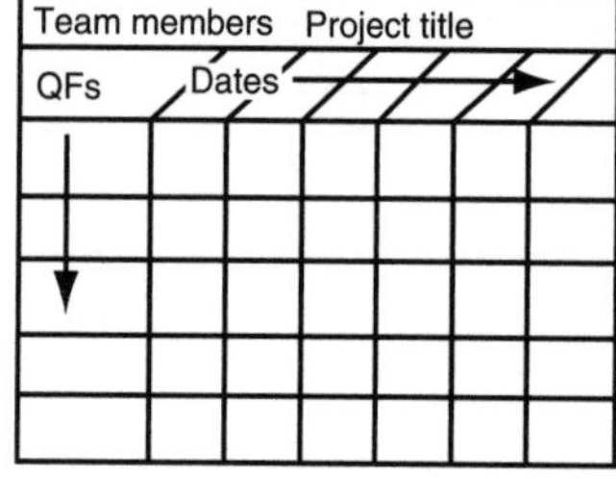

Pareto Chart

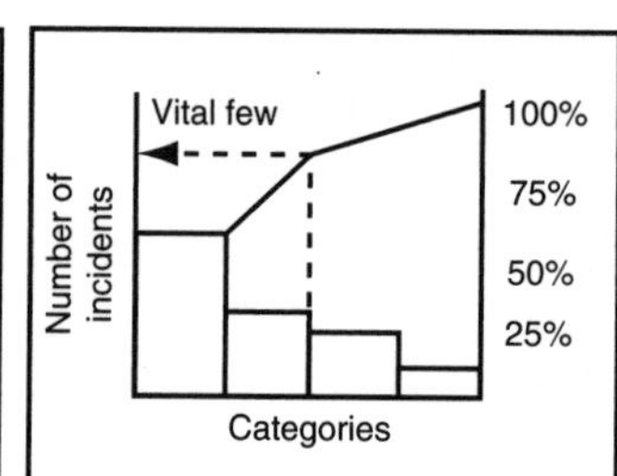

Product of this step: **All the tools are submitted with the project** and evidence of improvements made to eliminate all errors. See Figures 6.9 and 6.10.

Name **Norman** Project title **Ecosystems of the Ocean** Date **Nov. 15**

Fill in the box opposite the QF indicating the errors.

Process checkpoints

Quality factor	**1 Nov. 1**	**2 Nov. 7**	**3 Nov. 15**	**4**
Example: QF—Correct spelling	20 errors	10	3	3
Subject-verb agreement	6	5	3	1
Punctuation	23	15	15	5
Capitalization	0	0	0	1
Parts of speech	6	4	4	2
No sentence fragments	3	3	1	0
No run-on sentences	0	1	0	0

Figure 6.9 Example student error chart—QFs for learning.

Project purpose ______________________________

Deadline for completion __________ Process checkpoint # ________ Date ____________ Quality inspector ____________

Quality factor	Operational definition	Quality or not yet	Coaching tips

Figure 6.10 Sample student error chart: QFs for learning.

> Step 9: Team effectiveness and efficiency—How well does the team function together?

This is how the teams will assess their ability to work together and follow their mission on a daily or weekly basis. Each team's responsibility is to be honest and resolve its own issues while staying on task and becoming a high-performing team as evidenced in the HP Stages of Team Development on page 170.

Use the following tool: Social/Team Skills Assessment

Social/team skills					
Mission:					
Team:	Social skills ⟶				

Product of this step: A completed assessment from each team member and personal summary statement from each student: "*What I learned from doing this project and being a part of this team.*"

Example: "I learned about Pacific Islanders and their life, quality, and a lot about myself and how hard I could work. I am usually pretty stubborn and don't like to work, but this was fun."

Study: Assessment as Part of the Project

> Step 10: Effectiveness—How well did the team meet the expectations? Did each student meet the standards?

Provide each student with a QF for Learning Matrix. The teacher and each student will assess each team project. The entire class will collaborate and reach consensus on a fair, equitable approach to grading. Some classes determine a percentage of the total QFs that must be met and turn that into a grade. Others weight the QFs by assigning a number (5 points for the most critical, 3 points for important QFs, and 1 point for those of lesser importance to the project) to each and reaching a score based on the total number of points awarded the project. When students are empowered to collaborate on the decision of how the projects will be graded, there will be more student buy-in to the process. Once everyone scores all the projects, the teams will regroup to reach consensus on a score for each of the other teams, along with justification for the score in the coaching tips column. Final grades will be determined by combining the teacher's score with each of the other team's scores.

Use the following tool:

QF for Learning Matrix

Project			
OF oper.	Definition	Q?	Coaching

Product of this step: A completed matrix with an assessment of each QF and coaching tips for assigned team projects. The entire team contributes to this assessment process, and consensus is reached on a grade or score based on the agreed-upon scale.

After the Project

Assessment

Prepare an assessment covering the standards that were learned during the project. For example, if the team project had to do with preparing an estimate for hanging drywall in 20 homes from a particular development, the test would cover the geometry and other math standards necessary to complete the project. By making sure you have identified the appropriate content standards covered by any project, you diffuse any criticisms that may arise from parents when you ask students to participate in team projects of this sort. The link between the project and the standards *must be clear, strong, and visible or obvious to you and the students.*

We recommend the development of a test that requires student responses to several levels of learning as shown in Bloom's Taxonomy in Chapter 7, page 211. Figures 6.11 and 6.12 provide examples of the type of test we suggest at the secondary and elementary levels.

U.S. government

Secondary assessment example based on Bloom's Taxonomy

1. What are the three branches of the federal government? Name at least one key figure (person) from each branch. (Knowledge—remembering facts)

2. What are the roles and major responsibilities of each branch of the government? (Comprehension)

3. If you were going to make one change to our system of government, what would it be? How would that make things better? (Application)

4. Fifty years ago, *Brown vs. Board of Education* was handed down by the Supreme Court of the United States. What has been the impact of this decision on education? (Analysis)

5. Summarize major Supreme Court decisions on one of these issues: right to bear arms, freedom of speech, or separation of church and state. (Synthesis)

6. There was a major controversy over the 2000 presidential election. Describe the controversy, take a position about the outcome of this election, and defend your position. (Evaluation)

Figure 6.11 Sample assessment for U.S. government.

Science

Elementary assessment example based on Bloom's Taxonomy

1. Name the basic food groups. (Knowledge: remembering facts)

2. Give three examples of foods from each group. (Comprehension)

3. In what food group would you find candy? Give at least three examples of healthful substitutes for candy that would be in the same food group. (Application)

4. What are the most important things each food group contributes to healthy minds and bodies? (Analysis)

5. Plan three healthful, balanced meals for one day. (Synthesis)

6. What is your favorite "healthy" food? Explain what health benefits you gain from eating this food. (Evaluation)

Figure 6.12 Sample assessment for science.

Act—Planned Change

Upon completion of each team project and the assessment use a line graph or histogram to chart the class results. You might also want to analyze the results by level of learning to better understand the success (or not) of students' ability to advance their learning. Post all results in the classroom for all to see, but be sure results are anonymous.

Seek feedback from the students about what kept them from being successful and/or what contributed to their success and the overall success of the team. A variety of feedback tools can be used. The easiest to use are plus/delta charts and How Helpful Were These Resources? Surveys can also be helpful after major projects, and a root cause analysis ought to be done, especially after the first several team projects, to ensure improvements address barriers to success.

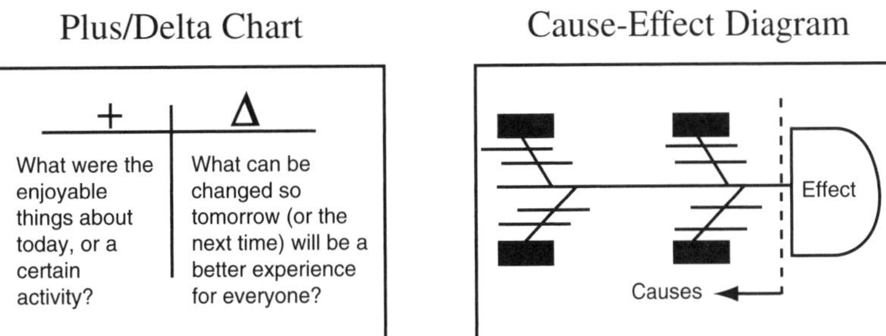

Have the entire class reflect on its ability to self-organize and work together efficiently and effectively on teams. You may want to draw the skeleton of a large Cause-Effect Diagram and post it for several days. Collectively determine the major causal bones, and allow students to add their comments to the chart using Post-it notes. To protect anonymity, give students the opportunity to put up ideas before or after school, class, lunch, or recess. That way you're most likely to get honest responses from everyone. When there are duplicate ideas, students can simply add a checkmark to the idea already noted. This will also help resolve the issue of common and special cause variation.

Once you have this feedback, you'll need to follow up with a root cause analysis and plan for improvement. Try out the new improvements with the next project.

The goal of the teacher, as the facilitator of learning, is to embrace the two Quality principles and take whatever action is necessary to eliminate any and all barriers to student and class success.

I am responsible for my own learning.
I am response-able to the success of the group.

Do Not Forget

If students report satisfaction with the team projects but haven't met the content standards, there is a system problem that must be analyzed.

Abbreviated team project steps for younger students are shown in Figures 6.13 and 6.14. Examples of team projects start below and continue on pages 195–197.

Sample High School Team Project Idea: Potholes 'n' Budgets

After a bad winter season, the main streets of the city have huge potholes. This situation was caused by unusually cold and wet weather from November through April. Constant expansion and contraction of the pavement coupled with wet weather (snow and rain) caused cracks, and as trucks and cars traveled over the roads, huge chunks of pavement were broken and ultimately removed.

Citizens have complained loudly about damage to their vehicles because of the potholes. The rising costs of auto insurance claims, coupled with personal injuries resulting from accidents, have created quite a stir among citizens and insurance companies. On Monday a 5-year-old child darted across the street and was severely injured by a teenage motorist who was swerving to miss a pothole that would likely have caused major damage to his parents' car. The citizens are outraged! They have come in force to a City Council meeting to protest and demand that the city fix the potholes at once!

Unfortunately, the city is experiencing a budget shortfall this year, mostly due to the winter weather. With all the storms, the city has spent three times the budgeted amount for

Plan Team organization	Task	Quality tools to use	Product for this step
Step 1	**Purpose** What is the team's purpose for this project?	Brainstorm Multivote (Might be led by the teacher for grades K–1)	A written purpose statement signed or initialed by all members of the team, stating its purpose.
Step 2	**Mission** How will your team accomplish its purpose?	Brainstorm Multivote	A mission statement signed by all students and the teacher which states how the team expects to behave and work together to accomplish the purpose.
Step 3	**Decide on quality factors for the project** What will the project look like when it is finished?	Lotus diagram	A completed lotus diagram with pictures and/or words describing what the expectations of the project are.
Step 4	**Responsibilities** Who is responsible for specific tasks related to the project?	Lotus diagram Affinity diagram Satellite diagram	Student assignments (volunteers) for parts of the project. Everyone is expected to assume responsibility for leadership for some part of the project. Everyone does research.
Step 5	**Resources** What resources are available to be used for this project?	Brainstorm Satellite diagram	A list of resources students can use to complete the project.
Do the project			
Study the results	**Task**	**Quality tools to use**	**Product for this step**
Step 6	**Assessment** How well did the team meet the quality factors for the project? How smoothly did the team work together to accomplish the task?	Plus-delta chart Force field analysis	Completed charts and an evaluation of the process
Act (teacher)	Use student results, feedback, and suggestions to make improvements in the next team project.		Assessment of student learning. Process improvements for next project.

Figure 6.13 Team project process for grades K–3.

Plan Team organization	Task	Quality tools to use	Product for this step
Step 1	**Purpose** What is the team's purpose for this project?	Brainstorm Affinity diagram Multivote	A written purpose statement signed or initialed by all members of the team, stating its purpose and evidence of the tool(s) used to write the purpose.
Step 2	**Mission** How will your team accomplish its purpose? What social skills will the team identify as critical to success?	Brainstorm Affinity diagram Multivote	A written mission statement signed by all members of the team that describes the way the team is committed to working together to achieve the purpose of the project. A team skills matrix listing the quality factors (verbs) from the mission statement and operational definitions for each.
Step 3	**Decide on quality factors for the project** What will the team need to learn about? What will the project look like when it is finished?	Quality factor matrix Lotus diagram	A completely filled out QF matrix and lotus diagram with the project title in the center and areas of 'need to know' in the surrounding boxes. Evidence of the approach used to consider the creativity QF, that is, Brainstorm, Affinity, Lotus, Satellite, and so on.
Step 4	**Responsibilities** Who is responsible for taking charge of specific tasks related to the project?	Brainstorm Affinity diagram Satellite diagram	A tool that shows who is responsible for specific tasks and signed by all team members. Everyone is expected to assume responsibility for leadership for some part of the project. Everyone does research.
Step 5	**Resources** What resources are available to students (in school and/or the community) to complete this project?	Brainstorm Affinity diagram	Team members will have signed off on a list of resources students can use to complete the project.
Do-learning	**Task**	**Quality tools to use**	**Product for this step**
Step 6	**Process information** Team members conduct research and/or experiments to accomplish the necessary learning and achieve the aim of the project.	QF for learning matrix	When the project is turned in, a completed QF matrix with a peer and self-assessment of each QF for learning is required.
Step 7	**Team effectiveness and efficiency** How well does this team function together?	Team skills assessment Personal summary Statement	Each person will complete a team skills assessment for each team member. Each student will be required to complete a personal summary statement: what did you learn from doing this project and being part of a team.
Study	**Task**	**Quality tools to use**	**Product for this step**
Step 8	**Peer and facilitator evaluation** When all the projects are completed, review the QFs and assess the projects of other teams.	QF for learning matrix	A completed QF for learning matrix with an assessment of each QF with coaching tips for assigned team projects. The entire team contributes to this assessment process and consensus is reached on a grade or score based on the agreed-upon scale.
Act (teacher)	Use student results, feedback, and suggestions to make improvements in the next team project.		Assessment of student learning. Process improvements for next project.

Figure 6.14 Team project process for grades 3–5.

street maintenance and snow removal. Additionally, in January, the heating system at city hall failed and could not be repaired. A new system cost nearly $300,000, leaving the city $500,000 in debt.

Your team represents the City Council. What will be your response to the citizens? What exactly is the problem? Who are the customers of this situation? What do they need and/or expect? How do you understand the problem? (What data have you collected?) Finally, what recommendations will you make to resolve the problem?

Your task is to research the problem systematically. Determine the data to collect. Then, after a root cause analysis, determine an improvement theory and measures. Here are a few hints:

- What is the extent of damage to the pavement?
- Has there been an increase in auto insurance claims?
- Has there been an increase in auto repairs?
- Has there been an increase in hospitalizations resulting from injury?
- What resources are available for resolving the problem?
- What are the alternatives available for repairing the damage?
- What are the consequences if the problem is not resolved?
- What type of future planning must be done to ensure the situation won't be repeated?

What action would you recommend? Prepare a full report. Using all the resources at your disposal, calculate the cost (show the work) and get three estimates based on different materials. Provide a cost/benefit analysis to substantiate your decision. Make a formal presentation to the citizens, using graphics for both the written report and the oral presentation with appropriate video and/or other multimedia to strengthen your points.

Sample Intermediate or Middle School Grades Team Project: School Beautification

Your school is not that old, but it is showing many signs of wear and tear. In the past, students have not been respectful of the property and considerable damage has been done. It is not easy to concentrate and learn when the building is dirty, drinking faucets don't work properly, the playground area is not safe anymore, the halls have ceiling and wall stains and marks, and the area around the school is littered with trash.

Your challenge is to organize and carry out plans to beautify the school. All your plans must be approved by the principal, and you'll need to put them in writing and make oral presentations at a Board meeting.

One team will have a responsibility for organizing a fund-raiser to get the money to complete the class's projects. The other teams are responsible for fixing and cleaning one area of the school. Each team will have five members. Select the team you wish to be on by signing your name to the lotus diagram (Figure 6.15). I encourage you to seek help from parents and the community to complete your projects, but remember you are the leaders.

Team ______ **Classrooms in "B" hall**	Team ______ **Fundraising**	Team ______ **Playground area**
Team ______ **Classrooms in "A" hall**	**School beautification project**	Team ______ **Hallways**
Team ______ **School grounds**	Team ______ **Gym and cafeteria**	Team ______ **Bathrooms and drinking faucets**

Figure 6.15 Selection of team members by using a lotus diagram.

Your team will begin by thoroughly researching the problem systematically. Determine the data to collect. Then, after a root cause analysis, determine a plan to fix the problem. Here are a few hints:

- What is the extent of the problem with your assigned area of the school?
- What must be done to improve or fix the problem?
- Have you researched the cost of fixing the problem?
- Have you planned how you will organize to solve the problem?
- Have you surveyed other classes, parents, and others in the community for willingness to help?
- What are the consequences of not resolving the problem?
- What is your team willing to do to ensure the problem won't be repeated?

What action will you recommend? Prepare a full report. Using all the resources at your disposal, calculate the cost (show the math work) and get three estimates based on different materials. Make a formal presentation to the principal, using graphics for both the written report and the oral presentation with appropriate video and/or other multimedia to strengthen your points.

Once fundraising is completed, carry out your plan.

Sample Elementary Grades Team Project: Recycle for Books

Our town does not require citizens to recycle trash. The class will study about recycling efforts in the region, take a field trip to a recycling center, and watch a science video about the environmental consequences of not recycling. With this as a project backdrop, the class will work in three teams to embark on a recycling project. Math, science, and language arts standards will be addressed with this project.

Students will be responsible for collecting recyclables, which each week will be taken to a recycling center by parent volunteers organized by the teacher. Teams will collect data on how much is being recycled and will collect the money, adding it up each week and filling in bar graphs and run charts with the data posted in the classroom. The project will last for six weeks. Money that is collected will be used to purchase books for our classroom.

Each of the three teams will collect one of the following: bottles and cans, newspapers and cardboard, or plastic and styrofoam. Different teams will be responsible for the following:

- Writing and/or illustrating a story about the environmental effects of not recycling
- Writing a survey or preparing oral survey questions about interest in recycling for parents, which will be copied and distributed to all
- Making posters about the need to recycle
- Collecting surveys and charting the data and sharing information with the class
- Collecting recyclables
- Counting and/or weighing the recyclables
- Packaging the recyclables for hauling to recycling center
- Collecting and counting the money
- Writing a final report on team results
- Making an oral presentation to the school and the city government

After the project, the class will decide what percentage of the profits will go toward buying some books to stay in the classroom and what percentage each student will receive to purchase books for her or his own use. This can become a math problem for appropriate grades; for younger students, the teacher will divide the amount of money according to the class's decision. The teacher will invite appropriate publishers to come and display the books for students to make their selections. Books to be purchased for the entire class will be selected by brainstorming titles and then multivoting.

Summary

This chapter has stressed the importance of helping your students learn to work in diverse team situations as well as tying your curriculum to real-life situations. The payoff for you, the teacher leader, is the "student as worker" shift that is occurring in your BBQ classroom. Yes, the students will make mistakes, and, yes, teamwork is often messier than the traditional model of teacher at the front doing most of the explaining. When you think about it, though, this is what school learning should encompass. When students work together to produce Quality products that frequently solve real-life problems, it teaches them important life lessons that cannot be learned through books and typical schoolwork.

Team projects address every one of the skills brought up in the Secretary's Commission on Achieving Necessary Skills. The topics are limitless, and we can almost guarantee that if you follow the model provided, your students will not forget what has been learned. Hooking the assignments to the real world and providing all students with meaningful work also greatly increases motivation and enthusiasm for learning. At the same time, a well-thought-out team project can address many content standards.

Team projects help students grow socially as well as master new skills and learn to work with diverse groups. Team projects help instill a sense of individual and group pride while providing opportunities for students to reach higher standards in a nonthreatening classroom climate. Yes, your classroom system is changing. Three cheers for the *team!*

Reflections

7

ENERGIZE STUDENTS, GET RESULTS, AND CELEBRATE

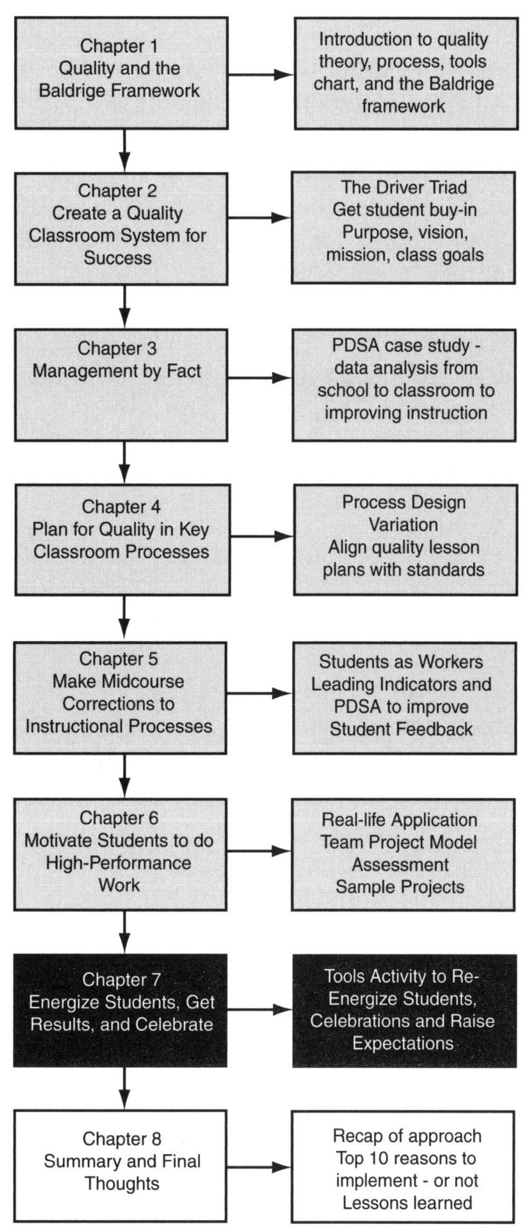

Conversation with the Teacher

We have explored several ways to rotate PDSA (formally and informally), and by now you have a sense of the significance of using leading indicators to measure progress in order to predict improvement of your results. You have also learned the importance of the two principles of a BBQ classroom (I am responsible and I am response-able) to ensure that everyone learns more. What we have not explored in depth yet is the value of using quality tools to assess in-process, as pre-tests to understand "where to start" or to uncover gaps and rework opportunities before the "real" test. You can also use some quality tools, as some of our trained teachers do, as instruments for final assessments.

Brain research has taught us that recall improves when students combine visual, kinesthetic, and musical/rhythmic approaches. BBQ teachers use this information to their great advantage, as described in Chapter 5, when they engage their students in-process and ask them how they want to learn. Quality tools such as the satellite chart and the lotus diagram act as graphic organizers, helping all students, even those with special needs, become better organized and able to see things more clearly. Some tools, such as the affinity diagram, lotus diagram, and satellite chart, help students break difficult topics into smaller bits that are easier to understand. Tools such as the flow chart show a picture of a process and can be very useful for understanding key instructional processes such as math operations or the writing process. Other tools serve different purposes, but most, if not all, can be applied to the instructional process in ways other than process improvement. While this chapter reveals ways you can use quality tools to assess how much students know, the use of quality tools in isolation does not equal a BBQ classroom.

We all know what it's like to maintain energy levels of students at the very end of the day or week. When students become lethargic, it is really difficult to stay on top of things. (We've visited some classrooms, though, where an hour before the end of the day students look as if they are too tired to continue.) In other schools, because of bus schedules, teachers begin the end of the day rituals long before dismissal time because they don't want to start something new. What if you knew of a way to immediately reenergize students and get them ready for the next day or next week's learning activities? The approach we're proposing in this chapter has never failed to work and it's amazing how everyone gets involved. If you are reading this as part of a training course, try some of the activities/problems suggested in this chapter. This is powerful information about how to increase the energy level of a class through the use of Q tools and teamwork. Enjoy the ride!

In this chapter you will learn:

- To use a variety of quality tools to assess students' knowledge
- To reenergize students with quality tools and teamwork
- The necessity and how-to for building celebration into a quality classroom to maintain energy to do high performance work

Use Quality Tools for a Variety of Purposes

Since students in school often lament how frequently the same topics are covered throughout their K–12 experience, wouldn't it be helpful to have the means to readily assess prior knowledge? If you had this ability, you would be able to do a better job of planning lessons and activities that would extend students' knowledge and skills without boring them (a major reason students give for why they dislike school). Figure 7.1 shows the linkage between Baldrige categories 1 (Leadership), 3 (Student, Stakeholder and Market Focus), and 5 (Student as Worker). You can see how important it is for the teacher/leader to be on top of student prior knowledge, and quality tools can help.

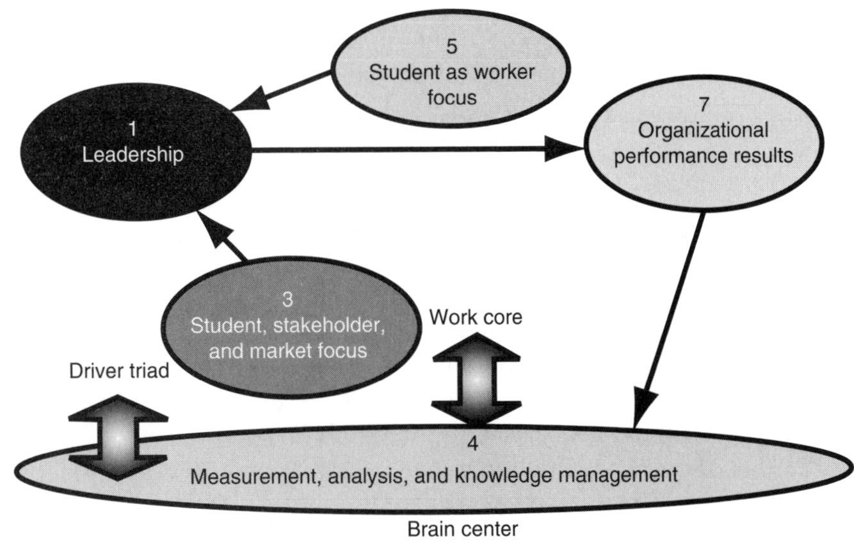

Figure 7.1 Linkages between leadership and students as customers and workers.

Quality tools can be used for two major purposes:

- To improve the processes within the classroom system or school system as we have described throughout this book
- To improve the quality and level of learning in the content areas

There are many more quality tools than the ones learned here; they include control charts and the Nominal Group Technique we listed in the Tool Selection Chart on page 13. For more information on quality tools, contact GOAL/QPC at 1-800-643-4316 and ask about the *Memory Jogger for Education* or other Memory Jogger books. This is an excellent and inexpensive resource. Only those tools previously learned are incorporated into this chapter.

Assess Prior Knowledge for Planning Purposes or As a Pre-Test

For planning purposes, several quality tools can be helpful in assessing what students know at any time during the school year. In some ways, the value of these as assessment tools supersedes online assessments because you can use these anytime and have more data points, instead of losing a whole quarter before making midcourse corrections. Examples include:

- Affinity Diagram
- Flow chart
- Cause-Effect Diagram
- Lotus Diagram
- Satellite Diagram

Teachers have used one or more of these tools before beginning a unit, before giving a test, and in many instances as the test itself. Refer to the Tool Selection Chart to find page numbers for tools' instructions.

Here are some suggestions for using quality tools as a pre-test:

- Ask students to flowchart a math problem.
- Pass out paper with a Satellite Diagram. Put the topic you've been studying in the head. Select four major aspects of the topic, and put one at the end of each arm. Ask students to put as much detail on each arm as they can.
- Pass out Lotus Diagrams with the topic under study in the center box. Identify four to eight aspects of this topic that you've studied and put one in each of the boxes around the center box. Ask students to fill in as many boxes as they can with important details.

Once you receive students' responses, it will be immediately apparent where the gaps are in student learning. This, in turn, informs the teacher about what reteaching must be done before the final assessment is given. Obviously, if most students made similar mistakes or errors of omission, teachers are wise to provide large-group, direct instruction to close the gap. However, teachers are not the only ones who can provide assistance. Perhaps you might divide the class into groups according to the gaps in their knowledge and give group leadership opportunities to students who had no gaps.

Here are some suggestions for using quality tools to determine what individual students already know about a topic. They can provide you with a proper starting point for instruction:

- *Cause-Effect Diagram.* In the head, place the words *abundant harvest.* Ask students to fill in the major bones and as much information as they know about what causes an abundant harvest.
- *Lotus Diagram.* In the center box, write the phrase *United States.* Fill in the boxes around the center with whatever approach you are going to follow. For example, you might use regions (northeast, southeast, southwest, and so on) and ask students to fill in the boxes with states of each region. Or, you might fill in the boxes around the center box with economy, government, weather, demographics, and so forth.
- *Affinity Diagram.* Provide students with Post-it notes and give them a specific amount of time to write down everything they know about a topic.

Quality Tools Contribute to Learning

Allow the tools to become a regular part of how students learn and draw meaning from lessons. Don't view them as something "cute" to do only when you're teaching about Thanksgiving or Christmas, Hanukkah, or Kwanzaa. Instead, allow the students to freely practice the tools often. You will be amazed at how much their recall and thinking skills improve.

Review the information on the SCANS skills and Multiple Intelligences from previous lessons. In what ways might the tools help students learn better, faster, and have fun in the process?

Once taught, the tools can help students as they learn new things or prepare for tests. Many of the tools contribute to critical thinking skills too, especially when used for process improvement. *But, one of the most significant reasons for using quality tools with students is that they conserve time, regardless of the tasks the students are expected to do.* We all know a picture is worth a thousand words, and when students learn the tools they will find myriad ways to use them.

Here is an example from an Ohio teacher. Girls in her fourth-grade class had a slumber party, and as you might expect, things began to deteriorate as the girls became more sleep deprived. The host decided to use some of the quality tools learned in class to save the night. After brainstorming, they used colored chalk to multivote on the activities they most wanted to do. Then, the young hostess flowcharted the slumber party with all the agreed-upon activities. From that moment on, there were no more tears and the girls came to school Monday morning all excited about what had happened.

The following is an overview of how quality tools can help teachers assess and plan activities:

1. Tools that help improve recall:
   - Affinity diagram
   - Satellite diagram
   - Flow chart
   - Lotus diagram
2. Tools that help improve organization or breaking down complex topics:
   - Affinity diagram
   - Satellite diagram
   - Flow chart
   - Lotus diagram
3. Tools that help with prioritization:
   - Multivoting
   - Nominal Group Technique
   - Relations digraph
4. Tools that help with data analysis:
   - Histogram
   - Line graph
   - Pareto chart
   - Run chart
   - Scatter diagram

5. Tools to help understand relationships:
   - Relations digraph
   - Scatter diagram
6. Tools that help understand cause/effect:
   - Cause-effect diagram
   - Relations digraph

Typically during training, we would ask teachers for specific suggestions about how they might use each of these tools in their content area to advance learning. Table 7.1 contains some of their ideas, and, of course, the list is almost endless.

Table 7.1 Examples of tools used for core subjects.

Tool	Social studies	Math	Language arts	Science
Run chart	Immigration data over time	Time of sunrise daily for a month	Books read by the class weekly for a semester	Plant growth over time
Cause/effect	Causes of the Civil War	Causes of types of math errors	Analysis of a good piece of literature	Causes of disappearance of ecosystems
Relations digraph	Motivation of early explorers	Causes of math anxiety	Events that lead to the actions of a character in any book	Contributors to global warming
Affinity diagram	Countries of each continent	Careers that require advanced math skills	Similarities of characters in Thurber's plays	Animals we will study for our trip to the zoo
Scatter diagram	Population density and crime	Attendance and quiz results	Fluency and comprehension quizzes	Temperature and plant growth
Pareto chart	Income data by ethnic groups in any city	Frequency of math errors by ethnicity or gender	Problems in our team study of great books	Scientific inventions with most world impact
Lotus diagram	Democracies around the world	Great mathematicians of the world	Study of a book, such as a biography of Winston Churchill	Planets
Satellite chart	Election process	Math facts	Parts of speech	Astrology

Reenergize the Class—Get Students Excited About Learning Again

Energy ebbs and flows from students and teachers at an uneven rate, often raised or drained by outside forces and influences such as impending weather, upcoming holidays, or state testing. Brain researchers realize that the adverse impact of stress on students' ability to learn can drain them of energy to recall facts or to solve problems. We must find a way to restore energy into classrooms and engage all students in the process.

In this day of Game Boys and intense media overload, motivating students to do high-performance work and to stay energized about learning requires teachers to add to their

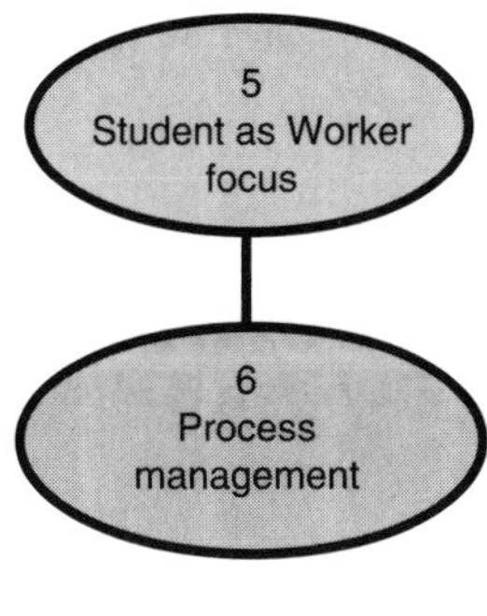

Figure 7.2 Work Core.

bag of strategies, which requires attention to the work core as shown in Figure 7.2. Motivation is part of the Student as Worker focus, and BBQ teachers realize that internal motivation makes all the difference in a teacher's work life as well as each student's future. In Chapter 2, we outlined an approach to flip motivation from external to internal by changing the essential culture of the classroom. This is key, yet we know that in reality there will be days or times during the day when the energy will wane. At times like these, the use of quality tools can be highly effective for reenergizing students.

In the following section, we describe an activity that can be used to assess learning in informal ways and provide direction for teachers to improve lessons and/or reteach where important concepts have been missed. It can be helpful during the Plan or Study phases of a PDSA cycle to ascertain how much students learned. For the activity, you might ask students to work individually, but we believe small teams work best. If students are required to work in teams, you can watch for how well they self-organize into a high-performing team, the group decision-making skills, and how effectively each group answers the problem. Give them a specific time limit for deciding on a tool to use and solving the problem. (Keep the time short enough to sustain enthusiasm and spark interest.)

When using this reenergizing activity in training, we generally keep the time limit to about five minutes because it is more important for our purposes to know if the teachers have a command of the tools and the use(s) for each. When using this type of activity with students, depending on the difficulty of the task, we suggest giving them about 10 minutes. Another approach might be to divide the task, giving a time limit for each part: "Your team has one minute to decide which tool is the best tool to solve this problem. At the end of that time, the team will have five minutes to solve the problem."

ACTIVITY: *Reenergize the students*

Teacher prep work:

- Prepare in advance a number of problems that are available for use throughout the semester or school year. It's a great idea to use problems that require recall of previously learned material. You can also use problems as a means to learn how much students already know about a topic. The use of any will depend on your purpose.
- Plan at least 15 to 30 minutes for this activity. (We don't recommend using it every day, or even on a scheduled day or time. One of its benefits is the element of surprise.)

- Have the flip chart paper, markers, and Post-it notes handy and organized into the number of teams in the class.
- Mix students up each time you use this activity so that everyone learns to work with everyone else.

Instructions to students:

1. Each team will need one or more pieces of flip chart paper (depending on the number of problems the teacher poses).
2. Organize yourselves around the table to make it easier to work together.
3. *Listen carefully to the problem.* (Read the problem only twice. This helps sharpen students' listening skills. You can take notes on the problem if you like.)
4. Your team task is to determine the tool to use to best solve the problem and then do it. You have only X minutes to determine the tool and solve the problem.
5. As soon as the team is finished, tape your paper to the nearest wall.

Examples of Problems to Energize Your Classroom

We're providing some examples of the general types of problems you could pose to your class, but the list is endless. Draw specific problems from your own content. We recommend you use a variety of problems from several content areas if you teach in a self-contained classroom. Our examples show the "script." With this activity and these problems, you are looking for self-organizing teams who can quickly make a decision about the appropriate tool to use. You learn how well the students know the tools and their logic. *Always, always, always* have the students tell you what level of learning they reached by using that specific tool. Most importantly, keep it light and moving at a pace that stretches the students but doesn't frustrate them. Emphasize how smart they are becoming!

> *Note to the teacher: After the answers for each type of problem, we have provided information about the level of learning (Bloom) or thinking skills (Marzano) required to complete the task. Make a decision based on which taxonomy your school district favors as to which of these two you will share with students. Some teachers make large posters for their rooms and ask students to identify the level of learning or thinking required. This is a powerful way to keep the focus on learning.*

Problem Type 1: What Tool Would You Use to . . .

- Identify everything you know about insects?
- Name all the states by region?
- Recall facts about your state's history?
- Write the times tables from 0 to 12?

Correct tool: Affinity Satellite Lotus

Level of learning skills when using a Q tool: *Knowledge*
Level of thinking skills when using a Q tool: *Recall*

Problem Type 2: What Tool Would You Use to . . .

- Break down the story of Cinderella, including at least plot, characters, and setting?
- Diagram the main elements of the story of Little Red Riding Hood?
- Relate the elements of weather patterns during the seasons?

Correct tool: Affinity Satellite Lotus

Level of learning skills when using a Q tool: *Analysis*
Level of thinking skills when using a Q tool: *Analysis*

Note: If the students added an additional category (such as the moral of the story or creating a different ending), they would have gone to *Integrating* (Bloom's Taxonomy).

Problem Type 3: What Tool Would You Use to . . .

- Review the following house plans and determine the cost of building it.
- Calculate the cost of buying groceries for a family of four for one week with a balanced diet.

Solving this problem requires two steps. The first is to determine what needs to be figured into the cost, and the tool(s) to use would be:

Correct tool: Affinity Satellite Lotus

The second step is to calculate the cost. The tool to use is a:

Flow chart

Level of learning skills when using a Q tool: *Analysis and Evaluation*
Level of thinking skill when using a tool: *Analysis and Evaluation*

Problem Type 4: What Tool Would You Use to . . .

- Solve any math problem?
- Identify the process for writing a story?
- Plan a trip to France?
- Organize a field trip to the zoo?

Correct tool: Flow Chart

Level of learning skills when using a Q tool: *Analysis*
Level of thinking skills when using a Q tool: *Analysis*

(You must provide data for problem types 5 and 6 in order for students to solve the problem.)

Problem Type 5: What Tool Would You Use to Gain an Understanding of . . .

- The relationship between weight and heart rate after exercise?
- Important information about human migration patterns and unemployment rates?
- Gas mileage and tire pressure?

Correct tool: Scatter Diagram

Level of learning skills when using a Q tool: *Evaluation*
Level of thinking skills when using a Q tool: *Inference*

Here are some examples of more complex problems designed to encourage students to become self-motivated to learn.

> *Note to the teacher: Save type 6 problems for last and use the category sparingly. It is very powerful, as you will see! Once your students realize they don't know enough to predict, you have succeeded in building internal motivation to learn.*

Problem Type 6: What Tool(s) Would You Use to . . .

- Predict what would happen to the animal life of the low country of southeast Georgia based on the following monthly rainfall data?
- Predict the annual life span for males and females in the United States in the year 2050 based on the following data on birthrates and life spans of the 20th century?
- Predict what will happen to the sea life over the next decade based on information on pollution and water temperature in the Pacific Ocean, as well as the impact this will have on the economies of Hawaii, Alaska, and California?

> *Hint to teachers: For this type of problem, do not simply provide students with data in logical sequence. Mix it up to require them to reorder it to make a run chart. For example: freeway fatalities caused by drunken drivers in 2001 [fictitious]: December, 39; April, 52; November, 17; August, 12; and so forth.*

Correct tool:

- To solve part one: Run chart and/or bar graph.
- To realize a prediction is impossible with current data and information: Use the lotus or affinity diagram to assess what must be learned in order to make a prediction.
- During their research, students may use other tools, such as the relations digraph, control chart, histogram, scatter diagram, and so forth.

Level of learning skills when using Q tools: *Analysis and evaluation*
Level of thinking skills when using Q tools: *Analysis, Inference, and evaluation when the project is finished*

When students realize they need more information to answer a question, you have "trapped" them into needing to learn. This is the best-case scenario for any teacher, because the students are now self-motivated.

Either the teacher or student teams can use the lotus or affinity diagrams to ascertain what the students need to research in order to answer the question posed by problem 6. These are "things we need to learn about in order to make any predictions." Each of the topics listed becomes a potential research project for one or more students. At this point, seek out volunteers who wish to study the topic and assign them to a group.

Groups can organize to divide the research into manageable bites. Give the entire class a deadline for completion of their research efforts, establish Quality Factors for the finished product, and let the students work. Using a variety of quality tools can help each group when presenting its information and data.

On the day set aside for reporting out, each group will report their research findings and then they will be asked to make their predictions, based on all the new information presented.

Debrief each reenergizing "problem" with students:

- What were the appropriate tools to use?
- What learning level or thinking skill set was your team using when using this tool to solve the problem?

> *Note to the teacher: We recommend that the problems be organized from simple to more complex to (1) get students involved early, get them excited, and allow them some success, and (2) cause them to think harder with each successive problem. The problems listed here are for example only. It's better for you to select things that are relevant to your subject matter and grade level. Keep it fun and nonpunitive; then stand back and observe the increase in student enthusiasm and interest.*

The Use and Benefits of the Reenergizing Activity

- To ascertain what the students know and can recall about a topic or concept before testing.
- To ascertain what students know about a topic before beginning a unit and creating lesson plans. This approach minimizes reteaching and can be used to expand a topic to greater depth.
- To ascertain the students' ability to follow oral instructions, and whether students can apply appropriate quality tools to solve problems.
- To provide examples of how quality tools can be used to push students to high levels of learning.
- To improve students' ability to organize quickly into teams and work together to solve complex problems.
- To summarize the day's learning and to keep the focus on learning (in a fun way) until the close of the day. Teachers study the results and use the knowledge gained to prepare lessons for the following day, with attention given to the "muddy" or missing points from the day's lessons.
- To begin the school day with a review of what was learned the previous day, to start the day off in a fun way, and to anchor previous learning.

The lessons for teachers are shown below in the PDSA cycle (Figure 7.3). Tables 7.2 and 7.3 contain Bloom's Taxonomy and Marzano's Thinking Skills, referred to in these examples.

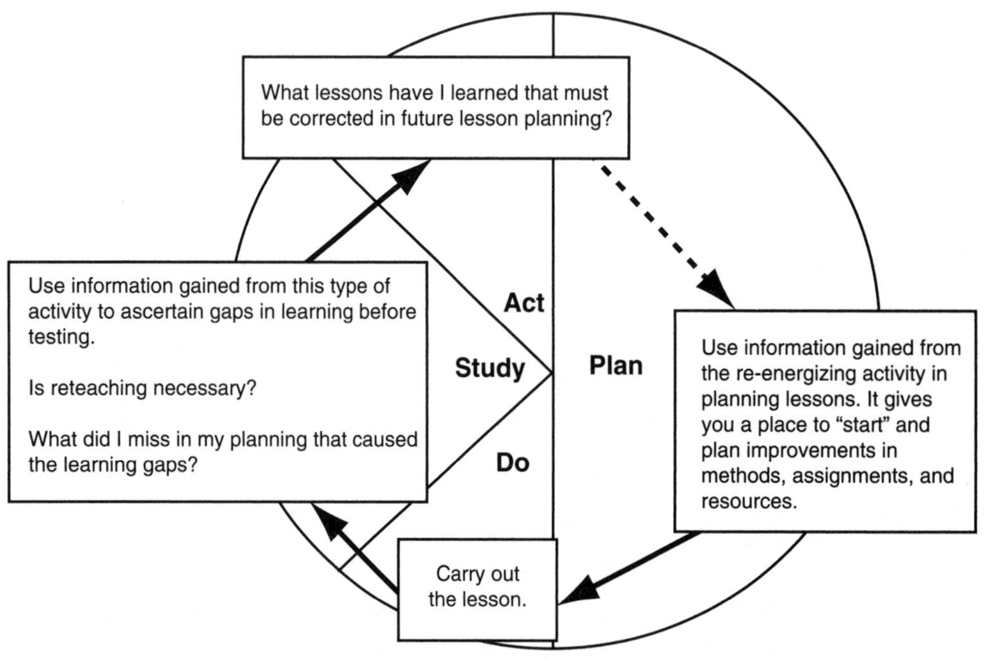

Figure 7.3 PDSA and lessons learned.

Table 7.2 Bloom's Taxonomy.

Learning level	Process verbs			Behavior description
Evaluation (appreciation)	appraise conclude justify validate	compare criticize interpret choose rate	contrast defend support predict judge	I am able to make a value judgment based on certain considerations such as usefulness or effectiveness. I'm able to write editorials and present my point substantiated with facts, theories, observations, and so forth. I can discuss and debate issues.
Synthesis (creative thinking)	categorize create formulate construct plan	compile design rewrite organize prepare	compose devise summarize manage	I use ideas to create something that could be a physical object, musical, communication, or abstract relations. I discuss, generalize, relate, compare, and contrast abstracts.
Analysis (thinking logically)	break down differentiate infer relate criticize debate test theory	deduce distinguish outline separate experiment question	diagram illustrate point out subdivide calculate examine	I analyze the application and understanding of knowledge by breaking it apart and realize how and when to put parts back together so that the organization of whole ideas becomes clear. I can break ideas into parts for logical analysis, assumptions, facts, and opinions, and I reach logical conclusions. I can use induction, deduction, or cause and effect processes.
Application (wisdom)	change develop produce transfer illustrate dramatize	compute employ relate use interpret	demonstrate modify solve translate operate	I can take knowledge from above and apply it to a new situation. I solve problems on my own and use other techniques. I recognize new problems and new tools to help solve them and this about the usefulness of this information so I can apply it to other problems.
Comprehension (understand)	convert discriminate extend infer report	defend estimate generalize paraphrase express restate	distinguish explain summarize predict compare contrast	I explain the idea or theory in written form or orally. I can do textbook assignments and recognize and extract information.
Knowledge (remember)	define label name recite memorize	describe list outline select record	identify match recall state repeat	I read materials, listen to lectures, view videos, take notes, and pass objective tests. I can recall facts.

Celebrations

To continue to encourage the class to practice the two principles of a BBQ classroom and to maintain enthusiasm for learning, it is wise to build in celebrations at critical points along the way, such as when a particular learning target has been met or when the class has reached a behavioral milestone. Celebrations are also a natural part of community-building. In a BBQ classroom there is a need to continue to impress all students with the joy that comes from achieving difficult goals as a group. High-performing teams understand the euphoria that comes from working together, often achieving heights beyond that which was anticipated.

In classrooms, the challenge of getting all students to work together to achieve the vision is sometimes more difficult than it might be with an athletic team, for example. The reason is that students are assigned to classes but students volunteer to participate on athletic teams, and we all know what happens to those students who are "not quite as good." BBQ classrooms must dispel the notion that some students are not quite as good. This is a part of why we believe so strongly in creating the culture for success through the creation of a different classroom system that was described in Chapter 2.

Table 7.3 Marzano's Thinking Skills.

Taxonomy	Action Words	Behavior Description
Evaluation	Evaluate, argue, judge, recommend, assess, debate, appraise, critique, defend	I can assess the quality, credibility, and worth or practicality of information or things. I use established criteria and can explain how these criteria are met or not. I can explain the interrelationship of evidence and reasons in support of my conclusions. For example, I can evaluate the credibility of arguments, decisions, and reports and evaluate their significance.
Inference	Deduce, anticipate, predict, infer, apply, speculate, conclude	I can make generalizations and explain the evidence that relates to it. I can deduce things from generalizations. Or, I can come up with generalizations from details or evidence. I can relate and integrate information and therefore am able to hypothesize, predict, conclude and synthesize information. For example, I can infer a characters' motivation in a novel.
Comparison	Compare, differentiate, contrast, distinguish, relate	I can recognize and explain simple or complex similarities and differences. For example, I can compare properties of objects or event; causes and effects of separate events; meanings, themes, plots, characters, settings and reasons.
Analysis	Subdivide, categorize, breakdown, sort, separate	I can divide a whole into component elements. I understand the part/whole relations and the cause/effect relationships that are essential components of more complex tasks. For example, I can identify the features of animate and inanimate objects.
Recall	Define, repeat, identify, what, label, when, list, who, name	I can recognize and remember key facts, definitions, concepts, rules, and principles. I can repeat verbatim or paraphrase given information. I can associate what I can recall to other, related concepts. For example, I can recall the names of the main characters in a story.

Based on the work of Robert J. Marzano.

Too often teachers reward students with stickers, treasure chest/goodie bag tokens, or food. Worse, these are often rewards for individual students, while others are not so lucky. Although these rewards may work to motivate some students, they actually end up being demotivators over the long haul. Imagine what it must be like for the students who are never good enough to get the rewards. What kind of attitude would that spark in you? On the other hand, if you were an exceptional student, continually rewarded in the above manner, would the rewards continue to motivate you over time?

When it comes to rewarding a class for achievement of a target or goal, we recommend the following:

- At the moment of establishing the targets, ask students how they would like to celebrate a specific achievement.
- Facilitate the discussion about how to celebrate by suggesting such things as 10 minutes at the end of the class to talk with friends, or an extra 5 minutes on the playground, or 15 minutes of free reading or using the computer or playing games.
- Encourage suggestions that do not entail cost and are not detrimental to anyone's health.
- Decide with the class about holding a grand celebration when the learning goals are met by everyone. These are huge accomplishments and should be

recognized as such. Have students make invitations and plan the event and encourage parents, the administration, and others to join in these celebrations.

- Celebrate mission specific (behavior related) accomplishments also.
- Avoid rewarding one or a small group of students for their accomplishments if the targets are not met by the class. Instead, foster a culture of "I am responseable to the success of the class."
- Exceptions can be made for special needs students who, the entire class agrees, have done exceptionally well.

Raise Expectations

Once a target or goal is met by the whole class, and after the celebration, it is time to raise the bar and ratchet up the expectations. Don't forget to engage the students in this process. Here's Candace (Allen) Smith's personal account of her experience at Centennial High School in Pueblo, Colorado.

Ratcheting Up Operationally Defined Quality Factors in a Ninth-Grade Civics Class

It was time for the students to do their first oral presentations of the year. The standard to be addressed was: Students will research, organize, and deliver an oral presentation relevant to a particular audience. I presented the standard to the students and asked the class what they thought a quality oral presentation would include—one that would really *wow* the audience. We conducted an affinity brainstorming and categorizing process and these are the categories that emerged:

- Interesting or funny
- Informative
- Good delivery
- Long enough

The class agreed that these were the areas that they wanted to be graded on and that would be essential in helping them meet the standard. I bit my tongue, knowing that what the students thought to be Quality Factor areas were not complete enough to use as assessment criteria for meeting the standard in the long run. But, I felt I needed to try something different this year, as the failure rate had been above 50% for my ninth-grade classes. I had already introduced many areas of quality and the students sought evidence that I really did want their input and feedback. (The class had decided that the acceptable level of quality should be 80%, and they were struggling with giving up the idea that 60% meant passing.) "It's quality or it's incomplete" was an idea that was very odd in their minds.

I purposefully didn't help the class develop operational definitions for the Quality Factor categories because I wanted the students to realize what happens when agreement *isn't* established operationally. During each speech, one-third of the class completed an evaluation along with me. The students were not happy with the wide variation of scores—after all, they had all decided on what was quality.

We then discussed the students' varying perceptions of "interesting, funny, informative, good delivery, and long enough" (the Quality Factor areas). I introduced the concept of "operational definition." The class then understood why the scores showed so much variation—they weren't operationally defined! They agreed that when preparing for the next oral presentation, operationally defining the Quality Factors would be a good idea.

In preparing for the next set of oral presentations, I wrote the Quality Factor areas from the previous speech on the board. I asked the class to brainstorm some ideas for improving the speeches, in general, from the last time. Discussion followed. I participated in the brainstorm, adding that I thought the speeches needed more substance, more research. Next, we used the Affinity process and these six quality factor categories emerged:

- Organized.
- Main points are clear.
- Good delivery.
- Interesting to this audience.
- Researched.
- Time limits set and observed.

Now we were ready for operational definitions. Following is what the class developed as operationally defined Quality Factors:

Organized:

- The talk had a beginning, middle, and an end.
- One idea was talked about before another began.

Main points are clear:

- The speaker stated the main points.
- The speaker gave evidence for the main points.

Good delivery:

- Note cards for notes (don't use rattly papers).
- Loud enough to be heard at the back of the room.
- Eye contact.

Interesting to this audience:

- Related to us and our interests.
- Made us think.

Researched:

- Showed research.
- Had to have at least two sources stated in speech ideas to prove it.

Met time limits:

- Speech lasted 4–5 minutes.

Each category had a "possible points" section, weighted according to importance as determined by the students. For example, "researched" could earn up to 20 points, whereas "met time limits" could earn only 10 points. (The weighting approach was similarly used by Jeff Burgard for his rubrics. For more information, see the Recommended Reading list.) After this round of oral presentations, there was less discrepancy between scores. Students thought the speeches were better, in general. I asked them if they were satisfied with the 80% acceptable level of quality, and, if not, did they want to raise it. Because they felt good about the possibility of personal success with the new process of operationally defining Quality Factors, students voted (three-quarters of the class was the determined majority) to accept 90% as the bottom line for quality. Speeches that failed to meet Quality Factor standards could be presented once again.

Throughout the year, we continued the process of ratcheting up the quality factors, brainstorming what we were missing in the categories and operationally defining that in the next speech. I was active in teaching necessary information as we went along. For example, when they suggested that "beginning" wasn't clearly definable operationally, the class was happy to hear that I could demonstrate different examples of what a good introduction was. They then wrote operationally defined Quality Factors for introductions. The process was evolutionary.

The final operationally defined Quality Factors for oral presentations were as follows:

Organization:

- The speech has clear divisions between the introduction, body, and conclusion.
- The speech revolves around one *big* idea, which is stated in the introduction.
- The big idea has three ideas that explain it and each can pass the "because test."
- Each supporting idea has examples to support it.

Introduction:

- The introduction has an attention-getter (story, question, or startling statement).
- The big idea of the whole speech is presented.
- A preview of the supporting ideas is given and clearly stated as a preview.

Body:

- The speech revolves around one big idea.
- Three ideas divide up the body and answer the "because test" for the big idea.
- Examples that develop each supporting idea are clearly there.
- Transitions are present. (They indicate that one idea section is ending and another is beginning.)

Conclusion:

- A summary of the speech is given.
- A closing thought—a "wind down"—is present.

Research:

- At least three sources of material are used and named in the speech.
- New information (information that isn't something "everybody knows") is presented.

Visual aids:

- Two visual aids are used.
- Each must be visible or readable from the back of the room.
- A costume or other "visual" counts as much as a poster.

Audience concern:

- The speech is interesting in that it can be related to personally to this class.
- The speaker used note cards and appeared practiced (as demonstrated in class).
- The speaker looked directly at individuals in the audience.
- The speaker talked loudly enough that everyone could hear.
- The speech doesn't waste time by repeating things we know and lasts 4-5 minutes.

Summary

In your quality journey for Chapter 7, you have added to your own list of ways to keep your students energized and motivated. Expanded ways in which quality tools can be used by your students in their problem solving are explained, and the theme of student work teams continues to be emphasized. What we aim for above all else in this chapter is that you take time with your students to experience the joy of learning and accomplishment. When students move from "fear of failure" and actually engage in the learning process, a gigantic first step has been reached in your Baldrige-based quality classroom. As a facilitator of learning (versus a dispenser of information), you also are evolving and exhibiting continuous improvement in your teacher leadership. With that in mind, never forget to celebrate *your* achievements.

Reflections

8

SUMMARY AND FINAL THOUGHTS

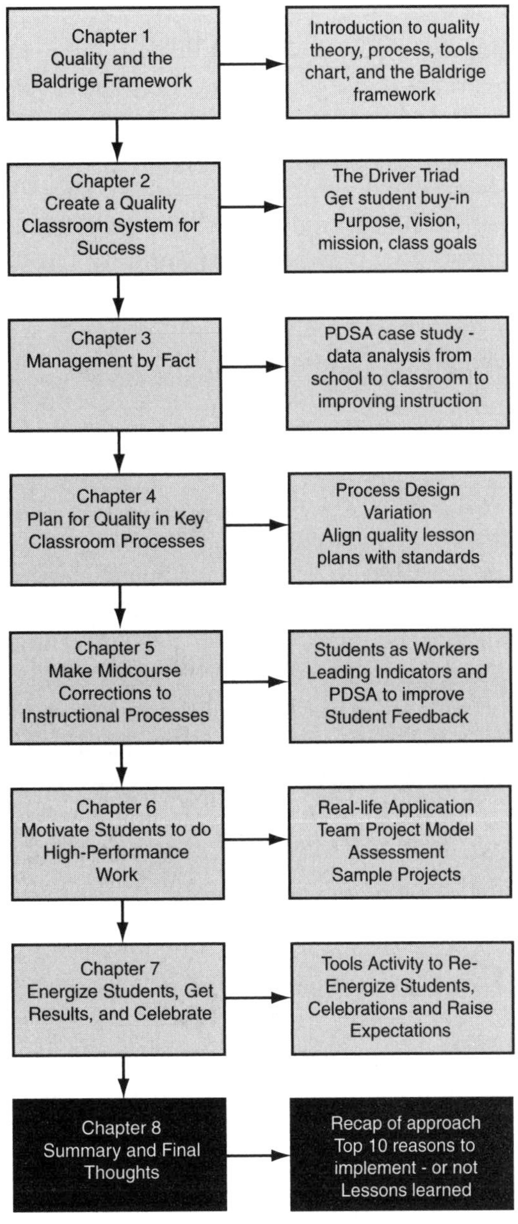

Congratulations! You have begun your Baldrige-based quality journey, one of the most challenging steps for any educator. There is hope for all students, but not without an effective, systematic fact-based approach of aligned and integrated processes within your classroom.

That, of course, is a short description of a Baldrige-based quality classroom. By reading and engaging in the activities in this book, you have learned about the Baldrige framework and now understand that your current system is yielding exactly the results for which you planned. While that may sting a bit when you consider your student's current learning results, once you change paradigms and accept this as truth, you are free to open yourself to the possibility that things can and do improve when the Baldrige framework is activated.

Performance excellence is not impossible to attain. You need to have courage and remain persistent in your dedication to personal and organizational learning. You have discovered that students are both workers and primary customers in your classroom. The next most important customer is the next-teacher-in-line or next-school-in-line or the world of work, depending on the age and level of the students with whom you work. You understand how the Baldrige framework yields a kinder, gentler atmosphere for students, yet requires more active participation in solving classroom system problems.

As you work to remove the barriers to student success, you realize the importance of engaging students as workers in a system created by management (you) so that together you share the burden. As the teacher-leader, you are a true facilitator of learning. In this way, students are empowered to help identify the barriers that prevent them from learning. You respond by making the necessary changes to improve the system. The whole system revolves around data: knowing what to collect, how often to collect it, and how to use it to inform and improve the system. This constitutes the brain center of your system.

In Chapters 3 and 5 you learned to use both a formal and an informal Plan-Do-Study-Act process, which is the improvement process used in Baldrige-based systems. The PDSA process is a scientific approach to system or process analysis and improvement. We have shown you the importance of using this approach for day-to-day operations as well as at the end of units, marking periods, or semesters. Remember that to predict better results at the end, you *must* rotate PDSA regularly and systematically and *learn by engaging all students* in this process. It is important to make midcourse corrections in the instructional process. While teachers may not have time to perform a formal PDSA to manage day-to-day operations, Chapter 5 provides you with a more informal approach that does work and provides many more benefits than the time it takes. This is the way to proceed if you want a sure-fire way to engage students actively as copartners in their education, and in the process keep them enthusiastic about learning.

To maximize the learning results, satisfaction, and student enthusiasm for learning, it is necessary to align and integrate all classroom processes. This begins by creating a culture and climate for success, as noted in Chapter 2. Chapter 4 provided information on how to design key classroom processes aligned with the desired results and how to reduce variation in deployment of the processes.

Chapters 6 and 7 focused on meeting student needs for active learning and aligning standards and curriculum with real-life application to improve student enthusiasm for learning and raise expectations. To address not only student needs, but also the needs and expectations of business leaders, a key stakeholder group, you learned a model for engaging students in team projects based on the skills recommended by the Secretary's

Commission on Achieving Necessary Skills. And because we don't work with widgets, student enthusiasm and motivation for learning sometimes wane. When they do, Chapter 7 provides an approach, using quality tools, to reenergize the classroom and discusses the important role celebrations play in maintaining enthusiasm in the classroom.

Point–Counterpoint

Over the years of training thousands of teachers around the country, we have accumulated a list of the most frequent reasons teachers give us for why this approach would not be feasible for them. No kidding! Here are the top 10 reasons why teachers can't create BBQ classrooms:

10. The district won't let me hang anything on the walls of my classroom.
9. Business models don't work with students—we don't make widgets.
8. Parents won't like it if I ask their kids to help others.
7. I teach special needs students. This won't work with them.
6. The reading (or) math program my district uses is scripted. I cannot deviate.
5. You don't understand my students – they are apathetic and undisciplined.
4. My students aren't capable of knowing how they want to learn.
3. The district requires me to teach to the state standards.
2. I've got to cover the curriculum.

And the number one reason why teachers can't create a BBQ classroom is:

1. I'm held accountable for students passing the state test.

In response to these reasons, we consulted teachers who *have* been successful in using the Baldrige framework and came up with these reasons why you must change your system. Here are the top 10 reasons why teachers can't afford *not* to create BBQ classrooms:

10. We don't produce widgets.
9. Parent communication and cooperation needed to improve.
8. Students in my class(es) come with a large range of abilities and interests.
7. My students were apathetic, bored, or disenfranchised.
6. I am tired, frustrated, and feel unappreciated by the district, parents, and students.
5. My students have to take the state standards test, and to be successful they need to learn the basics and critical thinking.
4. We have a new curriculum program but I knew it isn't working for all my students.
3. The district is holding me accountable for student learning results.
2. There's a lot the students are required to learn and know.

And the number one reason why teachers can't afford not to create a BBQ classroom is:

1. I invest a lot of time and take great pride in my teaching. I care about my students and I didn't know how to make it better for all of them.

The Time Issue

We will not avoid the fact that implementation of a BBQ classroom takes time. Anything new takes time, doesn't it? However, the reward of greatly reducing discipline issues and having many more students enthused about learning is worth it. Empowering students to become copartners in the classroom so you don't need to shoulder the burden all alone is also worth the upfront time commitment. Once you teach students the tools and PDSA process, it is amazing how much help they will be. As we said earlier, teachers tell us that for every minute spent teaching about quality, roughly 10 minutes of instructional time is saved. Imagine what you could do with 10 additional minutes each day. That adds up to 30 hours a year, or five school days. This is a savings of just 10 minutes a day!

Time is one of those finite things. There are, so far as we know, only 24 hours in a day. This holds true for everyone, yet some people seem to have a gift of finding time to accomplish much more than others. This is the fascinating thing about adopting the Baldrige framework and putting the quality process in use. It *appears* that there is more time for important work because all the players are focused on task, and there are many fewer classroom disruptions due to acting-out behavior or students coming to class late. (This would be a good time to speak with your building administrator about reducing or, better yet, eliminating PA announcements and other administrative interruptions.) Consequently, at the end of the day, week, or marking period, you realize that much more was accomplished and students actually learned a lot more than in the same amount of time spent previously.

Further, wouldn't it be nice to leave school and not have the sole burden of reading and grading hundreds of assignments, only to get exasperated by the number of errors? Rework is a killer. You not only have to read and grade all the assignments, but then you have the extra burden of reteaching what wasn't learned, taking more time away from new instruction. Wouldn't it be better to have students hand in quality work that has already been reviewed by peer assessors and revised before it reaches your desk? Using this process, the peers learn more too and eventually everyone saves time because there will be less rework and that reduces the burden of reteaching.

We think we are running out of time to change. Never in our recent history has there been a greater need to change the educational system and classroom systems to give every student an opportunity to gain the skills, knowledge, and abilities that must be learned. The Baldrige-based quality classroom represents the new culture of civility, respect, and cooperation. It is created through the two principles, class vision, mission, and goals combined with the use of PDSA that leads to continuous improvement. As you identify barriers that keep students from learning and improve key processes, you *will* see sustained, improved results.

Lessons Learned

We'll share our lessons learned in the hope that they might help you in your journey:

- There is never one "right" way to do something, but by using a management by fact approach and standardizing key processes after getting to "best practice," there's a greater chance of success.

- If you don't evaluate satisfaction and results regularly and frequently, in-process, you can never be sure of your effectiveness.
- Enthusiasm for learning is vital and both teachers and students need to have it.
- Every time we are *certain* that we are right, something happens to make us realize we are not. The antidote for this is to systematically ask for feedback and make changes accordingly.
- You have to identify and know your customer.
- Individuals who are angry have most likely been "hurt" by the system and feel disenfranchised. Look for ways to empower them to help fix the system.
- Many problems are more complex than can be described in a book or training. We leave it to you to build the bridges between these concepts and your own circumstances.
- Although critics may challenge our thinking, we need to remain open to what they say. It always follows that we are led to a better way to approach issues, training activities, and examples.
- Students who do not fit in with a traditional approach are the most likely to become missionaries and champions for BBQ over time. Conversely, students who have been highly successful with the traditional approach may be the most resistant to change. This is why the *two principles* and *building the culture of success for all* are so crucial to your success.
- Be very clear about your purpose. It frames everything you do.
- The School Board, PTA, and administrators are more likely to support a BBQ approach if students share their enthusiasm and improved learning results with these groups. It is hard for board members and other adults to ignore children and youth.
- If students are not learning more, no matter how enthusiastic they are, there are significant system problems that must be addressed. Ignoring this reality will cause more problems down the road.
- The more regularly and systematically you ask for feedback, share the results, and make improvements, the more "buy-in" and cooperation you'll receive from students and vice versa.
- Make and take time to regularly renew yourself so you have energy to continue over time. We encourage you to find a trusted peer who is willing to embark on the journey with you for support, feedback, and encouragement.
- Never, ever give up.

Good luck! Enjoy your journey, and let us know your thoughts, questions, or comments through our website, www.qualityeducationassociates.com, as your journey continues.

Appendix A

EXAMPLES OF STUDENT AND PARENT FEEDBACK INSTRUMENTS

Gaining feedback from students and other stakeholders is vital to any teacher's Baldrige-based Quality (BBQ) efforts. We have collected, over the years, a variety of instruments from teachers all around the country and offer them to you so that you might use the idea, if not the example. As we have mentioned several times in this guide, it is not possible to "copycat" any one teacher's approach, because every situation is somewhat different. We offer these as examples of the kinds of information you might find helpful in understanding the needs and expectations of your students and parents/guardians.

The first group of surveys is directed at getting to know a new group of students to understand their needs and expectations. The first example is for parents of pre-K, kindergarten, or first graders. After that, it is important to get feedback directly from the students. The value of this exercise is immeasurable when preparing for the opening of school and/or the start of a new semester. Teachers who are able to find out as much as possible about their students' interests can search out books and materials ahead of time that will (1) let students know you *care* about them and (2) pique their interest in reading and learning. You will also learn about what fears they may have, which, if paid attention to, can help relieve future stress.

The last document in this group is an elementary example used for determining parent expectations. The one used by Candace (Allen) Smith with high school parents appears in Chapter 2, page 35.

The second group of surveys relates to satisfaction of students and parents/guardians.

It is a mistake to imagine that giving parents/guardians a survey at the end of the year is sufficient to interpret their satisfaction. Likewise, it is insufficient to assume that anecdotal feedback guarantees accurate interpretation. Generally speaking, only individuals who feel strongly give you kudos or make complaints without solicitation. *Assumptions* about satisfaction levels of parents/guardians are often inaccurate. The worst mistake a teacher can make is to disregard the need to systematically seek satisfaction with what is happening in the classroom. This information is *gold* if used to improve. Teachers we have trained and who have implemented at least quarterly parent surveys all report that the process has led to greater parental support. Of course, as with students, our advice is *if you don't want to know and don't intend to share and don't use the feedback to improve, don't ask.*

If few parents/guardians respond to your surveys, it is important to try to understand the reasons. Here is a quick self-assessment:

- Do you communicate in the first language of parents? (Some schools translate any information that goes home into seven or more languages; most do so in at least two languages.)
- Are survey items nonbiased, short, and easy-to-understand? Have you created a survey in which all items are worded in the same (negative or positive) way?
- Have you structured the survey in a way that allows you to collect quantifiable, actionable data (yes/no or 3–5 point Likert scale) with space for additional comments, or is your survey entirely open-ended? (The latter is difficult to quantify or take action on because you cannot be certain whether the response is common cause or "special cause." You would not want to make system changes based on special cause.)
- What do you do with survey results? Do you chart or graph the responses and provide the results to *everyone* in a timely fashion?
- Do you tell parents what you intend to do in response? Do you ask parents for help in coming up with an action plan for improvement?
- Do you survey parents about *matters that are important to them?*

In short, we believe that a systematic feedback system is vital for any BBQ teacher and hope that these examples will help pave the way for your success. For students with limited English skills, we'd recommend translating the survey into their first language and putting the English translation immediately below each item. This will begin their journey to learning the vocabulary and increase the chance for success.

Getting to Know Your Child

Parents,

Please help me get to know your child. Be as specific or as vague as you feel comfortable with and return this to me by September 8th. *Thanks!*

1. What special talent (sports, music, etc.) does your child have?
2. Any hobbies?
3. What subject area is favored?
4. What is your child's best subject area?
5. What subject is most difficult for your child?
6. How does your child get along with siblings?
7. What does your child do during free time at home?
8. What would you like me to know about your child?

Introductory Student Survey—Elementary

Getting to Know You

My name is ____________________. Please call me ____________________.

My birthday is __________________. My phone number is __________________.

I live with ____.

My favorite color is _______________. Sports I like are ____________________.

My favorite sport is ____.

I don't like any sports. I like ______________________________________.

I have a pet ______________________________ named __________________.

The funniest thing that happened to me this summer was ____________________

____.

I am looking forward to this school year because _________________________.

My best or favorite subject in school is __________________________________.

Why ____.

My least favorite subject in school is ___________________________________.

Why ____.

I dread starting school because _______________________________________.

Tell me one (or a lot) thing(s) you would *really* like to learn in this class. _________

____

____

Introductory Student Survey—Middle School

Getting to Know You

My name is ____________________. Please call me ____________________.

My birthday is ____________________. My phone number is ____________________.

I live with ____.

Sports I like are ____________________. My favorite sport is ____________________.

I don't like any sports. I like ____.

I am a member of the ____________________ club(s) and participate in __________

____ after school.

I have a pet ____________________ named ____________________.

The funniest thing that happened to me this summer was ____________________

____.

I am looking forward to this school year because ____________________.

My best or favorite subject in school is ____________________.

Why ____.

My least favorite subject in school is ____________________.

Why ____.

I dread starting school because ____________________.

Tell me one (or a lot) of thing(s) you would *really* like to learn in this class. ________

____

Introductory Student Survey—High School

Hi,

I am looking forward to having you in this class. Please help me get to know you a little better and complete this survey. I will be asking for your help in making adjustments to our classroom system periodically throughout the semester and your assistance will greatly be appreciated. Thank you.

My name is ________________. Please call me ________________.

My birthday is ________________. My phone number is ________________.

I live with ________________________________.

Sports I like are ________________. My favorite sport is ________________.

I don't like any sports. I like ________________________________.

I am a member of the ________________ club(s) and participate in ________

________________________________ after school.

I don't participate in any after school activities. I work at ________________.

After graduating from high school I plan to ________________________.

My career hope is to work as ________________________.

The funniest thing that happened to me this summer was ________________

________________________________.

I am looking forward to this class because ________________________.

The thing I am dreading about this class is ________________________.

I learn best when I ________________________________.

The most important thing to know about me is ________________________.

________________________________.

It would be really great if we could learn ________________ in this class.

Parent/Guardian Expectations Survey—Elementary

I'm delighted to have your child in my third grade class this year. Because you are most likely concerned about what is taught in the class, this survey is intended to explore those interests.

Please answer the following questions. Thanks for your assistance. I will send a report informing you of how other parents/guardians have responded.

---

1. If you were the teacher of this class, what would you think is most important to teach? (We typically teach mathematics, language arts, social studies, science, writing, technology, physical education, music, and art.)

2. Other than academic content, is there anything else you hope your student will learn? (Skills, attitudes, etc.)

3. Is there any way in which you might be able to assist in the teaching of the class; that is, do you have expertise that might add value to this particular class? Would you be willing or able to help in any particular way?

4. What are some things I need to know to help your child learn this year?

5. Other comments, suggestions, expectations, etc.?

Please sign here if you're able to assist with this class. ______________________________

Intermediate Grades Student Math Satisfaction Survey

Please do not put your name on this paper.

You have been changing rooms for math class since the beginning of the year. The teachers and principal would like to know your feelings about having your math taught this way. Please circle the answer below that best describes you and your feelings about changing rooms for math.

1. I like having math class in other classrooms.		Lots	Some	Little
2. I like having different teachers for math.		Lots	Some	Little
3. I'm doing better at math this year by changing rooms.		Lots	Some	Little
4. I have no problem having all my supplies when I change classrooms.			Yes	No
5. I feel comfortable asking any of my math teachers for help.			Yes	No
6. I like having math class with kids who understand math at about the same level as I do.			Yes	No
7. I am bored in math class because I already know what we are supposed to be learning.			Yes	No
8. I like math.			Yes	No
9. Math is easy for me.			Yes	No
10. I have been made fun of or teased about the math class I am in.			Yes	No
11. I am:			Female	Male
12. My grades are usually:	E's & G's	G's & S's	S's & L's	L's & U's

Please write any comments you would like to make about your math classes.

Examples of Tools to Measure Parent Satisfaction

Parent Feedback on Flexible Math Grouping—Intermediate Grades

Please take the time to fill out this survey on the Flexible Math Program your child has participated in this year. We appreciate your time.

1. My child has benefited academically from this program.

   ____ Yes

   ____ No

   Comments: ____________________

2. My child's self-esteem has improved regarding his/her math skills this year.

   ____ Yes

   ____ No

   Comments: ____________________

3. My child has reacted positively to the transition made moving from group to group or teacher to teacher.

   ____ Yes

   ____ No

   Comments: ____________________

4. I would like to see this program continue in the future.

   ____ Yes

   ____ No

   Comments: ____________________

   Additional Comments: ____________________

Circle One: Grade 3 Grade 4

Name (optional) ____________________

Parent Satisfaction with Teacher—Elementary

Dear Parents/Guardians,

In my efforts to show continuous progress I have developed this Parent Satisfaction Form. I will use these results to help improve my teaching skills. Your input is very valuable to me so please take what I hope is just a few minutes, to fill out this form and return it to school with your student. There will be a box out on the hall table, outside my room, for students to drop off these evaluations. I'll summarize the results and make copies available to you. Thank you very much for filling this out and returning it to me as I feel we must always move forward!

Please return this assessment with your son/daughter as soon as possible. Results will be summarized and available should you like a copy.

In the PRIORITY scoring column, please tell me *how important each of these items is to you.* Regardless of how you think I am doing at the present time on the item, give each a rank from 1 to 5, with 5 being the most important and 1 being the least important.

In the EVALUATION scoring column, please tell me *how you think I am doing at the present time on each item.* Give a rank of 1 to 5 with 5 being excellent and 1 being unacceptable.

Overall Outcomes	**Priority**	**Evaluation**
High expectations		
Effective learning environment		
Amount of assigned work		
Classroom management		
Parental communication		
Grading and assessment		
Teacher availability		
Academic Outcomes		
The curriculum includes EXPERIENCES that:	**Priority**	**Evaluation**
provide opportunities for creative expression		
provide for a variety of learning styles		
provide for real life learning experiences		
provide for experiences in goal setting and decision making		
provide experiences to meet goals of courses of study as reflected on our new report cards		
develop an interest in lifelong learning		
develop citizenship skills		

Please use the reverse side for additional comments.

Signature ______________________________ Date __________

Example: Parent Satisfaction with Teacher—Middle School or High School Social Studies

Please return this evaluation form with your son/daughter as soon as possible. Results will be summarized and available should you like a copy.

In the PRIORITY scoring column, please tell me how important each of these items is to you. *Regardless of how you think I am doing at the present time on the item*, give a rank of 1 to 5, with 5 being the most important, and 1 being the least important. In the EVALUATION scoring column, please tell me *how you think I am doing at the present time* on the item. Give a rank of 1 to 5 being excellent and 1 being unacceptable.

Overall Outcomes	**Priority**	**Evaluation**
High expectations		
Effective learning environment		
Relevant curriculum		
Amount of assigned work		
Type of assigned work		
Multi-age environment		
Classroom management		
Parental communication		
Grading and assessment		
Teacher availability		
Academic Outcomes		
Curriculum includes EXPERIENCES that provide for the study:	**Priority**	**Evaluation**
of the ways humans view themselves over time		
of people within a given place, time, and environment		
of social identity		
of interactions among people and institutions of the time		
of how people have created and change structures of power and governance		
of how people deal with scarcity, choice, and costs in a given society		
of relationships between technology and society		
of global and cultural connections and interdependence		
of ideals, principles, and practices of citizenship in a democracy		
Non-Academic Outcomes	**Priority**	**Evaluation**
Adult life skills		
Thinking and decision-making skills		
Interest in lifelong learning		
Citizenship knowledge and skills		

Please use the reverse side for additional comments.

Your child's name ______________________ Grade __________ Period _______

Your signature: ______________________ Date: __________

Appendix B

PARTIAL EXAMPLES OF DISTRICT EXPECTATIONS

While we do not attempt to provide detailed expectations of districts around the country, we do want to give you some ideas in the hope that if your district has not yet accomplished this task, it will give you some talking points for discussion with your school administrator and/or the district. We cannot understate the importance of having specific, precise expectations at each grade level and in each course to engage in proper planning to meet the stakeholders' expectations. Included are partial benchmarks and targets for second, fifth, and sixth graders in Aldine Independent School District in Houston and Minuteman Science and Technology High School in Lexington, Massachusetts. The latter came from collaboration with employers. This school requires all teachers to align lessons with expectations so that the school can guarantee its graduates meet the entry-level business requirements. To do this, Minuteman faculty meet regularly with employers and must keep their courses aligned to the postsecondary and/or employers' requirements.

A BBQ teacher would align his or her lesson plans with the expectations and regularly measure student progress toward the achievement of each by all students. We recall working in a large district in one southern state several years ago, when this district was one of a few that instituted a third-grade reading *guarantee,* well before the No Child Left Behind Act. This forward-looking district assigned key skills at each grade level, starting in kindergarten. If each child mastered the skills, it would position him or her to read at grade level by the end of third grade. Teams of teachers, working with the Division of Curriculum and Instruction, made decisions about the building blocks for reading on grade level by third grade and then set up a coordinated system of required skills at each grade. This made decisions about lesson planning much easier for all teachers, and because of the alignment, many more students achieved the stated goals at each grade level.

Aldine ISD Benchmarks/Targets: Second Grade Language Arts (Partial Sample)

Assurances

By the end of Second Grade, the students will:

1. Write a "How To" composition and a personal or expressive narrative composition.
2. Know and be able to sight read all the High Frequency Words (Dolch) from PP—2nd grade.
3. Answer comprehension questions after reading a 200 or more word passage.
4. Use correct punctuation, capitalization, spelling and verb tenses in simple sentences.

   Commas → Friendly letter, commas in a series, commas between city and state, between day and year

   Capitalization → Proper nouns, cities, states, months and days, titles, verb tense (choose correct verb tense)
5. Use prior knowledge, context clues, and decoding strategies in order to find the meaning of unknown vocabulary words.

Language Arts—First Six Weeks

Vocabulary

Grade 1 Dolch				Grade 2 Dolch		
after again an any by could every fly from	give going had has her him his how just know	let live may of old once open over put round	some stop take thank them then think walk were when	again always around because been before best both	buy call cold does don't fast first found five	gave goes green its made many off

- After a skill is initially presented at a grade level, it is necessary to continuously reinforce and extend that skill, when appropriate, throughout the grade level to ensure mastery.
- Language Arts materials will be grade-level appropriate. The grade-level span will be 2.0–2.9.
- Upon completion of Grade 2, a student will be reading fluently at a minimum of a 2.9 level.

WORD STUDY/PHONICS/VOCABULARY STRAND

The students will:

WORD STUDY PHONICS (TAAS #1, TEKS 2.5A-B)

1. Recognize word families and/or rhyming words ow, ou, ar, or, oo, o, o-e, ph, gh, wh
2. Review beginning and ending consonants.
3. Review long and short vowel sounds.

Aldine ISD Benchmarks/Targets—Fifth Grade
Reading: First Six Weeks (Partial Sample)

Assurances

By the end of Fifth Grade, the student will:

1. Determine the meaning of unfamiliar words by using context clues.
2. Recognize and apply supporting details as they reinforce the main idea, directly or indirectly, in a variety of grade appropriate texts.
3. Identify the best summary of a grade appropriate text, and write a one or two sentence summary of a paragraph or a given text.
4. Make inferences and generalizations based on information in the text.
5. Determine whether details in a piece of writing are factual, nonfactual, opinionated, or false.

Reading: First Six Weeks

Vocabulary

FRY Words #501–521		Content Subject Area Words
can't matter square syllables perhaps bill felt suddenly test direction	center ready anything divided general energy subject Europe moon farmers	**General Science** absorb classify
		Physical Science density prey
		Life Science adaptation habitat
		Social Studies adjacent celebration

- After a skill is initially presented at a grade level, it is necessary to continuously reinforce and extend that skill, when appropriate, throughout the grade level to ensure mastery.
- Language Arts materials will be grade level appropriate. The grade level span will be 5.0–5.9.
- Upon completion of Grade 5, a student will be reading fluently at a minimum of a 5.9 level.

WORD STUDY/PHONICS/VOCABULARY STRAND

The students will:

WORD STUDY PHONICS (TEKS 5.6A&B)

1. Complete Diagnostic Evaluation Instrument—5th grade pretest (see Word Strand Curriculum Guide).

STRUCTURAL ANALYSIS (TEKS 5.6A&B)

2. Identify Latin roots: port, form.

Aldine ISD Benchmarks/Targets—Sixth Grade Math (Partial Sample)

Assurances

By the end of Sixth Grade, the student will:

1. Add and subtract decimal numbers through thousandths.
2. Compare and order nonnegative rational numbers.
3. Solve, recognize, and identify properties of 2-dimensional shapes using geometric vocabulary.
4. Generate equivalent fractions and identify the fraction reduced to lowest terms.
5. Solve problems involving proportional relationships.

Mathematics: First Six Weeks

Vocabulary

algebra	dividend	power
algebraic expression	divisor	product
associative property	estimate	quotient
base	evaluate	reasonable
commutative property	exponent	solution
cubed	identity property	solve
distributive property	inverse operation	squared
	order of operation	variable

Whole Number Review

The student will:

1. Read and write whole numbers to billions. (TEKS b6.1; TAAS 1.1) **M**
2. Compare and order non-negative rational numbers. (TEKS b6.1A; TAAS 1.1) **M**
3. Round whole numbers to approximate reasonable results. (TEKS b6.2D; TAAS 1.2) **M**
4. Solve problems using the order of operations. (TAAS 2.1) **D**
5. Use non-negative rational number properties (associative, commutative, distributive, and identity properties) and inverse operations. (TEKS a2; TAAS 2.1) **E, D**
6. Use addition, subtraction, multiplication, and division of whole numbers to solve problems where exact answers are not required. (TEKS b6.2D; TAAS 10) **D**
7. Use the operations of addition and subtraction of whole numbers to solve problems. (TEKS b6.11C; TAAS 6) **M**
8. Use multiplication and division of whole numbers to solve problems. (TEKS b6.2C; TAAS 1.4) **M**
9. Define and calculate whole numbers with exponents, a to the b power. (TEKS b6.1D, TAAS 1.4) **E,D**
10. Use letters to represent unknowns in an equation and evaluate expressions. (TEKS b6.5) **E,D**
11. Solve equations using inverse operations. (TEKS b6.5; TAAS 2.4) **D**

Minuteman Science-Technology High School, Lexington, MA Examples of Performance Competencies for the Biotechnology Manufacturing Technician

(The number before the competency gives the reader an idea of how many skills are required for each area)

1 = Excellent
2 = Good
3 = Adequate
NR = Not Rated

The student upon completion of his/her study of the Biotechnology Manufacturing Program will be able to:

		1	2	3	NR
TECHNOLOGY SKILLS					
T1	Follow appropriate safety procedures.	____	____	____	____
T8	Describe and explain the instrumentation used to measure media composition (i.e., nutrient probes and measurement devices).	____	____	____	____
T16	Program a robot using the "on-line" and "off-line" programming method.	____	____	____	____
T49	Isolate and identify bacteria in an unknown sample.	____	____	____	____
COMPUTER APPLICATION SKILLS					
CA1	Operate word processing software to record, edit, store, revise, and print correspondence, reports, forms, and other material in the PC environment.	____	____	____	____
CA5	Design and manage a computerized database using basic techniques and elementary commands.	____	____	____	____
BIOLOGY SKILLS					
B1	Describe the structure of a polymer and explain how polymers are formed and broken down.	____	____	____	____
B3	Describe the structure and functions of lipids in an organism.	____	____	____	____
B17	Distinguish between a bacteria and a virus and describe the structure of each.	____	____	____	____
B20	Explain the role of enzymes in metabolic pathways.	____	____	____	____

		1	2	3	NR
CHEMISTRY SKILLS					
C2	Express and solve a series of problems using exponential notation.	____	____	____	____
C10	Apply the principles of titration and know how to measure it.	____	____	____	____
MATH SKILLS					
M1	Add, subtract, multiply, and divide whole numbers, fractions, and decimal numbers.	____	____	____	____
M5	Solve problems using ratios and proportions.	____	____	____	____
M11	Use graphs, charts, and tables.	____	____	____	____
COMMUNICATION SKILLS					
CH1	Use reading, writing, listening, speaking, nonverbal and verbal skills to solve job-related problems and to help perform on-the-job tasks.	____	____	____	____
CH4	Use language, tone, style, format, and vocabulary appropriate for the purpose and audience.	____	____	____	____
READING AND WRITING COMPETENCIES					
CH11	Restate or paraphrase a written selection to confirm one's understanding of what was read.	____	____	____	____
CH13	Read and interpret data presented in tables, graphs, charts, maps, and blueprints alone or in combination with related texts.	____	____	____	____
WRITING AND VISUALS COMPETENCIES					
CH20	Write summaries of processes and events.	____	____	____	____
CH23	Prepare graphics (tables, diagrams, charts, graphs, drawing, maps, and photographs) for the purpose of communicating information.	____	____	____	____
LISTENING AND NONVERBAL COMMUNICATION COMPETENCIES					
CH24	Identify relevant information in oral messages.	____	____	____	____
CH29	Determine when more information is needed and ask appropriate questions to gain information.	____	____	____	____

	1	2	3	NR
SPEAKING AND NONVERBAL COMMUNICATION COMPETENCIES				
CH31 Participate in group team discussions.	____	____	____	____
CH32 Exchange ideas orally.	____	____	____	____
WORK HABITS COMPETENCIES				
CH34 Perform all tasks in a safe, disciplined, and efficient manner.	____	____	____	____
CH35 Maintain a good record of attendance and punctuality.	____	____	____	____
INTERPERSONAL COMPETENCIES				
CH42 Report errors, omissions, and/or malfunctions efficiently and according to school/company policy.	____	____	____	____
CH43 Demonstrate the ability to perform effectively and cooperatively as a member of a production team.	____	____	____	____
CH44 Demonstrate courteous and respectful relationships with fellow workers.	____	____	____	____

Appendix C

STUDENT DATA AND GOAL SETTING BOOKS

I am responsible for my own learning.

If students are to be our partners in their education, they have a responsibility to know how well they are doing. The idea that students can or will keep track of their own data puts the onus on each of them to realize that the teacher does not give grades arbitrarily; rather, they are earned. Another reason to have students keep track of their own progress is to teach them how to reflect, set goals, and create personal action plans for improvement.

This activity is a powerful experience for student-led parent conferences as teachers around the country are discovering. When students have to explain to their parents/guardians how well they are doing and what plans they have for improving, it emphasizes the importance of learning.

The basic elements of the Student Data Collection Book are:

- Class purpose, vision, mission, and class goals
- Two principles of a quality classroom (I am responsible and I am response-able)
- Some kind of learning styles awareness chart or sheet
- Sheets for weekly quizzes by subject—generally set out for the semester or grading period (run chart format)
- Sheets for monthly assessments for the entire year by subject (run chart format)
- Goal-setting sheets with action plans for improvement (one per subject per month)
- Blank radar charts for social skills improvement—quality student or mission
- Record of required skills/concepts needed to master for the year or semester

Added features that can make the experience more powerful:

- For students in grades 1 and above, a personal mission statement
- For students in middle grades and above, a personal vision
- A drawing of the quality student with Q factors operationally defined
- I AM PROUDEST OF . . . sheets (one per subject per marking period)
- Other?

What follows are some examples that might prove helpful to you. Select from the laundry list of examples and see what works best for you. Above all, feel free to revise anything. *The important thing is that students in your classes start keeping track of their own results.*

On pages 243–245, we have included an example of how powerful run charts can be when students keep track of their own data. You can see from the example how, if the teacher has a transparency of class results on a line graph, comparisons can be made for parents who may be interested in seeing how his or her child is progressing relative to his/her peers.

Expectations are raised when students set new goals at the end of each marking period. One way to accomplish this is to have each student average his or her weekly quiz results for the previous marking period. The average from the previous nine weeks becomes the lowest score acceptable for the next marking period. In effect, this new goal becomes a covenant each student makes with himself or herself. Students who set goals and articulate the strategies they will use to reach their goals will have a much greater chance of meeting the new goal. Teachers, meanwhile, do not need to remind or reprimand students if they fall below their own expectations once or twice during the marking period. The reason is simple—students know whether they studied or not. If, however, a teacher notices that the student is below his or her goal for two or three weeks in a row, there is a need for a private session to discover what the problem might be.

Example: Weekly Quiz Results

Subject *Math*   Class Goal: 8   My Personal Goal: 8   My Average for This Marking Period 6.88

Marking Period: 1st   I Will Improve by: *Using math flash cards at home 10 minutes each night.*

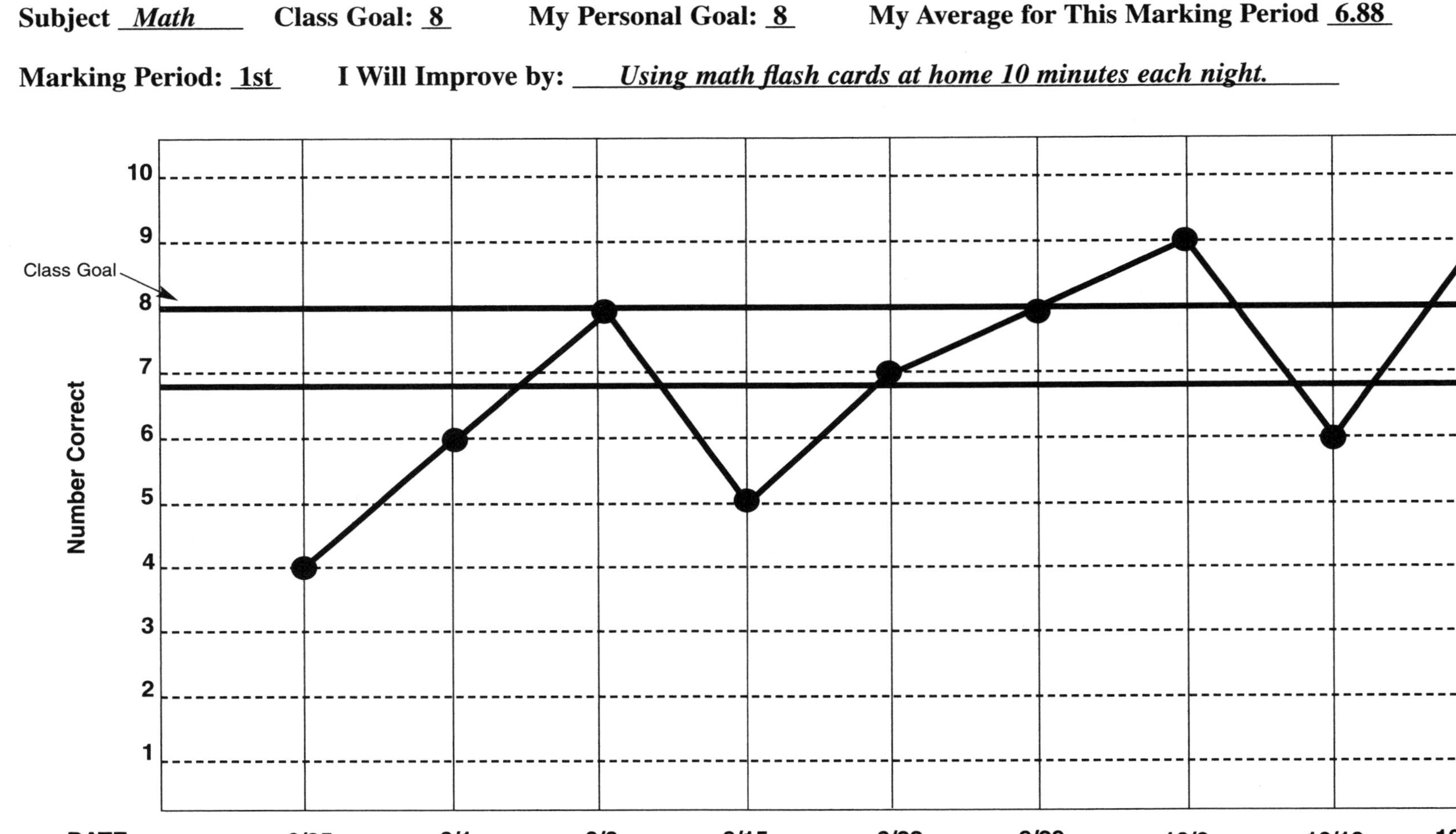

Example: Weekly Quiz Results

Subject *Math* **Class Goal:** 8 **My Personal Goal:** 8 none below 7. **My Average for This Marking Period** 8.5

Marking Period: 2nd **I Will Improve by:** *Using math flash cards 10 minutes nightly and have my parents quiz me the night before the class quiz.*

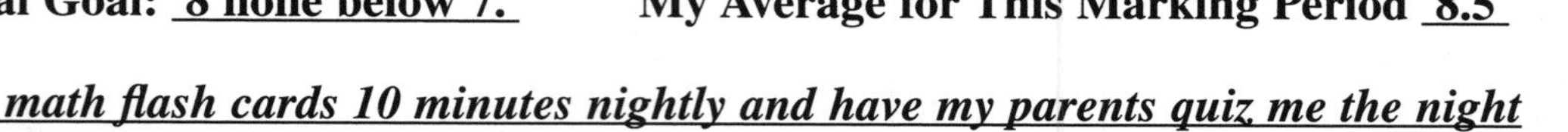

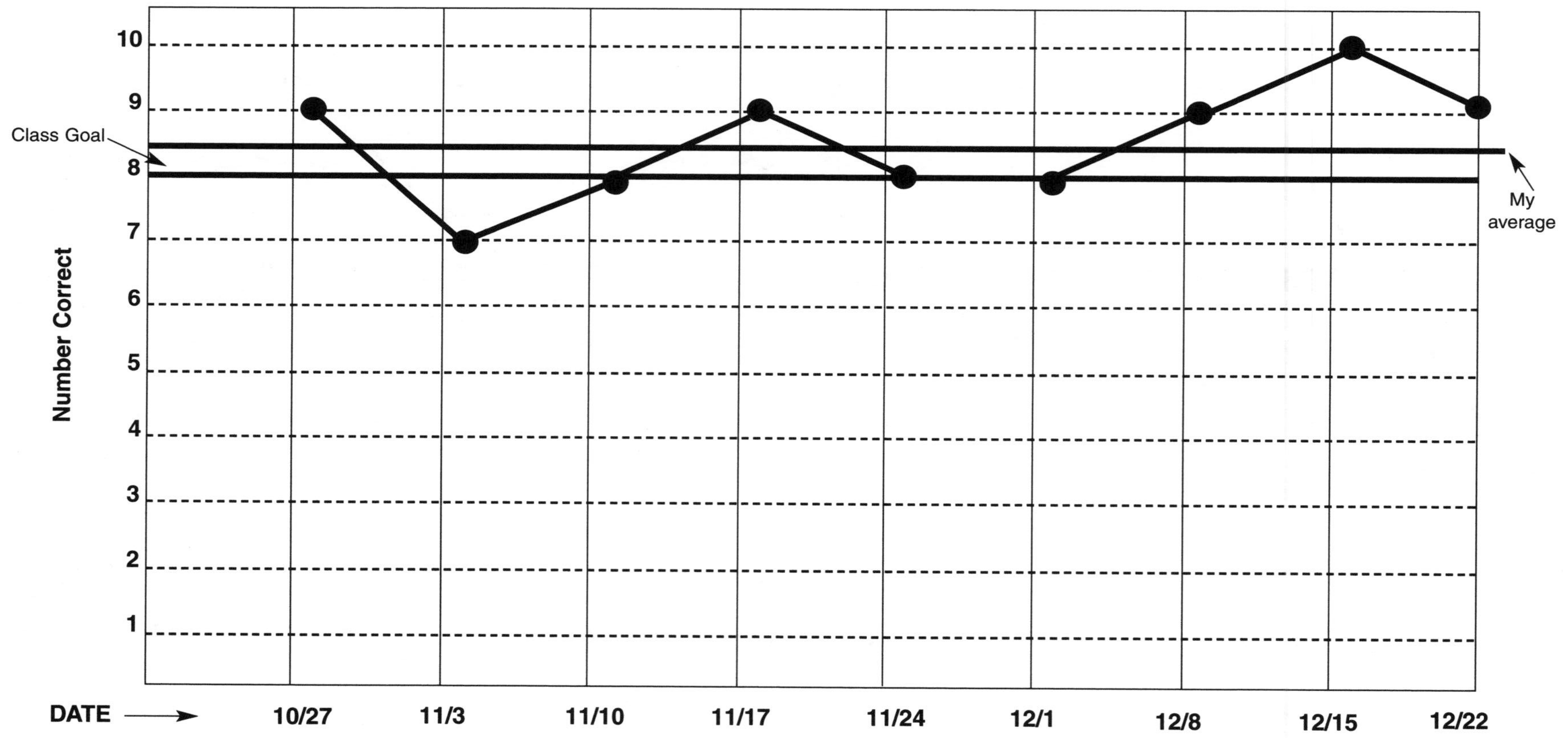

Example: Weekly Quiz Results for the Class

Subject *Math*
Marking Period: 2nd

Class Goal: 8
Number in Class: 20

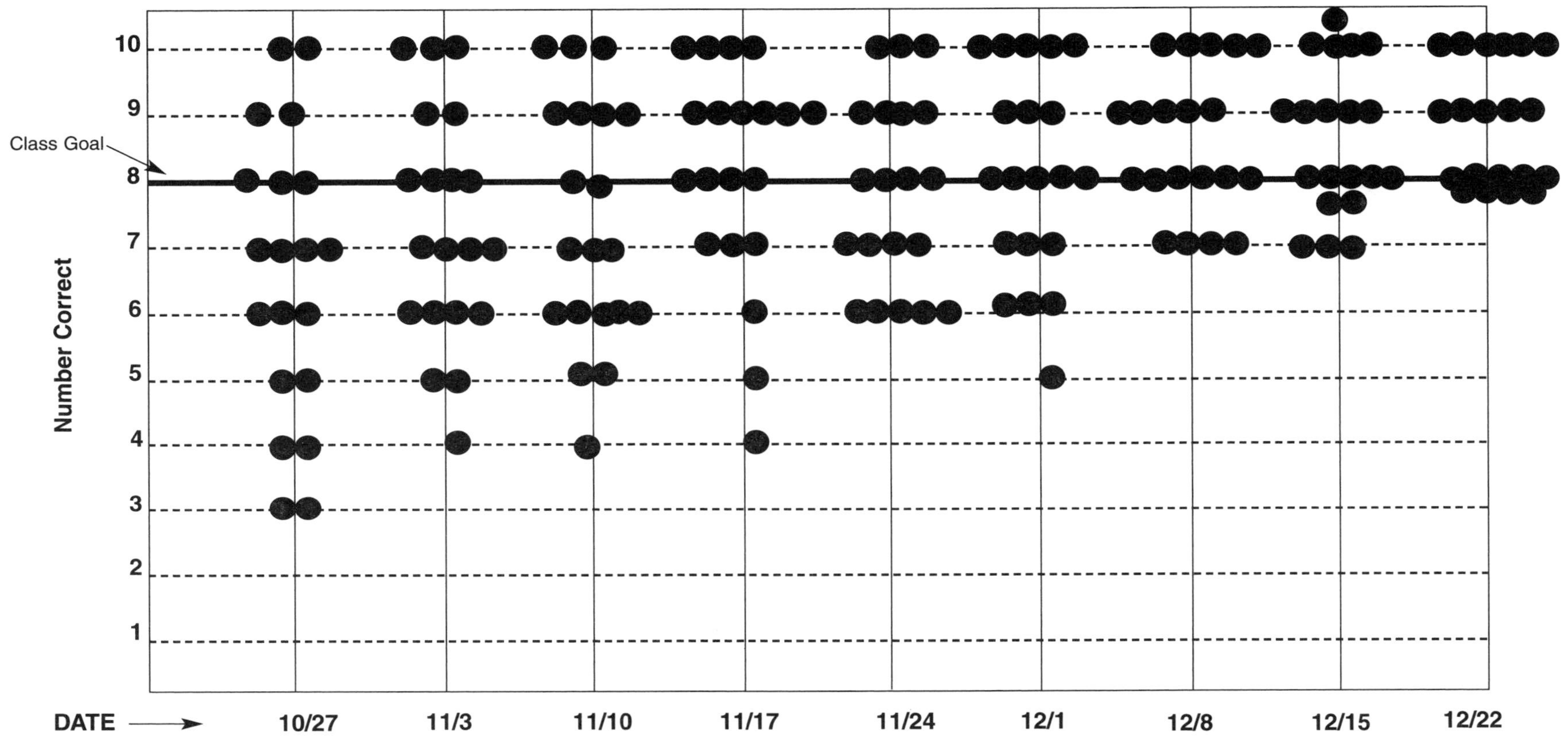

Weekly Quiz Results

Subject ____________

Marking Period: ____________

My Personal Goal: ____________

Class Goal: ____________

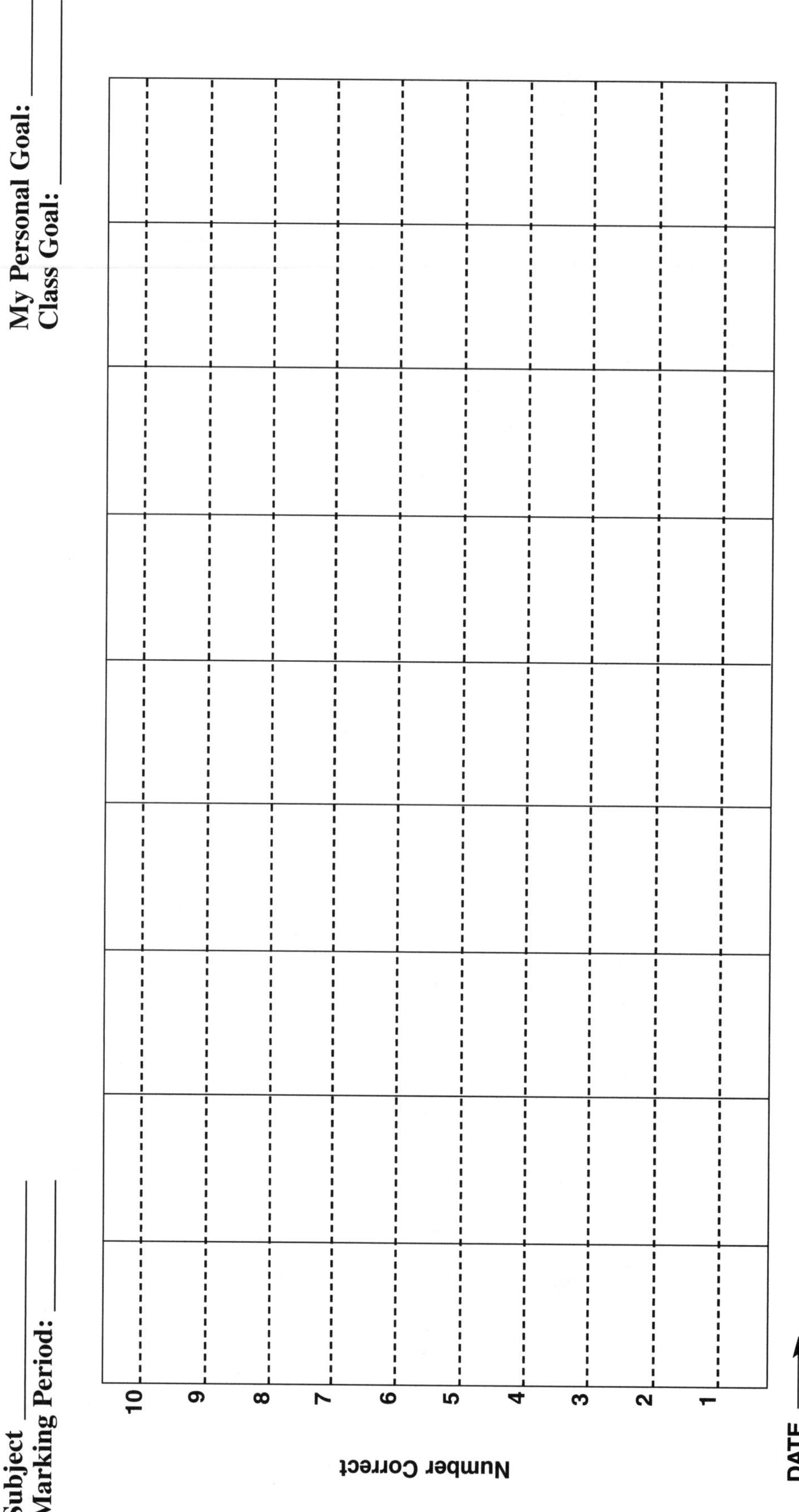

Weekly Quiz Results

Subject ____________________

# Correct	Date	Date	Date	Date	Date	Date	Date	Date	Date
10									
9									
8									
7									
6									
5									
4									
3									
2									
1									
0									

My Personal Goal: ____

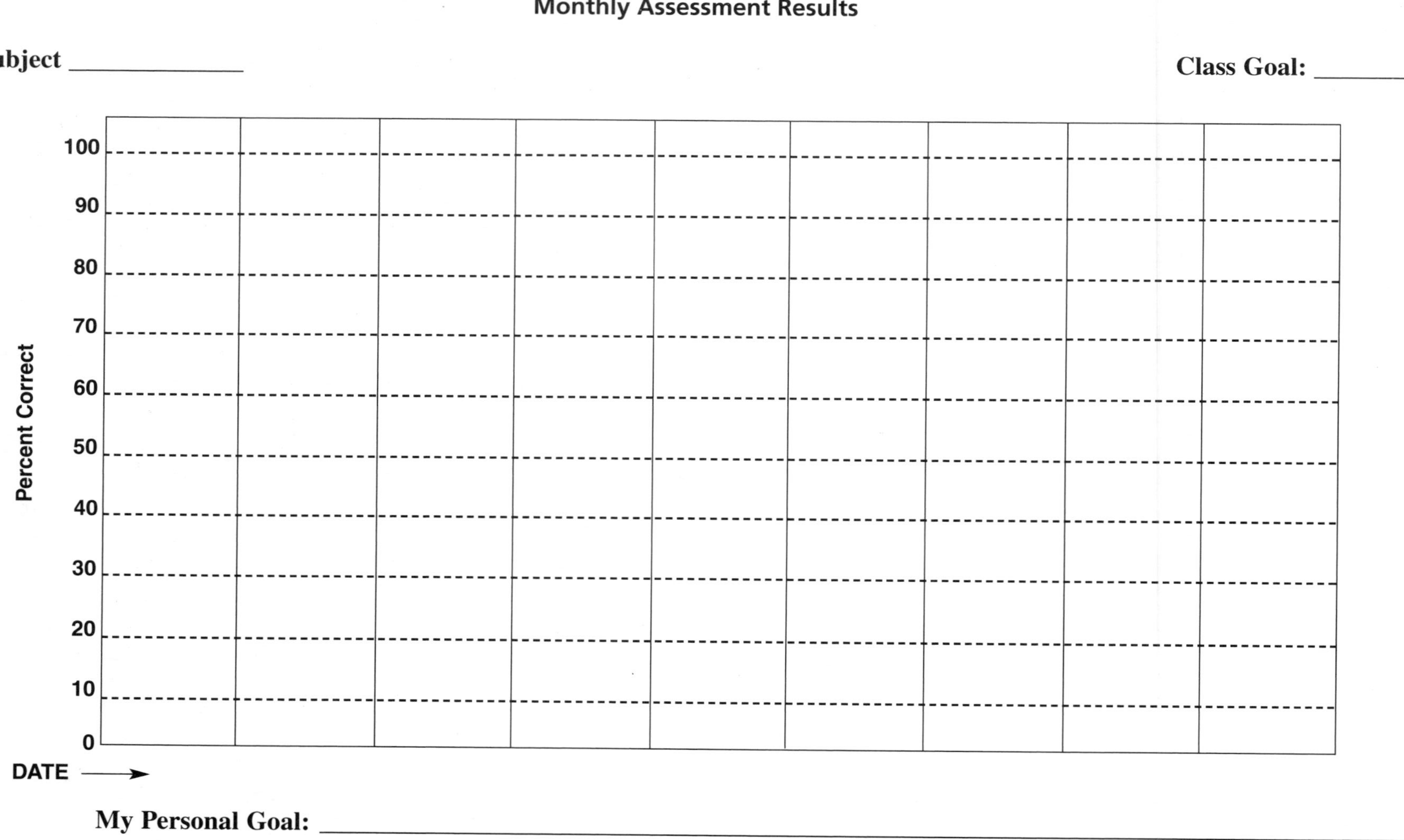
Monthly Assessment Results
Subject
Class Goal:
Percent Correct
100
90
80
70
60
50
40
30
20
10
0
DATE
My Personal Goal:

Personal Data Book

Name ______________________ School Year ________________________

Grade or Subject ____________________ Teacher ___________________________

Class Purpose ____

____

Class Vision ____

____

____

____

Class Mission ____

____

____

____

____

Class Goals ____

____

____

____

____

What I enjoy most about school or this class is ______________________

____

____

____

____

The subject I like best is ______________________________

Because ______________________________________

____

____

____

I have the most trouble with ____________________________

____

____

____

Learning Styles

I learn best when ______________________________

____

____

____

The best class(es) I've ever had was/were ______________________________

____

____

____

Because ______________________________

____

____

____

____

____

The things that get in the way of my learning are ______________________________

____

____

____

____

The strongest asset I bring to learning is ______________________________

____

____

____

The most difficult thing about school for me is ______________________________

____

____

____

To counteract this, I will ______________________________

____

____

____

Weekly Personal Goals and Action Plans

Date: ____________

This week I put about _____% effort into learning. I scored a _____ on the quiz.

The skills that I need to work on are

____

____

____

____

My action plan for improving and mastering these skills is

____

____

____

____

____

____

RESULTS

This week I put about _____% effort into learning. I scored a _____ on the quiz.

My action plan   worked   partially worked   didn't work

because ____

____

____

____

____

____

____

____

____

____

____

____

____

Social Skills

Name ______________________________ Dates ____________

My strongest social skill is ______________________________

The area I most need to improve is ______________________________

To improve, I will do the following ______________________________

____

Academic Skills

Name ______________________________ Dates ____________

My strongest academic skill is ______________________________

The area I most need to improve is ______________________________

To improve, I will do the following ______________________________

____

Student Record of Skills Taught and Learned

Name ______________________________

SUBJECT:____________________ GRADE or COURSE LEVEL: ______________

Skills or concepts to be mastered										
	Skill	**Date taught**							**Mastery**	**Application**
1										
2										
3										
4										
5										
6										
7										
8										
9										
10										
11										
12										
13										
14										
15										
16										
17										
18										
19										
20										
21										
22										
23										
24										
25										
26										
27										
28										

Appendix D

TEMPLATES

Method 1 Line Graph—Class

Subject ____________

What is being studied? ____________

Marking period ____________

Period: ____________

Class Goal: ____________

Number in class: ____________

Number of correct items for class

Quiz 1 | 2 | 3 | 4 | 5 | 6 | 7 | 8 | 9

Dates ⟶ ____ ____ ____ ____ ____ ____ ____ ____ ____

Methods used to learn

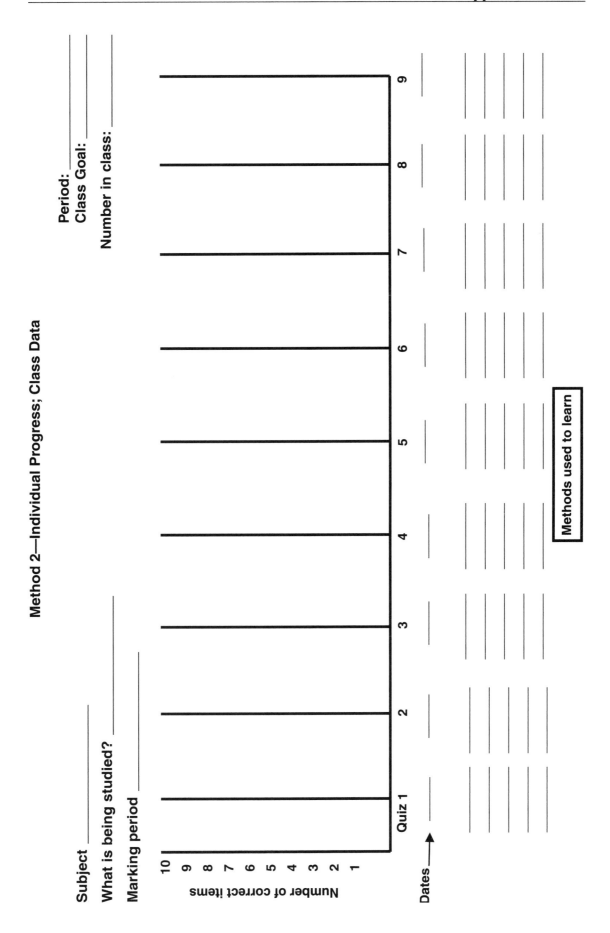

Method 2—Individual Progress; Class Data

Subject ____________

What is being studied? ____________

Marking period ____________

Period: ____________

Class Goal: ____________

Number in class: ____________

Number of correct items

10
9
8
7
6
5
4
3
2
1

Quiz 1 2 3 4 5 6 7 8 9

Dates → ____ ____ ____ ____ ____ ____ ____ ____ ____

Methods used to learn

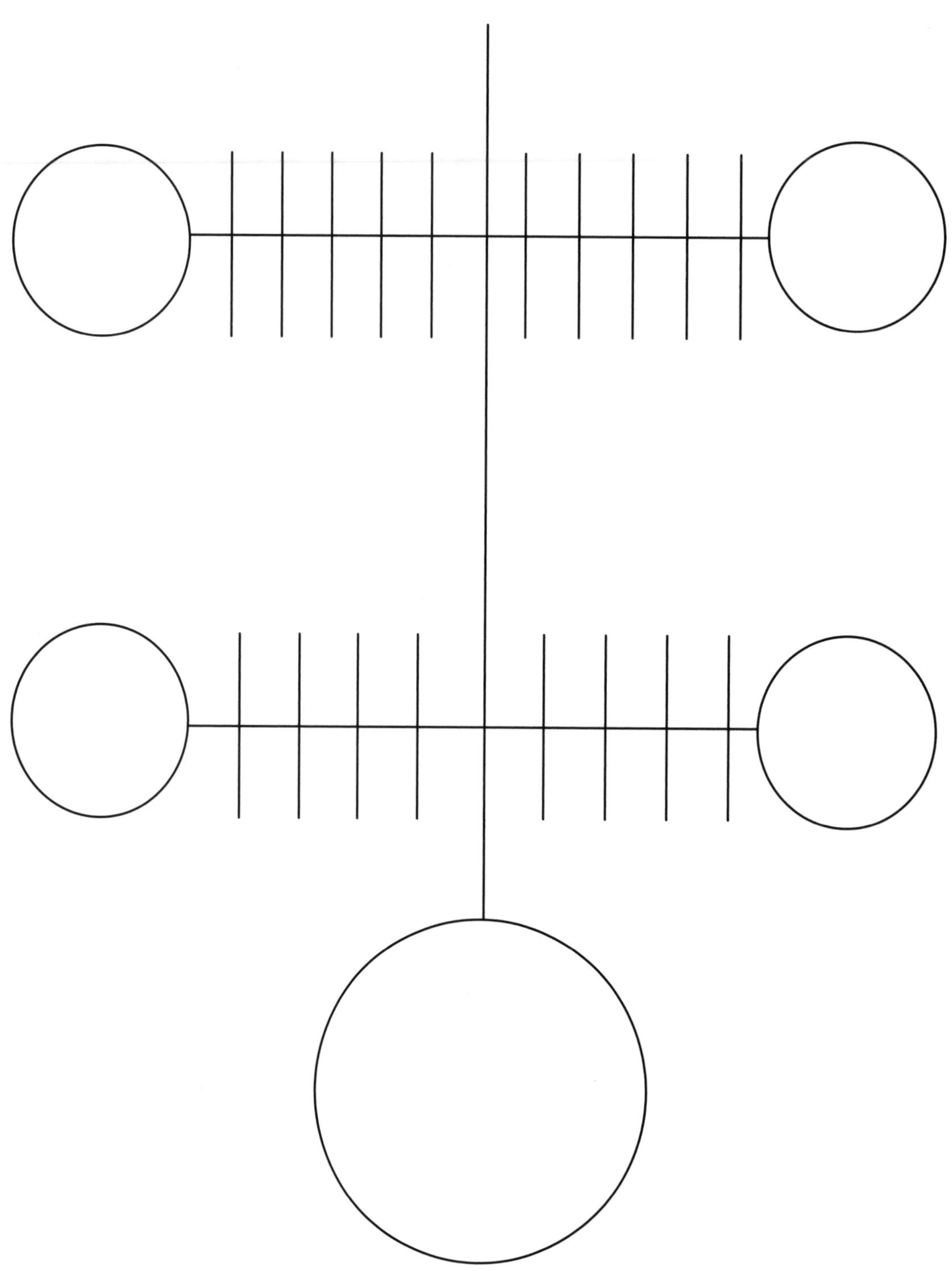

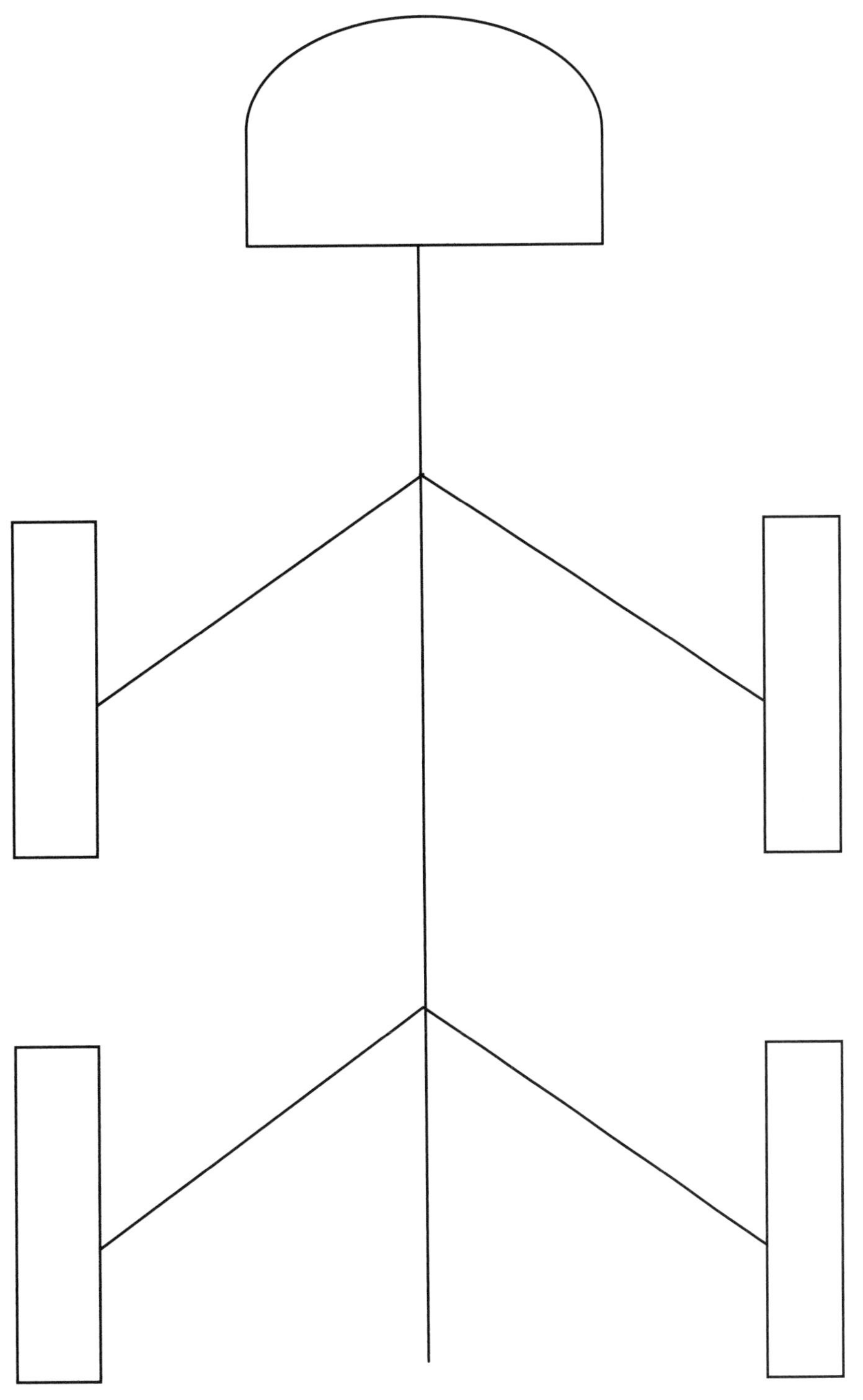

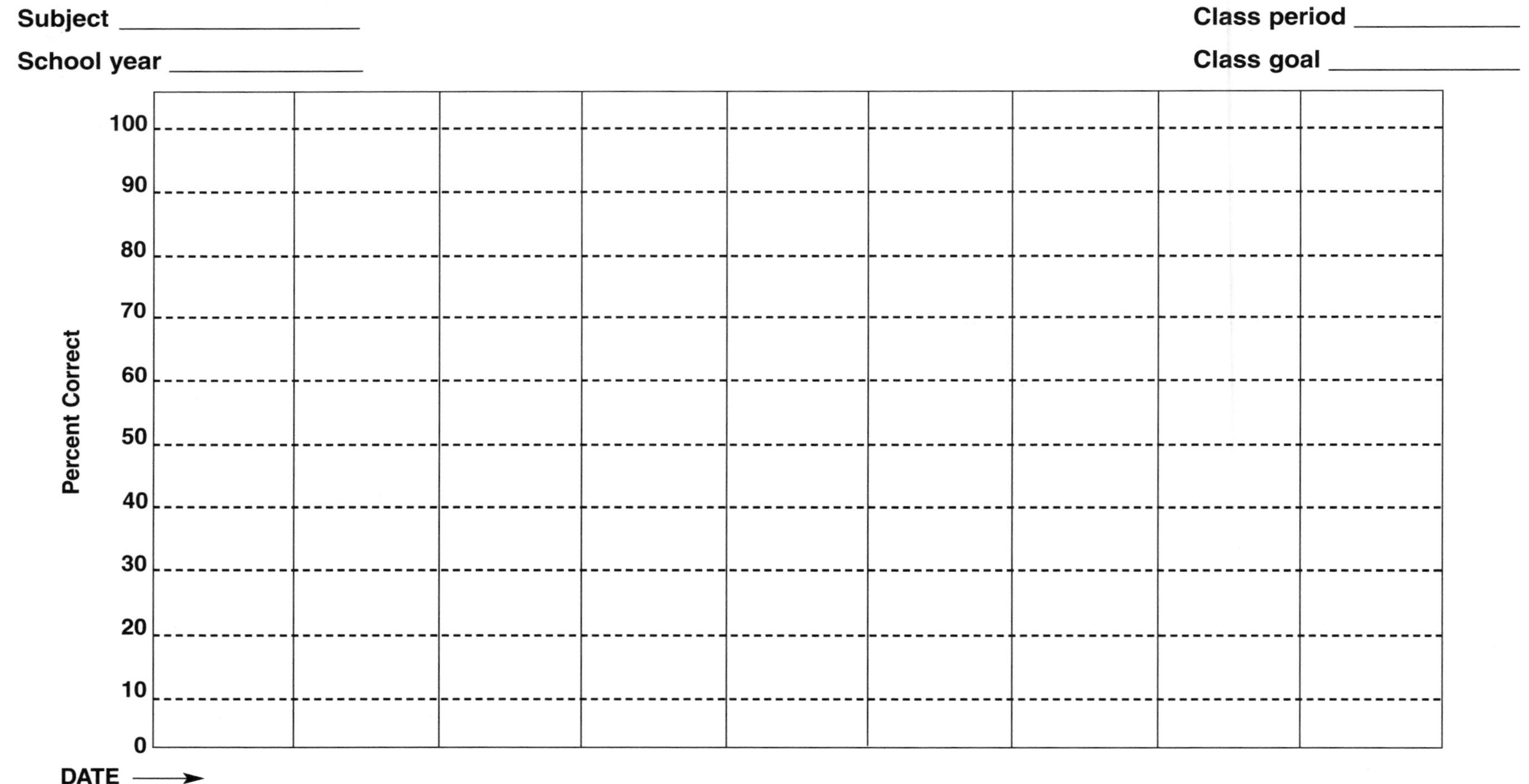
Monthly Class Assessment Results
Subject
School year
Class period
Class goal
Percent Correct
100
90
80
70
60
50
40
30
20
10
0
DATE

Monthly Assessment Results

Name ____________ Subject ____________ School year ____________ Class goal ____________

Percent Correct									
100									
90									
80									
70									
60									
50									
40									
30									
20									
10									
0									

DATE ⟶

My personal goal ____________

Data Collection Plan

Quality factor	Operational definition	How measured?	When?	By whom?

Data Collection Form

Name ______________________ Date __________________

Quality factor	Operational definition	How measured?	When?	Sample A	Sample B	Sample C

Noninstructional Process Design

Year ________________ **Class** ________________________ **Grade level** ___________

Requirements	Success measure(s)	Quality standards	Control strategies What, who, how often	Targets		
				September	December	February

Social/Team Skills Matrix

Team name: ________________ **Coach:** ________________

Project: ________________ **Date** ________

Team mission:

Mission-Specific Quality Factors

Names ↓ / Operational definitions →						

Has the QF, as stated in the operational definition, been met? Yes

Has the QF, as stated in the operational definition, not been met? Not yet

Team Project Quality Factors for Learning Matrix

State standards included: ____________________

Project due date: ____________________

Team members: ____________________

Quality factors	Operational definitions	Q? Not yet	Coaching tips

Student Error Chart–Quality Factors for Learning

For (Name) ____________________ Project title ____________________ Date __________

Process checker ____________________

Fill in the box opposite the Quality Factor and Operational Definition indicating the number of errors at each process checkpoint.

Quality factor	Operational definition	Process Checkpoints 1	2	3

Team Project—Process Checkpoint Assessment

Project purpose ______________________________

Deadline for completion __________ Process checkpoint # __________ Date ______ Process checker ______

Quality factor	Operational definition	Quality or not yet	Coaching tips

	1			2			3	
			1	2	3			
	8		8		4		4	
			7	6	5			
	7			6			5	

Radar Chart

Class/grade ______________________________ Date ______________

Check one: Social skills _______ Academic skills ______

Radar Chart

Class/grade __________________ School year _______ Marking period _________

Check one: Social skills _______ Academic skills ______

How Helpful Were These Resources?

Class: **Year:** **Project or unit:** **Date:**

Rating scale: E = Excellent; couldn't have done without it.
G = Good; was a big help.
O = Okay; wasn't that much help.
W = Waste of time; was no help whatsoever.

Please rate each of the following resources on how much it helped during this learning experience.

	E	G	O	W

Fast Feedback

Instructions: Circle the number that best represents your thoughts on today's lesson.			
I understand the logic of today's problem or concept.			
1 Strongly agree	2 Agree	3 Somewhat disagree	4 Disagree
I could apply this logic (or concept) to another situation.			
1 Strongly agree	2 Agree	3 Somewhat disagree	4 Disagree
The "muddy" points about today's lesson were:			
The pace of this class is (circle one)	Too slow	Just right	Too fast
I'd like some additional help, please. (signed) ____________________			

Fast Feedback

Instructions: Circle the number that best represents your thoughts on today's lesson.			
I understand the logic of today's problem or concept.			
1 Strongly agree	2 Agree	3 Somewhat disagree	4 Disagree
I could apply this logic (or concept) to another situation.			
1 Strongly agree	2 Agree	3 Somewhat disagree	4 Disagree
The "muddy" points about today's lesson were:			
The pace of this class is (circle one)	Too slow	Just right	Too fast
I'd like some additional help, please. (signed) ____________________			

Force Field Analysis

Name or ______________________________ **Date** ______________

Goal	
Driving forces +	**Restraining forces** –
Plan to reduce the restraining forces to meet the goal.	

Glossary

action plan—Plans that align with the class strategic goals and are set at the same time as targes are determined. Action plans include resources, lesson planning, student work systems addressed to meet the targets.

affinity diagram—A tool for organizing large amount of information or breaking down a complex topic. It is a silent brainstorming tool, which requires the group to work together to place ideas into "like" categories.

alignment—Consistency of focus of every aspect of the classroom system beginning with purpose, vision, mission, and goals. Work systems, key processes, and a measurement system must be in alignment (not conflicting or deviating from the purpose) with the classroom culture. This is important to assure everyone and everything is aimed towards achieving the class goals.

active learning—A way students work. Active learning engages students in higher-order thinking tasks such as analysis, synthesis, and evaluation and multiple intelligences. It promotes interdependence and individual accountability to accomplish a common goal.

Baldrige Criteria for Performance Excellence—The Baldrige Program was signed into U.S. law in 1987 and was named after deceased Secretary of Commerce Malcolm Baldrige for his managerial excellence. A framework for excellence includes seven interdependent categories of criteria that when aligned and integrated yield excellent results. The framework and criteria are now recognized as the best approach to system improvement in the world. The Baldrige Award is given to role model organizations with proven effective and efficient processes and excellent results in all aspects important to the organization. Awards can be given for large or small business, manufacturing, healthcare, education, and soon, nonprofit organizations. In 2001, the first education winners were announced: Chugach School District in Alaska, Pearl River School District in New York, and the University of Wisconsin-Stout. In 2003, Community Consolidated School District 15 in Palatine, IL, a K–8 district of 13,000 students, won this prestigious award.

bandwidth of variation—Every process has variation. The bandwidth is understood as the top and bottom score, or range of data points for any series of data. For example: In a class, five students score 100% and three students score 5%, while all others are in between; we would say the bandwidth of variation on that test was 95%. In a BBQ classroom, the goal is to continuously work to reduce the bandwidth of variation for every process, pushing the mean higher for instruction and other things you wish to improve and pushing the mean lower to extinguish negative behaviors.

bell curve—A normal distribution of data points more or less evenly split on each side of the average (mean). Generally, we speak about data falling about +/− three standard deviations from the mean. A bell curve represents a traditional model of "winners and losers." Many educators and policy makers who embrace traditional school models consider the bell curve to be about how the data will be distributed from any group of students.

benchmarks—From a Baldrige perspective, respresents "best practice." If you have a process that is not helping everyone be successful, or hasn't been changed in the past 5–10 years, you might benchmark other schools or classes having exceptional success in a similar situation. To benchmark another requires research for "best practice" as evidenced by a third party. It is another form of comparative data.

brainstorm—An active process for generating many ideas around a topic from a group of people. Formal brainstorming requires systematically asking team members for ideas.

cause-effect diagram—An analysis tool designed to identify the causes of an event or problem. Major causal categories are identified, and then subcauses are brainstormed under each category. Also known as an Ishikawa diagram (named for its creator).

cohort group—A single group of students from the same grade; used to compare how well a particular group of students performs over the course of time. For example, you want to compare the performance of a specific group of students in third grade in 2000 through fourth, fifth, or sixth grades on a normed test, to measure value added each year of enrollment. This constitutes a cohort group from 2000 to 2003. True cohort groups identify students by name and follow only those students over the years.

constancy of purpose—Focuses on the aim of the organization. What is it designed to do?

continuous process improvement—The Quality improvement process is known as PDSA, or Plan-Do-Study-Act. It is a systematic approach to problem solving and design of new processes.

customer—The primary customers of a classroom system are the students and the next-teacher-in-line. Other customers of a classroom system are the school, district, post-secondary institutions, and the world of work for those leaving high school.

data—Hard data are things that can be counted or measured, or factual data. Soft data are satisfaction and perceptual data. Both types are important to collect and chart. Data are the basis for decision making in a Quality classroom.

data-driven decision making—Decisions about what to change in any process are based on data analysis and a root cause analysis.

data collection plan—A systematic approach to collecting any data to inform the organization. The decision about what data to collect is important and must be aligned with any strategic goals. The data collection plan addresses questions of what, how, where, when, and an explanation of how the data are to be used.

differentiated instruction—Requires teachers to use different modalities and resources to meet the needs of a diverse student body within any class.

Dr. W. Edwards Deming—The Father of Modern Quality. A statistician (1900–1993) who taught the Japanese his quality management theory, which focused on involving the workers to improve processes and systems. Deming, born in Iowa, lived most of his adult life in Washington, DC. He received an MS degree from the University of Colorado and a Ph.D. from Yale. Deming believed that 95% of all problems within organizations were due to faulty systems and not people. His teachings and theory kept many U.S. businesses profitable and are the basis for the Malcolm Baldrige National Quality Criteria for Performance Excellence.

effectiveness measures—Learning gains, improved attendance, student joy of learning, and graduation rates are measures of an educational system's effectiveness.

efficiency measures—Reteaching, time away from learning, and drop-out rates are some of the efficiency measures of an educational system.

fast feedback—A short instrument that has three items to assess student learning and understanding. It is given to a random sample of students at the end of class and analyzed to give the teacher information about instruction and learning.

feedback—Information about the system or any process provided by customers, stakeholders, and partners. Systematic feedback implies collecting data on a regular basis either by using a random sample or by surveying the whole group. Informal feedback is usually anecdotal and not terribly useful for improving the system.

feedback instruments—Satisfaction surveys, needs assessments, focus groups, plus/delta charts, fast feedback, How Helpful Were These Resources?, Enthusiasm for Learning chart, and many others.

feedback plan—A well thought-out approach that uses a variety of feedback tools and approaches on a regular and systematic basis so that the information can be analyzed and improvements made in-process to ultimately delight the customer.

flow chart—Shows a picture of a process. Steps in the process are listed and arranged, using universal flow chart symbols. There are three types of flow charts: process—showing only the sequential steps; deployment—showing sequential steps and who is responsible for each; and those that include all elements of the depolyment flow chart along with the timetable for completion of each step. Flow charts help reduce variation.

focus on innovation—Making meaningful change to improve instruction and services and create new value for students. Innovation is a multistep process that involves development and knowledge sharing, a decision to implement, implementation, evaluation, and learning.

formative assessment—Frequent or ongoing evaluation in-process that informs the teacher of what students are learning, and their strengths and weaknesses. Formative assessment is used as to help teachers make real-time improvements in instructional methods, activities, or approaches.

goal—Addresses a future performance level. Longer-term goals for the classroom would be year-end or semester-end, if you teach a semester-long course. Short-term goals would be marking periods. Goals have targets associated with them that allow everyone to project future goal attainment.

hard data—Hard data are factual data that can be counted or measured. Examples include height, long jump in inches, weight, time to complete a task, and correct answers on a quiz or exam.

histogram—A bar graph that shows a snapshot of the spread of the data.

hold the gains—Each process demonstrates normal variation and over time, unless specific process checks are made, will deteriorate. To "hold the gains" means a decision has been made to periodically and systematically gather data and analyze it at specific key process points after an improvement project has been completed. In this way, if the data starts to exhibit a downward trend, targeted interventions can be taken immediately.

How helpful were these resources?—A feedback tool that asks students to assess the effectiveness of the resources used to accomplish any learning activity. Teachers use the results to make changes in resources available to students.

If/then improvement theory—A theory the team comes up with after identifying the root cause of any problem. The theory is written after a brainstorm session to determine actions to eliminate the root cause of a problem.

inputs—People, policies, and resources that flow into the system and influence it in some way.

key value-creation processes—Processes that produce benefit for students and for the organization (classroom or school). These are the processes most important to running the classroom and those that produce positive organizational results for students and next-teacher-in-line. These would include (1) instruction, (2) assessment, and (3) classroom management.

leading indicators—The best predictors of future success. These are also known as in-process measures. Some leading indicators for reading include vocabulary, phonemic awareness, phonemes, and comprehension. Systematically tracking leading indicators in-process is a key way for teachers to monitor progress towards the goals. When leading indicators indicate lack of progress, it signals that a PDSA improvement cycle is required.

learning-centered education—A strategic concept and one of the Baldrige core values that demands constant sensitivity to changing and emerging student, stakeholder, and market requirements and to the factors that drive student learning, satisfaction, and persistence.

levels of learning—Bloom's Taxonomy. The levels are from bottom to top: Knowledge, Comprehension, Application, Analysis, Synthesis, and Evaluation.

lotus diagram—A planning and organizational tool. The lotus diagram starts with a central idea or theme and expands outward with details.

measurement system—A systematic approach to collecting data with mission and vision specificity. The system includes measures for class goals that come from the vision and mission. It is used to inform teacher, students, and stakeholders about progress and to improve the classroom system.

multiple intelligences—Howard Gardner identified eight ways people learn. They are logical/mathematical, verbal/linguistic, visual/spatial, body/kinesthetic, musical/rhythmic, interpersonal, intrapersonal, and naturalist. Too often, educators rely heavily on verbal/linguistic and logical/mathematical and do not provide enough opportunities for students to learn through the other intelligences. It is the responsibility of the teacher to discover how students learn (by asking and observing) and then provide learning activities that use more of the intelligences. It is the combination of verbal/linguistic, body/kinesthetic, and musical/rhythmic that advances literacy skills rapidly.

operational definitions—Short, precise, detailed definition of a specification. A good operational definition yields either a "yes" or "no" response. Operational definitions provide clear communication to everyone about how something is to be measured. Operational definitions allow people to understand their jobs with less confusion.

outputs—The results of value-added and non-value-added processes. In education, the outputs include student learning results; student, stakeholder, and partner satisfaction and dissatisfaction results; and student enthusiasm for learning results.

output measures—Results measures. They are used to inform policy makers, administrators, and teachers about how well students achieve and to measure satisfaction at the end of the year. Results measures are only helpful to the teacher in terms of making system improvements for the following year.

Pareto chart—A bar graph that lines data up from most-to-least frequency. Pareto's principle is the significant few versus the trivial many. The significant few things will generally make up 80% of the whole, while the trivial many will make up about 20%. Pareto charts give teams an indication of where to start an improvement project. Pareto was an Italian economist.

performance excellence—An integrated approach to organizational performance management that results in (1) delivery of ever-improving value to students and stakeholders, contributing to improved education quality; (2) improvement of overall organizational effectiveness and capabilities; and (3) organizational and personal learning. The Baldrige Education Criteria for Performance Excellence provide a framework and an assessment tool for understanding organizational strengths and opportunities for improvement and thus for guiding planning efforts.

PDSA cycle—The seven-step quality improvement process that eliminates problems provided the true root cause is understood. P = Plan (four steps: identify the opportunity for improvement, assess the current situation, analyze the root cause, and write an improvement theiory); D = Do (put the improvement theory into practice); S = Study (analyze the results from the improvement theory); and A = Act (decide about expanding the improvement to the whole system or go back and understand the root cause).

plus/delta chart—An informal data collection tool that asks participants to provide feedback on what worked and what needs improvement.

process—A series of steps taken to achieve a task.

process measures—Predictors of success. They allow the teacher to make midcourse corrections leading to improved success at the end of the year. Data collected in-process ought to be the most critical predictors. These data, collected and analyzed regularly throughout the year, provide great insight for teachers to make adjustments in instructional and classroom management approaches.

process measures for literacy—The five in-process measures and best predictors of future success in reading, writing, and speaking are phonemic awareness, phonics, vocabulary, fluency, and comprehension. These are the important things teachers ought to regularly and systematically collect data on.

quality by fact—The product of the system actually functions as promised. In education, this means that students leave the grade or school with the required skills and ability to apply them to other situations.

quality by process—This measures effectiveness and efficiency of the processes making up the system. Graduation rates would be an example of the effectiveness and efficiency of the instructional process.

quality by perception—Perception is reality in the eyes of the customer and stakeholders. This measures whether or not customers believe the product is of high quality. When newspapers report the results of state standards tests, perception about the quality of instruction and education at each school is formed.

Quality Factors—The absolutely essential characteristics or elements that must be present to meet any standard and for someone to say "Wow, that was excellent." Quality Factors set expectations. The customer determines Quality Factors and constantly raises the bar on expectations.

Quality Features—Additional elements that delight the customer. These are not essential to the overall working of any product, but make it nicer, brighter, and more "alive." Quality Features often become Quality Factors over time. An example may be the expectation that students are required to use computers to write essays.

relations digraph—A tool that shows the relationship between any two factors among many factors; to identify and study the cause and effect between factors of a problem.

run chart—A tool that shows a picture of a process over time. It shows variation in a system or process from one point to the next and represents opportunities for improvement.

satellite chart—A planning and organizational tool. It can be used as a graphic organizer for students, but also has value when deciphering details about any topic or project.

scatter diagram—Shows the possible relationship between two different sets of data. Factors are selected to understand whether a potential cause/effect relationship exists. It is a statistical tool that shows how one factor influences (or not) another.

soft data—Perceptual data that reflect a person's feelings about something. Examples include satisfaction and enthusiasm.

student as customer—Students are the direct customers of teachers. They receive instruction, instructional support, and the climate for learning from teachers.

student as worker—Students are workers in a system traditionally created by the teacher. Students are expected to fit into the system; if they won't or can't, they are viewed as difficult students and often cause disruptions to the instructional process. Students are in the best position to identify the barriers to their success and it is up to the teacher to change the system. Unless teachers empower students to provide feedback and make suggestions for improvement, the barriers will remain and the results will be the same.

system—A series of processes linked together to achieve the aim of an organization.

system alignment—Consistency of plans, processes, information, resource decisions, actions, results, analysis, and learning to support the organization's key goals. In this case, the classroom is a subsystem of the school, and its mission must align with the school's and district's vision and mission. Class goals will be aligned with school and district goals and expectations.

system integration—Effective integration is achieved when the individual components of a system operate as a fully interconnected unit. That is, plans, processes, information, resource decisions, actions, results, analysis, and learning all support the key organization-wide goals.

teacher as leader—Teachers are leaders in the classroom, and as such they are responsible for removing barriers to student success. Most barriers are due to faulty systems and ineffective or inefficient processes. A teacher-leader empowers students to help identify system and process barriers and participate in finding solutions. Teacher-leaders are competent and of high character; they value all students, seek and engage in partnerships with students and parents, and view data as friends that allow them to learn and to engage in continuous improvement of self and the system.

teacher as service provider—Teachers provide instruction, support, and create the learning climate. These are all services. Students provide feedback in terms of achievement, satisfaction, and dissatisfaction manifest by behaviors, attendance, and attitudes. Teachers need to be customer focused to make changes based on student and stakeholder needs and expectations.

team projects—Total Quality Education–based team projects use all the SCANS skills and engage students in problem-solving and self-directed teams. The systematic approach to organizing students in teams, and the responsibilities they each assume, allows everyone to gain important social, academic, and workforce skills. Effective teams are the result of stage 4, in team development, and also demonstrate interdependence illustrated by Stephen Covey's Maturity Continuum.

work system—How students are organized to get work done and to accomplish the vision, mission, and goals. An effective work system is designed to align the components with the vision, mission, and goals and encourages students to contribute effectively and to the best of their ability.

variation—Every process exhibits some variation, whether in manufacturing or in education. The idea of a Quality organization is to minimize the bandwidth of variation and move the average higher for such things as learning, attendance, and enthusiasm and lower for such things as tardiness, absenteeism, failure, and acting-out behavior. The way to reduce variation is to provide precise operational definitions and expectations and then measure effectiveness and follow the PDSA cycle for improvement.

Recommended Reading

Armstrong, Thomas. *The Multiple Intelligences of Reading and Writing: Making the Words Come Alive*. Alexandria, VA: ASCD, 2003.

Ayres, Carolyn. *Continuous Improvement in the Mathematics Classroom.* Milwaukee, WI: ASQ Quality Press, 2000.

Blazey, Mark, et al. *Insights to Performance Excellence in Education 2003: An Inside Look at the 2003 Baldrige Award Criteria for Education.* Milwaukee, WI: ASQ Quality Press, 2004.

Blazey, Mark. *Insights to Performance Excellence 2005: An Inside Look at the 2005 Baldrige Award Criteria.* Milwaukee, WI: ASQ Quality Press, 2005.

Burgard, Jeffrey J. *Continuous Improvement in the Science Classroom (Grades 6–8).* Milwaukee, WI: ASQ Quality Press, 2000.

Campbell, Linda, Bruce Campbell, and Dee Dickinson. *Teaching and Learning through Multiple Intelligences,* 2nd edition. Boston: Allyn and Bacon, 1999.

Carr, Judy F., and Douglas E. Harris. *Succeeding with Standards: Linking Curriculum, Assessment, and Action Planning*. Alexandria, VA: ASCD, 2001.

Carson, Shelly. *Continuous Improvement in the History and Social Science Classroom.* Milwaukee, WI: ASQ Quality Press, 2000.

Cleary, Barbara, and Sally Duncan. *Tools and Techniques to Inspire Classroom Learning.* Milwaukee, WI: ASQ Quality Press, 1997.

Covey, Stephen R. *The Seven Habits of Highly Effective People*. New York: Simon & Shuster, 1989.

De Mente, Boye. *Instant Japanese: Everything You Need in 100 Key Words.* Boston: Tuttle, 2003.

Deming, W. Edwards. *The New Economics: For Industry, Government, Education*, 2nd edition. Cambridge, MA: Massachusetts Institute of Technology Center for Advanced Engineering Study, 1994.

Fauss, Karen R. *Continuous Improvement in the Primary Classroom: Language Arts (Grades K–3)*. Milwaukee, WI: ASQ Quality Press, 2000.

Fierro, Darlene M. "Is There A Difference in Learning Style Among Cultures?" ERIC Document Reproduction Service No. ED415974, 1997.

Gardner, Howard. *Multiple Intelligences: The Theory in Practice*. New York: Basic Books, 1993.

Glasser, William. *The Quality School: Managing Students Without Coersion.* Revised edition. New York: HarperCollins, 1998.

Harrington, Michael. *The Other America: Poverty in the United States*. New York: Touchstone, 1997.

Jenkins, Lee. *Improving Student Learning: Applying Deming's Quality Principles in Classrooms,* 2nd edition. Milwaukee, WI: ASQ Quality Press, 2003.

__________. *Permission to Forget.* Milwaukee, WI: ASQ Quality Press, 2004.

Kingery, Cathy, editor, et al. *The Six Sigma Memory Jogger II.* Salem, NH: GOAL/QPC, 2002.

Ritter, Diane, and Michael Brassard. *The Creativity Tools Memory Jogger.* Salem, NH: GOAL/QPC, 1998.

Senge, Peter. *The Fifth Discipline: The Art and Practice of the Learning Organization Field Book*. New York: Doubleday Dell, 1994.

Takaki, Ronald. *A Different Mirror: A History of Multicultural America.* Boston: Little, Brown, 1993.

Tomlinson, Carol Ann. *How to Differentiate Instruction in Mixed Ability Classrooms*, 2nd edition. Alexandria, VA: ASCD, 2001.

Interesting and Helpful Program

True Colors™. Sullivan Associates, 2929 Marsann Lane, Dallas, TX. 75234.

Helpful Websites for More Information

Baldrige Award Winning School Districts

Chugach Schools, Anchorage, Alaska www.chugachschools.com

Community Consolidated School District 15, Palatine, IL www.ccsd15.k12.il.us

Pearl River School District, Pearl River, NY www.pearlriver.k12.ny.us

Dolch sight words http://www.english-zone.com/reading/dolch.html

Kolb, David A. The Learning Styles: A Multiple Intelligences Approach http://pss.uvm.edu/ pss162/learning_styles.html

Malcolm Baldrige National Quality Award Program www.baldrige.nist.gov

To obtain a free copy of the Education Criteria Booklet www.baldrige.nist.gov

To obtain multiple copies of the Criteria www.asq.org

Thousand most frequently used words in the English language www.ezlearninglinks.com/freqwords.htm

UNESCO www.unesco.org/education

Click on icon on the right, Education for Sustainable Development

U.S. Department of Labor

SCANS Skills http://wdr.doleta.gov/SCANS/

Index

R

S

T–U

V

W–X–Y–Z